WESTMAR COLLEGE LIBRARY

THE

RISE OF THE

COUNTER-

ESTABLISHMENT

W9-BMI-073

Also written by Sidney Blumenthal
The Permanent Campaign

THE
RISE OF THE
COUNTER-
ESTABLISHMENT

FROM CONSERVATIVE
IDEOLOGY TO
POLITICAL POWER

90-181

SIDNEY BLUMENTHAL

PERENNIAL LIBRARY

Harper & Row, Publishers, New York
Cambridge, Philadelphia, San Francisco
London, Mexico City, São Paulo, Singapore, Sydney

For My Parents

Grateful acknowledgement is made to the following for permission to reprint previously published material:

The Boston Globe: Excerpts from articles by Sidney Blumenthal from *The Boston Globe Sunday Magazine.* Reprinted courtesy of The Boston Globe.

The Washington Post: Excerpts from articles by Sidney Blumenthal from *The Washington Post.* Copyright by The Washington Post. Reprinted by permission.

The New York Times: "David Stockman: The President's Cutting Edge," by Sidney Blumenthal from *The New York Times Magazine,* March 15, 1981. "Whose Side Is Business On Anyway," by Sidney Blumenthal from *The New York Times Magazine,* October 25, 1981. Copyright © 1981 by the New York Times Company. Reprinted by permission. All rights reserved.

Storm King Music, Inc.: Excerpt from "Which Side Are You On," by Florence Reece. Copyright 1947 by Storm King Music, Inc. All rights reserved. Used by permission.

A hardcover edition of this book was published in 1986 by Times Books, a division of Random House, Inc. It is here reprinted by arrangement with Times Books.

THE RISE OF THE COUNTER-ESTABLISHMENT. Copyright © 1986 by Sidney Blumenthal. Preface to the Perennial Library edition copyright © 1988 by Sidney Blumenthal. All rights reserved. Printed in the United States of America. No part of this book may be used or reproduced in any manner whatsoever without written permission except in the case of brief quotations embodied in critical articles and reviews. For information address Harper & Row, Publishers, Inc., 10 East 53rd Street, New York, N.Y. 10022. Published simultaneously in Canada by Fitzhenry & Whiteside Limited, Toronto.

First PERENNIAL LIBRARY edition published 1988.

Library of Congress Cataloging-in-Publication Data

Blumenthal, Sidney, 1948–
    The rise of the counter-establishment.

    Reprint. Originally published: New York : Times Books,
c1986.
    Bibliography: p.
    Includes index.
    1. Conservatism—United States. 2. Elite (Social sciences)—United States. 3. United States—Politics and government—1981-   . I. Title.
[JA84.U5B54 1988]   320.5′2′0973   88–45014
ISBN 0-06-097140-1 (pbk.)

88 89 90 91 92 FG 10 9 8 7 6 5 4 3 2 1

CONTENTS

ACKNOWLEDGMENTS vi

PREFACE viii

PREFACE TO THE PERENNIAL LIBRARY EDITION x

INTRODUCTION
SHADOW LIBERALISM 3

CHAPTER ONE
THE CONSERVATIVE REMNANT 12

CHAPTER TWO
THE BUSINESS OF INTELLECTUALS 32

CHAPTER THREE
THE BUSINESS OF AMERICA 55

CHAPTER FOUR
THE ROMANCE OF THE MARKET 69

CHAPTER FIVE
CAPITALISM AND FRIEDMAN 87

CHAPTER SIX
SHADOW LEFTISM, OR THE
IDEOLOGICAL LIGHT BRIGADE 122

CHAPTER SEVEN
A LOST CONTINENT 166

CHAPTER EIGHT
THE PROTESTANT ETHIC 210

CHAPTER NINE
THE MYTHOLOGY OF REAGANISM 240

CHAPTER TEN
THE WILL TO BELIEVE 262

CHAPTER ELEVEN
MORNING AGAIN 279

CHAPTER TWELVE
THE SECOND COMING 291

CHAPTER THIRTEEN
THE BEGINNING OF IDEOLOGY 311

NOTES 337

INDEX 349

ACKNOWLEDGMENTS

Shortly after Ronald Reagan was elected president I began work on this book, armed with only a few general ideas. As I tested them I was led to abandon some and adopt others.

I have rehearsed the ideas in this book almost endlessly with my friends. I'm sure that they will recognize the bits and pieces of conversations that appear here. I am delighted to be able to acknowledge the friendship and insights of Josiah Lee Auspitz, Ben Gerson, Hendrik Hertzberg, Christopher Hitchens, John Judis, Robert Kuttner, Robert Reich, William Schneider, Hillel Schwartz, Derek Shearer, Larry Smith, and Ralph Whitehead. I am also grateful for the friendship of Anthony Lewis and Margaret Marshall. Her wise counsel helped make this book possible.

At critical moments, this project would not have gone forward without support from those who believed in its potential merit. Martin Peretz, Charles Merrill, Philip M. Stern, Dr. Howard Hiatt, and Thomas Vallely helped fund the research. I am also indebted to the assistance of Richard Parker, the Bydale Foundation, Mark Green and the Democracy Project, and the Sabre Foundation's Project in Public Philosophy. I am especially grateful for the generous support offered by Richard Dennis, and for the friendship of Charles Wolff.

The book would have been very thin without the cooperation of many sources in the worlds of government, business, the academy, philanthropy, and politics. I am thankful that they confided their views and information.

ACKNOWLEDGMENTS

I am grateful to *The New York Times Magazine* for permission to reprint in different form articles that first appeared there. The *Times* editor I worked with was Robert Stock.

I have also adapted material that was initially published in the *Boston Globe Sunday Magazine,* where Michael Janeway presided. Michael Larkin and Al Larkin were also helpful editors there.

Material that first appeared in the *Washington Post* has been rewritten for this book. I am grateful to the *Post* for permission to reprint. Henry Allen and Robert Kaiser were particularly helpful editors. Maralee Schwartz assisted with the research.

I have been lucky to have had Hugh O'Neill as my editor at Times Books. His criticism and suggestions have been unfailingly incisive and helpful, immeasurably improving the manuscript. I'm also grateful for the careful copy editing of David Wade Smith. I thank my literary agent, Kathy Robbins, for placing me at this particular publishing house.

Above all, I am grateful to my family. My wife, Jackie, offered consistently intelligent advice. Our sons, Max and Paul, make the future real for us.

My sister, Marcia, and her husband, Dennis Fields, were supportive and encouraging. My grandmother, Minnie F. Stone, helped, too. We all miss her and cherish her memory.

Finally, my parents, Hymen and Claire Blumenthal, to whom this book is dedicated, have always given their confidence and love.

Brookline, Massachusetts
Washington, D.C.
May 1986

PREFACE

This book is a critical interpretation of the rise of a conservative elite, an event that is among the most startling and profound in modern American politics. Though in its own way *The Counter-Establishment* is a history and a report, it is intended to be neither a comprehensive survey nor a disengaged assemblage of facts. My aim is to advance the argument that ideas themselves have become a salient aspect of contemporary politics; that a conservative New Class, fortified within the battlements of the Counter-Establishment, has institutionalized a particular mode of ideological politics; that because of this the conservatives have determined much of the tenor of the 1980s; and that a principal consequence of the Counter-Establishment's rise has been a realignment of elites, not the much-heralded conventional realignment of the electorate.

From the beginning I conceived of *The Counter-Establishment* as a complement to *The Permanent Campaign*. In that book I advanced the notion that the traditional party system, personified by ward leaders and precinct captains, has been replaced by a new form of organization, personified by media consultants and pollsters. The conventional realignment many political scientists are anticipating, perforce, will never occur. The "realignment," if it can be called that, has already happened. But the party system, instead of being transformed along the lines of previous realignments, has been overcome by the permanent campaign system, rooted in the post-industrial technologies of telecommunications and computers, which cannot be uninvented. Since the past cannot be restored, the watch for a customary realignment may be the political scientists' version of *Waiting for Godot.*[1]

In the permanent campaign system, a politician must govern as if campaigning, using the techniques he employed in the effort to gain his office. A politics of imagery can neatly mesh with a politics of ideas. When individual candidates, especially at the national level, rely upon general themes, broadcast by media, to carry their message, ideas may serve their purpose well.

While the conservatives sometimes express perfunctory hopes for a realigned party system, they have become influential because of the vacuum opened by the old parties' decay. When speaking freely, the conservatives identify the regular partisans of both parties, particularly Republicans, as their foes. The realignment of policy the conservatives have wrought is a reflection, not of a realigned party system, but of a realignment of elites. And at the heart of conservatism is an intellectual elite, motivated mainly by ideology, and attached to the foundations and journals, think tanks, and institutes of what I call the Counter-Establishment, the subject of this book.

PREFACE TO THE

PERENNIAL LIBARY EDITION

The Rise of the Counter-Establishment appeared in the early fall of 1986, on the eve of Reaganism's fall from grace. The Senate had not yet been recaptured by the Democrats; the Iran-contra scandal had not been exposed; the Wall Street inside trader Ivan Boesky had not been led away in handcuffs; and Russia was still the "evil empire." Conservatives felt themselves in possession of the mandate of the nation, if not of heaven. They were certain that they were at the beginning of a long reign, in which they would steer easily around or ride over obstacles thrown up by a fading liberal establishment. It seemed inevitable to them that in a relatively short time they would come to dominate all of the command posts of the federal government and enact their agenda. In the second Reagan term—and beyond—they fully expected to gain ever greater control over the various agencies and departments, including the hated State Department; and they expected to rule within the Supreme Court, where their ideology would be translated into law for the rest of the century. The possibility that the golden age might be in its twilight rather than in its morning hardly occurred to any of them.

This failure of anticipation was shared not only among the conservatives. At this time, the Ronald Reagan who was later to appear in his former chief of staff Donald Regan's book, *For the Record*—as a vacuous, passive president—was barely revealed at all. The role at the center was assumed to be filled, in the words of *Time* magazine, by "a Prospero of American memories, a magician who carries a bright, ideal America like a holograph in his mind and projects its image in the air." This characterization was wrought in

July 1986, only four months before the disclosure of the Iran-contra scandal.

In the concluding chapter of *The Rise of the Counter-Establishment*, I suggested that the conservative movement was about to experience profound convulsions for several reasons. It was founded on an ideology whose elements were in conflict with one another. The rise of the religious right would inevitably accelerate this centrifugal sectarianism. Finally, the conservatives' devotion to movement over party would bring their movement into increasing conflict with traditional Republicanism, its most proximate and longstanding adversary since at least the days of Barry Goldwater and Nelson Rockefeller.

The members of the Counter-Establishment—a conservative elite, mostly concentrated in Washington—believed, above all, in their own idealized conception of themselves and their opponents. Though Reagan brought thousands of them to power in the Capitol, the responsibility that was theirs did not soften or alter their shadow liberalism, acquired by their habitual comparison of themselves to an omnipotent liberal establishment. On the contrary, their compulsions to take power and to justify themselves by exaggerating the power of the liberals intensified. In so doing, they contributed to their own downfall.

These actions and rationalizations led to disastrous consequences, most prominently in the Iran-contra affair. The Nicaraguan contras, conservatives believed, were "freedom fighters," on the front line of a worldwide struggle with the implacable "evil empire." The so-called Reagan Doctrine, an intellectual construct of neoconservative theorists, had as its goal the containment and rolling back of the Soviet Union in the Third World. What blocked this goal, so the theory went, was a liberal elite, entrenched in the Congress and the press. The reality, however, was that the contras were a highly ambiguous moral cause and a politically untenable one. Only after the administration systematically set out to deceive the Congress about its clandestine actions on behalf of the contra cause did the Congress seek to restrict it through successive Boland amendments. Also, public opinion never endorsed contra aid. The selling of missiles to Iran in order to get funds to divert to the contras was a means to get around the general will expressed by Congress.

The pattern apparent in this scandal was evident in other cases. In the law, for example, conservatives argued that liberals, lacking popular support for their programs, sought to enact them through an "imperial judiciary." To counter this, the conservatives quite deliberately attempted to gain control of the judiciary themselves. Attorney General Edwin Meese advanced a doctrine of "original intent," a jurisprudence evoking the motives of the constitution's framers, posed against what was assumed to be a coherent liberal activism. But in practice the Meese doctrine served as a rationale for the conservative activism to dominate the bench.

The culmination came in two stages. First, there was the nomination to the Supreme Court of the leading conservative judicial light, Robert Bork. In a week of televised hearings, he expounded his views, which met overwhelming rejection not only in the Senate but also in public opinion polls. Afterwards, conservatives vehemently insisted that Bork fell because of the organized liberal opposition, particularly a television ad produced by People for the American Way. The right denied the breadth and depth of the Bork rejection.

The second stage came in the form of Meese's ethical problems. He could not grasp the distinction between the public and private sectors and sought to apply the rules of an unfettered market to public service, which led him into many conflicts of interest and dubious business situations with dubious characters. His response to the storm of criticism was to fire the Justice Department's public affairs officer, Terry Eastland, for insufficiently defending him against ridicule. Eastland had been a major writer of Meese's speeches on "original intent." Here the ideology began to flail in a sea of mounting scandal.

The idea of neoconservatism itself fit the implosive pattern. Neoconservatives, most of whom had swung from left to right, believed that they articulated deep mass yearnings and, in fact, had even made the Reagan presidency possible by their appeals to alienated Democrats. Liberalism, they argued, had betrayed itself and become a self-delusionary proposition. "A neoconservative is a liberal who has been mugged by reality," said Irving Kristol, in a famous formulation. In the end, however, it was the neoconservatives' pursuit of their ideological imperatives that contributed most to their collapse. The quintessential case was that of Assistant Secretary of State Elliot Abrams, whose quest for a contra victory led him to a hotel room in London, under the assumed name of "Mr. Kenilworth," where he begged $10 million for the "freedom fighters" from a representative of the Sultan of Brunei. The money came across, but Abrams had mixed up the secret Swiss bank account's numbers. So the millions were lost, his tin-cup diplomacy gone awry. To cover his various actions on behalf of the contras, Abrams lied to Congress—and was exposed. (Inexplicably, he was kept in his office and went on to mismanage catastrophically the effort to oust Panamanian strongman Manuel Noriega.)

Before Reagan came to office, the neoconservatives promised that they would make America predominant in the world again, as it was in the immediate post-World War II period. They made extravagant claims about American weakness to justify their drive to power. In the 1980 campaign, Reagan himself drew an explicit comparison between Jimmy Carter and Neville Chamberlain, the British prime minister who pursued an appeasement policy toward Hitler. Reagan openly disdained arms control in favor of an arms race with the Soviets. America would seize the initiative, and Russia would be pushed into collapse. By the end, however, the Russian leader, not Reagan, had taken charge of the agenda. Gorbachev, in fact, was more popular in Western Europe than Reagan. Hundreds of billions of dollars had been spent in pursuit of an image that failed. By persisting in their ideology, the neoconservatives had fostered the conditions by which America lost much of its international prestige and influence.

As it turned out, neoconservatism had a scant popular base. Its preferred presidental candidate in the 1988 Republican primaries, Jack Kemp, received few votes and was knocked out of the process early. Reagan, moreover, was not their dependency but a figure indispensable to their rise; he may have needed their ideas, but, as his performance at the Moscow summit made plain, he could deliver startlingly new lines. Thus the neoconservatives finished the Reagan era as perhaps his most severe critics, certainly the most disillusioned, as he strolled through Red Square with Mikhail Gorbachev and declared the "evil empire" to be a phrase from the past. Reality had again mugged the neoconservatives.

They repaired to the redoubts of the Counter-Establishment—the think tanks and institutes, the journals and foundations. No matter what the next turn in the cycle of American history, they would be ready to attack the failure of others to live up to their ideology. Many of them will be distinguished formers, with access to the op-ed pages of the major newspapers and the public affairs shows on television. Their resources and institutional base, especially in Washington, is greater than in any previous period in which the right-wing has been out of favor. Any president who does not understand the power of ideas will provide them with a fresh opening.

But the conservatives will not be restored to influence by the harshness of their rhetoric alone. Their movement is at root ideological. And they expended much of their intellectual capital during the Reagan era; they had little of relevance to say by its end. Circumstances, of course, will help determine their political fate in the long run. But without new ideas this ideological movement is hollow and will become ossified. Many of the conservatives have come to seem almost eager for defeat, welcoming the familiar role of the embattled minority opposition and its tendentious point of view. From this position they can continue to avoid painful revisions and self-criticisms and to blame those who disagree with them for the country's problems. It is strikingly ironic that the Reagan era has concluded with the supposedly unchangeable totalitarians of the Soviet Union deeply engaged in re-examining their history and in self-analysis, while the American conservatives seem incapable of making even a gesture in either direction.

June 1988

THE
RISE OF THE
COUNTER-
ESTABLISHMENT

SHADOW

LIBERALISM

For more than a generation after the New Deal the world seemed permanent. Liberalism was the received wisdom, no longer a movement of experimental ideas. As the turbulence of the Depression years faded, intellectuals assimilated into the standing order by offering a new line of criticism that was less critical than celebratory: American history was the story of "consensus," not conflict. The Progressive interpretation of history, which explained the tides of reform and reaction, of public-spiritedness and private-mindedness, was filed on a dusty back shelf.

An "end of ideology" had been definitively reached. The sociologist Daniel Bell presented the most cogent analysis, arguing that disillusionment with the Soviet Union, coupled with the "rise of the Welfare State," had fostered "a rough consensus among intellectuals on political issues."[1] Ideology was once a "road to action," but had "come to be a dead end."[2] Organizationally and spiritually, the left was exhausted; and without the left there could be no ideology. "The end of ideology," wrote Bell, "closes the book, intellectually speaking, on an era, the one of easy 'left' formulae for social change."[3]

The last thing liberals expected was the rise of the conservatives. Operating on the assumption that their own intellectual authority was unassailable, it followed that conservatism was absurd. The notion of conservative intellectualism struck most as oxymoronic. Conservatives were ignored or disparaged as a fringe element. Certainly their shrill despair made no sense in an age of unspoken consensus. They were as

3

out of place as the old Progressive historians. The liberals, for the most part, had become a curious species of conservative, outspoken defenders of the regime. They specialized in suspicion of radical rhetoric, and their favorite word was "complexity."

Those who called themselves conservatives became the rebellious insurgents. Whenever the liberals stigmatized them as deviants they felt vindicated; for the liberal attitude confirmed their fundamental premise. They believed that the prevailing consensus the liberals heralded had been imposed from on high. Their own powerlessness and isolation were taken as proof that there was indeed an Establishment, that it was liberal, and that it ruled. Conservatives called this entity a variety of names: the "obliging order," the "hive," but mostly the Liberal Establishment. They viewed this juggernaut with a mixture of awe and contempt. How great was Harvard University, and *The New York Times,* the Ford Foundation, the Council on Foreign Relations, the Brookings Institution! And how great was the "hive's" invidious and pervasive influence! The key members always seemed to know each other, to promote each other's careers, and to further the same ends. If they were not a conspiracy, it was because among them everything important was tacitly agreed upon. According to the conservatives, it was a conspiracy of common assumptions.

Though there might have been an "end of ideology" for the entrenched liberals, there was no such thing for the conservatives. In 1965, the year after Barry Goldwater's pathbreaking run for the presidency as a conservative ideologue, M. Stanton Evans, a prominent right-wing writer, published his book, *The Liberal Establishment,* which elaborated a common assumption of the conservatives: "The chief point about the Liberal Establishment is that it is in control. It is guiding the lives and destinies of the American people. It wields enormous, immeasurable power . . . its control embraces the instruments of public scrutiny. It directs and instructs popular opinion."[4]

To counteract this Liberal Establishment, which conservatives believed encompassed both political parties, they deliberately created the Counter-Establishment. By constructing their own establishment, piece by piece, they hoped to supplant the liberals. Their version of Brookings—the American Enterprise Institute—would be bigger and better. The Olin Foundation would give millions, with greater effectiveness than Ford. The editorial pages of the *Wall Street Journal* would set the agenda with more prescience than *The New York Times*. And although the *Washington Times*, funded by the Reverend Sun Myung Moon, wasn't a formidable adversary for the *Washington Post*, a new generation of advocacy journalists, planted in a host of newspapers, would begin to create an alternative presence.

Conservatives crossed the empirical gap in their argument about the Liberal Establishment by taking a political leap. They imitated something they had imagined, but what they created was not imaginary. Through the making of a far-flung network they attempted to conquer political society. Their factories of ideology—think tanks, institutes, and journals—would win legitimacy for notions that would be translated into policy. The Counter-Establishment was a political elite aspiring to become a governing elite.

Conservatives have long believed that the force of ideas would lift them into power. One of the most influential books of the early conservative intellectual movement was in fact entitled *Ideas Have Consequences*. It appeared in 1948 and its author was the political philosopher Richard Weaver. In it he argued that the corrosive, modern liberal culture must be combated by creating a "metaphysical community."[5]

The Counter-Establishment is hardly an abstraction. Yet it is bound together by devotion to ideology, not tradition. Conservatism used to imply a defense of yesterday. Though contemporary conservatives claim to speak for a golden age of long ago, they are actually in revolt against the past half-century. The past is reverentially exhumed by conservatives in order to re-clothe it to fit their present wishes. They fulfill the ideal of the "metaphysical community" by organizing their institutions around their metaphysics.

"Shadow liberalism" is the main principle underlying the movement, pervading all its thinking and actions. When conservatism took institutional form as the Counter-Establishment—the opinion- and policy-making elite to counter the Liberal Establishment—it had more than a shadow relationship to liberalism. It had a shadow cause. Patrick Buchanan, the right-wing columnist and television personality who became the White House communications director, labeled the cause "a conservative counter-reformation."

Paradoxically, conservatism requires liberalism for its meaning. The conservatives' self-image, unchanging over time despite their hold on many offices in the federal bureaucracy, is rooted in their vision of the Liberal Establishment. Though they have a sense of mission, they also have difficulty rising above the adversarial stance. Even when conservatives are in power they refuse to adopt the psychology of an establishment. By accepting governmental responsibility, the conservatives' spirit as a lean and hungry movement of outsiders would be diminished. Their shadow liberalism spurs them on, but also marks the edge of their universe; if they sail beyond it, they fear they will fall off.

Among conservatives, one of the greatest fears privately voiced is that their cadres will lose sight of the ultimate goal—the dismantling of the infernal machine—and become dutiful bureaucrats, making the government run as efficiently as possible. Their psychology, however, renders them almost totally immune to the "Bridge Over the River Kwai" syndrome. Ronald Reagan himself has been exemplary, always campaigning as an anti-Establishment challenger, never as the incumbent, even while residing in the White House. For conservatives, liberals must always be in power; without the enemy to serve as nemesis and model, conservative politics would lack its organizing principle.

In the absence of a fearsome opponent, conservatives begin to lose their equilibrium; each faction of the "metaphysical community" argues heatedly that its version of conservative doctrine is the one true faith. No matter how weak the foe—Walter Mondale, for example—his menace is shown to be great. Mondale, in particular, was a necessary evil, indispensable to the conservatives as living proof of their ideological claims; he was more important to them than to the liberals.

Conservative depictions of the Liberal Establishment vary from faction to faction. Those in the evangelical right, the ultimate "metaphysical community," paint it like Hieronymus Bosch's vision of hell. Most conservative intellectuals, in the meantime, come and go, murmuring of the New Class, a force more insidious than any political movement, more influential than any political party—"the secret system," according to William Simon, the former Secretary of the Treasury and a major Counter-Establishment figure.[6] Once one learns about the New Class and its "secret system," it becomes clear that the source of modern liberalism must be located beyond the alluring superficialities of politics; it can be found in the hard reality of class. This is what lies at the heart of the Liberal Establishment: a class, as class-conscious as any prisoners of starvation, a liberal elite of "action intellectuals," simultaneously operating within and without government, imposing its desires on society.

Perhaps the most unself-consciously ironic lecture on this subject was delivered in May 1985 at a conservative conference held at Washington's Madison Hotel. Conservative after conservative, neoconservative after neoconservative, from *Commentary* editor Norman Podhoretz to American Enterprise Institute scholar Michael Novak, held forth on the dangers of "moral equivalence." This Counter-Establishment festival was intended to counter what was purported to be the liberals' habit of equating the United States and the Soviet Union; hence, "moral equivalence."

When the main course of polemics was cleared away and only dessert remained, the writer Tom Wolfe was served up. He wore pastels, the crowd wore gray. None dared call it chic. The ideological spoilsmen —conservative intellectuals with think-tank sinecures, foundation executives, political operatives, and federal jobholders—were congratulated on their "courage" for appearing at this lush affair in Reagan's Washington, incidentally funded in part by the State Department. Then came the rote attack on the New Class, those who really have power, "a class of ruling intellectuals trained to rule a country," Wolfe declared. The appeal of Marxism, he explained, was due to its "implicit secret promise . . . of handing power over to the intellectuals." In the Soviet Union there is even a name for the New Class in common usage: *nomenklatura.* About the "bad taste" of the liberal *nomenklatura* right here at home, Wolfe had many clever things to say. About the possible existence of a conservative *nomenklatura,* another item of "occupational sociology," he had nothing to say, perhaps as a show of hospitality to his hosts. The conservatives applauded, dispersed into the Washington night, and showed up at their New Class jobs the next morning.

Within Washington, the "metaphysical community" that had, through metamorphosis, become a *nomenklatura*—the Counter-Establishment—had a shape influenced by the nature of the capital. To conservatives, Jimmy Carter was a cautionary example. He left an imprint on them, and not only because he had been Reagan's victim. He was beaten, among other reasons, because he had won as a populist outsider against Washington, like Reagan. When Carter displayed confusion he was unprotected, and Washington helped defeat him. Conservatives believed that they could overcome the naturally fragmenting, centrifugal forces of the capital by providing a unifying principle. Whatever their agency or department, they would be motivated by a common ideology and held together by a political network established within the despised federal bureaucracy itself. Conservatives attributed the thwarting of change to government itself, not to the constitutional system of checks and balances. They also blamed the capital's familiar elites, whom they publicly lambasted yet enviously courted. Conservatives were incapable of tracing the cause of their ideological frustration to the founders' contrivance because they thought they were returning to first principles. In the past, the instrument of political cohesion, overcoming the separation of powers, was the party. But the conservative movement was set factionally against the regular Republicans, regarded as stalwarts of the Liberal Establishment. The movement was built upon the ruins of the old party. And in Washington the movement was to be the agent that the party once was.

Virtually every major policy initiative proposed by President Reagan percolated to the White House by means of an ideological filtration system. The outstanding case, of course, is supply-side economics, which traveled from lunatic panacea to official catechism in a few short years. The idea made all the stops: the *Wall Street Journal* editorial pages; the neoconservative journal *The Public Interest;* the foundations; the think tanks; Congress; a presidential campaign, desperate for a new theme; and, finally, the federal offices of a newly empowered conservative New Class. The Counter-Establishment had everything to do with it, the party almost nothing.

Reagan spoke often about rescinding the last half-century, thereby implying that Democratic and Republican administrations were all fundamentally alike. What we needed, he insisted, was a New Beginning.

Many political commentators were prompted to write about Reagan's potential for catalyzing a realignment of the party system, a realignment like that which his hero, Franklin D. Roosevelt, had wrought. But Reagan was operating beyond conventional partisan categories. He did not reinvent the Republican Party so much as transcend it. His primary political instrument was the conservative movement, which inhabited the party out of convenience. And his loyalty was not to the GOP, but to certain ideological tenets, which he dramatized as part of a mythology of small towns, small businessmen, and many small churches. The electorate's attraction to Reagan and his living theater, however, was not the same thing as a lasting attraction to a party.

One of the major motifs of Reagan's mythology was the battle of the "special interests" against "the people." Other names for the "special interests" were "big government," or merely "Washington." In Reagan's rendition of populism, conservatives would lead the righteous people, a crusading army of Norman Rockwell archetypes, in triumph over the corrupt and indolent cosmopolitans of the capital. This would be, Reagan announced at the beginning of his second term, the Second American Revolution.

In Washington, meanwhile, the conservative elite continued to concentrate the means of administration in its own hands. The Counter-Establishment cadres sought the commanding heights and the minor offices in the effort to control policy. And they measured their progress in wielding power by counting the jobs they held, compared with those held by regular Republicans.

While Reagan's personality and mythology sustained him with voters, the Counter-Establishment sustained him as a conservative President. At the center of the nation, the conservatives strove ceaselessly for a realignment of elites, a realignment that could never be gauged by an obvious index like the Gallup Poll; yet this extra-party realignment was an indisputable fact, unlike the party realignment, which was conjectural.

The Second American Revolution followed the pattern of the New Beginning: every important policy emanated from the Counter-Establishment: For example, the "Star Wars" outer-space defense scheme, a quintessential conservative panacea, came out of the foundations, the think tanks, and the *Wall Street Journal.*

The Counter-Establishment was also the pivot of the greatest public-private enterprise of the Reagan era: the *contra* war against the Sandinista government in Nicaragua. While the administration managed a secret war out of the National Security Council, the conservative movement raised funds to pay for it. Among the various right-wing groups set up to funnel the money to the *contras* was the Nicaraguan Freedom Fund. Its board meetings did not resemble Norman Rockwell's depiction of Thanksgiving dinner. The connections of its directors suggested the dimensions of the Counter-Establishment. Its chairman, big-business tycoon William Simon, is also president of the Olin Foundation, which disburses millions to conservatives. Jeane Kirkpatrick, the former United Nations ambassador, holds a portfolio in the Counter-Establishment's directorate as a Minister of Ideology, ruling over the fine distinction between totalitarianism and authoritarianism, between moral equivalence and the Reagan Doctrine. Michael Novak, the American Enterprise Institute scholar, is a jesuitical defender of the faith, even against the Catholic bishops, issuing conservative encyclicals against their statements on nuclear war and the economy. And Midge Decter, executive director of the Committee for a Free World and wife of *Commentary* editor Norman Podhoretz, is a thunderer against the sins of feminists, other miscreants from the 1960s, and crypto-Stalinists; she is also a trustee of the Heritage Foundation, a think tank that one conservative calls "the General Motors of conservatism." These notables represent, according to Reagan in a letter he sent Simon, "the noblest instincts of America."

The crowning event of elite realignment does not involve foreign policy or economics. It is a matter of law. By naming more than half of the federal judiciary, Reagan would install on the bench the legal wing of the Counter-Establishment. In this way he would entrench ideology in what has historically been a bulwark of conservatism. No matter who won the presidency in the future, conservatism would still exercise power as an appointive elite.

The central idea of this book is that ideas and ideology are now central to American politics. In my previous book, *The Permanent Campaign,* I described how the decline of party led to a fundamental transformation of the political system in which governing has been turned into a permanent campaign. The decline of party has had another effect: politics is now more open to ideological appeals, projected to attract the voters. Image and ideology, style and substance, are not opposites but complements. They are fused in Reagan. And behind him is arrayed the Counter-Establishment, which he brought from the political wilderness to dwell in Washington's ornate offices.

But the source of the Counter-Establishment's rise is more than a single cause, more than just the decline of party. Its ascendance was neither inevitable nor by chance. The conservative elite has been built by individuals who believe strongly, plan strategically, and move collectively.

The big money, the long green, was not much present at the creation. Will and intelligence preceded material interests and luck. To be sure, money and circumstances played their part. But in the case of the Counter-Establishment, ideas and intellectuals were in the lead.

CHAPTER ONE

THE
CONSERVATIVE
REMNANT

Albert Jay Nock was one of those rare people who physically resembled his philosophy. He was tall, dignified, and courtly. His white hair was full and his mustache neatly clipped. When he went out, he wore a cape and carried a walking stick. His style had everything to do with his substance; he was all of a piece. He was also one of a kind, a unique American species, a self-made aristocrat.

Nock was filled with apparent contradictions. He was an Episcopal minister who gave up his collar and disdained organized religion; an exponent of traditional values and free love; a defender of high culture and an obsessional anti-Semite; an anarchist who despised the masses. He was also a good writer and editor. His autobiography, *Memoirs of a Superfluous Man,* conveyed an elegant and elegiac tone about the triumph of the all-too-common man. At the age of sixty-five, still in the full bloom of his literary powers, Nock described himself as "a senile Tory."

In 1937, with Franklin D. Roosevelt and the New Deal triumphant, Nock published an essay entitled "Isaiah's Job," commending the calling of prophet. The masses, he argued, have been a hopelessly benighted group since the prophet's career opened up around 740 B.C. Posed against the masses is a tiny group of gentlemen and scholars who tend the flame of civilization. Borrowing from Isaiah and Matthew Arnold, the nineteenth-century English critic, Nock called this group "the Remnant." "There is a Remnant there that you know nothing about," Nock wrote in his version of what God really said to Isaiah. "They are obscure, unorganized, inarticulate, each one rubbing along as best he can. They need to be encouraged and braced up, because when everything has gone completely to the dogs, they are the ones who will come back and build up a new society. . . ."[1]

Yet, scanning the scene, Nock failed to detect a prophet who would lead the Remnant out of its cloisters. As World War II approached, Nock himself descended deeper into his hysterical anti-Semitism.

"It was thought that the battle was over," said William F. Buckley, Jr. In the beginning, back when Ronald Reagan was a "near-hopeless hemophilic liberal" (as he later described himself), conservatism was a deviant subculture. It was barely conscious of itself as a Remnant. And conservative intellectuals, those who might take up "Isaiah's job," were rare birds.

"It was implicitly denied that one could be conservative and rational, with the single exception of Senator Robert Taft, who was concededly brainy but thought of as an ideological automaton," said Buckley. "At the intellectual level the only people heard from were the Chamber of Commerce and the National Association of Manufacturers. They were treated as eccentrics. Nobody ever thought there was a body of learning there or that there lay ahead of the liberals a period in which empirical data would do a lot to demoralize their basic convictions."

The conservative intellectual movement built up force in successive waves. First, the conservatives were isolated, even from each other. In the second wave, with the founding of the *National Review,* they had a center. And, finally, with the establishment of think tanks, they achieved a stable institutional base.

The history of modern conservatism does not fit a conservative theory of history. Its story bears little resemblance to those of European conservatives. The native variant is not rooted in a landed gentry, in noble customs and tradition. Rather, it is a typically American story of discontinuity and self-invention. Many conservatives have convinced themselves that they are restoring the past, but the past was not kind to them. Nothing demonstrates this more clearly than the difficulty of their political odyssey. Despite their insistence that America is by nature a conservative country, they have had enormous trouble gaining a foothold. They are so haunted by the past that they still have the desperate fear that they may be sent back to the deep freeze. Even after Reagan's two landslides, they harbor the psychology of outsiders.

Conservatives did not share the vocabulary of New Deal liberalism. Like Communists, they had seen through it. Since nobody outside the Remnant shared their sectarian history, their rhetoric was exclusive. To succeed they had to become an expansive movement. The leap from first principles to politics required the aura of deep scholarship. Conservatives needed to justify their actions by learning beyond the liberal mainstream. Yet they constructed their institutions on their idea of the Liberal Establishment, usually interpreting its actions as the result of a grand design, or at least of conscious planning. Some conservatives had a vision of the opponent as a conspiracy, run by the Council on Foreign Relations, the Bilderberg Group, and Harvard University. Almost everything from foreign policy to reviews of Arthur Schlesinger, Jr.'s or John Kenneth Galbraith's latest books was seen as part of an overarching scheme. But most conservatives tended to agree with the more sophisticated account offered by William F. Buckley, Jr., who wrote:

> You need not be taken in by the solemn whisper that the Establishment has a president, an executive committee, a constitution, bylaws, and formal membership requirements, to believe that there do exist people of varying prestige and power within American Liberaldom; that we speak here of the intellectual plutocrats of the nation, who have at their disposal vast cultural and financial resources; and that it is possible at any given moment to plot with fair accuracy the vectors of the Establishment's position on everything.[2]

In the cold gray dawn of conservatism, just a handful of people, divided roughly into three ideological groups, attempted to halt the express train of liberalism. These figures represented distinct schools of thought, which thirty years later would be expressed as the mythology of Reaganism. Free-marketeers wanted to restore an austere marketplace, freed of the confounding mechanisms of the welfare state. Repentant ex-Communists, who had penetrated every concentric circle of the Inferno and seen its terrible heart, preached against the demonic power of the State. And cultural conservatives located philosophical ancestors in order to place a rootless American conservatism on the green branch of a venerable family tree.

The ex-Communists turned conservatives had once believed that the Russian Revolution was the brilliant sunrise of a new age. The Cold War was their personal dramaturgy. They underwent a complete political transformation and yet remained the same. Communists like Frank Meyer, who became a *National Review* editor, changed from true believers into true believers. They became crusaders against what had been the object of their passionate devotion. Still, they retained their desire for total victory. And their opinion of liberals remained remarkably constant. As Communists they had believed liberals were too "soft" to seize the Winter Palace and (depending on shifts in the party line) that reformism was an obstacle. As ex-Communists they believed liberals were "soft" on Communism and that their reformism demonstrated that they were in league with it "objectively," to employ the proper word from the Old Left lexicon. The ex-Communists brought to the nascent conservative cause ingrained habits of doctrinal hair-splitting and compulsive manipulation. They were always eager to engage in periodic purges, reading someone out of the "party" in order to purify it. Whether as Communists or as ex-Communists, they maintained the belief that the apocalypse was near ("'tis the final conflict"). They were always in a state of full mobilization: Red Alert.

In the 1940s and early 1950s, four signal events lit the bonfire of conservatism, awakening each of these groups. These events demonstrated that there were individuals willing and able to articulate the conservative case. Three of them involved representatives of the different schools of thought: Frederich von Hayek, a free-marketeer; Whittaker Chambers, an anti-Communist; and Russell Kirk, a cultural conservative. The fourth event was the emergence of William F. Buckley, Jr., and he would provide an instrument to unite the disparate factions.

The first happening occurred just a month after FDR won his fourth term of office in 1944, when the University of Chicago Press published two thousand copies of a book, *The Road to Serfdom,* by an obscure Austrian exile living in England, Frederich von Hayek. He argued in favor of the free market and that "planning leads to dictatorship."[3] Unexpectedly, his book became a popular success in America and Europe. *Reader's Digest* condensed it for its readers and the Book-of-the-Month Club distributed more than a million copies. Hayek lectured extensively in the United States and appeared on the serious radio discussion programs. *The Road to Serfdom* was generally conceded to be the first intellectually respectable defense of free-market doctrine to have appeared in decades.

Hayek was a living remnant—an expatriate classical liberal. When he was born in Vienna in 1899, the Hapsburgs still ruled the Austro-Hungarian Empire. All the trappings of feudalism, including monarchy, were contemporary; socialism, too, was a vital force. The upper middle class, the common origin of Austro-liberals, championed laissez faire economics and believed that order and progress would follow naturally. The historian Carl Schorske, in his magisterial *Fin-de-Siècle Vienna,* wrote:

> Far from rallying the masses against the old ruling class above
> . . . the liberals unwittingly summoned from the social deeps the
> forces of a general disintegration. Strong enough to dissolve the
> old political order, liberalism could not master the social forces
> which that dissolution released and which generated new cen-
> trifugal thrust under liberalism's tolerant but inflexible aegis.
> The new anti-liberal mass movements—Czech nationalism,
> Pan-Germanism, Christian Socialism, Social Democracy, and
> Zionism—rose from below to challenge the trusteeship of the
> educated middle class, to paralyze its political system, and to
> undermine its confidence in the rational structure of history.[4]

And all of these tumultuous events occurred at the turn of the century. Hayek came to maturity after Austro-liberalism was already in ruins, already a fossil. He transported this doctrine with him to England and eventually to America, where, after World War II, he secured a position, through connections in the nascent Counter-Establishment, at the University of Chicago. But even in Austrian terms, he was not representative of his time; he was part of the debris of an obliterated European culture. Still, he had the attraction of a perfectly preserved museum piece.

Hayek claimed that there was once a golden age of laissez faire, "the abandoned road," which led to the enduring ideals of Western civilization. His account of the glorious free market in England, however, did not mention the "dark satanic mills," mass poverty, or working-class discontent. His version of the Industrial Revolution was indifferent to Charles Dickens's version, much less Frederick Engels's *The Conditions of the English Working Class in 1844.* "There was nothing natural about laissez faire," the economic historian Karl Polanyi instructed in *The Great Transformation.* "Just as cotton manufacturers—the leading free trade industry—were created by the help of protective tariffs, export bounties, and indirect wage subsidies, laissez faire itself was enforced by the state."[5] Yet Hayek cast a romantic haze over the period, a past he wished could be revived.

Hayek's American appeal lay mostly in his advocacy of what appeared to be the old-fashioned native virtues of hard work and individualism. But he did not think in American terms at all. To the Austro-liberal, laissez faire economics would unshackle the bonds of feudalism—a breathtakingly revolutionary act. Whatever feudalism existed in America, however, was dispatched by George Washington long ago. Hayek's conservatism, consisting of a desire to conserve and extend the free market, had its source in the memory of a distant land. America wasn't what he had in mind.

Hayek, in fact, believed that the twentieth century was a mistake. He wanted progress, but yearned for a lost world, the age of fabled individualism. "Though we neither can wish nor possess the power to go back to the reality of the nineteenth century, we have the opportunity to realize its ideals—and they were not mean," he wrote. "We have little right to feel in this respect superior to our grandfathers; and we should never forget that it is we, the twentieth century, and not they, who have made a mess of things."[6]

In Britain, in 1945, during the election campaign, Hayek served as an adviser to Winston Churchill. At his instigation Churchill asserted that a "Gestapo" would be necessary to install the Labour Party's welfare state. Many Tories believe that this statement helped Churchill lose the election.

Hayek did not say where "the abandoned road" back to competition would lead in America. And who were "our grandfathers"? Should we go back to those proud individualists—the agrarian populists—who fought the industrial monopolists and the Republican Party? Or perhaps to the "New Freedom" of Woodrow Wilson, the president advised by Louis D. Brandeis to break up concentrated wealth in order to restore a free market? These traditions were not remarked upon by Hayek. To him, America was *terra incognita.* Still, his rendering of free-market doctrine struck a responsive note.

In 1948, another event occurred that advanced the conservative cause. When the ex-Communist and senior editor at *Time,* Whittaker Chambers, told House Un-American Activities Committee investigators that he had been part of a Soviet espionage ring operating within the American government, post–New Deal liberalism was shaken to its foundation. He identified a former highly placed State Department official, Alger Hiss, then president of the Carnegie Endowment, as his co-conspirator. Hiss and Chambers could not have been less alike. Hiss was the impeccable Eastern Establishmentarian: his career began as the law clerk to Supreme Court Justice Oliver Wendell Holmes; he was an ardent New Dealer; he had personal grace and social connections. Chambers seemed to be a character drawn from Dostoyevsky's *The Possessed.* (Appropriately, Dostoyevsky was among his favorite writers.) The rumpled and heavyset Chambers was suicidal and conspiratorial. He passed himself off under numerous false identities, and led a furtive life as a homosexual.

Hiss's ordeal put a "generation on trial," according to the acute British observer Alistair Cooke.[7] Ultimately Hiss was convicted of having given perjured testimony. Chambers's baroque version of subterranean Washington during the days of high liberalism, a capital crawling with Soviet spies and complicit New Dealers, seemed vindicated. Shortly before his death, Chambers wrote: "The Hiss Case was an epitomizing drama. It epitomized a basic conflict. And Alger Hiss and I were archetypes. That is, of course, what made the Hiss Case . . . what gave the peculiar intensity to the struggle."[8]

Liberals had little interest in Chambers's conversion or his philo-sophical beliefs, but were obsessed with Hiss's crisis. Chambers, mean-while, emerged from the case as a towering hero to conservatives in need of an icon. By casting clouds of doubt over the patriotism and integrity of the New Deal, he had created an opening for the right. On January 25, 1950, Alger Hiss was sentenced to prison. (And on Febru-ary 9, a little-known senator from Wisconsin, Joseph McCarthy, claimed to possess a list on which were inscribed the names of 205 Soviet spies in the State Department, which he described as "thoroughly infested with Communists.")

In 1952, Chambers's 808-page confessional, *Witness,* was pub-lished, a riveting statement of the ex-Communist position, lushly detail-ing Chambers's experiences in the Communist underground, his revelation of its perfidy, and his decision to inform. To him, the struggle with Communism was a religious crusade against the Antichrist. He saw darkness or light, demonic power or God, as the only choices. The battle of Armageddon was imminent. "The last war," he wrote, "simpli-fied the balance of political forces in the world by reducing them to two. . . ."[9] And he explained his defection as the consequence of a stark moral judgment: "A Communist breaks because he must choose at last between irreconcilable opposites—God or man, Soul or Mind, Freedom or Communism."[10]

While Chambers chose Freedom, he was fatalistic about Commu-nism's ultimate triumph. In his transformation from secret agent to "witness," his feelings about the revolution changed, but his belief in its inevitability did not. "The total situation is hopeless, past repair, organically irremediable," he wrote in a letter to his friend, William F. Buckley, Jr.[11]

Chambers believed, along with the Italian ex-Communist writer Ignazio Silone: "The final conflict will be between the Communists and the ex-Communists." In *Witness* he wrote, "No one knows so well as the ex-Communist the character of the conflict, and of the enemy, or shares so deeply the same power of faith and willingness to stake his life on his beliefs." In this climactic battle, he had no hope that conserva-tives would be of much use. "In the struggle against Communism, the conservative is all but helpless. For that struggle cannot be fought, much less won, or even understood, except in terms of total sacrifice. And the conservative is suspicious of sacrifice; he wishes first to conserve. . . ."[12]

While conservatives were "helpless," liberals gave comfort and aid to "the enemy." In fact, liberals were an aspect of "the enemy." The nature of liberalism itself was precisely what permitted Communism to flourish in dark corners. Chambers wrote:

> I saw that the New Deal was only superficially a reform movement. I had to acknowledge the truth of what its more forthright protagonists, sometimes unwarily, sometimes defiantly, averred: the New Deal was a genuine revolution, whose deepest purpose was not simply reform within existing traditions, but a basic change in the social, and, above all, the power relationships within the nation. It was not a revolution by violence. It was a revolution by bookkeeping and lawmaking. In so far as it was successful, the power of politics had replaced the power of business. This is the basic power shift of all the revolutions of our time. This shift *was* the revolution. . . . Whether the revolutionists prefer to call themselves Fabians, who seek power by the inevitability of gradualism, or Bolsheviks, who seek power by the dictatorship of the proletariat, the struggle is for power.[13]

From this insight, Chambers adduced "how it happened that so many concealed Communists were clustered in Government, and how it was possible for them to operate so freely with so little fear of detection." The answer was that liberals and Communists shared "common ends." And liberals, while they "sincerely abhorred the word Communism" were "unable to distinguish Communists from themselves."[14] This gave the Communists the opportunity to burrow deep into the recesses of government. By taking the witness stand and by writing *Witness,* Chambers not only discredited "the enemy" but helped establish a new conservatism.

In 1953, a small conservative press published a limited run of a book, *The Conservative Mind,* by an unknown writer named Russell

Kirk. After a favorable review appeared in *The New York Times, Time* magazine editors gave the volume to their former book editor, Whittaker Chambers, and requested his judgment. He portentously declared it "the most important book of the twentieth century," according to historian George H. Nash.[15] On July 6, 1953, *Time*'s entire book section was devoted to Kirk and his book.

The Conservative Mind was crucial in establishing the cause as a valid intellectual enterprise. It offered a genealogy of conservatism, an eclectic array of sources ranging from John Adams to the sour English novelist George Gissing. To Kirk, the fount of conservatism was Edmund Burke, stalwart of tradition and scourge of revolution. If one tampers carelessly with the present, the past is desecrated and the future imperiled.

Kirk described himself as having a "Gothic mind, medieval in its temper and structure."[16] Accordingly, this self-styled American medievalist referred to his residence in Mecosta, Michigan, as his "ancestral home." He was militantly antimodern, even attacking the automobile as a "mechanical Jacobin."[17] He believed that "a divine intent rules society" and that civilized society requires "orders and classes."[18] But he was no champion of capitalism, which he regarded as akin to Communism:

> The culmination of liberalism, the fulfillment of the aspirations of Bentham and Mill, and of the French and American democratic spokesmen, it is also the completion of capitalism. It is communism. Rockefeller and Marx were merely two agents of the same social force. . . .[19]

In his quest for historical legitimacy, Kirk ransacked the past for acceptable precedents. He did not believe the Chamber of Commerce–style Babbitry of the 1920s had much to recommend it. He saw the go-getting Republican ascendancy as the decadent corruption of the true conservative spirit:

> The principle of real leadership ignored, the mortal objects of society forgotten, practical conservatism degenerated into mere

laudation of "private enterprise," economic policy almost wholly succumbed to special interests—such a nation was inviting the catastrophes which compel society to reexamine first principles.[20]

To Kirk, businessmen were not the natural stewards of virtue, but money-grubbing philistines. "In the whole American nation," he wrote, "perhaps there are not a hundred important businessmen who take an intelligent interest in the problems of modern society."[21] They could not be the leaders of a new conservatism.

Kirk's dream was neo-feudal. He wished for an aristocracy to rule over a traditional culture. His elite—gentlemen and scholars—would defend values, not interests. Their status would derive from class and personal cultivation; they would conserve civilization against the onslaught of the masses demanding cheap and shoddy goods.

Kirk believed the conservative "great tradition" was sanctified by God, but failed to note when "divine intent" had settled on his heroes. When, for example, did the Founding Fathers become sacred leaders and cease being revolutionaries? He yearned for a preindustrial aristocracy in a country that had summarily executed feudalism, and he demanded tradition in a society whose imperative was change. Unfortunately, from Kirk's point of view, there was no Duke of Omnium here, but only Duke Snider and the Duke of Earl.

Kirk, moreover, rebuked democracy where the "great tradition" holds that "all men are created equal." He exalted a class hierarchy in the interest of moral values. And he did not appeal to reason, the Enlightenment virtue esteemed by the Founding Fathers, but worshiped the noble customs of imagined bygone days. He wanted to conserve society, yet the society he described wasn't America. His paradise more closely approximated the distant feudal kingdom that von Hayek, the Austro-liberal, had revolted against.

The novelty of *The Conservative Mind* aptly illustrated the lack of any conservatism with which Kirk could readily connect. He wanted to be part of an organic community, but his own alienation proved how far America was from his vision. Yet his book provided for the first time a scholarly backdrop against which the conservatives could see themselves doing honor to philosophical fathers.

Von Hayek, the philosopher of an Old World that had vanished, Chambers, the ex-Communist whose fatalism was out of step with perennial American optimism, and Kirk, the cultural conservative whose lineage was a swirl of arbitrary parentage—all awaited the figure who could lead the Remnant out of the wilderness. That figure would make his startling entrance onto the stage in 1951 when twenty-six-year-old William F. Buckley, Jr., published a precocious tract entitled *God and Man at Yale,* lambasting the faculty of his alma mater for perpetuating atheism and collectivism. He urged Yale alumni to break "the superstitions of 'academic freedom' " and restore the proper teaching of religion and individualism.[22] He raised the banner of tradition against the American tradition of liberal education. Thus Buckley's career was launched.

He stepped into the breach in a politically numb time. Everything about him was well defined when almost everyone else lacked definition. Conventional Democrats and Republicans were battling over which party best represented the dead center. "The struggle these days, if that is the word for it, is toward blandness; toward a national euphoria. . . . Dwight Eisenhower is the proper instrument of such an age," Buckley wrote in *Up from Liberalism.*[23]

The election of the first Republican President in twenty years, in 1952, did not provoke an ecstatic conservative revival. Americans were weary of Depression and war. Dwight Eisenhower, the former commander of the Allied forces, seemed to be a perfectly benign caretaker, his confident smile projecting paternal reassurance. Despite his worshipful praise of private enterprise, he was more the consolidator of the New Deal than the leader of a conservative departure; he had no intention of bringing about the restoration of the world before Roosevelt. He was, above all, a manager, who had so proven his mettle in the army that Roosevelt handpicked him to coordinate the Allied forces in Europe. Then the Eastern Republican Establishment, at the direction of Thomas Dewey, made him a presidential candidate. He liked and trusted his businessmen, kept the Foreign Service in charge of the State

Department, and warned against Asian land wars and "the military-industrial complex." He had no use for the conservative intellectuals, even as adornments. He may not have known they existed. Eisenhower's two-volume presidential memoir, *Mandate for Change,* makes not a single reference to "conservatism."[24] About the labels "liberal" and "conservative," he remarked during his retirement: "I have never found anyone who could convincingly explain his own definition of these political classifications."[25]

Buckley himself took on the task of defining conservatism. He wanted to revive the free market and forge a moral community. To him, Communism was the essence of evil—the Antichrist. Buckley was also a cultural conservative who wanted a country of Gothic buildings and stained-glass windows. He took the impulses of conservatism and offered a unifying principle. Buckley was distinctive in that he fit into no particular box. Perhaps most important, he knew how to stand in the spotlight.

Buckley's father, William F. Buckley, Sr., was an oil wildcatter and market speculator, a poor Irish Catholic boy from a small Southwest Texas town who became a multimillionaire. He was not a bland corporate manager. He was as fervently reactionary as he was devoutly religious. He wanted his children, growing up on the Great Elm family estate in Sharon, Connecticut, to possess both intellectual depth and cowboy daring.

At Great Elm, Albert Jay Nock made impressive appearances as the man who came to lunch. Young Buckley, then in prep school, was taken with Nock's style and his notion of the Remnant. It was from Nock that he first learned that there was an opening for the job of prophet.

There were other important influences on Buckley—among them Yale political scientist Wilmoore Kendall, an ex-Trotskyite turned conservative—but perhaps no one made a more profound impression on Buckley after his graduation from college in 1950 than Whittaker Chambers. His anguish and commitment, erudition and faith, attracted Buckley, who became one of his great defenders and friends. He often quoted Chambers on political strategy. "To live," Chambers wrote, "is to maneuver. The choices of maneuver are now visibly narrow. [But] a conservatism that cannot find room in its folds for the actualities is a conservatism that is not a political force, or even a twitch: it has become a literary whimsy. Those who remain in the world, if they will not surrender on its terms, must maneuver within its terms."[26]

One day, Willi Schlamm, "an old friend of Chambers in the hard anti-Communist cell at Time, Inc.," according to Buckley, appeared on the doorstep of Great Elm.[27] Schlamm was a Viennese expatriate, an ex-Communist and ideological adviser to Henry Luce, founder of Time, Inc., for whom Chambers had also worked. Schlamm had once almost persuaded Luce to launch a conservative intellectual journal as one of his stable of publications. Naturally, Schlamm would be editor, but Luce changed his mind, and Schlamm, seeking a financial angel for his magazine, came to William Buckley, Sr. He found Bill, who had boundless enthusiasm, intellectual poise, fame after the publication of *God and Man at Yale*—and his father's money.

At the same time, the small journal founded by Nock, *The Freeman,* the only conservative magazine in the field, was folding. The editorial staff split over the career and tactics of Senator Joseph McCarthy. Some cheered his rise; others deplored it. (Buckley, incidentally, was a cheerleader. In 1954 he published a defense of McCarthy, coauthored with L. Brent Bozell, entitled *McCarthy and His Enemies.*) The staff was also rent by the 1952 presidential campaign. Some supported Robert Taft as the only possible conservative standard-bearer, while a few liked Ike. *The Freeman* did not survive these controversies. With its demise, there was not a single conservative journal left in America.

Buckley began raising funds throughout 1954 for the projected *National Review.* His father gave him $100,000. "It was tough going," Buckley said. He discovered that businessmen generally were unreceptive to the renovation of conservatism. "They were demoralized as a result of being tainted by the New Deal as denizens of a dark underworld. They struggled very much to be liberal." In his search for money, Buckley approached Herbert Hoover, an almost forgotten and forlorn figure who, said Buckley, "liked the notion of a fairly high-brow journal speaking out for conservative values." Hoover, moreover, provided introductions to his friends, who provided some money. Thus Buckley raised $300,000, enough for a beginning.

The first issue of *National Review* appeared in 1955, in the wake of *The Freeman*'s collapse. It used the same typography, layout, and printer as *The Freeman,* but was wholly new. Gathered around Buckley were free-marketers, ex-Communists, and cultural conservatives. Quite purposely, there were no "modern Republicans" of the Eisenhower persuasion on the masthead. (When *National Review* was in embryo, Buckley wrote to a former comrade of John Reed and Leon Trotsky, Max Eastman, who had turned conservative: "I intend, in an early issue, to read Dwight Eisenhower out of the conservative movement . . . our principles are round and Eisenhower is square.")[28] If any of the eminences surrounding Buckley (who turned thirty shortly after *National Review*'s debut) thought they would dominate him or the journal, they soon discovered that they were mistaken. Buckley had a matchless combination of verve and editorial ability. Also, he emphasized, "I had the advantage of owning all the stock in this company. There was never any question of who ran the organization. It's amazing how many fights are avoided when you have total control."

In the lead editorial in the first issue, Buckley advanced the concept of the Remnant—the last defenders of the old values against modern liberal decadence. The magazine, he wrote, "stands athwart history, yelling Stop, at a time when no one is inclined to do so, or to have much patience with those who so urge it."[29]

National Review's first effect on history was to alter the chemistry of the conservative intellectual scene. "The magazine had an evangelistic and didactic function," said Buckley. "It brought a sense of community that had been lacking. The idea of a congregation wasn't realized until the formation of the *National Review.*"

Liberal intellectuals did not initially greet the magazine and the ideological currents that coursed through it with much respect. In an early review, the influential critic Dwight Macdonald dismissed *National Review* writers as "scrambled eggheads" and the journal itself as "the voice of the lumpen-bourgeoisie."[30] Buckley referred later to such depictions of conservatives as "hobgoblinization."

But there were more serious assaults than Macdonald's on the legitimacy of conservatism, assaults that gave Buckley and the *National Review* editors and writers the opportunity to defend their cause and establish its intellectual integrity. In 1955, the same year that *National Review* appeared, three significant books were published that classified American conservatism as, in turn, an impossibility, an impracticality, and a pathology. The historian Louis Hartz, in *The Liberal Tradition in America,* argued that American liberalism was "natural," and that the absence of feudalism meant the inevitable fall of Federalism, slavery, and socialism.[31] Just as there was no class-conscious proletariat in the European manner, there was no aristocracy; these exceptions were the rule, the logical outcome of liberalism's dominance. "The ironic flaw in American liberalism," wrote Hartz, "lies in the fact that we have never had a real conservative tradition."[32]

The political scientist Clinton Rossiter, in *Conservatism in America,* echoed Hartz's premise. The subtitle he appended to his book's 1962 edition was *The Thankless Persuasion.* Rossiter was a "modern Republican" attempting to provide justification for his creed. And he condemned the new conservatives as self-defeating:

> What disqualifies our Conservatives finally as suitable advisors in the realm of political ideas is the depth of their contempt, sometimes outspoken and always ill-concealed, for Liberalism. . . . The trouble is that they are too "real," that they have become so passionately attached to the resurgent tradition of Conservatism that they find themselves in a state of all-out war with Liberalism—and thus, in fact, with the American tradition.[33]

Rossiter didn't believe that those clustered around *National Review* fit the definition of true conservatism. He suggested that "a large wing of American conservatism, of which Buckley is the most eloquent and persistent voice, is not at all content to be simply and intuitively 'conservative' . . . its settled aim seems to be to restore a past rather than to conserve a present."[34] The only way Rossiter could see conservative intellectuals making a practical contribution to politics was through an alliance with the corporate managers. "American conservatism must, first of all," he wrote, "enlist and serve the interests of American business or abdicate responsibility for the future of the Republic."[35]

The third important critique published that year was an anthology entitled *The New American Right,* in which the leading liberal sociologists of the day attributed conservative political isolation to a reactionary status anxiety. Conservatism, they pronounced, was the last gasp of village values against modern culture. "Today," wrote Daniel Bell, "the politics of the radical right is the politics of frustration—the sour impotence of those who find themselves unable to understand, let alone command, the complex mass society that is the polity today."[36] He considered the right "outside the political pale, insofar as it refuses to accept the American consensus."[37] Seymour Martin Lipset stated that "it is extremely doubtful that the radical right will grow beyond the peak of 1953–54."[38]

Buckley answered such criticism in the pages of *National Review* and, in 1959, in *Up from Liberalism,* his most sustained argument. He believed that liberalism was dominant not because it was "natural," but because of a weakening of fundamental American values. "I think the attenuation of the early principles of this country has made America vulnerable to the most opportunistic ideology of the day, the strange and complex ideology of modern Liberalism."[39]

About democracy Buckley was ambivalent. "The democracy of universal suffrage is not a bad form of government; it is simply not necessarily nor inevitably a good form of government. Democracy must be justified by its works, not by doctrinaire affirmations of an intrinsic goodness that no mere method can legitimately lay claim to. . . . The commitment by the Liberals to democracy has proved obsessive, even fetishistic."[40]

As for "modern Republicanism," Buckley wrote that its "historical destiny . . . was to stay a radical impulse for a year or two, in exchange for a considerable erosion of the conservative position."[41]

He then took on the main criticisms of conservatism. First he summarized Hartz's argument—"Conservatism does not exist"—describing this interpretation as one of the typical liberal "techniques of indoctrination." Then he noted that another way to view "conservative dissent" was to label it a "pathology . . . a lowering political force that threatens to ring in a new Dark Age."[42]

Still, Buckley felt no need to offer an elaborate platform. Conservatism was a defense of values, not a political party. "It is not the single conservative's responsibility or right to draft a concrete program—merely to suggest the principles that should frame it. . . . Call it a No-Program, if you will, but adopt it for your very own. I will not cede more power to the state."[43]

But one thing conservatism could do was fight Communism. Buckley presented the Cold War as an Oxford Union debate in which the West was losing points. "Liberalism cannot teach Mr. Eisenhower to talk back effectively to Mr. Khrushchev, but conservatism can, and hence the very urgent need to make the conservative demonstration."[44]

Buckley may have wanted to restore the aristocracy of "the good, the rich, the well-born" (a definition offered by Federalist leader Fisher Ames). But he joined the only aristocracy really permitted in America when he became a celebrity.

His mastery of the infant medium of television was crucial in gaining conservatism a popular hearing. Buckley well understood that style served substance. "This was a period," he said, "in which it was supposed a conservative couldn't survive a confrontation with a liberal face-to-face. You'd make your arguments for rich people and run out of arguments. A few collisions had a tremendous effect. People on campus raised their eyes with new-found respect. I've always thought the panache of Keynes carried him farther than his facile arguments." Buckley was a champion debater. Television was an ideal podium for his sharp skills. "My own personal experience came terribly dramatically," he said. "After 1953, I never went anywhere unrecognized because of television. Those who matured in the 1950s were more keenly aware that television is an indispensable part of evangelization."

By 1953, Buckley was one of the first political television stars, perhaps the first who was not an elected official. He was outrageous yet insouciant, a hot message and a cool image. And in 1966, when Buckley's intellectual variety hour, *Firing Line,* went on the air, conservatism was established as a regular listing in *TV Guide.* The now-famous Buckley image was commonly taken for the essence of his philosophy.

But fame didn't temper his convictions. Rather, he used his personal renown to cover the conservative movement with the mantle of respectability. His acerbic elegance was in the service of the movement. In 1952 he became the first president of the Intercollegiate Studies Institute, the first national conservative student organization. In 1960 the founding meeting of the Young Americans for Freedom was held under his auspices at his Great Elm estate. In 1965 he ran for mayor of New York City on the Conservative Party ticket, winning about ten percent of the vote and in the process securing the new party as a force to be reckoned with in New York politics. And, of course, he provided an opening wedge in the press by establishing the first really successful conservative syndicated column. His example inspired a host of successors, from Patrick Buchanan to George F. Will.

Before Buckley, there was no common designation for people on the right. (Robert Taft, the old standard-bearer of the Republican right, had always referred to himself as a "liberal.") *National Review,* with an assist from Russell Kirk, was largely responsible for giving the believers an identity as "conservatives." (Ironically, neither von Hayek nor Chambers accepted this label.)

By becoming "conservatives," they drew upon intellectual resources beyond the American tradition, which they extolled as true Americanism. The cultural conservatives desired a fixed order of traditional values, which in Europe was sanctified by that most un-American institution, the Church establishment. The anti-Communists, though they dreaded the leviathan state, encouraged the building of a permanent and expansive national security state. And the "conservatives" assumed a continental belief in an absolute free market to an extent never before assumed in America, where the Grand Old Party was the party of the national government—the party of tariffs, land grants, and railroad subsidies.

The "conservative" label enabled conservatives to gloss over their incoherence by providing a convenient rubric under which to file everything. Identification as "conservative" also gave the conservatives a self-consciousness as a movement aspiring to power.

The discovery of an identity in the 1950s was followed in the 1960s by the discovery of politics. Some *National Review* editors urged immersion in electoral politics, while others veered toward more radical schemes. These fierce controversies raged mostly on the polemical plane and within the magazine's editorial offices. William Rusher, the publisher, believed that a principled conservatism might flourish within the Republican Party and perhaps even take it over. He was the first *National Review* figure to turn this thought into practice, casually hitting on the notion of a Draft Goldwater for President movement one day over lunch. In short order, using his contacts among veterans of the Young Republicans, a conservative activist network known as "The Syndicate," he helped field a Goldwater organization. Nobody at the magazine took his politicking very seriously until it was breathlessly reported in *The New York Times.*

With the Goldwater campaign, Buckley's mayoralty race, and Reagan's 1966 gubernatorial campaign, an immense process of political education of both the public and the conservatives themselves was set in motion. Reagan was an important figure in that he could make the conservatives' abstractions vivid in ordinary minds; he could turn the ideology into the mythology. Through his political skills, conservatism overcame the elitism of the Remnant and began to present itself as populism reborn. By 1980, conservative political activists numbered in the thousands, and political action committees were disbursing millions. But without the overwhelming sense of purpose, the movement's material resources would have lacked concentrated force. Conservatism's greatest political asset was conservatism, the intellectual capital bequeathed by the Remnant.

Behind Reagan and his alluring rhetoric stood the Counter-Establishment, which was vouchsafed the task of maintaining the power of the ideology. By 1980 the Counter-Establishment had grown from the Remnant into a vast apparatus of think tanks, journals, and institutes. And hundreds of its cadres, schooled in the movement's extra-party organizations, were recruited to serve in Reagan's Washington as a governing elite.

CHAPTER TWO

THE BUSINESS

OF INTELLECTUALS

Lewis H. Brown, chairman of the Johns-Mansville Company, wished to restore free-market economics in the aftermath of the New Deal. So in 1943 he founded what he called the American Enterprise Association. It had a budget of $80,000, no resident scholars, and no reputation. On its board were two former board members of the Liberty League, the right-wing business group that represented those Roosevelt had called the "economic royalists." In the days of Coolidge they were the lords of creation, paid national deference for their wealth, which was assumed to be the source of virtue. With Roosevelt as President, they felt that their status had been usurped, the country somehow stolen from them. Throughout the New Deal, these men desperately searched for a rational expression for their rage against Roosevelt: some issue, some study, some statistics. The AEA's founding appeared at the time to be among the minor manifestations of this impulse. In Washington, it was less well known than most corner drugstores. When Brown died in 1953, his project was still invisible.

In December 1980 the American Enterprise Institute staged a week-long festival of ideology. Its intellectual stars shone, its benefactors gave millions, and glad-handing politicians worked the crowd. *Hail to the Chief!* Enter President-elect Ronald Reagan, in black tie, happy speech in hand. "I just want you to know," he said to a beaming throng of triumphant conservatives, "that we'll be looking closely at your observations and proposals. Many of my staff have been with you during this week." Many of his staff, in fact, had just been hired from

AEI. "This kind of working relationship with AEI is one the next administration wants to maintain during the next four years."

Before Reagan's election, the Counter-Establishment cadres forged the theories; then they began putting them into action. The administration was a vast web of ideological patronage. Hundreds of officials with links to the Counter-Establishment were appointed to key jobs, from cabinet secretaries to receptionists.

In the past, Republican administrations had been staffed almost completely by big businessmen and party professionals. While these groups were still represented, they were now joined by the Counter-Establishment ideologues, whose network provided a ready reservoir of closely connected and intensely committed appointees. Through the Counter-Establishment, these conservatives had been raised to political and social eminence. But their spirit had not been tempered by the compromising charms of Washington. Under Carter, they could sense their influence growing, yet they were still removed from power. His shortcomings were an enormous incentive for them. At last, they felt, the Liberal Establishment could be toppled. "What's important isn't Ronald Reagan," explained Richard V. Allen, his National Security Adviser, during the anticipatory summer of 1980. "It's the set of attitudes he brings into office with him." The "set of attitudes" was not a cloud that happened to be drifting by. It was attached to individuals who would be brought into office. And the individuals were attached to the Counter-Establishment.

For years conservatives positioned themselves to work within the Republican Party and the government, without becoming absorbed as regular Republicans. Yet even after defeating the traditional partisans at Republican conventions ("It's no fun anymore without Nelson Rockefeller," lamented one prominent conservative), conservatives were often overwhelmed inside the Reagan administration by their rivals, who, conservatives frequently complained, were far more experienced and skilled at policy-making and bureaucratic infighting. So even after conservatives had gained control of Republican conventions and helped to elect a president, they were not fully prepared to act as a governing class. Their ambition to field a complete government, making it absolutely reliable on every issue, was far from realized. Many of their successes eventually turned out to be failures. Such conservatives as James G. Watt, Anne M. Burford, and Richard V. Allen were short-lived phenomena, and the Interior Department, the Environmental Protection Agency, and the National Security Council, respectively, fell from their grasp.

In spite of their shortcomings, conservatives inside the Reagan administration were proud of their efforts to turn their movement into a Washington establishment. "What is it Marx said about the class for itself instead of the class in itself, the class conscious of itself? The people know each other wherever they happen to be," explained Danny J. Boggs, deputy secretary of energy, whose appointment came after strenuous lobbying by the Heritage Foundation, a crucial Counter-Establishment redoubt. "It's very organic, as we used to say back in the sixties," he said. "It isn't created by grace from above. You expand outward into a network."

The credentials that carry the greatest weight among conservatives are affiliations with extra-party organizations ranging from the Heritage Foundation to the Intercollegiate Studies Institute, from the Leadership Institute to the American Conservative Union. "Having an endorsement from Heritage is important," said T. Kenneth Cribb, counselor to Attorney General Edwin Meese. "It's almost like shorthand. It cuts through the inquiries that would have to be made otherwise." He added: "We're conservatives, not party people. . . . Most conservatives are effective through the mechanism of the Republican Party."

Publication in conservative journals enhances one's credentials, especially when an article is subsidized by conservative foundations such as the Olin Foundation. The traditional old-school tie—having been an editor of the *Harvard Crimson,* for example—is not the credential of choice, and may even brand the bearer as ideologically suspect. Better to have been an editor of the *Harvard Salient,* the conservative alternative journal subsidized by a Counter-Establishment foundation.

Once AEI stood alone. By the mid-1980s, there were dozens of Counter-Establishment think tanks, foundations, and institutes devoted to virtually every public policy area, from taxes to law, from foreign affairs to family affairs. There was the Manhattan Institute and the Shavano Institute; the Center for the Study of Public Choice and the Center for Judicial Studies; the Scaife Foundation and the Bradley Foundation; the Ethics and Public Policy Center and the National Institute for Public Policy.

The Hoover Institution has had a special relationship with Ronald Reagan since 1974, when he was named an Honorary Fellow, a title shared only by Alexander Solzhenitsyn and Friedrich von Hayek. This Counter-Establishment stronghold was founded in 1919, after World War I, by that rising young Progressive Herbert Hoover. He needed a place to house the documents he had scavenged in Europe as famine relief administrator, including the best collection on the Russian Revolution. Years later the embittered and isolated former President wanted his institute to "demonstrate the evils of the doctrines of Karl Marx." He intended it to be free of the taint of "leftwingers," as he wrote to the widow of Joseph McCarthy.[1] A new director was sought, and in 1959 Hoover found his man: W. Glenn Campbell, an economist working as the research director at AEI. Soon conservative scholars were stacked in the Hoover Tower on the Stanford campus. Reagan's election as governor of California gave them an early opportunity to test their notions. All varieties of conservatism could be found at the Hoover, from libertarianism to neoconservatism. In electoral politics, almost all were Reagan partisans. During the 1976 primaries, Campbell drew the clear distinction for everyone by branding Gerald Ford a "leftist," another name for a traditional Republican.[2] Four years later, the inhabitants of the Hoover Tower prepared to assume their roles in the administration of their Honorary Fellow. Campbell himself helped select administration appointees. By 1985, fifty scholars and former fellows had served. And the budget of the institution had grown to $10.9 million, with a staff numbering about two hundred people.

Another phalanx of Counter-Establishment stalwarts came from the Center for Strategic and International Studies of Georgetown University, a mere six blocks from the White House. It was launched in 1962 as a direct offshoot of AEI; according to the de facto division of labor, CSIS handled most of the foreign policy work. Its director was David Abshire, who had been director of AEI's special projects. The first staff member hired was Richard V. Allen. In the beginning, CSIS issued short pamphlets on diverse subjects, quick hits. And a film on the energy crisis, starring the Flintstones, was produced there. But within a few years, respectability and an all-star cast were attained. Henry Kissinger joined as a fellow, triggering a rush of corporate giving. Then James Schlesinger, former Secretary of Defense and CIA chief, joined; and so did Carter's National Security Adviser, Zbigniew Brzezinski. During the Reagan administration's transition, Abshire boasted, "our center furnished more foriegn policy and national security advice than any other institution." Eighteen people affiliated with CSIS received appointments, and Abshire himself was named ambassador to NATO. By 1985, the center had a budget of about $8 million and a staff of 160 people.

In the immediate circle around the President, there was a strong commitment to the Counter-Establishment think tanks. When Reagan's term as governor ended, two of his closest associates, Caspar Weinberger and Edwin Meese, worked together in founding the Institute for Contemporary Studies in San Francisco, a small Counter-Establishment shop that held small conferences and published large books. Institutions like these were crucibles of conservative doctrine— and of conservatives.

The Counter-Establishment let Reagan be Reagan, giving him an ideological base within his administration that permitted him to be relatively independent of the conventional sources of Republican power. His rise, unlike that of Richard Nixon or Gerald Ford, was not dependent upon his standing with party regulars. The conservative movement, thriving beyond the boundaries of traditional partisanship, sustained Reagan's career, just as he sustained the movement. But he was larger than the sum of the movement's myriad parts; without him, conservatism would have lacked its political focus in the years before his election, and conservatives would never have assumed power. Reagan's indispensability allowed him to use the movement without becoming trapped by any of its factions.

"Our presence made Reaganism more acceptable," said Edwin Feulner, president of the Heritage Foundation. "Ideas are always ahead of the politicians. Ideas are refined through organizations like ours." Intellectuals, of course, had decisively shaped policy for years. But in the case of conservatism, an ideological politics was promoted by institutions that existed for that very purpose. When the parties declined, "politics became more ideological," William J. Baroody, Jr., president of AEI, observed. "The sophisticated ability to relate ideology to constituencies is what counts. And the ideology rests on technique." And both the ideology and the technique were vested in the Counter-Establishment. Without its unique resources, how could the "constituencies" be mobilized behind a conservative presidential candidate? The proposals the intellectuals promoted on the outside became those implemented on the inside. And those who formulated the ideas frequently became the administrators of their own policies.

Perhaps the two conservative think tanks that have had the most sway during the Reagan years are the American Enterprise Institute and the Heritage Foundation. They are also the most emblematic of the Counter-Establishment's history, the passage from isolation to influence.

AEI, which began as little more than a letterhead, by 1985 had 176 people on staff, ninety adjunct scholars, and a budget of $12.6 million. Thirty-four people from AEI were named to administration posts, boards, or commissions. More important, the notions that it had promoted were being turned into policy. AEI, for example, had championed the deregulation of markets. Some Democrats too, like Alfred Kahn, Carter's anti-inflation czar, believed in more deregulation. But AEI systematically promoted the issue for decades, not as a response to any immediate situation but as a matter of principle. The institute published a quarterly journal, *Regulation*, whose co-editor, Murray Weidenbaum, became chairman of the Council of Economic Advisers. And AEI ran a Government Regulation Studies program, whose director, James E. Miller III, became chairman of the Federal Trade Commission and later director of the Office of Management and Budget.

Compared to AEI, Heritage was "that feisty new kid on the conservative block," according to Reagan. It was begun in 1973, and by 1985 it had a staff of 105, a budget of $10.5 million, and thirty-six of its people had been appointed to administration jobs. Starting in 1980, the foundation published a series of thick volumes detailing the policies it wanted implemented. The books were more than wish-lists, for many of the proposals were carried out. These projects also served as a method for marshaling hundreds of cadres, focusing their energies, and bringing them to the attention of those who hired. Of the contributors to the first volume, *Mandate for Leadership,* more than thirty received jobs, among them William Bennett, who rose to become Secretary of Education, and James Watt, who became Secretary of the Interior.

When AEI was launched, Roosevelt was President and the Remnant roamed the wilderness. The Brookings Institution was the reigning think tank. Throughout the New Deal, Brookings was a constant antagonist of FDR's economic policies. Its president was a University of Chicago–trained economist, Harold Moulton, who worshiped at the shrine of the balanced budget. Roosevelt broke the idols of free-market theology, and the Brookings experts regarded him as a vandal. Brookings was an invaluable resource for those who opposed New Deal innovations, a kind of counter–brain trust, whose board was almost entirely composed of Eastern Republicans. Eventually, after Moulton departed, Brookings achieved the aura of bipartisanship by adding some Keynesians to its staff, a sign of the emerging postwar consensus. But the old economic model was not so much rejected as readjusted; classical economics became neoclassical. And Brookings presented this point of view as "value-free," which meant that the premises underlying it were not really debatable. Its experts filed through endless congressional hearings, served on whatever boards and commissions there were, and took jobs with both Republican and Democratic Presidents. Brookings produced more than "value-free" research; it produced crucial connections in the network that made up the permanent Washington establishment.

The people behind AEI envied Brookings's exalted status. To them, the imposing gray Brookings building on Massachusetts Avenue was irrefutable physical evidence of a Liberal Establishment. How could conservatism become so accepted that everyone believed it was "value-free"? The credo of William Baroody, Sr., who built AEI, was a defensive plea for tolerance: "Competition of ideas is fundamental to a free society. A free society, if it is to remain free, cannot permit itself to be dominated by one strain of thought." His mission was to make conservatism the dominant "strain of thought."

Three years after Lewis Brown died, the board of the moribund organization he had left behind asked Baroody to become its president. He was a soft-spoken and anonymous Chamber of Commerce employee, the son of a Lebanese immigrant who was a stonecutter. After graduating from St. Anselm's College, Baroody became a statistician in the New Hampshire state employment agency. A congressman named Sherman Adams befriended him and brought him to Washington, where Baroody got a job as a minor bureaucrat in the Veterans Administration. He was a nondescript functionary, but he had faith in the power of ideas. So he set out to make conservatism the reigning public philosophy and the basis of government policy. He understood that without conservative theory there could be no conservative movement.

Baroody invented a role that hadn't previously existed: impressario of intellectuals. AEI was his stage. Conservative thinkers would rehearse ideas there, and then present them to political leaders. The atmosphere—the political ether surrounding Washingtonians—would change gradually.

As a first step, Baroody altered the name of Brown's group to the American Enterprise Institute so that it sounded less like a trade association and more like an intellectual center. Then he brought in Milton Friedman, who would become a Nobel Prize–winning economist, but was little known at the time. Baroody was making his mark quietly. By the early 1960s, conservatism no longer seemed an abstraction, but a movement.

In early 1963, Baroody began planning for a presidential bid by Senator Barry Goldwater. Denison Kitchel, Goldwater's attorney and later his campaign manager, was lovingly and successfully courted. When John F. Kennedy was assassinated, Goldwater was shaken, but his advisers convinced him that the cause demanded his candidacy. "If such a candidacy could not win, it was argued, particularly by Baroody, it would at least begin a principled opposition and the educational effort needed for a subsequent victory," wrote Karl Hess, an AEI scholar.[3]

In Goldwater's campaign, Baroody controlled policy and speechwriting, all the cerebral functions. Potential competitors, like William F. Buckley, Jr., were edged out of the picture. Within the campaign, Baroody's shop was known as "the think tank." Milton Friedman was the economic adviser and Karl Hess the chief speechwriter. Hess took a suggestion from the conservative philosopher Harry V. Jaffa and inserted the most memorable lines of the campaign into Goldwater's convention acceptance speech: "Extremism in the defense of liberty is no vice, moderation in the pursuit of justice is no virtue!"

"In your heart you know he's right"—that was Goldwater's slogan. But what does your brain say? Reasoning was Baroody's specialty, but conservatism was still too novel to be convincing. Everything seemed to go wrong. The candidate was a gaffe machine running against peace and prosperity. Baroody wanted to stick to the main themes, but the political professionals resorted to desperate measures. They wanted to buy television time for a speech by the most celebrated Hollywood personality supporting Goldwater—Ronald Reagan. Baroody was livid. He mustered all his influence to try to block the speech, to keep this *actor* out of his campaign.

But Reagan learned of Baroody's maneuvering. On his way to the television studio to deliver the speech, according to Buckley, Reagan stopped his car at a gas station to use a pay telephone. He had decided he had to speak directly with Goldwater, man to man, conservative to conservative. Eventually Baroody was overruled because Reagan had more than ideology; he had the power of persuasion. On October 27, 1964, those powers were illuminated for the first time before a national audience in a political setting. Reagan's speech was entitled "A Time for Choosing." Goldwater was mentioned in passing five times, not quite an afterthought, but not the main event either. At the climax of his impassioned performance Reagan resonated with the words of Franklin D. Roosevelt. "You and I," he said, "have a rendezvous with destiny. We will preserve for our children this, the last best hope of man on earth, or we will sentence them to take the last step into a thousand years of darkness." The speech stirred a great commotion in conservative ranks. A small group of California entrepreneurs quietly discussed whether they ought to finance a Reagan run for the governorship. Reagan returned before election day to the set of "Death Valley Days" to film a tale of the Old West in which he starred as a cavalry officer captured by Indians.

Baroody, for his part, returned after election day to the think-tank business. Even though he had exposed himself as a movement ideologue, he still sought respectability. (On his office wall he displayed a letter from Hubert Humphrey as proof of AEI's broad acceptance.) At first the Goldwater campaign appeared to be a setback, stigmatizing conservatism as anachronistic and even psychotic. Richard Hofstadter, the distinguished historian, labeled it "the paranoid style in American politics." "We are all sufferers from history," he wrote, "but the paranoid is a double sufferer, since he is afflicted not only by the real world, with the rest of us, but by his fantasies as well."[4] Yet, despite the Goldwater debacle, Baroody's assessment in early 1963 of its long-term value was not all that wrong. While he feared during the campaign that conservatism might be seen as a fringe movement and that his role in the campaign might make him an outcast in political life, the Goldwater campaign was a conservative advance. A large base was created within the GOP; many voters were introduced to conservatism; the future leader, Ronald Reagan, was cast up; and AEI survived and flourished. "We had by the late 1960s a certain academic reputation. Whatever we did was credible," said Robert J. Pranger, director of AEI's international programs.

AEI, however, was not seen as an obvious resource by the Nixon administration. As late as 1969, it had only two resident scholars. "There is a clear need for a conservative counterpart to Brookings which can generate ideas Republicans can use," Patrick Buchanan, then a Nixon speechwriter, wrote in a memo to the President in 1970. And the administration seriously contemplated setting up an alternative Brookings. Charles Colson, a presidential aide, wanted to hire a former CIA agent he knew, E. Howard Hunt, to direct it. The think tank was tentatively to be called the Institute for an Informed America or the Silent Majority Institute. Another aide, Jeb Magruder, was charged with coordinating the project. Hunt suggested to Magruder that it would be a good cover for covert activity.[5] Other work was found for Hunt, as a Watergate "plumber." Gerald Ford was soon President.

Ford's tenure was brief, and his defeat was AEI's opportunity. Many prominent Ford administration officials, including the former President himself, became visiting fellows for a season or two. Arthur

Burns, the former Federal Reserve chairman, became a permanent fixture. AEI had finally attained the stature of Brookings as a government-in-exile.

Ford's special relationship with AEI had been arranged by former Secretary of Defense Melvin Laird, a catalyst in the creation of the Counter-Establishment. The presidents of the American Enterprise Institute, Georgetown's CSIS, and the Heritage Foundation all served as his congressional assistants. Laird's attachment to AEI was formed during the Goldwater campaign, when it acted as the candidate's brain trust. He began to raise large sums of money for it in the early 1970s. But the Ford *coup* meant far more than money. With the former president as a fellow, the institute's prestige was immeasurably boosted. This legitimacy extended to the ideas AEI advanced, ideas once dismissed as marginal.

The money, of course, was hardly insignificant. It was the token of AEI's tie to the corporate managers. When William Baroody, Jr., joined AEI in 1977 it had reached what he called a "critical mass." "Historically," he observed, "the funding of AEI was 25 percent corporate, with 75 percent from foundations and individuals. Today, it's 45 percent corporate, from a much larger corporate base." More than six hundred major corporations give to AEI. John Post, the Washington representative of the Business Roundtable said, "It used to be that practically every policy committee meeting would talk about making contributions to support AEI. We want to know where the country should be going. You had to have an organization that knew who was doing what in which universities. AEI knows what's going on. If I wanted an economist I'd call Bill Baroody to give me a list. I can remember the early days when chief executive officers didn't want to have anything to do with these goddamned professors. Now we understand more about the impact of ideas."

In the late 1960s and early 1970s, Baroody senior cultivated neoconservative intellectuals, who had previously been outside the conservative sphere. The neoconservatives, leftists moving right, would become an important component of the Counter-Establishment. Baroody managed their institutional attachment to conservatism. After a long discussion with Irving Kristol, the neoconservative who had the least ambivalence about going over to the other side, Baroody signed him up as a "senior fellow." Soon other neoconservatives followed, almost all of them social scientists, a weak point at AEI, where free-market economists had predominated.

One AEI project, the Political and Social Processes program, especially reflected the neoconservatives' concerns. After 1968, internal reforms within the Democratic Party changed the way presidential candidates were nominated, making primaries rather than brokered conventions the path to glory, a change that reduced the influence of the neoconservatives and their political allies. Grassroots Democratic Party activists were overwhelmingly liberal, and neoconservatives labeled them "McGovernites," after George McGovern, the first beneficiary of the alteration of party rules. The label, in the polemical style of the Old Left to which the neoconservatives were accustomed, was intended to be a term of opprobrium. At AEI, neoconservatives lamented the decline of the old party system and pondered how to revive it; they hoped their former influence could be revived. Austin Ranney, the neoconservative Democrat who ran the Political and Social Processes program, said, "It's possible that only a system managed by insiders will produce the kind of presidential candidates we'd like to have."[6] Yet the Counter-Establishment think tanks, not the traditional parties, were the ascendant institutions. The AEI neoconservatives, however, never investigated how the think tanks may have undermined the parties by usurping their policy-making function.

In 1978, AEI's president handed his office to his son. Two years later, Baroody senior died. He had brought his people to the outskirts of the promised land, but he could not enter. William junior had been press secretary to Melvin Laird when he was a congressman and later Secretary of Defense in the Nixon administration. In the Ford White House, Baroody established the Office of Public Liaison to help organize support from constituencies for the President's program. (Under Reagan, this office coordinated the "business coalition," and the task initially fell to Wayne Valis, who had been Baroody's personal assistant at AEI.)

"I make no bones about marketing," said Baroody. "We pay as much attention to dissemination of product as to the content. We're probably the first major think tank to get into the electronic media. We hire ghost writers for scholars to produce op-ed articles that are sent out to one hundred and one cooperating newspapers—three pieces every two weeks. And we have a press luncheon monthly." AEI produces a monthly television show on public policy shown on more than four hundred stations, a weekly radio talk show on more than 180 stations, four magazines (*Regulation, Public Opinion, The AEI Economist, Foreign Policy and Defense Review*), legislative analyses, and books. It sponsors conferences on important issues in which the press and policy-makers participate. And it runs seminars for corporate managers. "It's important for them to deal with public policy issues that permeate the environment in which they have to do business," said Baroody. "That has become clear to them."

In the 1980 campaign, the preferred candidate of almost everyone at AEI was George Bush. While the institute had been indispensable in the creation of supply-side economics, it also housed the doctrine's principal critics. The skepticism of economists like Herbert Stein was in line with the wariness with which the corporate managers approached the supply side. When Bush attacked the theory as "voodoo economics," belittling Reagan's belief in it, there was much affirmative head-nodding at AEI. But Bush faltered, and Reagan inherited his brain trust. In his campaign, all the various tendencies of the Counter-Establishment merged as one.

AEI's research was now accorded the deference that Baroody had hoped for. In its alliance with corporate executives, espousal of traditional free-market economics, and criticism of liberals, AEI became almost exactly what Brookings was in the 1930s. Its mission was fulfilled. Tribute was paid by the experts at Brookings, who edged rightward. The Democratic politicians who reflexively relied on Brookings's judgment were dragged to the right, too.

"We are on the front lines of policy," said Robert Pranger. "We were there when the times needed us, but we helped create the times. We're the flagship of conservatism." But the institute gained respectability at the expense of some of its insurgent spirit. The militance that easily came to outsiders came harder to insiders. By the mid-1980s,

AEI's influence rested less on its eagerness for combat than on its connections and bureaucratic stability.

While AEI's rise paralleled the political parties' decline, there was no obvious connection. Heritage, however, is self-consciously a para-party organization. Ideology is its deliberate instrument for power. The foundation cultivates promising politicians, who in turn attempt to gain prominence by using the ideas. The result can mean publicity, a favorable image, and reelection.

"AEI is like the big gun on an offshore battleship," said Burton Yale Pines, Heritage's vice-president for research. "We are the landing party. If they hadn't softened it up, we wouldn't have landed." Heritage wants liberalism to tender an unconditional surrender. It enlists intellectual marines eager to fight for every inch of beach.

If AEI had Brookings as a model, Heritage had AEI; and whereas AEI emerged in the dark ages of conservatism, Heritage was born in the conservative dawn. "Here at Heritage we believe without hesitation that our conservative ideas are right," said Edwin Feulner. "We don't worry whether other people think they're respectable or not. That is not the way AEI thinks about it." AEI wants to be at the center of a new center that has shifted right. Heritage knows it is at the center of the Counter-Establishment.

The Heritage leadership has actively fostered the disintegration of the old political system. The right is built on the ashes of the old center. Like much of the rest of the new conservative *apparat,* Heritage is dependent upon the money of entrepreneurs, fascinated by the political uses of high technology and impatient with traditional conservatives.

Heritage was begun with a $250,000 grant from Colorado brewer Joseph Coors. (Coors was also the financial angel behind James Watt's Mountain States Legal Foundation.) Whereas AEI relies upon the managers of the big corporations for its sustenance, Heritage counts on new money, mostly from the Sunbelt. The self-made men, who view themselves as rugged individuals on an economic frontier, still run their enterprises. Their firms have not matured to the point where management and ownership are separated, the common condition among the Fortune 500 companies.

The entrepreneurs view the Liberal Establishment as a foreign, occupying power. Archetypal Establishment institutions such as the Council on Foreign Relations do not reflect the newly successful capitalist's outlook. He sees them as liberal, effete, and not truly American. He wants his own establishment, which can govern America as he understands it. Heritage is part of this scheme.

Heritage also relies heavily on direct mail to generate funds. It claims at least 140,000 contributors who give a minimum of twenty-five dollars. These givers enable Heritage to have the courage of its convictions. "We can be principled because we have a broad base of public support," said Feulner. "If a corporation that gives us $25,000 says our position on something is unacceptable and that they can't fund us, we can say 'Sorry.' "

"A lot of people were struck on the road to Damascus," he said. But Feulner himself is no convert. He dates his adherence to the conservative faith to his early intellectual awakening in 1959, his freshman year in college. In a history course at Regis College in Colorado, he read Russell Kirk's *The Conservative Mind* and Eric Kuehnelt-Leddihn's *Liberty or Equality.* After turning the last page, his mind was set in a pattern that would never waver. Thus began a career that has covered most of the stations of the conservative cross.

Feulner's appetite for conservative literature prompted him to subscribe to the *National Review,* where he noticed an advertisement for the Intercollegiate Studies Institute, a conservative student group. He joined, making connections that would serve him well over the years.

A year after gaining an MBA degree from the Wharton School in 1964, he attended the London School of Economics, where his studies were underwritten by an ISI fellowship program named after Richard Weaver, the early conservative philosopher and author of *Ideas Have Consequences.* And while he did graduate work from 1965 to 1968 at Georgetown University, his roommate was another ISI member, John F. Lehman, who was later appointed Secretary of the Navy.

Three years after conservatives set up CSIS in 1962, Feulner received another fellowship, this one from a program run by Richard V.

Allen, another ISI member. Then, through Allen, Feulner became a Hoover Institution fellow, where he worked as a policy analyst for Melvin Laird, then head of the House Republican Conference. After he left Laird's staff, he joined that of Representative Philip Crane of Illinois, a pre–Reagan era conservative idol and, incidentally, an ISI member.

Feulner was struck by the conservative failure in Congress. He wanted to change the congressional as well as the public debate. Along with other conservative staffers on Capitol Hill, he became convinced that the traditional House Republicans lacked imagination, will, and strategy. "There was a feeling among the younger ones of us that in this town the old conservative system wasn't working," said Philip Truluck, executive vice-president of Heritage, who was an assistant to Senator Strom Thurmond of South Carolina. "Conservatives ended up losing most of the time. There was no strategy. We had a pretty clear idea of what we wanted to do. We felt we needed a research group that could address legislative issues. There was no lack of talent and manpower for the liberal perspective. They had Brookings and the majority of the committee staffs. The conservatives did not have the staffs. They didn't have too many places to turn to for research work." So Feulner founded the Republican Study Committee to fill the vacuum. (His 1981 Ph.D. dissertation at Edinburgh University was about the committee.) This group was a forerunner of Heritage.

In the meantime, Joseph Coors, the brewery tycoon, was looking for new ways to propagate conservatism. With his money, Feulner and another Capitol Hill aide, Paul Weyrich, founded Heritage in 1973. Weyrich eventually left to lead New Right political action committees. And Feulner became president of Heritage.

Heritage energetically expounds conservative doctrine. It produces a theoretical journal, *Policy Review;* stages symposia on subjects like "Objections to Conservatism"; hosts "Distinguished Scholars"; sponsors an annual "Growth Day" devoted to free-market economics; and publishes numerous papers. But its main effort is in the daily world of government.

As Heritage embarked on its mission, Congress itself was undergoing a transformation. First, party discipline was breaking down. "[House Speaker] Sam Rayburn could cut a deal with Ike and it would be kept. The system has disintegrated," said Feulner. Then the congressional staffs expanded. "Fifteen or twenty years ago," he noted, "a congressman took for granted that his party mates on a committee were looking out for him. He would vote without paying too much attention. He had two or three staffers. Now, you've got bright Ph.D.'s trying to make their mark by writing new laws. Think tanks have opportunities for impact and input. The congressional staffers have to get their ideas from someplace. Getting it to the right staff guy is as important as getting it to the congressmen."

Heritage has several dozen policy analysts who are the heart of the organization. Almost all are under forty years old; many are new Ph.D.'s or are still writing their theses. Each analyst has a specialty, such as energy or taxes. They are expected to develop contacts on the key congressional committees dealing with their subjects. They cultivate staffers, taking them out for *de rigueur* Washington lunches, to learn the progress of issues and bills. Among the cadres, this is known as "tracking." If a hearing is coming up, they will attempt to shape it. A study will be prepared; the average time for preparation of a Heritage paper is six to eight weeks. The paper will be given to a receptive staffer or congressman before the hearing. "We feed into Congress," said Truluck.

Another way Heritage "feeds" this process is through its Academic Bank, directed in the early 1980s by Willa Johnson. (Her successor was Robert Huberty, an ISI member and a researcher for Richard Nixon during the writing of his memoirs.) This operation was instrumental in transforming isolated conservative intellectuals into a network. Johnson was a circuit rider, discovering policy groups and individuals "without an institution to plug into," she said. "They have an expertise and they don't know how to get it into channels. Heritage is an institution by which they can do that." Johnson had 1,600 scholars coded into her computer, the Heritage reserve army. Press "C-5" and a list of business economics experts is printed out. Johnson added new names continually. (In 1977 she recruited Edwin Meese, who became an active participant at Heritage meetings and conferences.)

Heritage disseminates news of the Academic Bank intellectuals through a publication called *Insider Newsletter*. It also publishes a thick volume entitled *Annual Guide to Public Policy Experts*—experts on tap for political action.

The foundation then "feeds" these experts into legislative hearings. When a Heritage staffer learns of a hearing, the Academic Bank is set in motion. For example, Johnson was informed by a staffer that a hearing on health policy was coming up in a month. She knew of a group in California working on a relevant book. She rushed the scholars to mail draft chapters, which were forwarded promptly to the interested congressman. The experts were called to testify. And while they were in Washington, Heritage gave a press luncheon for them to spread the message.

Through this process, Heritage alters the experts' attitudes. "We impart to them a sense of timing," Johnson said. "Dealing with the academic community can be frustrating. They're used to their own deadlines with no concept of how to plug it in here. We've given them a sensitivity. It's helped refine their product. This community lacks marketing. We do that."

"We don't just stress credibility," said Feulner. "We stress timeliness. We stress an efficient, effective delivery system. Production is one side; marketing is equally important." Every congressional staffer is in the Heritage computer. So are about 3,500 journalists, organized by specialty. Every Heritage study goes out with a synopsis to those who might be interested; every study is turned into an op-ed piece, distributed by the Heritage Features Syndicate to newspapers that publish them. "Our targets are the policy-makers and the opinion-making elite," said Pines. "Not the public. The public gets it from them."

Heritage's mastery of what Pines called the "decision-making loop" was illustrated early on by the progress of the idea of "urban enterprise zones." These are depressed city areas where, according to the proposal, taxes would be reduced in order to attract business. The first paper on the subject was written by a Heritage staffer, Stuart Butler. It was then circulated in Congress, and Jack Kemp, the ardent supply-sider particularly attuned to ideological politics, was excited by it. Heritage conducted a seminar for a select group of congressional aides, while Kemp, according to Feulner, "worked the political process." George Will, the conservative columnist, who began his Washington career as a member of the conservative network on Capitol Hill, working as an aide to right-wing Senator Gordon Allott of Colorado, entered the act, writing a laudatory column in *Newsweek*. During the 1980 campaign, Reagan endorsed it. In early 1981, Butler published a book detailing the argument. Heritage also held a conference on it, with mayors and black businessmen in attendance, in Atlanta. In the summer of 1981, the idea was discussed by senior aides in the White House; by fall, it had solid support. In January 1982, the President proposed it in his State of the Union address.

On virtually every issue of the moment Heritage has a position and attempts to steer the debate in the right direction. On the eve of the 1985 Summit between President Reagan and Soviet leader Mikhail Gorbachev, the foundation circulated an unsigned paper within the administration, on the Hill, and throughout the media calling for non-compliance with the Anti-Ballistic Missile Treaty, cleverly explaining in precise detail how such an action could be defended within the legal terms of the treaty itself. Among the intransigent hard-liners this was a welcome document, and within the top echelons of the Pentagon and the White House an attempt was made to push it in an effort to prevent any potential arms control agreement.

Policy after policy, week after week, the routine is the same. But Heritage does more than move ideas; it moves people. "People are policy," said Feulner, a maxim that has entered the folklore of the conservative movement. "We can point the White House to the infantry officers to fire the guns," he said.

During Reagan's first term, Heritage collected thousands of résumés that were regularly carted over to the administration's personnel office. Not all of the job-seekers who mailed their curriculum vitae to Heritage were ideologically desirable. "A lot of them were like Republican operatives. . . . They weren't interesting; we didn't know them," a Heritage official said. "They simply worked on the campaign. Heritage was in no position to recommend them. They weren't in the circle."

Before the 1984 election, Heritage altered its approach. It no longer stockpiled résumés. Instead, it helped place trustworthy applicants solely on the strength of the foundation's contacts within the administration. "Occasionally," a Heritage official said, "a staff aide to a cabinet secretary will call and say, 'We have twenty positions to fill. Do you have any résumés?' I'll say, 'Tell me what you want. Give me a list. We'll see what we can do.'"

"Conservatives don't come to Washington looking for jobs," said Herb Berkowitz, Heritage's public relations director. "It requires an effort by someone on the inside to staff the administration with true believers." But Heritage's incessant demands do not always result in instant gratification. "You can never be satisfied by White House personnel," said a Heritage official. "They can never accommodate just one institution."

Yet the foundation's ties to the administration were sufficiently intimate so that Edwin Meese, veteran of many Heritage conferences and meetings, wrote a letter on White House stationery endorsing the group's President's Club, composed of donors who give more than $1,000. "The President's Club," Meese wrote, "will provide a vital communications link between policy makers and those key people who made possible President Reagan's victory."

On October 3, 1983, at Heritage's black-tie tenth-anniversary banquet, Reagan himself declared: "Historians who seek the real meaning of events in the latter part of the twentieth century must look back on gatherings such as this."

The Counter-Establishment think tanks, seeking to make profound changes in the economy and society, succeeded also in making procedural changes in politics and governing. "Party considerations are secondary," declared Feulner. "Ideology," proclaimed his colleague, Philip Truluck, "is *it!*"

The alliance of the party of principle with the party of interest—the intellectuals and the corporate managers—was not easily arranged. There were hesitations on all sides. The intellectuals distrusted the businessmen's lack of principles, while the businessmen distrusted the intellectuals' insistence on consistent belief. The entrepreneurs came to the Counter-Establishment early; the corporate managers lent support later and were never true believers. "The events of the last few years have emboldened the corporate managers to be more conservative and socially conscious," Buckley observed. "This wasn't easy for them."

Until the mid-1970s the corporate managers had been indifferent, at best, to the conservative intellectuals. They felt they had little need for abstract and ideological theoreticians. "The great frustration my father faced," William Baroody, Jr., said, "was convincing the business community of the relevance of ideas to the practical world of American society. That wasn't what they were about. They were about business. They were not in the business of politics. But there's been an evolution over the past twenty years, epitomized by the issues AEI has worked on."

With the growth of the federal bureaucracy, accelerating even under Republican presidents, and the threat of economic stagnation, the corporate managers suddenly began paying attention. The increasingly technical nature of economic production had compelled elaborate planning of operations and consumer desire. Now the most advanced chief executive officers realized that policy must be influenced to make their planning successful. Economic development depends upon the ability to marshal resources, including the resources of ideas and persuasion. Power in a democracy rests ultimately upon belief. Feeling challenged by the consumer movement and by the federal government as planners, the CEOs wanted to shape events, not react to them. Conservative intellectuals no longer seemed peculiar, but essential. Corporate managers became convinced, upon hearing the conservatives tell them, that they needed to support an intelligentsia to advance their goals.

The CEOs did not need to control intellectuals directly to get the ideas to enhance their position. Intellectuals, after all, do not work well when strictly supervised; they require autonomy. Moreover, intellectuals who are considered by their peers to lack independence have no reputation and hence no value. Investment in ideas is necessarily speculative; they cannot be contracted for with an expectation of immediate return. "What comes out of AEI is the statement of an individual," said John Post, the former Washington representative of the Business Roundtable, the leading policy group of corporate managers. "We have to *not* influence them in any way. We don't say, 'Write a brief.' They do some of the essential research to build a good case."

Irving Shapiro, former chairman of Du Pont and the Roundtable, said, "AEI supplied a framework for a lot of business beliefs. There's value in getting the flow of ideas."

Clifton Garvin, chairman of Exxon and former chairman of the Roundtable, said, "I'm a supporter of AEI. I support others, too, like Brookings. The ability to articulate and present well-reasoned views isn't easy. To have a group like that, even though they're biased in one direction—conservative—has been helpful."

And David Rockefeller, the former chairman of the Chase Manhattan Bank, observed, "AEI has moved much more to the middle-of-the-road approach. And Brookings has moved more to the center. Both are moving to what I happen to feel is a better position. AEI now has very solid people working for them. These are respected middle-of-the-road economists. They're not far out in their thinking."

To propagate the ideas that they believed would lead to political triumph and economic revival, the CEOs began supporting AEI and other Counter-Establishment think tanks. These institutions were a political New Class version of what John Kenneth Galbraith called the corporate "technostructure," which he defined in *The New Industrial State* as embracing "all who bring specialized knowledge, talent or experience to group decision-making. This, not the management, is the guiding intelligence—the brain—of the enterprise."[7] The "technostructure" inside corporations jealously protects its prerogatives to plan. Think-tank intellectuals belong, in some loose sense, to an external technostructure. They are micro-planners, who think not in terms of particular firms but particular policies; and they are macro-planners, who think of the political economy as a whole. Thus the free-market economics espoused by the think-tank intellectuals may serve the interest of the private planners. Unraveling the government becomes a form of control over it and a method to concentrate planning in private hands. In seeking to liberate markets, the intellectuals may open the way for the CEOs.

Walter Wriston, the former chairman of Citicorp and a member of AEI's development committee during the early Reagan years, explained, "It takes about twenty years for a research paper at Harvard to become a law. There weren't any people feeding the intellectual argument on the other side. Brookings is fat with liberals out of office. AEI is the other side of the operation. It puts an idea in the market. We figured it out." And what was "it"? Wriston misquoted a lyric from a Barry Manilow song: "I write the songs the world sings."

CHAPTER THREE

THE BUSINESS
OF AMERICA

Business is not an all-powerful, unified force. The wealthy do not rule by decree, with hired agents carrying out the orders. Of course elites do exist, but they cannot be adequately explained by any crude theory of economic determinism. Moreover, business is an intricate mosaic presenting an often perplexing picture.

The most important business elements involved with the Counter-Establishment are Sunbelt entrepreneurs and corporate managers. Each has its own relationship with this infrastructure, its own notion of capitalism, its own view of the future. The contrasts between the entrepreneurs and managers are significant and sometimes sharp. Their positions within the economy and politics differ, and so do their ideologies. They are often at odds.

Throughout the 1970s, the chief executive officers of major corporations began to play a much more personal and direct role in the political arena than ever before. They became profoundly disillusioned with the post–World War II consensus. Federal regulatory agencies, they believed, hampered productivity; government expenditures, under the rubric of Keynesian economics, produced inflation; and taxes inhibited investment. In 1972 the CEOs formed the Business Roundtable to shape public policy. By the late 1970s, many corporate managers were giving money to Counter-Establishment institutions such as the American Enterprise Institute, which incidentally set up a special seminar program to educate CEOs. In the 1980 campaign, most CEOs initially supported John Connally and then George Bush; they backed Reagan only after it was a certainty he would be the Republican nominee. "On the East Coast," said Walter Wriston, then the chairman of Citicorp, "a lot of us underestimated his skills and his great political strength." Through the Roundtable, the top managers backed the initial Reagan economic program. They are concerned, above all, with results, and they will move with any new political trend that promises to benefit them. Still, for all their emotional adherence to the romance of the free market, they have little taste for the risks and terrors on which entrepreneurs thrive.

The Sunbelt entrepreneurs possess neither authority endowed by inheritance nor authority stemming from bureaucratic function. For almost all Sunbelt entrepreneurs, social status is derived entirely from crisp new money, not any prior rank in the community. Often their communities are new and their public leadership untested. They are part of a great geopolitical shift that has occurred since World War II. Indisputably the Sunbelt has been a region on the rise, and just as indisputably the Northeast and Midwest have been in decline. The major cities there are losing population; relative income and the share of the federal budget are down; and basic industries are decaying. One consequence of this historic change is that the Establishment that arose on the wealth of this region is no longer unchallenged.

The Sunbelt entrepreneurs generally don't view the corporation as a social institution with communal obligations. Instead, they see it as the projection of an individual: they preach economic egoism. This new plutocracy lacks both the patrician heritage of noblesse oblige and the managerial instinct for conformity. To the entrepreneurs, private success is the fulfillment of social responsibility. Members of the larger community, they believe, should strive to emulate their example and become successful, too. Work-and-win is the way for everybody.

The entrepreneurs identify with an old version of business ideology, which they believe is completely contemporary. To them, free-market doctrine is autobiography. For the most part, they think of themselves as country boys who have made good in the city. Entrepreneurs believe that the American frontier is still vibrant in the Sunbelt. They see themselves near the beginning of time, the New World still unexplored, its riches barely tapped. Free enterprise, individualism, survival of the fittest—these are their dogmas. They believe that this is the true Americanism and that the inherent legitimacy of go-getters derives from universal truths. If the entrepreneurial worldview isn't correct, then the very terms of American success that made this country great are wrong. And that can't be.

Although the Sunbelt entrepreneurs have accumulated great wealth, they are envious and resentful of the Eastern Establishment, which they equate with the Liberal Establishment. The parvenu entrepreneurs tend to be practical men who are often obsessed with the prerogatives of caste superiority, especially those they may not possess, such as an Ivy League education. Their own rise is recent, a postwar phenomenon, and they feel excluded because of an Eastern Establishment monopoly of prestige and political power. To be wealthy and yet to be an outsider engenders an extremely powerful emotion of resentment.

At the same time that they may harbor envy for Ivy Leaguers, the entrepreneurs are affronted by them. They regard the values of the Liberal Establishment as antipathetic to their own, somehow unpatriotic and vaguely alien. By breaking the hold of the Liberal Establishment on national affairs, they believe they can redeem the American Dream of individual opportunity. They see in the crisis and decline of old Establishment institutions their main chance.

Just as a compliant public authority was necessary for the Robber Barons of the nineteenth century to consolidate their positions, so it is today for the Sunbelt entrepreneurs. The rugged individual alone cannot maintain a strategic political position for long; individuals require institutional support. For the entrepreneurs, the Counter-Establishment is a means of linking economics to politics and thereby making their power systematic. The nature of entrepreneurial enterprise doesn't permit the owner to preside over a system like that of the corporate managers. While an entrepreneur may be able to have his way locally, his money is never enough to dominate national politics; his business by itself can't give him a commanding position in Washington. Old-fashioned partisanship is not necessarily the entrepreneur's answer, and it's noteworthy that there is little Republican tradition in most

Sunbelt states in the manner of the Northeast and Midwest. The new men of money seek to create new avenues to power, a new political system. They want the respectability that only lasting political power can confer.

The first President to base his political strategy explicitly on the regional shift of forces to the Sunbelt was Richard Nixon. He and his advisers sought to realign American politics along the lines suggested by Kevin P. Phillips in *The Emerging Republican Majority.* Phillips argued that Sunbelt voters and disaffected blue-collar voters in the Northeast and Midwest could be united by social issues such as opposition to "acid, abortion, and amnesty," as Vice President Spiro Agnew put it. This mass coalition was arrayed against the Eastern liberal elite, yet implicit in the Phillips strategy was the rise of a new elite.

Nixon's Sunbelt strategy informed his administration. More than half of his cabinet appointments were from the Sunbelt, as well as about a third of the agency chiefs, half of his nominations to the Supreme Court, and about two-thirds of the senior staff positions within the White House. Sunbelt entrepreneurs were a pillar of his support. Nixon's homes in Key Biscayne, Florida, and San Clemente, California, anchored the Sunbelt's far ends, symbolically proclaiming the regional power shift.

Significantly, Nixon's career had been financed over the years by an exclusive group of 160 entrepreneurial types known as the Lincoln Club, headquartered in Newport Beach, California. Herbert Kalmbach, Nixon's personal lawyer, was the club's chief strategist and fund raiser. His offices were in the Irving Tower, along Newport Beach's "Millionaire's Row," near the docks where the entrepreneurs parked their yachts. A short distance away were the offices of Stuart Spencer, the political consultant who managed Ronald Reagan's gubernatorial campaigns and later would have a hand in his 1980 presidential bid. John Wayne, the cowboy icon, lived here too, and Kalmbach often had drinks with him. Among Kalmbach's corporate clients was Dart Industries, owned by Justin Dart, one of Reagan's friends and most important money men. (Kalmbach would later be convicted of Watergate-related crimes, having run the secret slush fund that financed dirty tricks and provided hush money to the Watergate burglars.)

Nixon was neither a pure conservative nor a pure Sunbelt entrepreneurial figure. He was, after all, Dwight Eisenhower's Vice President; a Wall Street lawyer; and the one who installed Harvard professor and Rockefeller adviser Henry Kissinger as his National Security Advisor and later Secretary of State.

In personality, Nixon and Reagan could not be more different. Nixon never escaped the dark resentments of growing up poor. Reagan, despite a childhood of relative deprivation, accepted the good life easily. His conservatism is not an attempt to get even with enemies, real or imagined. He stands for the sunny side of the Sunbelt, where everyone optimistically hopes for stardom.

Nixon was a keeper of "enemies" lists. He considered all sorts of people, from politicians to movie actors, to be his sworn enemies. But he believed his biggest enemy wasn't so much a person as a powerful network—the "Establishment." On March 13, 1973, Nixon met with his counsel, John Dean, to plot the Watergate cover-up. Their conversation was immortalized on the White House tapes. "I tell you," Nixon said about the unfolding scandal, "this is the last gasp of our hardest opponents. They've just got to have something to squeal about it. . . . They are having a hard time now. They got the hell kicked out of them in the election . . . the basic thing is the Establishment. The Establishment is dying, and so they've got to show that despite the success we have had in foreign policy and in the election, they've got to show that it is just wrong just because of this."[1]

In Nixon's mind, the Watergate affair was used by the "dying" Establishment to stymie him. And what was his intent? Ultimately, it was to realize the Phillips scenario, to create a political realignment using the Sunbelt as his bastion. His personal instrument, the Committee to Re-elect the President (CREEP), was a prototype of the organization to replace the traditional Republican Party. Throughout his career, Nixon had been a staunch party man. The party sustained him through good times and bad. His rise, after all, hadn't been fueled by charisma or the conservative movement; in 1968 he even had to head off a right-wing challenge from Ronald Reagan in order to secure the presidential nomination. But by the early 1970s, Nixon was no longer operating in the old-fashioned partisan mode. After his landslide 1972 election victory, "we even deliberated for several days about starting a new party," he wrote in his memoirs.[2]

According to his speechwriter William Safire, Nixon "saw in the quiet abandonment of party loyalty, a higher loyalty—the ability to build a new majority based on the principles so long espoused by the largest part of the minority party, and by so doing to reconstitute the Republican Party as a majority party."[3] Nixon's post-partisanship was not post-ideological. As he saw it, American politics in the future would become more ideological and the dominant factions would be based on ideological rather than classically partisan divisions. Safire locates the impulse of Nixon's new politics in his psychology. His "us-against-them syndrome," Safire writes, "led to a demand for a two-ideology system, rather than a two-party system."[4] To be a dominant leader in this system, Nixon believed that a political mythology would be essential. Myth raises ideology to a truth beyond facts and cloaks the politician with a compelling and indestructable mystique. Safire writes that Nixon was "too conscious of the need to create a myth. By surrounding power with mystery, Nixon believed he would gain a momentum and fashion a shield in times that called for unpopular actions."[5]

In 1968 Richard Whalen, a conservative intellectual, worked as a speechwriter for Nixon. When Nixon contemplated vice presidential choices, Whalen urged that he select Ronald Reagan. "Why, if the momentum of events and the mood of the people are running toward conservatism, should we deny ourselves access to this potential majority?" he wrote in a memo to Nixon. "If the Democrats had a governor of the most populous state in the nation, who had sex, glamour, and expert proficiency on the tube, who projected the image of the 'citizen' politician to an electorate fed up with 'professionals,' would they rule him out for a place on the ticket because of ideological qualms? They would not."[6]

Whalen departed from the Nixon entourage before Nixon entered the White House, explaining his rift in a book, *Catch the Falling Flag.* Whalen felt that Nixon did not have any "guiding ideals" or commitment. In 1970, in Whalen's last letter to Nixon, he analyzed the problem of conservative politics in America as one that extended beyond immediate political concerns. Conservatives, Whalen stated, didn't have an array of institutions on their side that would create an environment making conservatism part of the atmosphere. "In the long run, ideas are the decisive force in a free society," he wrote. "Our side is woefully short of the institutional resources necessary to complement and consolidate our present political strength. . . . On our side there is no Ford Foundation, no Brookings Institution, no Kennedy Institute; and yet we have intelligent, resourceful men, instinctively aware of the deficiency, who need only inspiration, leadership, and a strategy to do what is required." Nixon, upon reading Whalen's letter, told him to "proceed discreetly."[7] Whalen despaired. He withdrew to his own business consulting firm.

The failure of the conservatives to develop their own infrastructure, Whalen believed, left Nixon exposed to the attacks of the Liberal Establishment. Nixon's frustration was epitomized by one of the many bizarre incidents that eventually were collected under the heading Watergate: presidential assistant Charles Colson's attempt to organize a firebombing of the Brookings Institution. Burn, liberals, burn!

Whalen himself was fascinated by the Kennedys as a family and a political dynasty. His first book was *The Founding Father,* a best-selling biography of Joseph P. Kennedy, patriarch of princes in the sense that Machiavelli meant. Although Whalen was a conservative, he found a great deal to admire in John F. Kennedy. He wished his side could produce a figure of comparable grace and appeal. In his writing on the Kennedys, he implied that the family provided the political infrastructure that made their careers possible; it was something the conservatives couldn't match.

Whalen bided his time. And in 1980 he served as a speechwriter and adviser to Reagan.

By 1980, the shift of electoral power to the Sunbelt states, the entrepreneurial frontier, was self-evident. Carrying exactly the same states Richard Nixon did in 1960 against John F. Kennedy, a candidate would win. "Under the new electoral calculus," Kevin Phillips pointed out, "William Jennings Bryan would also have been an easy winner in 1896."[8]

The first businessmen to recognize the political potential of Ronald Reagan were Sunbelt entrepreneurs, and his immediate circle of friends is largely composed of these men. As owners of their own enterprises, the entrepreneurs answer only to themselves. They are not subject to the constraints and compulsions of shareholders, as are corporate managers; their careers are not at the mercy of quarterly earnings reports, so they can afford to take the long view. When they first scouted Ronald Reagan, they saw him as a man like themselves, a self-made man who shared their values and could fulfill their dream for the reshaping of America. He was their ticket to national power.

The friends of Ronald Reagan offer a case study of how an economic group uses politics to expand its influence. Their enterprises by themselves never added up to an overarching system. Consider the men and their businesses: Jack Wrather, oil, entertainment, real estate; Henry Salvatori, oil; Alfred Bloomingdale, Diners' Club; Holmes Tuttle, auto dealerships; Justin Dart, drugstores; William Wilson, cattle ranches; Walter Annenberg, publishing; Earl Jorgensen, steel; Charles Wick, nursing homes. They were very rich, but, with the exception of Annenberg, not titans. They were not founders of crucial enterprises like General Motors or IBM. If they had never existed, what well-known products would be missing? Tupperware, Duracell batteries, *Lassie, TV Guide,* and the Diners' Club credit card. Without politics, final success would have eluded them.

Their decades-long association with Reagan was intimate, more so than is commonly assumed. Their attachment to him was personal, not a cold calculation. Reagan played opposite actress Jane Bryant in the 1938 movie *Girls on Probation* and in two later films. He dated her, too, before she married Justin Dart. In 1938, Reagan appeared with Bonita "Bunny" Granville in *Angels Wash Their Faces.* She married Jack Wrather. Nancy Reagan befriended Betsy Bloomingdale when their children attended the same summer camp. And when young Ron Reagan, Jr., was estranged from his parents during his senior year in high school, he moved into the home of Charles Wick, whose children had been Ron's playmates since elementary school.

Charles Wick was an early Reagan appointee—as head of the United States Information Agency. He shares a show-business background with the President. Wick has a law degree, but he has never practiced. Instead, he was a musical arranger for the Tommy Dorsey band and an actor's agent, a "packager," for such stars as Pinky Lee, a television kiddie-show host during the 1950s. Wick also helped produce a movie called *Snow White and the Three Stooges*. He made his fortune in nursing homes.

"The goal of the entrepreneur is to be successful," Wick said. America, as he sees it, is "just a giant business." Like his friend the President, Wick was once a Democrat who became disenchanted with big government. The Watts riot of 1965—"a lot of people on welfare with free time on their hands"—convinced him that society was falling apart.

When Ronald Reagan made his dramatic entrance into national politics in 1964 with his rousing television speech on behalf of Barry Goldwater's presidential candidacy, the entrepreneurs saw in him great political promise. They were eager to venture capital on his stock. "We recognized," said Wick, "that he had a certain magic quality—he didn't lose the audience. You trust him." So the entrepreneurs financed his campaign for governor of California as a "citizen-politician." Then they acted as his personnel office during his first days in Sacramento, recruiting and screening at least thirty-five top job-holders, almost all of them businessmen or corporate employees. During his tenure, the governor turned to them often for advice, and they were celebrated as the "Millionaire Backers."

Clearly, Reagan's next step was the presidency, and the millionaires backed him with millions. (Wick claimed that he and his wife alone raised $15 million for the 1980 campaign. "We played a vital role," he said.) It would have seemed that their American Dream was fulfilled. What more could be done?

Even before Reagan's election the group around him, allied with other entrepreneurs, was planning for the distant future. They wanted a legacy to last beyond Reagan, beyond a particular political leader, no matter how successful. In order to make permanent Reagan's accomplishment, they invested their hopes and funds in the Counter-Establishment. One of their chief agents was a figure unlike Reagan. Instead of a generational peer, a father figure, who could becalm the multitudes with his mellifluous manner, the entrepreneurs wanted a young warrior, a son they wished they had, an aggressive businessmen in his own right, eager to battle the liberals. If Reagan was a father, William Simon was a son. Justin Dart so admired him for his fundamentalist free-market views that he gave him a seat on the board of Dart Industries. Dart also urged Reagan to name Simon as his vice-presidential running mate. Reagan-Simon—a dream ticket for those who helped dream up Reagan.

Simon was a full partner in the Salomon Brothers investment house, earning several million dollars a year, when President Nixon named him energy czar in 1973. According to Simon, Nixon "likened the job he was giving me to that of Albert Speer in the Third Reich when he was put in charge of German armaments. Nixon told the Cabinet that if not for the power that Hitler had given Speer to override the German bureaucracy, Germany would have been defeated far earlier."[9] Thus anointed, Simon embarked on his mission as the bureaucratic *Übermensch*.

The greatest challenge Simon faced, as energy czar and later as Secretary of the Treasury, was the energy crisis, which reconfirmed his principal opinion: Big government is to blame. "All government knows how to do is create another entity to compound the problem that government created to begin with," he said. "That's why we have the energy crisis. Look at the economic illiteracy of the American people, the glee we have in punishing people."

If the energy crisis exemplified the economic problem on a macrocosmic level, then Simon saw the default of New York City in 1975 as the problem on the microcosmic scale. As Treasury Secretary, he decided that New York should be denied a federal bail-out, an action that led to the notorious *New York Daily News* headline: "Ford to City: Drop Dead." That headline contributed to Ford's loss of New York State and the 1976 election. Eventually New York City technically defaulted, the federal government assumed its debt, and the city was placed in a de facto receivership under which its budget was cut. Simon welcomed this as an opportunity to demonstrate the fallacies of liberalism. For him, New York's default was an idea whose time had come.

Whether in the fields of energy or municipal finance, Simon believed he was battling the forces of ignorance. His enemies, above all, are "stupid." Liberalism, of course, is stupid, "a hash of statism, collectivism, egalitarianism, and anticapitalism, mixed with the desire for the results of capitalism. This murky conceptual mess renders even the most innately brilliant of men stupid."[10]

In 1979 he published *A Time for Truth*, detailing his views of the liberals' "New Despotism," rooted in the desire for equality—"a morbid assault on both ability and justice."[11] The egalitarian impulse did not come from outsiders, but from insiders. "Equality" was an ideological weapon of the Liberal Establishment, used to maintain its own power. "The powerful political intelligentsia that determines the trends in social democratic nations today is as stubborn and ruthless a ruling elite as any in history and worse than many because it is possessed of delusions of moral grandeur."[12]

The Republican Party, to Simon, was not the instrument of redemption. It was, alas, "stupid." Only an ideological movement could rescue the country. The method would require "multimillions" from business, channeled to a "counterintelligentsia." By assuming a new identity, becoming a "party of principle," the GOP could own the future. But without this "counterintelligentsia," it was "destined to remain the Stupid Party and to die. It might even deserve to die."[13]

Simon's tract for 1980 was entitled *A Time for Action*, and in this volume he exposed once again the Liberal Establishment, the "secret system" linked by veiled connections among "the media, the public interest groups and think tanks, the second and third echelons of the bureaucracy and, increasingly, the courts."[14] The Liberal Establishment was nearly omnipotent, thwarting economic growth, bloating government bureaucracy, distorting the news, and undermining defense. It had a "death grip" on the country.[15] Only if it was shattered could America be saved. As for the press, willful twister of facts, Simon warned: "Freedom is indivisible and the media spokesmen who have been working overtime to deny liberty to others may someday discover that they have forfeited their own."[16]

Before Reagan the "secret system" had always managed to triumph, especially when it seemed as though it might lose. "I really believe that Richard Nixon's second term would have done wonders," said Simon. "Watergate destroyed that. Gerald Ford did as much as one could. His greatest accomplishment was vetoing 64 bills, all spending proposals." Ford dealt with the "New Despotism" by containment. Reagan's strategy must be rollback. "And I think," said Simon, "Reagan can fulfill the promise of Nixon's second term."

But there was always the possibility that the Republicans would once again prove themselves to be the Stupid Party, liberals would confound the best-laid plans, and conservatives would fail to dislodge the "New Despotism." So Simon sought to develop the "counterintelligentsia," which would define a framework for lasting change. The members of the "counterintelligentsia" Simon cultivated would assail the conventional wisdom of an antiquated system. The Bastille to which they laid siege was the fortress of liberalism, the hollow doctrine of the old regime. These intellectuals impressed their thoughts on public activity, staffing the new institutes, writing policy papers and newspaper editorials, and serving as political advisers, lending the power of the word to the defense of ideology.

Simon gained personal prominence as president of the U.S. Olympic Committee and the wealth of a sheik as director of a Saudi holding company. But his political imprint has been made as a pivotal figure within the Counter-Establishment. There are several tycoons and scions whose money has been put at the service of the movement. Joseph Coors and Richard Mellon Scaife, for example, have funneled millions of their own into a host of conservative institutions. While Simon has his millions, too, his pile has been insufficient by itself to raise him to the level of a Coors or a Scaife; he is not the paymaster of the foundations he commands. But no other person within the Counter-Establishment has his hands on more money that isn't his own.

How much money? One foundation, the John M. Olin Foundation, of which Simon is president, had assets in 1983 of more than $61.3 million and dispensed about $5 million to Counter-Establishment sources. Simon is also the chairman of the Institute for Educational Affairs (IEA), which he founded in 1978 with neoconservative Irving

Kristol and which doles out additional millions. He is also on the boards of the Heritage Foundation, the Hoover Institution, and the Manhattan Institute. His *Who's Who* listing is an index to much of the Counter-Establishment. By controlling the wellsprings of funding, Simon makes the movement green. Thus the Olin Foundation and IEA generate the cadres who staff the institutions that create the issues to stir public opinion.

IEA, for its part, specializes in developing young cadres. Between 1980 and 1983, the foundation's funding brought into being 33 student publications. The IEA's 1983 *Annual Report* describes these newspapers and magazines as "alternative," a word evoking memories of the alternative press of the sixties. This student movement, however, is the alternative to the alternative, a new aspect of shadow liberalism, intended to combat "the liberal orthodoxy strangling opinion on the campus," according to the IEA's *Annual Report.* The most promising cadres are then financed in internships to prepare them for "media careers." Individual articles by these up-and-coming ideologues are also underwritten; and some "former apprentices have taken their places as regular employees at such publications as *Reason, The Journal of Contemporary Studies,* and *The Wall Street Journal.*"

In the spirit of shadow liberalism, the IEA has funded studies demonstrating that members of the New Class, in all the opinion-making professions, are conclusively liberal. The foundation also develops responses to policy issues, even long-resolved ones, that its directors believe liberals have dominated. The Vietnam War is a special sticking point because conservatives believe that if they refight the war of interpretation and win, then support for their sort of foreign policy can be mustered. That's why the IEA offered "major support to the reinterpretation now underway of this country's Vietnam experience and of the results of American defeat there." The sixties can be replayed in reverse, with the conservative version prevailing.

The foundation also supports a journal, *This World,* on religion and politics "intended to counter" the "current ideological guerrilla warfare" of the left. Its articles have included attacks on the mainline National Council of Churches, a moral defense of Reagan's "Star Wars" scheme, and an attack on "the theology of Carl Sagan's *Cosmos* series."

The impulse animating all this funding by the left is a desire to root out the Liberal Establishment, "an established cultural system that condemns the society which sustains it," according to Simon and Kristol in their signed "Statement of Purpose."

The Olin Foundation, for its part, is a pillar of the Counter-Establishment. It supports the think tanks by endowing chairs and fellowships—$294,000 in 1983 to the Heritage Foundation, $450,000 to the Hoover Institution, and $99,425 to the American Enterprise Institute. It creates entirely new institutions—$50,000 to establish the Center for the Study of Religion and Society. It supports a network of publications, ranging from *The New Criterion* ($100,000) to *The American Spectator* ($25,000). And it backs a variety of groups devoted to harassing the Liberal Establishment, including the Media Institute ($20,000) and the Capitol Legal Foundation ($45,000), the latter of which encouraged retired General William Westmoreland to sue CBS for libel and then provided him with counsel.

Both the Olin Foundation and IEA operate as 501(c)3 tax-exempt institutions. In that they are not linked to the old political parties, even to the Republican "Stupid Party," they are nonpartisan. More precisely, they are institutions of an ideological movement. "It's been," Simon said, "quite effective."

As for the "Millionaire Backers" and Reagan: They still influenced the President, but their influence was mostly in the realm of sensibility. One by one—Justin Dart, Alfred Bloomingdale, Jack Wrather—they were dying off. True, some remained within the Reagan court in appointive positions. William Wilson, for example, was named U.S. ambassador to the Vatican, and Charles Z. Wick was always close at hand. Most of them, however, saw the Reagans only at parties. Their success had made them superfluous. These individualists had helped create Reagan and the institutions of the Counter-Establishment, which could endure without their efforts.

The old crowd of new money, of course, remained steadfastly conservative. But it wasn't quite the same for them, not like the glory days when Reagan was governor of California. A President must take other individuals into account—for example, the chief executive officers who comprise the membership of the Business Roundtable.

THE ROMANCE
OF THE MARKET

T he two hundred or so members of the Business Roundtable manage corporations ranging from the American Telephone and Telegraph Company to United States Steel. Their firms' combined revenues are roughly equivalent to half of the Gross National Product. The members inducted into this American business peerage share common characteristics: devotion to impersonal company goals and appreciation of the byzantine mechanics of vast bureaucracies. These are not traits apt to be cultivated by entrepreneurs.

The nondescript offices of the organization in Washington are located several floors above Brooks Brothers on L Street. The staff is small. The first principle of the Roundtable is personal involvement; surrogates are eschewed. The CEO himself is expected to attend meetings of the various task forces that formulate public policy initiatives and to lobby for them. When the chairman of General Motors calls, a congressman tends to pick up the phone.

The CEOs were not convinced to help finance the Counter-Establishment on the strength of ideology alone. Pressured by world recessions and rising wages, they abandoned the old consensus and discovered new allies. Big business was hardly incorporated into the Counter-Establishment, yet its support was crucial to its flowering. Nor was the Counter-Establishment its sole means in fashioning a new corporate politics. Political action committees, for example, were used to fund politicians. And a unique form of lobbying emerged in which the lobbyist not only worked on behalf of issues but created them. Then the CEOs themselves, through the Roundtable, directly represented their interests.

The CEOs are not the heirs of primeval capitalists, the economic buccaneers of the nineteenth century with whose spirits today's entrepreneurs commune; nor are they mere caretakers for the original family proprietors. The CEOs have not risen to their positions because of Yankee ingenuity, chance, or celebrity. With the growth of a national market and the rapid pace of technological development in the late nineteenth century, the corporations expanded and diversified. They required technical expertise, a complex hierarchial system, internal stability, and a permanent managerial elite. The CEOs are the supreme bureaucrats of private enterprise, and they have long exercised control over the important decisions of the corporations they run.

In the early Reagan years, Clifton C. Garvin was the chairman of Exxon and of the Business Roundtable. In his enormous plush office, fifty-six stories above Manhattan, bounded on two sides by twenty-foot-tall glass windows, he supervised the largest corporation in the world, with annual sales roughly equal to the GNP of Sweden. He conducted secret negotiations with European ministers and Arabian sheiks. He constructed boomtowns and turned them overnight into ghost towns. His fleet of more than five hundred ships sailed on the seven seas. When he telephoned the President of the United States, he was not put on hold.

Garvin was a company man, a chemical engineer by training. He began his ascent from the Baton Rouge refinery, known as "the Academy" within Exxon because it is a prep school for many top executives. As he rose in the ranks he learned how to manage larger and larger divisions of the company until he was finally chosen to coordinate all plans. He had the rugged good looks of the Marlboro Man (the frontier individualist), but he wore a Countess Mara tie (the expensive accoutrement of the organization man). He appeared impeccably self-confident. And yet, in early 1981, shortly after Ronald Reagan submitted "A Program for Economic Recovery," which Garvin believed was sure to succeed, he felt uneasy.

"I don't have a sense of power," Garvin said. "When I think of all the times we don't sell what we're after . . ." His voice trailed off. "The only power we have is to survive as an entity because we do a job well enough that the public accepts it. There's some power in that. In terms of influence with Congress, Ralph Nader has more power than we have. I don't have a sense of power," he repeated. "I have a sense of frustration, in fact. How come I can't sell the country on the direction I see it ought to go? We don't get the results. The press pays much more attention to Nader than it does to me. That's a statement of fact. The plight of the downtrodden attracts all the attention."

This is not the speech of an entrepreneurial hero, but of a thwarted manager. Garvin was concerned with his—and other CEOs'—power. As planners, they make things happen every day within their companies, but they are frustrated because America does not operate like the private corporation. Given their way, the corporations and their managers believe they could convert wealth into happiness, matter into spirit, in a way that no single entrepreneur could, since no single entrepreneur will ever control all the forces necessary for such social magic. But Garvin feels his hands are somehow tied because people don't understand the larger design, a design he can't really explain himself.

The pure free-market myth does not really serve the CEO as a completely convincing rationale. In the free-market myth, only the market is impersonal. But corporations, those curiously legal individuals, are not actually people. Within them, the CEOs enforce a regime of impersonality. The willful risk-taker is generally not rewarded because he does not adhere to organizational purposes and conduct. The entrepreneur is, in effect, the corporate misfit. For the entrepreneur the market is much riskier than for the CEO, because the entrepreneur must really be alone. To the CEO, the entrepreneur may appear narrow, selfish, and parochial, a throwback to a more primitive time. The entrepreneur, for example, believes that adversity is the teacher of success. The CEO, however, knows that adversity is usually needless and inefficient; it is not something that should be built into corporate plans.

Yet the personal motivation of the CEO is never at issue; only his results matter. The entrepreneur believes his success reflects his character, and he uses the firm to advance his own ends. The entrepreneur invents his own title; he places the crown on his own head. But no matter how vast his kingdom, he cannot match the powerful system of the CEOs.

The entrepreneur can't represent anyone but himself: he's a supply-sider. For the manager, however, the consumer is essential in establishing a moral justification. His definition does not come from himself. The entrepreneur believes he supplies what people need; that's why they buy his products. (Yet even entrepreneurs like Joseph Coors, an important movement conservative, try to plan markets.) But the CEO will not supply without trying to assure demand through market research and advertising. He goes beyond consumer need to consumer desire. Once the CEO knows what the desires are, he will plan for the future; desires can always be transformed into needs. He helps the public define its dreams, and the CEO who gains his identity through this pursuit of dream believes that he speaks for the public interest in a way the entrepreneur never can.

The CEOs want profits, power, and respect. But managers believe people distrust them and do not sufficiently honor them. The consumer movement manifests disrespect by promoting excessive regulation by big government; it suspects the executives' best intentions. For decades, through both Democratic and Republican administrations, distrust has been built into the government/business partnership. And regulation is costly. It has contributed to such a substantial capital shortage, the managers argued, that big business couldn't fulfill its obligation to society through new investment. The CEOs of the 1980s have sought to recapture the public's esteem as well as their own image as selfless servants. This is the romantic vision of the gray flannel men.

In medieval literature, a romance was a narrative of adventures about a quest for the recovery of love or purity; the subtext was about the loss and regaining of identity. These stories were never about the poor serf making it big or the good peasant getting a lucky break, but about archetypal Knights of the Round Table who upheld a chivalrous ideal. Their adherence to their code of honor proved that they were worthy of their privileges.

Our contemporary knights of the Business Roundtable would like to regard themselves as emissaries for the public good, and their corporate identification resembles the knight's sense of belonging to one of the basic orders of society. The CEO is unlike the entrepreneurial hero, who makes his way alone through a society without fixed orders. The manager asserts his loyalty to the order, just like the Round Table knight, and without that loyalty the Round Table collapses: individual pride and turmoil replace collective identity and security. If they can win esteem they will be acknowledged as the men they really are— stewards of society upholding the chivalrous ideal of public service.*

The romance of the market reflects the deep corporate crisis of legitimacy. William Vanderbilt, the remorseless Robber Baron, proclaimed, "The public be damned!" Such power without justification and wealth without mythology was not calculated to win public esteem. Capitalists who are generations removed from the age of primitive accumulation feel the need for a more palatable rationale. The free-market myth, which equates fortune and merit, does not properly fit the CEOs. The great sociologist Max Weber, with free-market entrepreneurs in mind, wrote:

> The fortunate is seldom satisfied with the fact of being fortunate. Beyond this, he needs to know that he has a *right* to his good fortune. He wants to be convinced that he "deserves" it, and above all, that he deserves it in comparison with others. He wishes to be allowed the belief that the less fortunate also merely experience their due. Good fortune thus wants to be legitimate fortune.[1]

*When planning fails and the CEO beseeches big government for rescue, the other managers must cast him out because he has betrayed the romance. When Chrysler was nearly bankrupt in 1979 and its managers pled for assistance from Washington, the leadership of the Business Roundtable issued a statement of condemnation: "Whatever the hardships or failures may be for particular companies and individuals the broad social and economic interests of the nation are best served by allowing this system to operate as freely and fully as possible." Chrysler's CEO, Lee Iacocca, who believed he had no choice but to quit the Roundtable, replied that it was "ironic not to oppose similar guarantees to the steel, shipping, airlines and housing industries." From the point of view of the other CEOs, Chrysler was too openly and abjectly supplicating; the unwritten code of honor was besmirched.

This is the free-market myth in which the luck rides with the good. It isn't the corporate manager's romance, in which the public good they do is planned, not merely luck.

"Business represents the public will," said Thomas Murphy, former chairman of General Motors and of the Business Roundtable. "The public goes into the market and votes. It buys or it doesn't buy the product. Business is the greatest consumer group in this country." The more market surveys the CEO orders, the more advertising he commissions, the more the CEO insists that the consumer is sovereign. "We live in the future," said Murphy. "Next year's product? That's done. The decisions were made years ago. The product in two years? That's the day after tomorrow. In every case, you're trying to anticipate where the customer will be. You're taking a hell of a risk."

"We *are* entrepreneurs," claimed Murphy. "Our business is a risk business." But the manager's sense of excitement and adventure, unlike the entrepreneur's, is vicarious because he casts the corporation as an individual. To argue that the law treats corporations as individuals is one thing; to claim that the corporation is actually an entrepreneur is another. Both entrepreneur and manager accept capitalism, but the free-market myth that makes the entrepreneur a hero is formed out of perceptions of capitalism of the eighteenth and nineteenth centuries. The manager's capitalism is a different concept of the market. John D. Rockefeller's desk is preserved on the top floor of the Exxon Building, where Clifton Garvin presides. But claiming spiritual continuity with the founders cannot resolve the crisis of legitimacy.

The Business Roundtable is the political flowering of managerial capitalism, a consequence of the managers' prosaic tasks as planners and their search for a higher justification. Without planning, a firm lacks elementary security. Coordination of the far-flung parts of the modern corporation—raw materials, capital, pricing, transportation, distribution, and consumer demand—requires extraordinary administration. But, as planners, the managers are not without competition from government, and they do not much like competition because it introduces the factor of uncertainty.

When government created a bureaucracy of regulators and planners, business created its own cadre to cope with them. The managers believed that without these professions working in the interstices between business and government, planning would become an impossible job. "Who are these intermediaries?" inquired Harvard professor Robert B. Reich in a *Harvard Business Review* article:

> They are approximately 12,000 Washington-based lawyers who represent business before regulatory agencies and the federal courts, the 9,000 lobbyists who represent business before Congress, the 42,000 trade association personnel who keep close watch on pending regulations and legislation, the 8,000 public relations specialists who advise business executives about regulatory issues, the 1,200 specialized journalists who report to particular industries on government developments that might affect them, the 1,300 public affairs consultants who help business organize to deal with regulation, and the 3,500 business affairs consultants who provide regulatory officials with specialized information about particular industries.[2]

But even with the presence of this standing army of lobbyists bivouacked in Washington, the CEOs still felt nervous. No matter how much actual influence they had with government agencies, they believed they had little control.

Whereas in Europe businessmen view the state as the creation of the aristocracy, American businessmen see the state as the creation of New Deal brain-trusters. In Europe, the state preceded the bourgeoisie; in America, businessmen consider the state a latecomer. The CEOs see government the way consumer activists see some corporations, as bureaucracies dangerously out of control.

The emboldened CEOs of the Roundtable can see a valuable role for big government and still believe in the romance of the market. They want big government to be the marketing agency and brokerage firm to big business. The CEOs appreciate the methods of big government, when they serve their interest, because they seem so similar to those of big business. What they always want from big government is faster service and preferential treatment. They believe government should be run like a subsidiary. So they think of reforming government, not eliminating it. Ultimately, they wish big government to respect big business as the true spokesman—the chivalric knight—for consumer desire.

To make government work in their favor, the managers believed they had to increase their market share of policy. To do that they had to increase their investments in politics. But with the decline of political parties, politics itself had changed. "Either party has a whole lot of difficulty," said Garvin. "Discipline isn't there." The managers discovered that public opinion was even more difficult to plan than consumer desire.

As financiers of both parties in the past, businessmen had been integrated into the old system in which parties were necessary for almost every detail of campaigning and government. Businessmen prefer to deal with stable institutions, as close to the corporate image as possible. When corporate leaders used to confer with ranking political leaders, they felt assured that the politicians had the machinery to enforce their authority. With the advent of television, political consultants, computerized polling and direct mail, and sophisticated media advertising—the mechanisms of the permanent campaign—parties were rendered insecure and began to disintegrate. With the collapse of the traditional party system, no relatively autonomous institutions existed to mediate with the public on business's behalf. At the same time, businessmen were subject to more public criticism than ever before. They felt isolated and yet exposed.

Garvin discovered this uncomfortable situation when he appeared on the Phil Donahue show in 1979 during the gasoline shortage. Lines of motorists waiting their turns at the pumps snaked for blocks through city streets; a full-scale riot in which a gas station was burned took place in the working-class section of that stereotypical suburban community Levittown, Pennsylvania; and not many people believed the oil companies were blameless. As a ranking member of the Roundtable, Garvin felt obliged to defend his corporation himself. He kept his composure when asked what he later called "nasty questions." He denied that the shortage was contrived to increase profits. It was a jarring experience, and it taught Garvin fear. "The laws are made by the public," he said.

"Exxon has lived in a hundred countries only because the public wants us. If they don't want us, they kick us out. It's not personal. They've decided they want to do it some other way. The decision can be made in this country, too, just as easily." Public opinion, therefore, was crucial. But how could it be influenced to support policies favorable to business?

Back in the early 1970s, when poll after poll showed businessmen to be held in about as low repute as politicians, the CEOs felt hurt. "The notable parallelism in the two trends suggests that feelings about business and government may have been part of the same syndrome, an apparently broad loss of confidence in the leadership of our major political and economic institutions," wrote the sociologists Seymour Martin Lipset and William Schneider in *The Confidence Gap,* a study funded by the Roundtable.[3] As practical men, the CEOs prided themselves on making things work; without public support they couldn't affect legislation the way they wanted. "We were not effective," recalled John Harper, a founder of the Roundtable and former chairman of Alcoa. "We were not involved. What we were doing wasn't working. All the polls showed business was in disfavor. We didn't think people understood how the economic system works. We were getting short shrift from Congress. I thought we were powerless in spite of the stories of how we could manipulate everything." To Harper, public contempt for the corporation was a measure of business weakness. If the CEOs exercised political power, they might earn respect.

On a 1971 business trip to Washington, Harper asked some friends what was to be done. Secretary of the Treasury John Connally and Federal Reserve Board chairman Arthur Burns counseled him to form an organization of CEOs beyond party politics. Despite the legions of lobbyists present in the capital, no authoritative business group was really setting larger themes and acting on them, until the founding of the Roundtable in 1972.

When John Post, a lawyer and oil-company consultant, was hired as the Roundtable's first Washington director, one of the corporate lobbyists who had been around town for years tried to show him the ropes. He instructed Post never to talk to Democrats, advice Post instantly dismissed. Business now needed the studied neutrality of the seller who doesn't favor customers because of their political allegiance. Both Democrats and Republicans required cultivation; the larger the market, the larger the sale. In any case, the CEOs weren't interested in partisanship so much as power. "The Roundtable tries to work with whichever political party is in power," Garvin said. "We may each individually have our own political alliances, but as a group the Roundtable works with every administration to the degree they let us."

The managers have an unsentimental view of politics. To them, it is not a matter of pressing the flesh of constituents; it is a hard economic question. Politics is a game, but they are not in it for pleasure or ego. Nor do they see politics as a contest of principles. For the CEOs, politics is simply a way they now have to do business. They have interests, not favorites. "Others from the outside impute feelings to us," said John Post. "We have no feelings. That's the way it is. That's the way CEOs are. We're pragmatic."

In the 1980 election, most CEOs backed Ronald Reagan, but with some private misgivings. They didn't know him well, and they were nervous about his enthusiasm for ideology. "One of the reasons the business community went for Connally first," said Martin Anderson, "is that they knew down deep that Reagan meant what he said on free enterprise. CEOs are for free enterprise, but they don't necessarily understand what it is."

One of the most important connections between big business and the Reagan camp in 1980 was Charls Walker, a lobbyist for the Roundtable and many of its constituent companies. His good-ol'-boy style is deceptive, for his method is novel. Walker's lobbying is based not only on corporate fees but partly on ideas he manufactures. He is a mini-Counter-Establishment. He holds a doctorate in economics and has taught at the University of Texas and the Wharton School. Walker is an ambassador from the corporate world to the higher precincts of politics, a Texas back-slapper with a mind for econometrics who travels in style. "Yeah, boy, I still have my Cadillac," he drawled. "Vintage 1975 model. Got it depreciated down to the value of zilch. Got a hundred and fifty thousand miles on it."

One gets the impression that no problem is too difficult to be worked out in his quiet, thickly carpeted office on Pennsylvania Avenue, down the street from the White House. Reasonable men can always make a deal. Have a cigar? Walker will open his humidor to light discussion. This is a congenial smoke-filled room. On the wall behind his desk are autographed pictures of Dwight Eisenhower, Gerald Ford, and Lyndon Johnson. Walker served in the Treasury Department under Eisenhower and Ford (also Nixon, but no picture), and Johnson is the patron saint of Texas wheeler-dealers who find their way to Washington.

"In 1959, the government was basically run by four people," Walker said. "Dwight Eisenhower, Robert Anderson—my boss, who was then Secretary of the Treasury and had Eisenhower's complete confidence and respect—[House Speaker] Sam Rayburn, and [Senate Majority Leader] Lyndon Johnson. It's no accident they were all born in the state of Texas—I thought I'd just throw that in for an extra. And they'd get together at the White House every week or two for a drink. Eisenhower would say, I think we ought to do such and such. Rayburn and Johnson would say, That's a good idea, but change it this way, or let us propose it, it'd be better coming from Democrats than Republicans, or no, there's no chance of that. They were leaders. When you had Speaker Rayburn and Wilbur Mills [chairman of the House Ways and Means Committee] and the others on a tax issue, you were 99 percent sure. It's all different now. You have a democracy with a capital D right now."

When Walker left the Eisenhower administration, he became executive head of the American Bankers Association and registered as a lobbyist. He returned with the Nixon administration, serving as the Treasury Department's legislative liaison and as deputy to Secretaries John Connally and George Shultz. "The smart money in the White House was that Connally was going to kick my ass out," he said. "But we hit it off like ham and eggs."

When he finally left the Treasury Department in 1973 to start a private consulting firm, a roster of corporations—including GE, Ford, Proctor and Gamble, and Alcoa, which were still Walker's clients in 1980—asked him to represent their interests on tax matters before Congress. Walker was also asked to represent the Business Roundtable.

"The Roundtable has made a lot of difference," he said. "They know how to get the CEOs into Washington and lobby; they maintain good relationships with the congressional staffs; they've just learned a lot about Washington they didn't know before. There's a fiction around that you can't do anything with Congress, particularly if it's a Democratic Congress. But that is not true. You can get things done over there if you know how to do it."

In the early 1970s, William Simon had raised the "capital formation" issue without much effect. Then in 1975, the efficacious Charls Walker was designated chairman of the newly formed American Council on Capital Gains and Estate Taxation. (Later, the group changed its name to the American Council on Capital Formation.) The group was begun with seed money provided by the Weyerhauser Company, a lumber and wood products concern, and the National Forest Products Association, looking for ways to change the tax code. By 1984, more than 340 companies and trade associations contributed to the council, which also received significant grants from conservative foundations. The money enabled Walker to hire bright young policy professionals, churning out papers, organizing conferences, and promoting their proposals. Thus Walker entered the business of ideas.

The logic of capital formation seemed clear—prosperity depends upon productivity, which depends upon investment, which, in turn, depends upon savings. Cutting taxes for business would create the savings that would lead to a boom. The case, however, wasn't as obvious as it may have seemed on first glance. Investment as a percentage of GNP had remained about constant since the early 1950s; productivity rates in the 1970s were more affected by "oil shocks" than by investment rates; and while the savings rate in the United States was lower relative to those of the Western European nations and Japan, tax rates there were far steeper and welfare programs more extensive. Finally, cutting taxes did not guarantee that the released capital would flow into productive investments; it might just flow into the most profitable ones, like mergers or speculations. Savings is not quite the same thing as investment, a postulate of classical economics first defined by Turgot, the French *philosophe*.

The capital formation school was not the supply-side school. The former wanted tax breaks only for the corporations and the wealthy, who, after all, were the ones making the big investments. The supply-siders, on the other hand, argued for tax breaks for everyone. They were in their way more rigorous Keynesians—that is, demand-siders—because by making a tax cut universal, consumer demand would be stimulated and boost production.

In 1978, Walker's group won a swift and decisive campaign in Congress. The council developed a bill that would greatly reduce capital gains taxes. This, Walker claimed, would make the financial markets flush. His group by now had bipartisan support within the Washington establishment. On its board, seated alongside supply-side wizard Arthur Laffer, were venerable Democratic superlawyers Clark Clifford and Edward Bennett Williams; the council's president was Robert Keith Gray, a high-powered lobbyist with close ties to prominent Republicans. The council lobbied hard, buoyed by stories in the business press (including one by supply-sider Jude Wanniski in the *Wall Street Journal*), and released studies showing the beneficent effects the bill would have. Robert Kuttner, the economics correspondent for *The New Republic,* wrote in his book *Revolt of the Haves*: "Many of these studies later were shown to be based on unverifiable assumptions about how the market was *likely* to respond to a cut in the capital gains rates; yet they were presented as scientific fact, and by the time the liberal economists reassembled their forces and challenged the methodology in the various tax journals, the political battle was over and Charlie Walker's capital formation council had moved on to other issues."[4]

Although the 1978 capital gains tax cut bill passed Congress overwhelmingly, there was no spurt in investment. Other factors were over-riding—for example, the Federal Reserve's monetarist policy. Walker, however, was undaunted. In November 1979, he told the annual meeting of the council that the tax cut had saved the economy from deeper troubles.

The council had won what Walker considered an ideological triumph. "The consensus is cohering on a different basis than the consensus Lyndon Johnson had. There's a crossover of party lines, an ignoring of party lines," said Walker. "The American people deep down understand about capital. They don't use the same words. A survey in 1976 asked people what they thought about capital formation. They said huh? Then you put the question this way: Do you think American business is putting enough money into new machinery? And they say no. There it is."

In the 1980 presidential campaign, Walker was the chief economic adviser to candidate John Connally, his former colleague, fellow Texan, and the favorite of his clients. When Connally withdrew from the race, Walker was freed to dispense his wisdom to Ronald Reagan. "I think I provided the key memo," he said. It offered a rationale for cutting taxes and government spending—and increasing the defense budget.

His clients were relieved to know his steady presence hovered near Reagan. "The Business Roundtable didn't know Reagan, and they tend to identify him with right-wing positions and extremism," he said. "But the publicity that me and these 'moderates' are in there makes them feel a lot better. None of us who started working on capital formation in the early 1970s thought the consensus would come along this fast. The American people are basically closet capitalists. They're not dumb."

Walker may have assuaged the anxieties of most big businessmen, but in 1980 not all were at ease.

For David Rockefeller, the 1980 campaign had been traumatic. The banker had been the founding father of the Trilateral Commission, a forum in which American, European, and Japanese economic and political leaders could discuss common problems. Many members of the Carter administration, including the President himself, were members. Some right-wing groups supporting Reagan's candidacy charged that the internationalist, detente-minded commission was part of a conspiracy, a plot by the Liberal Establishment. Edwin Meese, Reagan's campaign issues adviser and later the President's counselor and Attorney General, asserted that "all these people come out of an international economic industrial organization with a pattern of thinking on world affairs" that led to a "softening on defense."[5] On February 7, 1980, Reagan himself observed that nineteen key members of the Carter administration were members of the Trilateral Commission. Their influence, he claimed, had led to a "softening of defense" because of the belief that commerce "should transcend, perhaps, the national defense." George Bush gingerly dropped his Trilateral membership. (He also quit the Council on Foreign Relations, another Establishment institution.) Rockefeller was uncertain, after Reagan's election, whether he would enjoy the kind of access to the White House that he had had in the past.

The relationship of the Rockefeller family and the Republican right had long been volatile. In the nineteenth century, opposition to the international bankers' syndicate was a staple of agrarian populism. In the twentieth century, the "international Communist conspiracy" became the embodiment of evil for the right wing. The Rockefellers, with their far-flung interests, support for big government and internationalism, and influence in the GOP, seemed to many fervent right-wingers to personify both the nineteenth- and twentieth-century symbols of conspiracy. This sentiment was stoked by frustrated conservatives who were sure that if the Rockefeller grip on the party was broken, the right would sweep the nation. Senator Robert Taft, thwarted for years in his bid for the Republican nomination, declared after losing once again at the 1952 convention, "Every Republican candidate for President since 1936 has been nominated by the Chase National Bank."[6]

In 1964, Phyllis Schlafly, an Illinois housewife and Goldwater militant, later to become the most prominent female leader of the New Right, wrote a book, *A Choice Not an Echo,* whose thesis was that the Republican Party was controlled by a conspiracy of "secret New York kingmakers . . . to insure control of the largest cash market in the world: the Executive Branch of the United States Government."[7] One of Barry Goldwater's manifestos was entitled *The Conscience of a Majority*; the message was clear. At the 1964 convention, when Nelson Rockefeller appeared on the podium at midnight to deliver a short speech on the dangers of extremism, the Goldwater delegates on the floor and supporters in the galleries jeered him. "This is still a free country, ladies and gentlemen," Rockefeller responded, which only raised the decibel level.

It was no surprise that in 1980 the Reagan campaign explicitly tapped anti-Rockefeller resentments. David Rockefeller's apprehension, however, was soon dispelled. Reagan the President was far friendlier than Reagan the candidate. When the annual meeting of the Trilateral Commission was held in Washington in March 1981, Bush, who had earlier distanced himself, appeared as a speaker. "Bush came to speak and in fact," Rockefeller said with a measure of vindication, "he was very eloquent in his support of the commission and the good work it had done." Another speaker was Secretary of Defense Caspar Weinberger, a long-time Trilateral member and a Reagan confidant who had never sought to excuse his affiliation. "Perhaps surprisingly to them," said Rockefeller, "they're finding that we have a lot in common."

Rockefeller is a centrist, and he believes the center is wherever he happens to be. According to this logic, the friendly President of the United States must be in the center, too. "My enthusiasm has grown," Rockefeller said. "I didn't adequately recognize the strength of his leadership." But Reagan and the Counter-Establishment are a force apart from the center as Rockefeller understands it. Their gestures of accommodation were a form of detente on their own terms, not a capitulation or moderation.

As soon as Reagan became President, the White House attempted to harness corporate power to serve his ends. The administration assumed the leading role as the broker for an aggressive new business politics. "We try to stay on top of all the different segments," said Elizabeth Dole, who was chief of the Office of Public Liaison before she became Secretary of Transportation. The White House role in the "business coalition" was to help business transcend the narrow interests of individual companies and industries. The coalition included trade associations, organizations like the Chamber of Commerce, and groups like the Roundtable.

Wayne Valis, bearded, youthful, and enthusiastic, was the presidential assistant charged with coordinating the business coalition. He was a true product of the Counter-Establishment: a disciple of Milton Friedman's teachings; a minor official during the Nixon and Ford administrations; assistant to William Baroody, Jr., president of the American Enterprise Institute; editor of a book about Reagan and conservative policy. "We didn't have the business coalition under

Nixon," said Valis. "We didn't have it under Ford. Carter went right through the forest and didn't see a tree. The business resources are almost scary, they're so big."

On February 19, 1981, the day after the President unveiled his "Program for Economic Recovery" before a joint session of Congress, hundreds of corporate lobbyists crowded into Room 450 of the Old Executive Office Building to hear Valis issue a call to arms. "Like the Confederacy, you have only won defensive victories," Valis declared. "That leads to defeat. If you will march with us this time, you will win offensive victories!" (Stormy applause.)

But unlike the entrepreneurs, the corporate managers had no interest in the withering away of the state. To the degree that President Reagan sought to remove government's role as the underwriter of economic risk, they came into conflict with him. These conflicts reflected a more fundamental fissure between entrepreneurs and managers. Both the conservative intellectuals, who advocated the entrepreneurial viewpoint, and the CEOs gave lip service to the free market. But at the same time that some CEOs funded the think tanks of the Counter-Establishment, they opposed its ultimate goals. This difference led to fractious combat during the Reagan presidency. The party of principle and the party of interest, ostensibly united in the conservative cause, were often deeply divided.

The managers' motives are rooted in the nature of the modern business firm, which in fact if not in rhetoric places them beyond free-market orthodoxy. To them, Reaganism was an unprecedented opportunity to extend their planning in the name of the free market. But they could not win the White House by their own power alone. Money without ideas is merely great wealth, not great influence.

In perhaps his most celebrated passage, John Maynard Keynes observed that "the ideas of economists and political philosophers, both when they are right and when they are wrong, are more powerful than is commonly understood. Indeed, the world is ruled by little else. Practical men, who believe themselves to be quite exempt from any intellectual influences, are usually the slaves of some defunct economist."[8]

THE RISE OF THE COUNTER-ESTABLISHMENT

Keynes's description aptly fits the case of conservatism, with one glaring exception. The most influential economist was hardly "defunct" during Reagan's presidency. Milton Friedman, the bright young man of the Remnant, the movement's most prestigious intellectual star, central to the rise of the Counter-Establishment, had survived to see his ideas tested by the acids of conservatism.

CAPITALISM

AND

FRIEDMAN

"I often tell the story of a breed of duck which flies in a V with a leader in front," said Milton Friedman. "Every once in a while the ducks move off. The leader keeps going on until he looks behind and sees that they're off, and then he gets in front of them. Every other president has been that kind of a duck. Ronald Reagan is the first one in which the ducks came behind him while he was flying all by himself. This says a great deal about his character. Every politician has to compromise, but he didn't get elected by compromising. There has been a very dramatic change in the public at large. It's the result of three parts experience and one part the effects of people like me. People have experience over fifty years now with great promises and miserable results. They have become disillusioned."

The metaphor of the duck is a perfect one for the free market: If you do what you do best, you may be rewarded. The lead duck gains respect without compromising. He refuses to follow the crowd, blown about by various wind currents, and instead sticks stubbornly to the path he knows to be true. His orthodoxy is nonconforming and his virtue rewarded.

It's hardly surprising that Milton Friedman thinks in free-market terms, or that he describes Reagan this way. But the duck in the metaphor can also be taken to be Friedman himself. The story he tells is of an economist triumphant.

In the heady days of the New Frontier, when Keynesianism—the New Economics—was fervently and explicitly embraced by President

John F. Kennedy, Friedman's ideas were generally considered outlandish, beyond the pale of reasonable discussion, an atavism from a dreadful past. He was a certifiable individualist—the lone member of his profession to advise Barry Goldwater during his 1964 presidential campaign. Yet within a few years, Friedman's opinions were taken seriously by a wide audience—and they were tested.

More than anyone else, he was responsible for reviving free-market ideas in the post–New Deal era. For years he wrote a column for *Newsweek.* He was a one-man think tank, author of numerous public policy proposals, including the volunteer army, who served both the American Enterprise Institute and the Hoover Institution, those Counter-Establishment ships of the line; he joined Ronald Reagan and Alexander Solzhenitsyn as one of only three Honorary Fellows at the Hoover Institution; he starred in his own television series, *Free to Choose,* which, with his wife, he adapted into a best-selling book. And he was the leading man in an influential television commercial in favor of California's Proposition 13, the opening wedge of the tax revolt that contributed so much to Reagan's political momentum. In 1976 he won the Nobel Prize in Economics, thereby becoming a figure of worldwide renown and distinction. His advice has been sought by presidents and prime ministers—and even a Latin dictator.

Friedman offered instruction in microeconomics, through his empirical studies, and macroeconomics, through his grand theory. He advocated reanimating the classical free market through a specific means: money. Almost singlehandedly he revived monetarism, the idea that the regulation of the money supply could stifle inflation, liberate markets, and produce prosperity, an idea discredited in the aftermath of the Depression. Friedman's monetarist prescription, however arcane it might seem, has been no abstraction in the daily lives of hundreds of millions of people. Whether most ordinary Americans, Britons, or Chileans have ever heard of Friedman or monetarism is doubtful, but his theory, implemented by the reigning economic policy-makers, has directly affected their most important decisions. Monetarism has determined whether they could buy homes or cars, afford to have children or comfortable retirements; or, in more extreme cases, whether they would have jobs or even enough to eat. Friedman has proved conclusively that ideas have consequences.

As an academic and a political advocate, Friedman made a signal contribution to the making of the Counter-Establishment. As the greatest popularizer of free-market doctrine, he helped prepare public opinion. And as the formulator of monetarism, he provided a crucial component of the Reagan economic program.

He is an astonishingly effective communicator—especially so because this short, bald, bespectacled professor does not have an immediately prepossessing presence. He lacks the caustic and elegant wit of his fellow economist, the liberal John Kenneth Galbraith, as well as Galbraith's arresting height. Friedman is not a great literary stylist like Galbraith, but he learned to write serviceable prose accessible to the common reader. And he cultivated a glibness that gave his arguments, once dismissed by liberals as "flaky," a convincing ring.

Friedman has a rare combination of qualities. He is both a first-rate publicist and a scholar. His influence as a public personality has enhanced his influence as a man of ideas. His celebrity, moreover, never debased his thought; fame was always in the service of ideology. "Friedman's emergence as a preeminent economist among conservatives constituted a major landmark in the evolution of the postwar Right. . . . By the end of the 1960s he was probably the most highly regarded and influential conservative scholar in the country, and one of the few with an international reputation," wrote historian George H. Nash in *The Conservative Intellectual Movement in America*.[1] Friedman, however, doesn't regard himself as a "conservative" at all. "I'm not a conservative," he averred. "I'm a liberal in the traditional sense." He is, as he claims, the fullest flower of classical liberalism, a forceful proponent of free markets and laissez faire economics, who has attempted to reprise the thought of Adam Smith in the twentieth century.

The ideas Friedman espoused were in retreat within the academy since the late nineteenth century, when Herbert Spencer, the Victorian philosopher of Social Darwinism, propounded the iron "law" of nature: the wealthy were "fittest" to enjoy their wealth and the poor had earned their poverty. The roots of both modern American sociology and economics can be traced to the nineteenth-century assault on the Social Darwinist viewpoint.

In 1884, Lester F. Ward, the father of American sociology, published a piercing essay entitled, "The Laissez Fair Doctrine Is Suicidal." "Is it true," he asked, "that man shall ultimately obtain dominion of the whole world except himself?"[2] It was in this spirit that the discipline of sociology in America was born.

A year later the American Economics Association was founded by Richard T. Ely, who declared: "The avenues of wealth and preferment are continually blocked by the greed of combinations of men and by monopolists. . . . We hold that there are certain spheres of activity which do not belong to the individual, certain functions which the great cooperative society, called the state—must perform to keep the avenues open."[3] It was in this spirit that the profession of economics in America was born.

A long war of ideas was waged, in discipline after discipline, generation after generation, the consequence of which was a conservative rout. Even before Franklin D. Roosevelt became president, John Maynard Keynes published an essay, "The End of Laissez Faire," which had an air of finality:

Let us clear from the ground the metaphysical or general principles upon which, from time to time, laissez-faire had been founded. It is *not* true that individuals possess a prescriptive "natural liberty" in their economic activities. There is *no* "compact" conferring perpetual rights on those who Have or on those who Acquire. The world is *not* so governed from above that private and social interest always coincide. It is *not* so managed here below that in practice they coincide. It is *not* a correct deduction from the Principles of Economics that enlightened self-interest always operates in the public interest. Nor is it true that self-interest generally *is* enlightened; more often individuals acting separately to promote their own ends are too ignorant or too weak to attain even these. Experience does *not* show that individuals, when they make up a social unit, are always less clear-sighted than when they act separately.[4]

After Keynes, free-marketeers seemed to occupy something like the eighth ring of the Inferno, the special place for soothsayers, diviners, and magicians, where they are condemned to walk backward with their heads twisted around. But the needs of classes and the efforts of intellectuals can bring ideas back from the netherworld of history. Largely because of Friedman's exertions, free-market economics has had a life after death. His preeminence was recognized even before 1967, when he was elected president of the American Economics Association, which had been founded to counter laissez faire notions. And then he covered conservatism with glory by becoming a Nobel laureate.

The influence of his ideas is partly due to his personal consistency. He has never veered from the path he set for himself, and has always excoriated those who have deviated from this path. To him, the free market is a complete system of enduring principles. Whenever Friedman's principles are not scrupulously followed by a politician, he blames "opportunism" or "bureaucratic inertia." He regards his ideas as "objective" and "scientific," indisputably correct. And he believes that the others worship false idols. Such an unshakable orthodoxy has sources beyond the laws of economics. Friedman alone cannot explain Friedman. His thought is inextricably entwined with his own rags-to-riches tale.

The winding road to the Royal Swedish Academy of Sciences and, beyond that, to the White House, where Friedman would be greeted by that other Hoover Honorary Fellow, Ronald Reagan, began in Brooklyn, where Friedman was born to poor immigrant parents. His father ran a small dry-goods store and his mother worked as a seamstress in a sweatshop. When Milton was a very young child, the family moved to the small town of Rahway, New Jersey. There were few Jews there, yet Milton felt no anti-Semitism; still, his Jewishness decisively shaped his thought.

"I have very little tolerance for hypocrisy in intellectual affairs," he said. "When I was very young, thirteen years old, I went to *cheder,* Hebrew school." Thirteen, of course, is the time for bar mitzvah, when a boy stands alone on the synagogue altar before the congregation to chant from the *haftorah,* proving that he has grasped a portion of traditional knowledge and is now an adult, a full member of the community. Friedman's first intellectual crisis occurred as he assumed the mantle of manhood. "I was brought up in the Jewish religion and I took it seriously. I insisted to my parents that if this was right we had to do it right. I would insist on keeping kosher and not doing things on Saturday you shouldn't do. My parents did keep kosher, but they were not radically observant in the way I was trying to be. At age thirteen, I became convinced that the fundamental basis of it was wrong. I no longer believed there was a supernatural God required to give validity. I was intellectually maturing. I decided the whole thing was a bunch of nonsense. I shouldn't use such language because many other people believe it isn't nonsense. But for me the authenticity and validity of the doctrines disappeared. If you believed in it, you ought to do it right. If you didn't, you ought not to pretend."

In time Friedman displaced the faith of his fathers with the faith of Adam Smith. Although he is criticized by some conservatives for substituting the almighty dollar for the Almighty, his system is concerned with values, especially hypocrisy. Big government, to him, encourages activity uncongenial to the spirit of the market. It makes you do things you shouldn't be doing; it encourages hypocrisy. When the government assumes an economic role, the market is violated and its heart destroyed. Left alone, the free market permits no hypocrisy. Deception of consumers may be possible in the short term, but it is in the businessman's long-term interest to maintain a good reputation. The market won't let one deceive oneself, or others, for long; it's a wrathful god.

Friedman upholds an absolute standard. He wants politicians, economists, and bankers to adhere faithfully to the monetarist rite that will bring about the market's salvation. He is continually perplexed and upset by their worldly hypocrisy. The demands of orthodoxy and the sin of hypocrisy have troubled him since boyhood: *If you believed in it, you ought to do it right. If you didn't, you ought not to pretend.*

Milton graduated from high school at the age of sixteen and won a state scholarship to attend Rutgers University. He was a mathematical prodigy and decided to become an actuary, passing the examination while still in college. But two teachers at Rutgers inducted him into the mysteries of economics, saving him from a life of white-collar anonymity. One was Arthur F. Burns, who would later become chairman of the Federal Reserve Board and Secretary of the Treasury; he imbued his young student with a sense of statistical "objectivity." Another teacher, Homer Jones, was a product of the University of Chicago. He encouraged Milton to apply there, too. In 1932, Friedman graduated from Rutgers and won a scholarship at Chicago.

Among economists the free market was a fading passion, but not at the University of Chicago. During the New Deal it was a redoubt of laissez faire ideas. But the economics department was divided. At one end stood Frank Knight, a theorist of the free market, and at the other stood Paul Douglas, a theorist of the welfare state. "The main influences on me undoubtedly were from the University of Chicago," said Friedman. Obviously these influences did not include Paul Douglas.

The Chicago experience imprinted free-market ideas deeply on Friedman's mind. But Chicago also taught him a harsh financial lesson. The school gave him only a $300 tuition grant, and in 1933 he had to drop out. Promptly, he won a $1,500 fellowship at Columbia University, where he studied statistical analysis under such teachers as Wesley Mitchell, who eschewed the idea that theoretical presumption should guide the study of the economy. Friedman claimed to have found inspiration in this "scientific spirit."

While at Columbia, Friedman discovered for the first time Jews who did not share his small-town background. It was something of a shock. "When I went to Columbia University as a graduate student," he said, "I made friends with people who had grown up in the New York City environment. There was no doubt that there was a big difference between them and me. I have been very much impressed with the difference between myself and those friends of mine who grew up in New York. To them, their Jewishness was a matter of everyday importance. They were very self-conscious of being Jews, self-conscious in being discriminated against. When you grow up in a small town in New Jersey like I did, with very few Jews, where classes in school had maybe two or three Jews out of thirty or forty people, I never had that kind of feeling at all. I never really personally experienced the effects of prejudice. So it didn't play any role in my intellectual development."

But his experience as a Jew was critical; for his provincial youth and the absence of persecution were atypical for his generation. Almost all Jews lived in big cities, in tight-knit communities, where they suffered discrimination in education, housing, and employment. And yet they held the highest aspirations for life in America.

Friedman experienced theological pangs, but not ethnic solidarity. Having decided that Judaism was "nonsense," he had categorically dispensed with it. But the Jewishness of the graduate students he encountered at Columbia was unavoidable; they could not escape the prejudice directed against them. This entrapped them in a ghetto, yet they also knew that the community thrived precisely because it was a community. Jewish life was sustained by a dense network of institutions, from educational funds to burial societies. Jews as a group got ahead also by voting together for certain liberal politicians and social programs. Friedman didn't know from this. "If I had grown up in New York I'm sure I would have had different feelings," he said. "No question. Historically, Jews have been socialists. In my case, no." Thus he was open, as few Jews of his generation were, to the free-market doctrine. His attraction to it was partly made possible by his special social background: he was a Jew familiar with Judaism, but not Jews. And in spite of the formative influence of his own personal sociology, he went on to attribute human behavior almost entirely to economics.

In 1935, Milton Friedman joined the New Deal, working on the National Resources Committee, headed by Gardiner Means, coauthor of *The Modern Corporation and Private Property,* which argued that power within the corporation had been transferred from the original entrepreneurs to the managers. Means wanted to use his agency as an instrument of national industrial planning. Friedman, therefore, found himself at the heart of modern liberalism. Still, he considered his work as a statistician "value-free." Moreover, his Chicago training inoculated him against an outbreak of liberal enthusiasm. "I was working in the New Deal not in any policy area whatsoever," he said. "I was working on a major survey of consumer spending. I was never disillusioned with the New Deal. It never had that effect on me." One must first believe, after all, in order to become disillusioned.

In 1937, Friedman joined the National Bureau of Economic Research in New York, a leading center for the statistical study of the business cycle. He was assigned the study of independent professionals —lawyers, doctors, dentists, engineers—and the project became the basis of his doctoral thesis. By 1941 he had completed his manuscript, but his results were highly controversial and his degree was withheld for five years. Friedman argued that physicians limited the number of medical students in order to increase their own incomes. This was a classic case of restraint of trade, demonstrating how interest-group regulation distorted the market. At the bureau, some senior members regarded Friedman's thesis as an intemperate attack on an honorable profession. Only when he hedged his conclusion—"an adequate judgment of this explanation would be exceedingly difficult and is well outside the scope of this study"—was he awarded his doctorate.[5]

Throughout the war years, Friedman served in government, first as the chief economist of the Treasury Department's Division of Tax Research and then as a statistician for the Division of War Research, working on projects such as the development of high-temperature alloys. His role was entirely technical. When the war ended, he spent a year teaching at the University of Minnesota. Finally, in 1946, he returned to the University of Chicago, where he would stay for more than thirty years. He had come home.

Conservative intellectuals then were an endangered species—a "remnant." Their tone was filled with the frustrations of isolation and defeat. FDR may have been dead, but Harry Truman, his feisty successor, offered no surcease from New Deal policies. Conservative intellectuals were scattered, ineffective, and plain irrelevant. But not at the economics department of the University of Chicago. What was occurring nationally—the continuing liberal rout of conservatives—was reversed at Chicago. There liberals were on the run, conservatives ascendant. Within the narrow confines of the economics department, Friedman was the leading figure of a rising generation assuming power (or at least gaining tenure). Paul Douglas, the liberal light of the department, returning from hard war years in the Marine Corps, found that conservatives had usurped all the important departmental decisions and had won the ideological upper hand in his absence. In his autobiography he lamented:

> I was disconcerted to find that the economic and political conservatives had acquired an almost complete dominance over my department and taught that market decisions were always right and profit values the supreme ones. The doctrine of non-interference with the market meant, in practice, clear the track for big business. Inequalities of bargaining power, knowledge, and income were brushed aside, and the realities of monopoly, quasi-monopoly, and imperfect competition were treated as either immaterial or nonexistent. . . .
>
> The opinions of my colleagues would have confined government to the eighteenth-century functions of justice, police, and arms, which I thought had been insufficient even for that time and were certainly so for ours. These men would neither use statistical data to develop economic theory nor accept critical analysis of the economic system. Though expounded with intellectual subtlety, their unrealistic view did not furnish adequate answers to the problems that beset us. It was too much like the economics of the period prior to World War I. So I found myself increasingly out of tune with many of my faculty colleagues and was keenly aware of their impatience and disgust with me. The university I had loved so much seemed to be a different place.[6]

Douglas ran for the U.S. Senate in Illinois in 1948 and was elected. He probably did not carry a majority of his former colleagues' votes.

Friedman takes strong exception to Douglas's history. He disputes the notion that the economics department was uncongenial to liberals, that it lacked tolerance. "What really happened to Paul Douglas was that he got the political itch," said Friedman. "So I think you have to take his reaction to the postwar department of economics with a little grain of salt. But he was unhappy with it because back before he left, before 1940, he and Frank Knight had been at very, very serious odds with one another. There was a feud. When he came back after 1945, he says that Knight had taken over the place and there was no more place for him. Well, you can understand. But still it was not true that the University of Chicago had become monolithic. While I was there we tried to hire on the faculty every one of the names you would think of when you think of the leaders on the other side. We tried to hire Jim Tobin at one time. [Tobin, a leading Keynesian at Yale, was Kennedy's Council of Economic Advisers chairman and later won the Nobel Prize.] My point is that what distinguished the economics department of the University of Chicago, since it was founded in 1892, is its diversity. But the University of Chicago was for many years the only school where you had this strong substantial group, always a minority in the department, that held these [free-market] views. That made us distinctive, and that's why we were considered the 'Chicago School.' But it's a misconception that it was a homogeneous department. All of us, so-called members of the 'Chicago School,' would have been opposed to having a homogeneous department." And yet it was undeniable that the free-marketers were in control and that the University of Chicago economics department was *the* stronghold within the academy of laissez faire thought. The almost complete superiority of liberals in the intellectual field made this bastion that much more significant to conservatives. Safe within the Gothic buildings of the University of Chicago, Friedman was not in the minority, constantly on the defensive. He could elaborate his ideas with confidence.

Outside of Chicago, however, Keynesians were preeminent. They believed, along with Paul Douglas, that the old free-market doctrine was "unrealistic." And they sought to describe the intricate patterns of the economy more precisely, paying attention to monopolies and oligopolies, a world of imperfect competition. Adam Smith was not their lodestar. One of the results of Keynesianism was econometrics, the computer-based modeling of the economy. Friedman believed, however, that too much knowledge was a dangerous thing. Knowing every detail of the economy, he felt, was beyond human comprehension, and in any case shouldn't be attempted because it would lead inevitably to central planning; temptation would lead to sin. So he set out to defend free-market doctrine from the criticism that it was "unrealistic" and to defend the market itself from the planners. His self-justification, a monograph entitled "The Methodology of Positive Economics," appeared in 1953. He divided the economic realm among those who practiced the discipline as a positive science, a normative science, and an art. (These distinctions were first made by the economist John Neville Keynes, John Maynard's father—an ironic citation.) Friedman cast himself as a positive economist. He wrote:

> Positive economics is in principle independent of any particular ethical position or normative judgments. As Keynes says, it deals with "what is" not with "what ought to be." Its task is to provide a system of generalizations that can be used to make correct predictions about the consequences of any change in circumstances. Its performance is to be judged by the precision, scope, and conformity with experience of the predictions it yields. In short, positive economics is, or can be, an "objective" science, in precisely the same sense as any of the physical sciences.[7]

Positive economics would produce "conclusions that are, and deserve to be, widely accepted."[8] Friedman implied that those with whom he disagreed were unscientific and that his dispute with them centered less on political aims than on their adherence to professional standards.

To him, a theory was not necessarily proven by its "realistic" description of the economy. The theory of "monopolistic and imperfect competition" was a case in point. He argued that this notion was an attempt to prove free-market economics a "false image of reality."[9] Yet he claimed that the "realists" did not demonstrate that "predictions" based on classical doctrine were wrong, and this to him was crucial. "A hypothesis is important," he wrote, "if it 'explains' much by little, that is, if it abstracts the common and crucial elements from the mass of complex and detailed circumstances surrounding the phenomena to be explained and permits valid predictions on the basis of them alone."[10] The sole criterion for judging a theory was "whether it yields sufficiently accurate predictions."[11] It was more important to have a "truly useful general theory" than reams of data.[12] "A theory cannot be tested by comparing its assumptions directly with 'reality.' . . . Such criticism is largely irrelevant."[13] Thus he defended free-market economics from the "realists."

His credo was more than a statement of intention. It also had a theological drift, for Friedman had not shed his orthodox temperament. His free market could not be modeled because, he insisted, it could not be caught in one shape, a single body; economic modeling was like idolatry. The "realists" worshiped the graven images of the Keynesian conception. But Friedman didn't want the market to be so well defined, out of fear that it would be defiled; the true god would be blasphemed.

The Keynesians, however, tampered with the economy, and Friedman sought to counter them. Acting on the principles of positive economics, he devised a doctrine that " 'explains' much by little." "Monetarism is a very limited statement," he said. Indeed, its tenets are simple, consisting of only two main points: (1) the money supply is the only significant factor affecting the Gross National Product; and (2) by fixing the growth in the money supply to the real annual growth of the GNP—from 3 to 5 percent—the Federal Reserve can guarantee prosperity. Inflation can be held down, unemployment can reach the vanishing point, and the economy can stabilize yet remain dynamic. Consequently, government spending and social programs on the New Deal scale would become superfluous—in fact, become a burden on growth—and could be discarded without causing anyone real suffering. Government would then atrophy to a minimal state. The market would be free at last.

Monetarism, as conceived by Friedman, was both an answer to Keynesianism and its continuation—the "bastard progeny" said Joan Robinson, the British economist and a Friedman antagonist.[14] For although it concentrates on monetary rather than fiscal policy, monetarism, like Keynesianism, prescribes regulation of demand to achieve economic equilibrium. The Keynesians raise consumer demand by government expenditure, where the monetarists try to stop the inflation they believe flows from liberal profligacy by tightening the money-supply spigot. Monetarism is an economics of "shadow liberalism."

In seeking a response to the liberal New Economics, Friedman reanimated an old idea. He did not come to his theory overnight, but developed it gradually. If he had not been at the University of Chicago, where free-market ideas dismissed elsewhere as moribund were kept alive, he would almost surely never have made his most important contribution. Monetarism, he wrote in an essay, was part of "an aberrant tradition. Chicago was one of the few academic centers at which the quantity theory [of money] continued to be a central and vigorous part of the oral tradition throughout the 1930s and 1940s, where students continued to study monetary theory and to write theses on monetary problems."[15]

Friedman reformulated the ideas of Irving Fisher, who had reformulated the ideas of John Stuart Mill, the quintessential nineteenth-century classical liberal. Fisher was a Yale economics professor, whose quantity theory of money in the 1920s had made its way into the textbooks as conventional wisdom. He termed the business cycle the "dance of the dollar" because he believed it spun to the tune of the money supply. In Fisher, Friedman found the missing link for free-marketers, a theory apparently bridging empiricism and principle. Other free-marketers, such as Friedrich von Hayek, reiterated the philosophy of laissez faire economics with perhaps more nostalgic eloquence than Friedman. But Friedman alone showed how the restoration of the market might actually be attempted. He did more than state the eternal verities and implore society to return to them. The appeal of his theory rested both on its hypothetical simplicity and its apparent practicality.

Friedman published occasional essays on monetarism in academic journals. And finally, in 1963, his magnum opus, *A Monetary History of the United States 1867–1960* (written with Anna Schwartz), was published, dense with charts, figures, narrative, and interpretation, a labor of many years. In it Friedman attempted to prove the primacy of the money supply and disprove the most damaging claims against the absolute free market. The Depression was crucial in his scheme, for it had resulted in the discrediting of laissez faire ideas and the rise of Keynesianism. He felt obliged to explain it in a way that vindicated the market. The Depression, after all, was generally seen at the time as a revelation of the market's failure. If the business cycle was caused by gyrations in the money supply, poorly managed by the Federal Reserve, an agency of big government, then it would follow that the Depression and recessions in general were not caused by surplus production and weak demand, income inequality and corporate incompetence. The inability of the economy to right itself after 1929 could be blamed on the conservative's enemy—the state.

A Monetary History is a history of the United States as told by a dollar bill. But Friedman did not believe this was a one-dimensional presentation. "Money is a veil," he wrote. "The 'real' forces are the capacities of the people, their industry and ingenuity, the resources they command, their mode of economic and political organization and the like."[16] He proposed to lift the veil.

His account of the events that led to the creation of the Federal Reserve deserves some attention because of the stress he places on the Fed's importance as the chief confounder of the market. The origins of the Fed can be directly traced to the panic of 1907, a Wall Street upheaval that almost triggered a general economic collapse. Friedman assiduously presented numerous statistics about the panic. And he attributed the stemming of the crisis to the banks' refusal to convert deposits into currency. His tone was dispassionate, but he was scoring points. To him, government intervention always destabilizes the market. And the creation of the Fed is an ideal case study. In Friedman's view, the Fed's formation was precisely the wrong conclusion to be drawn from the 1907 experience. What was needed was *not* a central bank because, he claimed, market forces themselves achieved balance without outside interference. If the Fed had not existed, he continued, the Depression of the 1930s might have been avoided. The Fed's policies worsened the crisis, which eventually might have been halted just as he insisted the 1907 panic ended: by the banks' restrictions on withdrawals. He is so certain about his conclusion that he repeats it in *Free to Choose*:

> Had the Federal Reserve System never been established, and had a similar series of runs [on the banks] started, there is little doubt that the same measures would have been taken as in 1907 —a restriction of payments . . . by preventing the draining of reserves from good banks, restriction would almost certainly

> have prevented the subsequent series of bank failures in 1931,
> 1932, and 1933, just as restriction in 1907 quickly ended bank
> failures then. . . . The panic over, confidence restored, economic
> recovery would very likely have begun in early 1981, just as it
> had in early 1908.[17]

Friedman's economic solution, according to his own logic, must depend
upon the cogency of his history. The 1907 panic, therefore, is a particularly critical example of his historiography. Consider the following: The
precipitating event of the panic was a speculators' battle over stock in
the United Copper Company, controlled by a youthful buccaneer of
industry named F. Augustus Heinze. In Montana, where he owned a
copper company, he waged war against the Amalgamated Company,
which controlled the giant Anaconda mine and lay within the orbit of
the Standard Oil/Rockefeller group. Heinze, unlike Amalgamated,
recognized the workers' union and paid relatively high wages. Eventually he sold out to the Rockefeller interests to enter New York banking
and stock-market speculation. But because of his labor policy he had
made powerful foes who had once been upstarts like Heinze but were
now the ruling powers. When one of his schemes failed ignominiously
—United Copper stock fell from sixty dollars to ten dollars a share
within two days—he and his business associates went to the wall. The
Clearing House, a condominium of the leading New York banks, demanded their resignations from the boards of the Mercantile National
Bank and the Knickerbocker Trust Company. A run promptly began
on the Knickerbocker when word leaked to the public that the Clearing
House had lost confidence in the bank. On October 20, 1907, from nine
in the morning until noon, its reserves of $8 million were depleted by
panicked depositors. The bank closed its doors. Within hours, crowds
began besieging other banks.

Secretary of the Treasury George Cortelyou quickly took a train
from Washington to New York, where that evening he closeted himself
in his room at the Manhattan Hotel with the banker J. P. Morgan, who
had mobilized the leading financiers, including his rivals, behind him.
Cortelyou was quite familiar with Morgan and the men he had assembled. The Treasury Secretary, after all, had been chairman of the

Republican National Committee, assuming the role that had belonged to Mark Hanna, the old party boss who had died shortly before the 1904 election. As RNC chairman, Cortelyou collected millions of dollars in corporate contributions for the presidential campaign. Now he pledged direct and immediate government help to the financiers, which was forthcoming four days later in the form of $25 million dollars. It must be emphasized that this was not a simple case of quid pro quo: the national economy was imperiled; something had to be done swiftly. The Treasury money, which would rise to the sum of $36 million, was transferred to the banks, then to the threatened trust companies and then to the falling stock market—all under Morgan's direction. Morgan also threw in $25 million of his own money to stem the panic. And he sent his agents to Wall Street to instruct the frenzied sellers to cease and desist. This had the force of a command. Behind Morgan stood James Stillman of the Rockefeller-controlled National City Bank, George F. Baker of the First National Bank, Edward Harriman of the Harriman-Brown Brothers investment firm, Henry C. Frick of the Morgan-controlled U.S. Steel Company, and Thomas Fortune Ryan and August Belmont, the financiers who provided most of the funding for the Democratic Party. Most important, Morgan had the authority and money of the federal government behind him. Morgan himself judged how these amassed resources would be used; he proposed and he disposed. And still the crisis continued.

Within a few days the Trust Company of America, a Morgan holding, was badly hemorrhaging, losing $34 million in deposits. Then another event occurred that suggested to Morgan the possibility of ending the panic. This event appeared initially to resemble the United Copper debacle, a seemingly minor episode containing within it the potential for vast mischief. As it happened, George F. Baker's brother-in-law, Grant B. Schley, an important stockbroker, was in financial difficulty. He had put up as collateral against his substantial debts shares of the Tennessee Coal and Iron Company. If he failed, the company might collapse and the market would be plunged into a deeper abyss.

On the evening of November 2, Morgan gathered the Clearing House bankers in his marble library at 33 East Thirty-sixth Street, where the walls were lined with red silk, and Shakespeare folios were on private display. At midnight he presented his own ultimatum. He would purchase the Tennessee Coal & Iron stock and merge the company with his U.S. Steel, if the bankers would raise another $25 million to underwrite the Trust Company of America and other beleaguered institutions. One of his lawyers read the agreement aloud to them. "There you go, gentlemen," Morgan said. The bankers, all priding themselves on their caution and prudence, hesitated. Morgan put his hand on the shoulder of one and placed a gold pen between his fingers. The banker signed, and the others followed suit.

One obstacle, perhaps insuperable, now remained: the President of the United States, Theodore Roosevelt, who had railed against "malefactors of great wealth." Would he press antitrust action against U.S. Steel, which wanted to add the valuable Tennessee jewel to its crown? Elbert Gary and Henry Frick, managers of U.S. Steel, traveled to the White House to breakfast with Roosevelt on November 4. They explained that the stock purchase was motivated by altruism; that it would avert further panic; that it was of "little benefit" to U.S. Steel; that it was the "only means of avoiding failure." The President acceded on the spot, hoping that the panic would finally end. When his decision was announced, the stock market rallied and bankers everywhere were relieved. Thus the panic concluded, followed by a bracing but brief depression.[18]

The panic, as it turned out, was the pinnacle of Morgan's power—the power of America's greatest "money trust." And his enhanced glory meant increased monopolization, as the relentless destruction of Heinze and the purchase of Tennessee Coal & Iron made so clear. The weakness in the financial structure, however, taught the big bankers that there must be a systematic means of mobilizing reserves. Even Morgan, the Jupiter of Wall Street, and all the resources he commanded, was ultimately an inadequate substitute for a central bank.

In 1908, Congress passed the Aldrich-Vreeland Act, which permitted banks to issue currency against securities during emergencies. Another provision of the measure established the National Monetary Commission under the chairmanship of Senator Nelson W. Aldrich, described by the leading journalist of the day, Lincoln Steffens, as "the boss of the United States."[19] Aldrich was dedicated to the free enterprise of big bankers, and he prepared plans for a central bank that reflected his commitment. A host of other engaging actors appeared, among them Paul M. Warburg, a partner in the Kuhn, Loeb investment house, and an independent-minded thinker who came up with the design of a central bank; and William Jennings Bryan, the agrarian populist, Woodrow Wilson's Secretary of State, who demanded that the bank serve the interests of farmers.[20] The Federal Reserve Act of 1913 was amended by the various conflicting forces, and in the end the bankers were satisfied too.

In preparation for the new monetary legislation, the House of Representatives authorized the Committee on Banking and Currency to determine whether there really was a "money trust." A subcommittee under the aegis of Arsene Pujo of Louisiana began work. On December 18, 1912, J. P. Morgan was called to Washington. The titan of finance offered arresting testimony. He declared that he granted loans to borrowers not on the basis of collateral, but on their characters. "Is not commercial credit based primarily upon money or property?" inquired the committee's counsel. "No, sir," Morgan replied. "The first thing is character."[21] He celebrated the free-market myth, although time and again he had buried competition. Despite Morgan's disavowals, the Pujo Committee in its final report produced voluminous material to suggest that a "money trust" did indeed exist.

"Money is a veil." In *A Monetary History,* Friedman set out to penetrate it with scientific precision, the mark of "positive economics." And he dealt with the 1907 panic, the turning point that led to the creation of the Federal Reserve, in a seemingly technical manner. He duly noted that the crisis ended when the banks refused to allow deposits to be withdrawn as cash. He observed in a single terse sentence and a footnote Cortelyou's $25 million deposit with the "chief central reserve city banks in New York."[22] In passing, he mentioned Morgan's $25 million fund to abate the panic. But he offered little else. What he did not convey was a sense of business as a political force and how this might have translated into economic policy. He also neglected to discuss how financial interests might have used the crisis for their own ends. Cortelyou's political connection, Morgan's ubiquity, the Pujo Committee—these are a few of the things missing from Friedman's history. What was absent was not merely detail, but the heart of the matter. According to Friedman, the market corrected itself. To have written this, he must have confused Morgan with the market.

Friedman's deficient history proved his own assumptions, at least to Friedman. The Fed, to him, was solely the device of big government; yet he unfairly slighted the bankers. His history of 1907 incited him to dramatic claims about 1929. If the Fed had not been created, he asserted, we would have been spared the Depression. He insisted that its cause was the Fed's imprudent reduction of the money supply. Unfortunately, on this point, Friedman suffered a shortage of facts, namely that from 1929 to 1932, the money supply fell by less than 3 percent, prices dropped by more than 30 percent, and unemployment rose to 25 percent. Leonard Silk, the economics columnist of *The New York Times,* wrote that it is "difficult to see how such a catastrophe could have resulted from so small a decline in the stock of money."[23]

Despite the black holes in Friedman's analysis, *A Monetary History* contributed greatly to solidifying his reputation as a major thinker. His notion that the Depression was not produced by an unbalanced market system but was artificially induced by the Fed was seized upon eagerly by conservatives. "Friedman's liberating revisionism rapidly became part of the conservative scholarly arsenal," wrote the historian George H. Nash.[24] For conservatives, Friedman's respectability was taken as their own.

While *A Monetary History* was an important landmark for conservatives, it was not—at over eight hundred pages, replete with abstruse economic language and numbers—a popular work. It was intended for the community of scholars, particularly the community of economists. Friedman's *Capitalism and Freedom,* published in 1962, was intended for the general educated reader. In this book the uncompromising professional economist became a polemicist and advocate. By no means, though, was it a tract; it was carefully argued so that the reader might be led to Friedman's ironclad conclusions.

On one level, *Capitalism and Freedom* introduced the free market as a philosophy. On another, the book was a practical program, a guide to right-wing public policy. Friedman's catalog of government programs was a battle plan. Whatever government did, he wanted to undo:

farm parities, tariffs, rent control, minimum wages, industry regulation, social security, public housing, conscription, national parks, the post office, public roads, and the licensing of professions.[25] His litany was a conservative *What Is Not to Be Done.* Over the years, he and his disciples fashioned many public policies to limit government functions. In so doing, he demonstrated that his philosophical critique was neither antiquated nor an affair of the armchair; it was an impetus for politics.

Capitalism and Freedom was one of the early products of the burgeoning conservative Counter-Establishment. The book began in June 1956 as a series of lectures at Wabash College in Crawfordsville, Indiana, underwritten by one of the first conservative foundations, the Volker Fund. Every summer the Volker Fund financed a program to bring about thirty young scholars from around the country together with about six older professors to discuss ideology, a program designed as shadow liberalism. "It was the same kind of thing the Young Socialist League does with its summer sessions," said Friedman. "It was very effective for quite a while. Then it more or less died out."

Friedman was always more important to the Counter-Establishment than it was to him. He was secure at Chicago, where he produced the bulk of his work without outside funding. But the conservative network offered him an opportunity to make contacts and a means to inject his ideas into the public debate.

In the late 1940s, the free-market cloister at Chicago was bolstered by the arrival of Friedrich von Hayek, already famous for his best-selling attack on the welfare state, *The Road to Serfdom.* Von Hayek's appointment was facilitated by the Volker Fund, which, according to Friedman, "provided the finances." Von Hayek, an expatriate Austrian who had resided for years in London, had a broad range of international connections. He knew conservatives in many countries, but they didn't know each other. In 1947 he gathered forty prominent scholars from Europe and America for ten days in the Alpine village of Mont Pelerin, Switzerland. The money that made this extraordinary conference possible was provided by the Volker Fund. A statement of high philosophical intent was issued and the group, named the Mont Pelerin Society, met every year thereafter.

"I was there at the time," Friedman recalled. "Its major importance as an institution—it's hard to realize this now—was that in 1947 the people who believed in the market economy were mostly isolated individuals, almost completely separated from their intellectual environment. The whole thrust was toward central planning. Britain was dominated by the Fabian Society. The real function of the Mount Pelerin Society, which it served magnificently in the early years, which function has disappeared largely now, was that it provided an opportunity for isolated people from around the world to get together for a week in which they could let their hair down and talk to one another about the things that really concerned them without looking over their shoulders all the time. It gave them a feeling that they weren't speaking in a vacuum, that the views they held were respectable, worth pursuing. The Americans had a large group there. The function it served for me was a very different one, and it didn't have very much to do with my ideas. It brought me into contact with a variety of very interesting and able people from a variety of countries whom I never would have met. Some of them are now involved in policy-making. In Britain, for example, Ralph Harris runs the Institute for Economic Affairs, which was the original think tank for Margaret Thatcher."

Back home, ideas were becoming the road to action, too. Friedman met an obscure conservative, William Baroody, who had no great ideas of his own and no independent reputation as a scholar. Baroody was a new political type: the entrepreneur of ideas. He wanted right-wing intellectuals to gather their strength in his American Enterprise Institute and turn ideology into power.

Friedman had little to gain by way of academic standing through such an untried endeavor. His incentive was less personal than ideological gain. "AEI had no significance to me particularly, but I hope I was important to it," he said. "I was a member for years of its academic advisory group, which took itself very seriously, both in terms of proposing projects to be studied and in terms of going over manuscripts submitted, giving editorial advice and judgment. We were mainly assuring quality and giving some coherence."

In the early 1960s, AEI, though obscure and small, was at the center of Washington's conservative movement. Baroody was a prime player, becoming a senior political adviser to Barry Goldwater. When

Goldwater ran for the presidency in 1964, partly upon Baroody's urging, the AEI president assumed control of the issues and speechwriting staff. He brought in his AEI stable, including Friedman, the only one of the group having impeccable academic credentials in economics. Goldwater went down to an ignominious defeat, but for the conservatives it was an advance. The campaign, Friedman said, "was premature in the sense that there was no chance of his getting elected. In the first place, the assassination of Kennedy made an enormous difference in the whole atmosphere. The emotional wave that followed Kennedy's assassination made it impossible for almost any Republican to be elected. But I do not believe Reagan would have been elected in 1980 if Goldwater had not carried out his campaign in 1964. You've got sets of political ideas and values that take a long time to develop and have an enormous momentum. It takes a long time to turn them around. Goldwater was enormously important in providing an impetus to the subsequent move away from New Deal ideas, away from Fabian socialism."

When the next Republican candidate for president, Richard Nixon, was elected in 1968, it appeared that monetarism would finally have its chance. In his seminal paper, "Methodology of Positive Economics," Friedman stated that a theory's validity depends upon "whether it yields sufficiently accurate predictions." Monetarism was to be proven by its divining power, and Friedman was its soothsayer. Now the test had arrived, with Nixon indicating his desire to follow the general Friedman line. As his chairman of the Council of Economic Advisers he appointed Paul McCracken, who immediately pronounced himself "Friedmanesque." And in 1970, Nixon named Arthur F. Burns, Friedman's mentor at Rutgers, chairman of the Federal Reserve. Everything seemed to be in place for a proper experiment. Friedman had high expectations. "Richard Nixon," he said, "is an enormously able person with a high IQ. I have met only one other major political figure who had a higher sheer academic intellectual IQ. That was Robert Taft, Sr., a brilliant person who would have been a delight on any academic faculty in the country. Nixon is an intellectual in the sense he's interested in abstract ideas. Moreover, prior to his election, the principles he expressed were the principles I expressed and agreed with."

Friedman prescribed growth in the money supply from 3 to 5

percent, and for the first six months of 1969 the Fed stayed the course. George Shultz, who had been dean of the University of Chicago's business school, became Nixon's budget director, and coined the monetarist catchphrase "Steady as you go." In the last six months of 1969, the Fed tightened up to a virtual no-growth money supply. Then Burns was appointed chairman of the central bank. He faced increasingly alarming conditions. The monetarist solution, it seemed, was not working exactly as advertised. The constricted money supply was followed by an inflation growth rate of 6 percent, an increase of unemployment from 3.5 percent in 1969 to 5 percent by May 1970, and an unbalanced budget. Businesses also suffered from the credit squeeze. The Penn Central Railroad went under—its mismanagement exposed in the crunch—the largest failure in business history.

Burns was profoundly troubled. On May 27, at a dinner at the White House, the Fed chairman gravely told a gathering of prominent corporate leaders that he "would not let the economy collapse." He quickly disposed of Friedman's formula and raised money-supply levels to rates double and triple those that Friedman wanted. But the damage was done, and the recession resulted in a political setback to the Republicans in the 1970 midterm elections. Nixon rethought his economic policy.

On August 15, 1971, the President froze wages, prices, and rents. And he declared, "I am now a Keynesian." The New Economic Policy arrived, its outline suggested by John Connally, personification of the corporate state, who became Secretary of the Treasury. As Connally rose, Friedman fell. In the beginning, Nixon had wanted to use free-market policies, but abandoned them; he had intended to reduce the government role in the economy, but wound up presiding over an expansion.[26]

Friedman denounced the NEP in stentorian rhetoric. "The controls are deeply and inherently immoral. By substituting the rule of men for the rule of law and for voluntary cooperation in the marketplace, the controls threaten the very foundations of a free society."[27]

Friedman faulted Nixon for not staying the course. Yet political necessity, as the President understood it, required veering away from monetarist assumptions. Whether Friedman's predictions of a virtually inflation-free, prosperous economy, achieved through control of the money supply, would ever come to pass was too problematical a proposition for the politician. "The Nixon administration was an enormous disappointment," reflected Friedman. "It was a disappointment because it turned out that what were our principles were Nixon's prejudices. If there were not immediate political matters at stake he would go with his principles. Of course, every President must have the capacity to rise above principles. It would not be good for a country to have a completely doctrinaire ideological president who insisted on going according to his principles. So it's a matter of degree. The threshold at which Nixon could rise above principle was very, very low. The most extreme example was the end of my own connection with the Nixon administration, when he introduced wage and price controls. It was a terrible mistake. If you hadn't had wage and price controls, then you would not have gone through the inflationary episodes you did. Nixon coupled that with a sharp stimulation of the economy. Wage and price controls gave him, in the short run, the best of both worlds. He could seem to be holding down inflation while at the same time stimulating the economy with what looked like prosperity for the 1972 election. And that worked from a short-term political point of view. Its long-term effects were disastrous. I once had a conversation with Nixon in which the point came out. This was in the summer of 1971, before wage and price controls. He was trying to get me to press Arthur Burns to increase the money supply more. I objected that that would be a bad policy because it would produce inflation. My recollection is that what I said was that there's no point in getting elected by means of making the country ungovernable after the election. Inflating now might help you get elected, but it would leave you with a situation after the election when it will not be worth having been elected. I recall Nixon having said, 'Well, let's first get reelected.' That was typical. I'd like to hear the White House tapes to see if my recollection is correct."

It did not seem that Friedman's brand of economics would get another test soon. But in 1975 another president beckoned him, a president unyielding in his principles, confident of his mandate, and unwilling to bend to voters—Augusto Pinochet of Chile.

After the coup, Pinochet was handed a three-hundred-page economic blueprint prepared by Chilean protégés of Milton Friedman. (According to a 1975 report of the U.S. Senate Select Committee on Intelligence Activities, they had received CIA funds for their efforts.) These economists—known as "Los Chicago Boys"—became the top advisers to the junta. Many of them had been trained at the University of Chicago. Others came from the economics department of the Universidad Católica de Chile, where the teachings of the "Chicago School" were stressed; the curriculum there had been crafted by Arnold Harberger, a Chicago professor.

In March 1975, Harberger and Friedman were summoned by Pinochet to design his economic policy. Friedman justified his action as a contribution to the defense of "capitalism and freedom," which to him were the same thing. "There's no doubt that Allende brought the coup on himself," he said, "but not necessarily through his inflationary policies. It was because he was trying to turn the country into a standard Communist totalitarian state. He was aware of the danger of a coup, but he thought he was going to be able to carry through this plan. I don't think there's any doubt that Allende was driving the country toward a straight Marxist dictatorship. Why should I have had qualms about going down there? I'm not going down to help the government. I'm going down to say what I believe. If they're willing to have me, that's that. The military hadn't overthrown a democracy. It had overthrown a regime headed toward Communist dictatorship. Between the two evils, I have no doubt the military junta is the lesser evil."

Friedman met with Pinochet in his office in the presidential palace, La Moneda, which had been bombed during the coup and where Allende had died with a submachine gun in his hands, fighting junta soldiers. The economist found the president attentive. "He seemed a perfectly reasonable human being. It's very hard to make a judgment on that. I don't know. For all I know he goes home and beats his wife. He could be the kindest father and husband in the world. But he seemed intelligent. He asked sensible questions. He was able to understand the answers. I had a very favorable impression of him on that level. We did not talk about any of the political aspects." To Friedman, Pinochet was like a graduate student. If he took instruction well, he was regarded well.

Friedman prescribed the monetarist cure: a 20 to 25 percent cut in government spending, a severe restriction in money-supply growth, and a laissez faire approach to private business. *Business Week* reported: "The idea of taming inflation once and for all by a sharp cutback in government spending and money-supply growth has frequently been advocated. Chile is almost a laboratory experiment to see how well this kind of program works."[28]

The junta followed Friedman's advice to the letter, and the austerity policies were ardently administered by "Los Chicago Boys." A phrase of Friedman's, "shock treatment"—*tratamiento de "shock"*—was borrowed by the regime in its propaganda effort to shore up support. Inflation was beaten back, but unemployment and bankruptcies soared. There were other consequences. Juan de Onis, a *New York Times* correspondent, reported on Chile seven months after the Friedman-inspired measures went into effect:

Scenes of daily life here now resemble the darkest days of the depression of the 1930s. The privation in the shantytowns where the unemployed are in the thousands is ameliorated only by food kitchens and relief efforts through a government program and church charities. Often the only hot meal a child gets is the school lunch program. At home it is a piece of bread and a glass of tea. In the wealthier residential areas it is a nightly experience for some child in wretched clothes to knock at the door for bread.[29]

To those who believed the monetarist medicine would result in a healthy economy, such suffering was therapeutic. Pablo Baraona, the president of the Central Bank and the chief junta adviser, declared that the fact that "more than 90 percent of the people are against our policies is proof that the model is working. . . ."[30] And yet, although it possessed the unique ability to maintain a policy heedless of public opinion, the junta ruled over an economy in virtual ruins.

Chile was more than a test of monetarism. It also tested the philosophical premises of free-market doctrine as rightly understood by economists from the "Chicago School." In *Free to Choose*, Friedman had written: "In the past century a myth has grown up that free market capitalism . . . is a system under which the rich exploit the poor."[31] And: "Economic freedom is an essential requisite for political freedom."[32] This point was the entire purpose of *Capitalism and Freedom*. But in Chile the market is dominated by oligopolies and multinational corporations, and presided over by a dictatorship that enforces its fiat by the torture, "disappearance," assassination, and internal exile of political opponents. Is Chile an unfair experiment? Is Pinochet a poor student? Or has he understood the implications of Friedman better than Friedman has understood them?

Friedman spoke defensively of his association with the junta. "I don't know any of the details. I am not going to defend the Chilean government on grounds of human rights. The fundamental principles of a military government are antithetical to the principles of a free market. The military government is organized from the top down and the free market from the bottom up. It was a great exception. I don't know of any other military regime that's adopted free-market policies. I think that the political pressures are all in the direction of suppressing freedom. On the other hand, the people of Chile have a long tradition of a democratic society. I'd like to see that happen. I'm not going to predict one way or the other. I am hopeful that Chile will be in the tradition of military regimes replaced by democratic governments."

Some of Friedman's critics argued as though the relationship between free-market economics and political dictatorship were logical and natural. But this connection, in the case of Chile, was not inevitable. Friedman could have refused to collaborate with the dictatorship. He made his decision voluntarily; he was, after all, free to choose.

Controversy swirled around Friedman because of his Chilean consultancy, but soon after he advised Pinochet he received his highest honor—the Nobel Prize. He was now a monument. And he was marketable as never before.

In 1980 he appeared as the star of his very own television series, *Free to Choose*, where, in ten one-hour programs, he elucidated the principles he had taught for decades. The series became the basis of a best-selling book, also called *Free to Choose*. The television programs were financed by a host of large corporations, but Friedman was no mere corporate mercenary. They sought his reflected glory; they had had little to do with promoting him in the past, and he didn't need them. But the CEOs sponsoring him now felt that he could help turn public opinion in their favor. Thus, in the midst of a presidential election year, Friedman emerged as the most important mass media popularizer of Counter-Establishment notions.

The book was a synthesis of his previous work; there was nothing new here. He recapitulated his history of the Federal Reserve and how it had manufactured the Depression; he invoked the spirit of Adam Smith; and he proposed monetarism as the answer to our woes. *Free to Choose* was filled with glib, insupportable statements on almost every page: "You can travel from one end of the industrialized world to the other and almost the only people you will find engaging in backbreaking toil are the people who are doing it for sport."[33] Friedman's slickness usually made his arguments fall down. There was also plenty of trademark quirky history. Still, he sounded his themes forcefully and clearly.

Even if his interpretations of historical events were often bizarre, he did offer a general theory. He is a classical liberal who views history as the linear unfolding of progress. "Indeed," he wrote, "the very progress of society made the residual evils seem all the more objectionable."[34] The success of the market then inspired misguided do-gooders, who sought in big government a corrective instrument. But the state really leads, Friedman reminds us, to von Hayek's "road to serfdom." The hour was late, yet not too late to appreciate the "intimate connection between political freedom and economic freedom."[35] The book concluded with a plethora of proposals that would encode free-market doctrine and forbid heresies like the unbalanced budget. Friedman called his ideas an "economic Bill of Rights."[36]

In *Free to Choose*, Friedman was at once philosopher, economist, historian, and policy-maker. Above all, he was a propagandist. The project was a huge success. And even as his programs were airing on television and his books stacked high in the stores, monetarism was undergoing yet another critical test.

In 1979 the Labour government in Britain collapsed and was replaced by voters with a staunchly Conservative one headed by Prime Minister Margaret Thatcher. She was not a Tory of the old school, whose sense of noblesse oblige led to paternal concern for the working class. Thatcher was the daughter of a shopkeeper, a prim and proper *petite bourgeoise* filled with ideological certitude. "The lady's not for turning," she declared. Her Conservative supporters disdainfully regarded the old Tories of the Harold Macmillan variety, stigmatizing them as "wets," or soft-headed wimps.

The influence of conservative intellectuals in the rise and rule of Thatcherism has been strikingly parallel to the American experience of Reaganism. Thatcherism diverged from the old Toryism just as Reaganism diverged from the old Republicanism. Among the philosophers who most impressed Thatcher were Friedrich von Hayek and Milton Friedman. She dismissed the Keynesian economics pursued by Tory and Labour governments alike, and she disavowed the role of government in negotiating agreements between labor and management. Further, she attacked the very notion of consensus itself. "To me," she proclaimed, "consensus seems to be the process of abandoning all beliefs, principles, values and polices. . . . It is the process of avoiding the very issues that have got to be solved merely to get people to come to an agreement on the way ahead."[37]

Behind Thatcher's ideology stood a new array of right-wing intellectual institutions—a British Counter-Establishment. The Centre for Policy Studies was founded in 1974 as a direct alternative to the Conservative Party's own Research Department. Its director, Alfred Sherman, became a speechwriter for Thatcher. The Centre's guiding light, Sir Keith Joseph, became Thatcher's personal intellectual mentor. Then there were the Salisbury Group and the Conservative Philosophy Group, which held informal seminars attended by Thatcher. The Institute for Economic Affairs was directed by Ralph Harris, whom Friedman met at the founding of the Mont Pelerin Society. The institute's chairman was Antony G. A. Fisher, who played an active role in Counter-Establishment networks on both sides of the Atlantic. He helped found the International Center for Economic Policy Studies (later known as the Manhattan Institute) with William Casey, the Wall Street speculator who became Reagan's CIA director. (Casey was the lawyer who incorporated the *National Review*.) Another British think tank, the Adam Smith Institute, was founded by a brother of a Heritage Foundation researcher and directly modeled on the Heritage example. Under Thatcher, its researchers served as party advisers. And after her 1983 reelection, the Adam Smith Institute embarked upon the "Omega Project," a plan to draw up detailed proposals for her second term.

Once ensconced at 10 Downing Street, Thatcher summoned the monetarists. From America she imported a disciple of Friedman's to serve as her personal economic adviser—Alan Walters, a Johns Hopkins economist with close ties to the American Counter-Establishment, who served, for example, on the Academic Advisory Board of the Manhattan Institute.* Friedman himself made a personal appearance. At last, here was a test of monetarism in a democracy inculcated with the Dunkirk spirit of national sacrifice.

Thatcher's monetarism had three immediate economic effects: (1) unemployment skyrocketed to levels not seen since the Depression, consumer demand plummeted, and the resulting deflation depressed the domestic market; (2) high interest rates forced British industry to pay more for its money, pushing up its costs, which undercut productivity and competitiveness; and (3) the pound became overvalued, which priced British goods out of world markets and shattered Britain's export trade. The social costs were high, too. In 1981, riots by youths without hope of getting jobs engulfed major cities. Opposition to the Thatcher policy was mounted not only by Labour, which was wholly expected, but also by the "wets" of her own party, who reflected rising business discontent. One critic, Christopher Hitchens, referred to Thatcherism as "sado-monetarism." Until the short war over the Falkland Islands, her future appeared bleak.

---

*Walters was knighted, and when he returned to America he became a Resident Scholar at the American Enterprise Institute.

On June 11, 1980, Friedman submitted a memorandum to the House of Commons supporting the Thatcher monetary "strategy." But he attacked her monetary "tactics," labeling them "egregious" and "simply wrong."[38] To him, once again, what was occurring was not true monetarism. "No, of course Britain is not a fair test of monetarism," he said. "And yes, of course. A test is never provided by one episode. It's got to be repeated. It's false to say that any one of these circumstances is a crucial experiment. None is." According to Friedman, monetarism was still untried.

But the possibility of a decisive experiment loomed when Ronald Reagan captured the Republican nomination for president. He was a true conservative and a great admirer of Friedman to boot. "Superb!" read Reagan's blurb on the paperback edition of *Free to Choose*.

"I first met Ronald Reagan in 1970 when I was spending a semester at UCLA as a visiting professor," said Friedman. "I was very, very favorably impressed. I thought he was a very serious, thoughtful person. He is interested in the principles, and he has reached them by thinking them through and by reading. In terms of sheer IQ, I'd have to say that Nixon had a higher IQ. They're both, in a way, intellectuals interested in abstract ideas and principles. I have found Reagan will discuss and understand complicated ideas." Another graduate student.

By now, Friedman had entered the conservative Valhalla. All bowed before him. Yet some conservatives wondered if perhaps the Nobel Prize winner was too narrow. "It is possible," wrote William F. Buckley, Jr., "that his theories suffer from the overriding disqualification that they simply cannot get a sufficient exercise in democratic situations—because it takes longer for them to produce results than the public is prepared to wait."[39]

Was the trouble with Friedman's economics precisely that it was merely economics and not political economy? To Friedman, politics is little more than economics, a system of incentives. Voters are always seeking to maximize their interests; and politicians, purveyors of goods and services, are trying to offer incremental advantages to gain votes. According to this view, politics is a market driven by consumer demand.

In Friedman's free market, people don't have to believe in anything, not even in the virtue of competition; they just have to compete. Though the market is a wrathful god, ultimately punishing hypocrisy, it does not necessarily make the competitor virtuous. One of the market's virtues is its impersonality.

Friedman occasionally talks about individuals, but he always comes back to the bottom line. To him the aggregates are real, the individuals unscientific. He doesn't offer anybody Utopia. Unlike von Hayek, he has written no rhapsodies about the golden age of the past. "The free enterprise system," he wrote in *Free to Choose,* "is a *profit* and *loss* system."[40] Friedman doesn't say that once you are "free to choose," success will follow. His belief is captured by the title of another of his books: *There's No Such Thing as a Free Lunch.* There's no promise in his promise. For him, the hero is the free market, an abstract mechanism, not the people involved in it.

He has a vision, but it's not in Technicolor. Friedman sees changes occurring gradually. He has an actuarial sense of time, and why not? After all, he did pass the New Jersey actuarial licensing exam.

Reagan, on the other hand, was thunderstruck on the road from Sunset Boulevard. He has a mythological sense of time, a belief that we are at a turning point of history and yet that his ideology is timeless.

Unlike Friedman, Reagan has a political economy. He views economic exchanges as social relationships. He knows from personal experience that the race goes to the good, except when big government meddles. He has flesh-and-blood winners in mind: himself and his friends. And he believes that everyone can win because Americans are good at heart.

Friedman focuses on the medium of the exchange, not on the people making it. The medium, of course, is money, the ultimate rational object lacking all subjectivity. It has no consciousness; money doesn't care who owns it. And money is never hypocritical. It is scientific.

If one focuses on the medium, the method of solving economic problems becomes obvious: monetarism. But if one focuses on people, there's more to the market than money; there's faith. But Friedman's system can't operate on faith. The more one relies on faith, the more likely it is that expectations will be raised that can't be fulfilled. And then politics will interfere; monetarism will again be thwarted.

Reagan, however, acts as though the economy should respond to him the same way voters do. He attempts to establish a personal relationship with the market just as he establishes a personal relationship with the unseen audience on the other side of the camera. To him, the essence of politics and economics is psychological, a confidence game.

To Friedman, leadership is solely legal, a contract between the electorate and its chosen representative. All that is missing from his vision is the vitality of politics: persuasion, cunning, ideology, loyalty, resentment, friendship, partisanship, *Robert's Rules of Order,* and personality. There is no place in his system for a charismatic leader, a leader with special grace because he appears to embody the dreams of the masses, a leader whose leadership rests upon enthusiasm that must be tested by crises, whose authority is not merely legal but personal. In other words, there is no accounting in Friedman's system for Ronald Reagan.

On the eve of the 1980 presidential campaign, on October 6, 1979, a dramatic monetarist experiment began in America, when Paul Volcker, chairman of the Federal Reserve, announced that in order to combat double-digit inflation, the Fed would directly regulate the money supply. *Newsweek* called Volcker's bold move "radical shock treatment for the economy," evoking Friedman's Chilean rhetoric. Alan Greenspan, the influential Wall Street investment analyst, said that "if adhered to, [it] would be the most important change in monetary policy in a generation."[41] Friedman himself, in a *Newsweek* column, praised the Fed's action as "excellent anti-inflation sentiment," but he reserved judgment. It was "promise, not performance."[42]

In 1980, the critical election year, real income dropped to zero, workers' real weekly earnings fell by almost 3 percent, unemployment rose to 7.5 percent, and interest rates shot up past 20 percent. It was under these gloomy conditions that Jimmy Carter had to conduct his reelection campaign. His message was one of sacrifice and pessimism. Reagan, for his part, was uplifting and positive. He campaigned against the dolorous effects of monetarism while embracing the ideas of Milton Friedman, its foremost advocate. Friedman, he announced, was one of his closest and most trusted economic advisers. And in October 1980,

Reagan declared, "We must establish a stable, sound, and predictable monetary policy"—vintage Friedmanism.

Reagan, however, was an inveterate optimist. He promised no pain. It had no place in his world. For Friedman, though, pain was inevitable and necessary. "If you cut down the rate in the money supply," he said, "you will go through a period of unemployment, slow growth, *pain*, in return for which you will come out after an interval into a period in which you'll have rapid economic growth without inflation. Now, if you are going to do it, it will be most effective if you can persuade people that's what you're really doing. The worst of all worlds is to start on that course and reverse yourself, because you get all the pain without the benefits."

Monetarism, in fact, was a policy whose consequences could have been predicted, if the experiences of Nixon, Pinochet, Thatcher, and Carter were any guide. The results were similar each time: deflation, unemployment, bankruptcies, increased monopolization, constriction of the market—but only if one believed that monetarism had been tried. To Friedman, each of these examples was, as he said about Chile, "a great exception." He awaited the leader willing to go the limit. *"If you believed in it you ought to do it right. If you didn't you ought not to pretend."*

He hoped that in Reagan he had at last found his man. And in 1980, Reagan expressed no misgivings; on the contrary, he expressed zeal. Though monetarism as formulated by Friedman was a recent doctrine, it was regarded by most conservatives as the wisdom of the ages, one of the greatest legacies of the Remnant. Friedman had become the grand old man of the right. And within the Counter-Establishment even those who had spent decades in the internecine ideological debates of the New York intellectuals were regarded as newcomers.

CHAPTER SIX

SHADOW LEFTISM,

OR THE IDEOLOGICAL

LIGHT BRIGADE

Every Halloween, at nightfall, the largest annual gathering of neo-conservatives convenes. The revelers come in the guise of the Pumpkin Paper Irregulars, a double identity that recalls the Ur–Cold War passion play, the Alger Hiss case, whose memory they intend to keep burning bright. At least one speaker retries and resentences Hiss, while others deliver orations on the onset of Cold War: "Bliss was it in that dawn to be alive!" At the 1985 dinner the featured speaker was Richard Nixon, who was presented with a scroll making him an honorary member. By these rituals the Irregulars commune with the spirit of Whittaker Chambers, who progressed from Bolshevik to conservative, from true believer to true believer, and whose act of hiding stolen government documents in a pumpkin patch inspired the group's name. The neoconservatives, too, are witnesses, and the conversion from left to right is the central political experience in their lives. These are people for whom card-carrying membership still has meaning.

"The definition of a neoconservative is someone who wasn't a conservative," said neoconservative Harvard professor Nathan Glazer. Over the course of two generations, neoconservatives have been transformed from leftist intellectuals, congregating in cafeterias and small magazines, into high officials and courtiers of the Reagan administration. Their political journey, however, cannot be explained simply by reference to a calibrated ideological scale. Although they are frequently inclined to the formulaic, they are less coherent as an intellectual movement than as a social group. Some are welfare-statists, others are free-marketers; some proclaim the moral mission of America in global terms, others urge the hardheaded practice of realpolitik. What really binds them together is their common experience.

The neoconservatives are sufferers from multiple forms of alienation—personal, professional, and political. They are mostly second-generation Jews, torn between cultures. To their own surprise, they found themselves achieving tenure in the elite universities—which used to prescribe quotas limiting their numbers—at the very moment that students rejected all mentors. Then, as they prepared to assume an expected role as the intellectual helpers of the traditional New Deal coalition, especially blacks and labor, blacks sought their own counsel and the party regulars were supplanted by the insurgent New Politics forces. The neoconservatives' success was a failure. They had done everything right, and everything came out wrong. Their writings became an encyclopedia of disaffection; they presented themselves as the *philosophes* of the counter-reformation.

As former leftists they are powerful legitimatizers of conservatism. They serve as proof to conservatives that their cause is righteous. Their conversion holds out the hope of final victory; they have been in the camp of the Liberal Establishment, learned the gnostic rites, and yet emerged disenchanted. Despite their assimilation into the Counter-Establishment, they still maintain a distinct identity, marked by their unique history. In many important respects, neoconservatism is the political culture of the Old Left preserved in aspic.

They are a minority within a minority in one city: neoconservatives among conservatives, conservative Jews among liberal Jews, and parochial New Yorkers, who instinctively regard events between the Hudson and East rivers as exemplifying America, only on a higher level. Yet their strength is as the strength of ten because of their fervent faith in ideas. They are an avant-garde leading a retreat. And they view themselves as heirs to the tradition of the European intelligentsia.

Many people traversed the same social territory as the neoconservatives. Yet only a few gave themselves over so completely in the 1930s to the world of the left, an experience that still sets the neoconservatives apart. Not the least of their assets is a conceptual method of thinking from which conservatives have shut themselves off: Marxism.

As a generation of prospective intellectuals in the 1930s, they came to Marxism already steeped in the disputatious heritage of the Talmud. In the alcoves of the City College of New York, they learned the political value of universal principles, the dynamic movement of history, and the crucial role of the vanguard. Even within the left-wing movement, the future neoconservatives occupied a special place of alienation. Most were Trotskyists, followers of Leon Trotsky, the Russian revolutionary leader who was purged by Stalin after Lenin's death. Stalin's tens of thousands of followers in the American Communist Party, with their array of front groups and their entrenched base within the labor movement, dwarfed the minuscule Trotskyist sects. While a few isolated Trotskyists aroused a constituency beyond their own slight numbers—teamster organizers in Minneapolis being the most striking example—this brand of Communism remained rarefied. In order to join, one had to define oneself primarily in terms of the outcome of the internal power struggle within the Kremlin. Then one had to identify with the loser Trotsky and his analysis of the Soviet Union as a "degenerated workers' state." To the Trotskyist, the Stalinist had the upper hand on the left wing. This granted the Trotskyist, almost totally removed from any sort of political influence anywhere, a kind of intellectual freedom. Not surprisingly, most Trotskyists were intense young intellectuals invigorated by day-long sessions of ideological charge and countercharge.

Training in the discipline of Marxist cell groups, even after one rejects the cells' confinement, is rigorous preparation for what is to be done. Many of the neoconservatives still inhabit the theoretical style of the Marxists; some have adapted the practical framework of the Leninists; and some of the former Trotskyists who have gained influence under Reagan have assumed the tone of Stalinist commissars. When aligning themselves as defenders of the captains of industry they see themselves in the familiar role of a self-conscious vanguard at the forefront of the class struggle, sneering at the lily-livered liberals. No position could carry more world-historical weight.

In an age of expertise, the neoconservatives are not specialists. They are publicists, sociologists, litterateurs, and generalists, an intellectual elite defending what they believe to be first principles. Unlike many conservatives, they were not economics majors. Imbued with the spirit of liberal-arts education, they are an ideological "light brigade," able to move fluidly from field to field, generality to generality.

Their ideas are married to powerful emotions, a combustible mixture. Most neoconservatives were suspended between the traditional immigrant culture of their parents and the enticements of America. In their homes, English was often a foreign language. Although learning was revered, usually nobody in the family had been to college. These precocious children were neither greenhorns nor fully assimilated natives. To escape the dilemma, they identified themselves with a cosmopolitan intellectualism beyond social background; they remade themselves into aristocrats of high culture. Yet they had none of the ease of aristocrats. Instead, they were frequently consumed by the insecurities of arrivistes. Their striving has been fierce, and they write about it endlessly, often directly in the form of raw personal testament, as in Norman Podhoretz's *Making It.* They sought order and acceptance in the world of ideas, and when their ideas were challenged they felt the challenge was to civilization itself.

For the neoconservatives, two decades matter most: the one in which they were student radicals, the 1930s, and the one in which they reacted against student radicals, the 1960s. At the moment of their arrival at their properly tenured stations, when they believed they had earned deference for their accumulated wisdom, hordes of longhairs screamed that they belonged in the dustbin of history. This generational conflict was heightened by a cultural conflict, for the youth were Americans for whom the painful ordeal of assimilation didn't exist. The "adversary culture" that the neoconservatives condemned as nihilism incarnate was an extravagant assertion of the native culture. And the harsh criticisms leveled by the young at *Amerika* implied an American innocence that was being violated; even in their "infantile leftism," the sixties radicals were at home. The neoconservatives, in the meantime, felt more alienated than ever. Their sense of estrangement moved them closer in sentiment to the conservatives, who had always believed themselves to be true-blue Americans and yet out of place.

The neoconservatives became embittered parents, in rebellion against the young. Long after Yippies had become yuppies, many remained filled with a desire for vengeance, determined to wage the generational war: *Totem and Taboo* in reverse. This unabated desire led some neoconservatives to feel a measure of vindication when John Lennon was killed, a symbolic slaying of the sixties, a month after Reagan's election in 1980. Now the old would leave the primal battleground triumphant, the sixties dead forever.

The neoconservatives represented themselves to the conservatives as indispensable brokers of the traditional Democratic coalition, speaking for the disaffected rank and file. Yet those few neoconservatives who had actual experience within the Democratic Party were never principals themselves, but aides, mainly to Hubert Humphrey. Max Kampelman, later Reagan's arms-control negotiator, was Humphrey's administrative assistant; Ben Wattenberg, the neoconservative publicist, was his campaign speechwriter; Evron Kirkpatrick, his political-science professor and colleague at the University of Minnesota, and Kirkpatrick's wife, Jeane, were advisers. Unfortunately for the neoconservatives, the Humphrey connection was not an entitlement program. Laying claim to his mantle did not grant them clear leadership within the Democracy. The Humphrey legacy, in fact, was a problematic one: in 1968, Humphrey had lost his moral authority through his loyalty to Lyndon Johnson over the issue of the Vietnam War. Within the Democratic Party, Humphrey's position crumbled. The dimming of Humphrey's luster was more than a personal eclipse; it was an ideological one. In the short run, the failure led to the rise of Richard Nixon, and in the long run to the rise of conservatism.

In 1972, when George McGovern captured the Democratic presidential nomination through the primaries, defeating Humphrey, the old party establishment felt that its power had been illegitimately expropriated, stolen by legerdemain, leaving their candidate unfairly at the mercy of the voters. The neoconservatives, who had wielded influence almost exclusively by membership in Humphrey's personal coterie, believed that the party was their rightful property. They had felt a sense of entitlement as presumptive rhetoricians of an overthrown faction. And this contributed to their general sensation of disenfranchisement, having quickly lost preeminence in the universities, the literary culture, the civil rights movement, and even within the Jewish community. By

July 1972 they had a method, but a severely constricted base. Humphrey, their champion, was an exhausted volcano who disgraced himself not only by his association with Vietnam and Johnson but by his last presidential campaign, during which he launched a personal attack against his old friend George McGovern and an ideological attack against the social welfare state he had helped to construct: "Humphrey will stop the flow of your tax dollars to those who chisel their way onto the welfare rolls through fraud," ran a radio ad.[1]

The neoconservatives generally read the primary results through Old Left lenses as a victory for Stalinist fellow-traveling. Opposition to the Vietnam War, after all, "objectively" placed McGovern on the same side as the Soviets. And didn't he, as a college student in 1948, briefly back the candidacy of that fellow traveler of fellow travelers, Henry Wallace? Some neoconservatives, such as former Trotskyist dialectician Max Schachtman, whose arguments were influential with top members of the AFL-CIO hierarchy, offered reasons for voting for Nixon in purely Marxist terms: If the AFL-CIO isn't backing McGovern and it represents the proletariat, then which side are you on? To describe the alien force that had usurped the Democratic Party, the neoconservatives invented a new category, a new "ism"—McGovernism. After 1972, all Democrats who failed to heed the advice of the neoconservatives were considered infected with this dread affliction.

One neoconservative may have had more than a political motive for demonizing McGovern. In the mid-1960s, Norman Podhoretz invited the senator to dinner at a French restaurant. McGovern arrived early. As he took his seat he noticed two attractive women sitting behind him and what he regarded as two rather unattractive, heavily rouged women facing him. When Podhoretz finally showed up, McGovern tried to put him at ease by making small talk about the women in the room. "Norman," he said, "you get to look at those good-looking ones while I have to look at those turkeys." Podhoretz scowled. "That's my wife," he muttered. McGovern instantly apologized, trying to smooth over a rough spot. But Podhoretz maintained his scowl throughout the meal. McGovern recalls the incident with embarrassed regret and a laugh. (Podhoretz denies that the incident occurred.) And *Commentary*, under Podhoretz's direction, later went on to become the principal scourge of "McGovernism."

In the 1976 Democratic primaries, the neoconservatives supported Senator Henry Jackson, a black hole of charisma who could not fill the vacuum left by Humphrey. By now some of them were beginning to become an entrenched element within the Counter-Establishment. Their flagship publications, *Commentary* and *The Public Interest,* set the line, critical of Great Society social policy and a non-interventionist foreign policy. At think tanks such as the American Enterprise Institute, they occupied chairs newly endowed by corporate benefactors seeking intellectual guardians. Some neoconservatives who, amazingly, still regarded themselves as socialists belonged to the Social Democrats U.S.A., which had intimate ties to key figures within the AFL-CIO leadership. These Social Democrats had battled for decades against the sins of Stalinism, and they viewed their position as unchanged. As they allied themselves with the right wing, they still quaintly called each other "comrade." Other neoconservatives belonged to the Committee on the Present Danger, trying to persuade the public that the Soviets had achieved military superiority and that the threat was immediate. Every deviation by the Democrats from the neoconservative line was assailed by the entity they founded in the wake of McGovern's intra-party victory, the Coalition for a Democratic Majority. The name expressed their desire more than the reality, for they were not the majority and many of them were moving out of the Democratic Party. The CDM was the neoconservative party shadow.

When Jimmy Carter was elected President, the neoconservatives, through their various organizations, presented him with fifty-three names to fill top jobs. "We were completely frozen out," said Elliott Abrams, Henry Jackson's aide, who later became Reagan's Assistant Secretary of State. "We got one unbelievably minor job. It was a special-negotiator position. Not for Polynesia. Not Macronesia. But Micronesia. The Carter administration turned out to be ideological, a New Left administration." Carter, the neoconservatives swiftly decided, was another McGovernite.

They also came to believe that by undermining the Democratic Party they could somehow re-create their factional position. All

Democrats who failed to maintain an ossified stance, frozen in time, pre-McGovern, must be annihilated. Then the neoconservatives' ideological preeminence would be assured.

The neoconservatives traded on their former liberal identities for a new importance; they liquidated their Democratic assets when the bidding price was high. As Democrats for Nixon (and Reagan), they had more leverage than they would ever have had as Democrats for McGovern (and Carter). So they took the tattered remnant of their political base, their still viable method, and put them in the service of another cause.

The sudden demand for neoconservatives excited them a great deal; they suddenly saw themselves as intellectual power brokers, deliverers of the stalwart Democrats. Reagan, they felt, owed them a lot, nothing less than his election to the presidency. Podhoretz wrote that

> if the grip of the conventional liberal wisdom and leftist orthodoxies in the world of ideas had not been loosened by the criticisms of the new-conservatives; if a correlative willingness to entertain new ideas had not thereby been created; and if these new ideas had not been plausibly articulated and skillfully defended in the trials by intellectual combat that do so much to shape public opinion in the United States—if not for all this, Ronald Reagan would in all probability have been unable to win over the traditionally Democratic constituencies (blue-collar workers, white-ethnic groups like the Irish and the Italians and a surprisingly high percentage of Jews) whose support swept him into the White House.[2]

According to this reading of the election, Reagan's victory was based upon a "New American Majority," the old Democratic coalition on a new footing.

Conservatism, some convinced themselves, was a new form of the neoconservatives' old beliefs. "We had, Reagan suggested, lost or forgotten the principles through which we had become the most productive, the most prosperous, the strongest and most respected nation on earth," wrote Podhoretz. "In 1980 . . . the Republicans completed the usurpation of the abandoned Democratic tradition."[3]

The fundamentalist right, meanwhile, was interpreted as the latest extension of the neoconservative *Kulturkampf* against the sixties. And supply-side economics became nothing less than the economics practiced by Hubert Humphrey. "The reason Republicans are winning now," said neoconservative Ben Wattenberg, "is that they stole our ideas. Supply-side economics? The numbers may not work, but economics is symbolic. Forget the numbers. It's growth economics. That's New Deal economics. That's Democratic economics. That ain't Republican economics."

The neoconservatives created a Reagan in their own image. Upon close examination he appeared to be a neoconservative. He, too, had been a Democrat, a left-winger, from a working-class family, a union official even. Although they had trod the same path, Reagan crossed the aisle long before them. The neoconservatives provided *ex post facto* justification for Reagan's defection, a justification for ideological metamorphosis especially vivid in their own minds.

Neoconservatism is the final stage of the Old Left, the only element in American politics whose identity is principally derived from its view of Communism. Like the conservatives, the neoconservatives depend upon their enemy for their own definition. The difference between shadow liberalism and shadow leftism is subtle but crucial. The conservatives believe that the Liberal Establishment has been running the country. Neoconservatives add to this general notion the belief that liberals are either a species of Stalinist fellow traveler or operate "objectively," whether they know it or not, in the broad interest of the Soviet Union. Conservatives would like to believe this, too. But the neoconservatives, many with the benefit of the Trotskyist background, offer an unmatchable authenticity and intensity on the subject.

Curiously, the notion that the liberals are "objectively" contributing to the Communist cause parallels one of the most perverse notions ever advanced by the Communists. In the ultra-left Third Period of the Communist International, during the late 1920s and early 1930s, a doctrine known as "social fascism" was declared to be the basis of the movement's politics. Liberals and Social Democrats were charged with being the "objective" allies of the fascists, but more deceitful because they pretended to be opposed to fascism by talking about democracy.

This fantastic ideological dogma had the practical effect of preventing any possible coalition between the German Communists and Social Democrats against the Nazis. "After Hitler, our turn," was the Communist slogan. In America, the proponents of "social fascism" physically assaulted the socialist followers of Norman Thomas. This was more farce than tragedy.

In an odd historical refraction, the neoconservatives regularly denounce liberals employing a tactic that bears a through-the-looking-glass resemblance to that of "social fascism." But instead of exposing liberals as dangerously disguised agents of fascists, neoconservatives now unmask them as helpers of Communism. The chief doctrinal device used to prove the point is the notion of "moral equivalence." Many liberals, the neoconservatives claim, criticize official policy by somehow equating the Soviet Union and America, "objectively" aiding the other side. This is "social fascism" upside down and, therefore, can be called the ideological technique of "social communism."

Communism in America, however, is a matter solely of memory. The neoconservatives have been drawing their own meaning from something that has lost its meaning here; so they must insist that world Communism is still vital in order to lend their position vitality. Communism, they argue, is on the march, gaining strength and overwhelming us. By contrast, the United States is viewed as weakening, always losing strength. From the neoconservative viewpoint, we are either approaching the appeasement of Munich or the last stand of Masada. For decades, they say, we have been disarming under the tutelage of the Liberal Establishment, guided by a fatal doctrine of appeasement called detente, a doctrine that can "objectively" make liberals act like fellow travelers. Cyrus Vance is Lillian Hellman in pinstripes.

In style, the neoconservatives are true to their left-wing pasts, sectarian to a fault. They will not cut out their denunciations to fit today's fashion. The denunciation, in fact, remains their favored mode of expression, often in the form of wonderfully crafted private letters to their objects of contempt. These exorcisms are animated by the literary spirit of the Karl Marx of *Critique of the Gotha Program*— mean, personal, and vindictive. Such habits have been sharpened for more than a century in the Old Left, handed down from International to International, from generation to generation, until only the neocon-servatives are left.

Perhaps the most distilled statements of shadow leftism can be found in *The New Criterion,* edited by Hilton Kramer, the former *New York Times* art critic, defender of high culture against lowlife Stalinoids and other liberals. In "Turning Back the Clock: Art and Politics in 1984," Kramer sent his rhetorical missiles flying against exhibitions organized around the themes of nuclear war and Central American intervention, which he decried as "radical pacifism." Even the Hirsh-horn Museum's exhibit "Dreams and Nightmares," inspired by Orwell's *Nineteen Eighty-Four,* without "an explicit condemnation of current U.S. government policy," was still "pacifist in spirit; and clearly owed its inspiration to the anti-nuclear movement." Kramer has an uncanny ability for recognizing, especially when unstated, the "objective" mean-ing of art. And this art isn't just "objectively" pacifist. It is a conscious attempt to "turn back the cultural and political clock," not to the "counterculture of the sixties," but to something even more devious, "the hypocritical 'social consciousness' of the Stalinist ethos."[4] Al-though most of the artists Kramer describes were not alive during the 1930s, he has been able to see through their veneer with his ideological X-ray vision and detect their "objective" Stalinism. If the enemy is Communism, then the neoconservative ideology works perfectly, and the neoconservative knows that he is the critic we need. When his moral righteousness is unacknowledged, his role as a sentinel of fearless integ-rity is validated; he has proven his willingness to stand against the crowd for the sake of his penetrating insight.

Just as shadow liberalism requires a Liberal Establishment for its cosmology to make sense, shadow leftism needs an ideal foe. Stalinists, who can be conjured up by "objective" analysis, serve best. But even longtime anti-Communists, if they happen to be hostile to neoconserva-tism, will do. When Irving Howe, a democratic socialist and lifelong opponent of Stalinism, delivered an address at the New York Council for the Humanities, noting that the "conservative outlook seems domi-nant or at least increasingly powerful," Kramer was ready for the return volley. Howe, the despairing socialist, is a representative of a "closed culture . . . the left-liberal American cultural establishment" that rules all, a rule that can be measured by the "indices of 'established power,' " such as lucrative book contracts. To clinch his case, Kramer writes: "If we look uptown, to the activities of the American Academy and Institute of Arts and Letters, we find that John Kenneth Galbraith has just succeeded Arthur M. Schlesinger, Jr., as president."[5] The invocation of the names Galbraith and Schlesinger, among old conservatives and (apparently) neoconservatives alike, is always the ultimate proof of liberal conniving.

How, then, can Kramer and his comrades rise to glory when the liberals control "uptown"? If they can't gain admission to "the left-liberal American cultural establishment" club, they'll start their own—the Counter-Establishment. *The New Criterion* itself, begun as a bodyguard of Western civilization, with a start-up grant of $100,000 from the Olin Foundation (William Simon, president), is an excellent example of the method.

"Neoconservatives," observed Diana Trilling, "such as Joseph Epstein [neoconservative editor of *The American Scholar*], Norman Podhoretz, and Hilton Kramer, all of them editors of important periodicals, are not so young but that they have to be fully aware of the irreparable damage that was done to the cultural and even the political life of this country by their Stalinist forebears who, instead of honorably debating issues, poisoned the intellectual atmosphere with lies and personal invective. By what process of self-hallucination do they now persuade themselves that just because they operate from an opposite premise, the anti-Communist premise, they do us any better service with such methods?"[6]

Norman Podhoretz, a mandarin general in the neoconservative camp, understood well how a sustained campaign of ideas could transform politics in ways that were not readily apparent. "Most of those in the Reagan upper echelon are readers of *Commentary*," he said, a month after the first Reagan victory. "Some of my contributors have become important, such as Jeane Kirkpatrick. What a magazine like *Commentary* really does is affect the ideological atmosphere. It gets into the air. Sometimes it has tangible influence, but that is not the main thing. People can consider it purifying the air or polluting it, but it is doing *something* to it. We have been very successful in altering the terms of the debate."

On election night, 1980, the neoconservatives felt redeemed. Many of their illuminati gathered in a Manhattan apartment, eagerly awaiting the returns, which, as liberal senator after liberal senator fell before the conservative onslaught, they toasted and cheered. When Carter conceded, they were, according to Podhoretz, "so jubilant at the news of the mounting landslide that a passing stranger might have taken them for professional Republican Party workers or perhaps for fervent ideological conservatives."[7]

Podhoretz appeared on the scene in the late 1940s as the latest incarnation of the intellectual rags-to-riches story, a disheveled, foul-mouthed youngster from working-class Jewish Brooklyn, transformed into the rising literary star of Columbia University.

He was of the generation that just missed the Sturm und Drang of the Depression decade, arriving after the wrenching left-wing wars had been fought and decided. The Stalinists were in hasty retreat, if not in actual hiding, and the most brilliant Marxists opposing them, like Seymour Martin Lipset, had become sociologists. The "end of ideology" was descending.

Among the New York intellectuals, Podhoretz's teacher Lionel Trilling was the most brilliant among the brilliant, the most accomplished literary critic of his generation, and one of the first Jews awarded tenure at Columbia. Like many others during the 1930s, he had flirted with Communism. The moral crisis of one comrade he befriended—Whittaker Chambers—deeply affected him. Trilling wrote many volumes of criticism and one novel, entitled *The Middle of the Journey.* Its subject was Chambers and Alger Hiss. His presence and teachings set much of the tone of the postwar period. Among his teachings, expressed in his essential text, *The Liberal Imagination,* was that conservatives do not "express themselves in ideas but only in action or in irritable mental gestures which seek to resemble ideas."[8]

Podhoretz was one of Trilling's prize students, and much of the teacher's hopes for an intellectual succession were placed upon him. Despite the apparent closeness of their bond, the Trilling and Podhoretz personalities could not have been less alike. The mentor was a man of subtle grace, the student a man of anger and often uncontrollable passions. Although Podhoretz admired and tried to emulate Trilling, his friends say that he could not help feeling that his mentor was somehow inauthentic, suppressing his true self, feigning the false air of an English gentleman. At crucial junctures in Podhoretz's career, he would hurl violent verbal abuse at Trilling, these assaults couched in ideological terms, initially from Trilling's left and later from his right. Podhoretz's charge—that Trilling lacked the courage of his convictions, that he was faithless to his own teaching—remained constant.

Podhoretz regarded himself as self-made, and he considered his own self-promoting efforts to be the universal condition for success—a tawdry but elemental truth denied by more delicate and less honest souls. To be sure, he had talent, worked hard, and was a self-promoter. But he was not as self-made as he suggested.

After Podhoretz completed his work at Columbia, Trilling's recommendation helped gain him entrance for graduate work at Cambridge University in England, where he studied under F. R. Leavis, the leading English critic. When Podhoretz came home, Trilling lined up a job for him reviewing books for *The New Yorker.* Then Trilling got him a job as an assistant editor at *Commentary* magazine, then emerging as a leading journal of the New York intellectuals.

But Podhoretz was restless, and he left *Commentary* for a career as an entrepreneur. In partnership with an old Columbia classmate, Jason Epstein, he started a publishing house specializing in children's books. The venture failed, and he was out of work.

At that moment, *Commentary*'s editor, Eliot Cohen, suffered a mental breakdown. The magazine's board of directors promptly offered Cohen's job to Irving Kristol, who turned it down. Next, an offer went out to Daniel Bell, then writing for *Fortune* magazine and later to become a distinguished sociologist. He, too, refused. Finally a proposal was made to Podhoretz, and he gladly accepted. At the age of thirty, he became one of the most important intellectual arbiters in Manhattan.

When Podhoretz had returned from England, he had tried mightily to fit the image of a latter-day Trilling. His criticism was self-consciously marked by efforts at irony and complexity. Within his generation, however, the Trilling style suddenly became retrograde. The avant garde were the Beats, some of whose leading lights were from Columbia, like Allen Ginsberg, whose work was not marked by ironic detachment but by howling. Initially Podhoretz adopted a superior tone, calling his peers a mindless "non-generation," who "know nothing, stand for nothing, believe in nothing."[9]

Then, say his friends, he changed. Instead of resisting the coming wave, he put himself on top of it. He befriended the hippest literary hipster, Norman Mailer, and joined in the Mailer frolics on Fire Island. And at *Commentary* he showcased the work of Paul Goodman, the forgotten man of the New York intellectuals. His *Growing Up Absurd*, first presented in *Commentary*, overnight became essential reading for the new existential generation. Podhoretz could also claim credit for lifting to intellectual fame Norman O. Brown, the analyst of polymorphous perversity. These people were not in the Trilling tradition.

In his sharp move to the left, Podhoretz drew a line in the sand. On one side stood he and Mailer and friends; on the other side stood the old fogies, the palefaces, as cowardly as they were irrelevant. These political differences, he wrote, could be seen most clearly in the differences between the old *Commentary* and the new *Commentary*:

> From *Commentary*—in this it was a true spokesman for the spirit of the fifties—one got the impression that the United States of America, for all its imperfections (the persistence of discrimination against Jews and Negroes being the main one), was the best society a human nature beset and limited by its own built-in imperfections . . . was likely to be able to build. American society was, therefore, Reality . . . and any large dissatisfaction with it was to be attributed to the Human Condition itself, against which it was of course "childish" or "foolish" or "infantile leftist" or pathological to struggle. . . . My ideological strategy for the "new *Commentary*" . . . was to say goodbye to all that: to hard anti-Communism and to celebration, however quiet, of American virtue.[10]

Thus Podhoretz became a pioneer of the New Left, founded in contempt for the old. But for him this was not simply an "ideological strategy." It was a personal strategy, too.

It was not enough for him to tack his manifesto to the door and start his own church. For the battle was not just a battle of opposing opinions. In the political schism Podhoretz was creating, he apparently felt the necessity to antagonize Trilling. The task of disengaging himself from his mentor's influence was not easy.

In the early 1960s, at three successive dinners where the two men appeared, those present recall Podhoretz's ferocious, almost hysterical lunges at Trilling. He wasn't a socialist at all, screamed Podhoretz, but a phony, a sellout.

One night Kristol, Bell, Epstein, Trilling, Podhoretz, Sidney Hook, Steven Marcus, William Phillips, and other eminent New York intellectuals gathered at the Columbia faculty club, "the last time everyone was together," said Bell. At previous dinners Podhoretz had vented his wrath at Trilling. Now he turned on Hook, screeching, "You're a fraud! You're not a social democrat!" Trilling paled and abruptly stood up. "Gentlemen," he said, always the ironist, "good evening." And he left. "He wouldn't take it any longer," said Bell.

Still, Podhoretz sought Trilling's approval. And when he completed his first manuscript he presented it to the master, anxiously awaiting his judgment. It was to be entitled *Making It,* a confessional on literary success, which Podhoretz called the "dirty little secret."[11] Exposing that "secret" was, he wrote, an act of bravery morally equivalent to "breaking with the Communist Party."[12] At last he would speak the truth that could not be told. By admitting what the others would not admit, he was purifying himself and revealing their corruption. *Making It* would hide nothing. It would be "a frank, Mailer-like bid for literary distinction, fame, and money all in one package."[13] Thus Podhoretz presented himself as a virtuous arriviste, a Mailer *manqué* with a difference, the bad boy as good boy.

Trilling's verdict was absolute and shattering. Do not publish this book, he advised. It is a gigantic mistake. Put it away and do not let others see it.

Podhoretz turned to Daniel Bell, Trilling's close friend, another authoritative figure. If you must publish this, Bell said, then add a final chapter showing some ironic distance, some perspective on yourself.

Podhoretz felt like an outcast. Just as Trilling and Bell rejected his book, he rejected their advice. *Making It* was published in 1967. Podhoretz expected that it would be embraced by the younger generation. In particular, he expected a favorable review from Mailer, who had been encouraging but hadn't yet read through the manuscript. Then came the Mailer pronouncement: *Making It* was a "blunder of self-assertion, self-exposure and self-denigration."[14]

"I felt very betrayed by the literary world," said Podhoretz. "I had written that book in the spirit of my education, which inculcated in me certain values: honesty and the supreme importance of writing well and precisely. I thought I had done that. But instead of being defended I was abandoned." He was pure, the others corrupt. And, according to Podhoretz, this explained the reaction. "I attributed to the intellectual class the same feelings and motives that the enemy was supposed to have, that is, the bourgeoisie, the businessmen. It seemed to me an absurd pretension that intellectuals represented a superior human alternative to everybody else. *Making It* was a book which said no, we were people like any other. That was an offensive statement. The way to protect against it was to say it was only true of me, that I was a very bad person. So the book was offensive on cultural and political grounds."

The betrayal of intellectual honesty that he attributed to his peers (Mailer) and the older generation (Trilling and Bell) he also came to attribute to the younger generation. Somehow, as Podhoretz saw it, they were all in league, united by a common false spirit. "Well," he said, "1967 and 1968 was the moment that this idea reached its height, that there was a perfect human possibility. You can see this in relation to the death of John Lennon . . . this posthumous orgy of self-congratulation and self-pity."

Podhoretz, the cultural radical and Mailer pal, cast himself as a cultural cop and anti-hipster. For one who had trafficked with "white Negroes," no reversal could be more startling. He would no longer shock the bourgeoisie, whom he redefined as the oppressed; instead, he would shock the bohemians, whom he relabeled the ruling class. Once again, the battle was between the pure and the corrupt, the honest and dishonest.

"I look at the experience of the 1960s as a gigantic public experiment in the validity of radical ideas," he said. "If you're intellectually honest you are obligated to say these ideas were wrong. I discovered that a lot of people were lying about the results, refusing to admit that the results were what they were and getting angry at those of us who were telling the truth. I didn't feel betrayed by such people. I felt contempt for them. I continue to. There are people for whom I will never again have any respect. The parallel with the experience of ex-Communists is very striking and interesting. It's a question of loyalty to an ideology or a party. It doesn't matter if there is no party there."

His enemies were somehow "objectively" Stalinist, requiring the revival of the entire Old Left gestalt, the ideological *Late Show* he had once so vehemently condemned. This time Podhoretz would play the leading man, an impassioned witness and an Olympian critic, a composite of Whittaker Chambers and Lionel Trilling. In his re-creation of the atmospherics of the past, he wrote about how he courageously broke with the "radical party line" and the "fellow travelers" of the counterculture, and how he resisted the reign of "terror" they imposed.[15]

"No one was fired," he explained. "But unquestionably people failed to get assignments that they might have, or invitations to appear on television programs that they would have otherwise have gotten, or lucrative book contracts, things of that sort. There is not the slightest doubt in my mind that it went on. In my own case, I was in a protected position, but if I hadn't been I would have suffered very badly in my career. As it was, I suffered. You were subject to vilification and serious damage to your reputation if you disagreed with a whole series of positions."

Podhoretz opened the 1980s with the publication of *Breaking Ranks,* a hymn to neoconservatism. In it he presented himself as a Candide who learned through bitter experience the wisdom of the patriotism he had once dismissed. His conversion to neoconservatism was not, however, a rejection of the social climbing of *Making It. Breaking Ranks* was volume two of *Making It* yet another effort at success. The crucial difference between the two books was that the notion of success in *Making It* was personal, where in *Breaking Ranks* it was elevated to ideological status.

While Podhoretz insisted that he was "breaking ranks" with his past—goodbye to all that—he still felt the need for the repetitive ritual of breaking with Trilling. Before, he had abused his mentor from the left. Now he abused him from the right. Once again, he charged, Trilling was inauthentic and weak. He had been the first one to define the "adversary culture" that flowered in the 1960s, but his criticism was meaningless. "In criticizing the cultural radicalism of the sixties and its historical sources," Podhoretz wrote, "Trilling increasingly seemed to use both the idea of complication and the prose embodying it not so much to clarify and deepen his own point of view as to disguise and hide it." In his assaults on the "adversary culture," Podhoretz believed that he was true to the meaning of Trilling's teachings. But to act on them he had to discard the Trilling method.

Breaking Ranks was the prelude to his bravura performance of the 1980 campaign, a manifesto on the world crisis, *The Present Danger,* a title taken appropriately from the Committee on the Present Danger, which Podhoretz had helped found. Through his relationship with members of this group he exercised his greatest influence.

The committee's guiding lights were Eugene Rostow, former Under-Secretary of State under Lyndon Johnson, who believed that U.S. power was paralyzed by a "Vietnam syndrome" that needed to be dispelled; and Paul Nitze, an architect of the original Cold War policy, who had come to believe that the Soviets threatened us with their increasing nuclear arsenal, opening a "window of vulnerability" that could be closed only by vastly increasing our military armaments. The Soviets, according to the committee, had achieved nuclear parity, which translated into geopolitical superiority—a view given the stamp of canonical truth by the report of what came to be called the B-Team.

During Gerald Ford's administration, conservative dissent from the old foreign-policy consensus, forged around notions like detente and deterrence, rose to a high pitch. To satisfy this rising right-wing faction, a small group of experts was appointed by the President to investigate their own assertions of American decline and Soviet strength. All were conservatives or neoconservatives—the B-Team. The A-Team was the

CIA itself, under suspicion for slipshod intelligence work because of faulty political premises: the agency was insufficiently conservative. Not surprisingly, the B-Team's findings confirmed its hypotheses; its official character lent it an air of final authority.

Almost all the B-Team members belonged to the Committee on the Present Danger. Also present among the committee's directors were a sprinkling of disaffected figures from the old foreign-policy establishment like Nitze; conservative cadres like Richard V. Allen; Washington lobbyists like Charls Walker; and a sizable contingent of neoconservatives. Thirteen of the eighteen members of the Coalition for a Democratic Majority foreign-policy task force, chaired by Rostow, joined.

Shortly after the committee was started in 1976, Jimmy Carter became president. He promptly conferred with the august Nitze, who lectured him sternly with charts and graphs on how the Soviets would win a nuclear war. When the committee's short-lived efforts to persuade Carter to support their policies failed, they went on the offensive. Week after week, month after month, year after year they attacked in newspaper columns, lectures, and conferences. *Commentary* became the committee's forum for many of their most important pronouncements, just as *Foreign Affairs* had been for the old foreign-policy elite.

Carter's appointment of Paul Warnke, a liberal, to head the Arms Control and Disarmament Agency, offered the committee's Cold Warriors an early opportunity for opposition. In the end Warnke was approved, but it was a pyrrhic victory. The battle had, in effect, discredited him as a spokesman for the treaty he was supposed to negotiate. The committee's members were emboldened.

Virtually everything Carter did, from human rights to Iran, was attributed to his weakness, which in turn was blamed on liberal ideology. In spite of the relentlessness of the assault, Carter and his team never comprehended the root of this new brand of right-wing politics. The pressure the conservatives exerted, in the meantime, accentuated the incoherence the President was suffering from the Vance-Brzezinski fissure on the inside. Since Carter couldn't control or even make sense of these conservative forces, his reputation for weakness was underlined. Ironically, the public began to agree with the conservatives that Carter was weak, but for reasons different from those that the conservatives suggested. If the President had directly confronted his lethal foes, his image might have been altered. But to do that, he would have had to define his own position sharply. So the committee flourished at least as much from the Carter administration's internal confusion as from the energy of their arguments.

Vice President Walter Mondale, for his part, occasionally attempted to placate the neoconservative committee members, whom he viewed as disgruntled Democrats, not as part of a radically novel political formation—the right-wing Counter-Establishment. In fact Mondale was linked to the neoconservatives by personal history and common affection for Humphrey. Kampelman, Evron Kirkpatrick, and Mondale had all grown up together in Minnesota politics. His response to their attacks was shaped by his long-standing friendship and alliance with them. He believed that by appealing to the neoconservatives in the shared language of "real Democrats," they would be calmed. Still held in thrall by fond memories of the past, Mondale was instinctively incapable of mounting a counterattack against these old comrades. Even as late as his 1984 campaign against Reagan, he would reveal his lack of understanding of their political intent by including Kampelman in the circle of his intimate advisers. An instant clarification occurred immediately after Mondale spent his last advertising dollars on television spots against Reagan's Star Wars plan and lost the election. Kampelman, now a Star Wars defender, stood in the Oval Office with Reagan, appointed as his chief arms-control negotiator.

The Committee on the Present Danger, therefore, captured ground that was mostly uncontested. And when Reagan was elected, they assumed dominance over critical parts of the national security apparatus, especially the areas dealing with arms control. More than fifty of the committee's members received appointments.

The Present Danger was Podhoretz's campaign contribution. He is the literary critic as ideologue, and appropriately, his categories of analysis are governed by metaphor, simile, and analogy. He tends to regard a well-designed metaphor as sufficient empirical proof of an argument. *The Present Danger* is 101 pages of metaphor, yet it is devoid of irony and complexity.

The first metaphor he used was that of "Finlandization," a coinage referring to Finland's quiet submission to Soviet will. If the United States allowed a "tilt in the balance of power" to the Soviet Union, as he believed was occurring, then, "we would know what name to call the new era into which we have entered . . . the Finlandization of America, the political and economic subordination of the United States to superior Soviet power."[17]

Undermining American will to resist "Finlandization" was, according to Podhoretz, a "culture of appeasement"—another metaphor. "As a movement the radical movement of the sixties is dead," he said, "but its ideas are not only not dead but more entrenched in a bowdlerized form than they ever were in the past, all over the liberal culture. You can't pin it down that easily. Obviously, it is in the universities, certain sectors of the media, in the publishing industry. The incessant harping on the danger of confrontation and nuclear war, all of this is part of a culture of appeasement. It is made up of fear of a powerful adversary and a lack of belief in the legitimacy of our own position."

Podhoretz derived his concept of a "culture of appeasement" from an interpretation of literary history. "This is all very carefully documented," he said. His main source was *Children of the Sun,* Martin Green's chronicle of English literary life between the world wars. "One of the interesting similarities between the two periods [England then, America now] was the prominence of homosexuals in the literary worlds. The homosexual ethos in England between the wars was anti-English: English society had been criminal in sending the flower of its youth off to war; it was bourgeois and dull. The writers who were propagating these attitudes did a good deal to undermine the feelings of confidence and belief in the legitimacy that there was something to defend in England. This could extend all the way to treason or to simple sourness about the society. The American homosexual literary world has been saying the same kinds of things about this society. This is an absolutely important element in the culture of appeasement."

The principal thrust of the "culture of appeasement," according to Podhoretz, is "anti-American." "The term anti-American is not vague, scurrilous, or sweeping. It refers to a position that is against America and the use of American power. This position flourished in the 1960s. A lot of the younger foreign policy people in the Carter administration were influenced by the anti-American case. A lot of them seem to feel that American power was and is a great problem, not American powerlessness." This proposition and other corollaries of what he called "liberal isolationism"—an analogy to the 1930s—aroused his ire. "What is immoral about the liberal argument is that it suggests we collaborate with the Soviet Union in maintaining its hold over its empire. It is also a stupid argument."

Podhoretz's division of the world into pro- and anti-Americans is a construct based on disillusionment with Communism, which Podhoretz has cited persistently to elucidate his own travails. Podhoretz himself missed the great disappointment with "the God that failed"— the decisive experience of his mentors. In its place he substituted a stylized version. The "anti-Americans"—from Jimmy Carter's State Department officers to literary homosexuals to liberals in general— assumed the place of the Communists, as defined by Podhoretz himself, not by card-carrying membership. He was pure; they were corrupt.

His argument in *The Present Danger* won rave reviews from the Reagan camp, where it was widely read. To Podhoretz, the 1980 election represented a stunning repudiation of the neoconservatives' enemies, the enemies of the Coalition for a Democratic Majority, of the Committee on the Present Danger, of *Commentary,* of Podhoretz. In an article entitled "The New American Majority," he argued that Reagan's triumph was the dramatic completion of Nixon's 1972 victory, which had been "nullified" by a "coup d'etat" called Watergate. In 1972 "the new leftist liberalism" personified by the Democratic nominee George McGovern "humiliated their centrist rivals within the Democratic party." But Nixon won because "the new majority . . . among them large numbers of Democrats" were repelled by the "adversary culture." In 1980 "the disgust" with the "new culture," which had infected "larger and larger areas of American society," had "grown." This was the key to the election. "As Nixon had before him, Ronald Reagan spoke for those disgusted."[18]

As the new administration prepared to take office, Podhoretz made some gestures at securing an appointment as head of the U.S. Information Agency. That plum, however, went to Reagan's old friend Charles Z. Wick. Podhoretz received something of a consolation prize. A red and white band was wrapped around copies of *The Present Danger.* On it was a directive from the new President: "I urge all Americans to read this critically important book."

"I've met Reagan twice," said Podhoretz at the beginning of the New Beginning. "He listens, and they tell me he reads. But I can't vouch for that."

Eventually Podhoretz did manage to get himself appointed to an official postion. If he wasn't the director of the USIA, at least he was on the advsory board. He became part of the Reagan team through some old-fashioned string-pulling: his wife, Midge Decter, had become a trustee of the Heritage Foundation, whose president, Edwin Feulner, was chairman of the USIA advisory board.

Several neoconservatives achieved high positions, all in the field of foreign policy: Elliott Abrams, Podhoretz's son-in-law, a former aide to Henry Jackson and Daniel Patrick Moynihan, was named Assistant Secretary of State for Human Rights, certifying the moral character of "authoritarian" and "totalitarian" regimes; Richard Perle, a former Jackson aide and an unyielding opponent of arms-control agreements with the Soviets, was appointed Assistant Secretary of Defense and assumed virtual dominance over the arms-control agenda; Kenneth Adelman, a close friend of Perle's, a former student of Jeane Kirkpatrick at Georgetown and her deputy at the United Nations, was appointed director of the Arms Control and Disarmament Agency; and there was Kirkpatrick herself, the UN ambassador during Reagan's first term, always pushing for a harder line. Through these and other comrades, the neoconservatives exercised influence in Reagan's Washington.

They also exercised influence by loud playing on their Wurlitzer of publications. By remaining editor of *Commentary*—a job that apparently has the security of that of a Supreme Court Justice—Podhoretz was able to continue in his self-appointed post as the neoconservative vicar of U.S. foreign policy. He took upon himself the ambitious tasks of reopening the debate about the Vietnam War, reprimanding the Reagan administration for its deviationism, and commending all proposals for Pentagon spending, with a gold star for Star Wars.

During the 1980 campaign, Reagan had called the Vietnam War "a noble cause." On February 18, 1982, at a press conference, he offered his own history of the war, consisting of the usual factual errors, five in this case, covering everything from the origin of North and South Vietnam as two separate entities to the reasons for the U.S. entry into the conflict.

About a month after Reagan's statement, Podhoretz's *Why We Were in Vietnam* was published. In it he attempted to provide the scholarly underpinning for Reagan's approach. Podhoretz wanted to overturn the outcome of the "debate over Vietnam," which he asserted "had already been settled in favor of the moral and political position of the antiwar position."[19]

His argument, however, was not persuasive. He took Richard Nixon's and Henry Kissinger's accounts of events as authoritative, although he did not grant similar status to those of Arthur Schlesinger, Jr., a Kennedy adviser. And to prove many of his points, Podhoretz relied almost entirely on Guenter Lewy's *America in Vietnam,* a hawkish interpretation of history that is the subject of heated debate. Podhoretz's own outspoken opposition to the war, once voiced in *Commentary,* was never acknowledged. That was now down the memory-hole.

He analyzed the Vietnam War in the categories popularized by Jeane Kirkpatrick, her ideas providing the underpinning for his operatic denunciation. "The truth is," he wrote, "that the antiwar movement bears a certain measure of responsibility for the horrors that have overtaken the people of Vietnam; and so long as those who participated in that movement are unwilling to acknowledge this, they will go on trying to discredit the idea that there is a distinction between authoritarianism and totalitarianism."[20] The antiwar critics, by this reasoning, had displaced their responsibility and created a myth of national guilt. They preserved their retrospect purity, but were now incapable of making the distinctions honest people must make; their opposition to neoconservatism stems from their blindness. And this failure is not just political, but moral.

Against the "Vietnam syndrome" of national guilt, Podhoretz posed the notion of national innocence. He does not see America as one great power among other powers, attempting to achieve its ends through the traditional means of statecraft and motivated by the same impulses as other nation-states. If America harbors no guilt for the Vietnam War, then Reagan's crusade for the restoration of American might must be righteous, and those who oppose it must be damned.

To Podhoretz's dismay, though, Reagan was squandering his historic opportunity. After martial law was declared in Poland and the free trade union movement Solidarity was suppressed, Reagan did not apply draconian measures. Podhoretz began to doubt Reagan's commitment to his own tough rhetoric. Was Reagan pure enough? On May 2, 1982, *The New York Times Magazine* published a cover story by Podhoretz, "The Neo-Conservative Anguish Over Reagan's Foreign Policy," an attack from the right. Reagan, he charged, "has in practice been following a strategy of helping the Soviet Union stabilize its empire, rather than a strategy aimed at encouraging the breakup of that empire from within."[21]

Shortly after the *Times* piece appeared, Podhoretz's telephone rang. "Hello, Norman?" It was President Reagan, assuring him that they were really not so far apart after all. Reagan was listening, if not reading.

Podhoretz kept up the pressure, and the praise. The carrot and the stick seemed to produce concrete results, like phone calls. But for more than a decade no new Democratic political figure had bothered to dial the neoconservatives' number. The exception was Moynihan, who, once elected senator from New York, displayed such deviationism that the neoconservatives came to consider him a turncoat; he was an alumnus, no longer a comrade. But now the President of the United States seemed to care what they were saying. The good news was that even the bad news they delivered was good for them. Through their assimilation into the Counter-Establishment, they had arrived. Even while his advice was not heeded, Podhoretz was making it.

Irving Kristol had no compunction about crossing over the bar to the other side. He is a registered Republican, one of the few neoconservatives to embrace the label before 1980. "Slowly, slowly, the rest of them are accepting the term neoconservative," he said. "And they are becoming Republicans. The question of becoming a Republican, to put it bluntly, is often a matter of class. Neoconservative intellectuals are too snobbish to join the Republicans and the country club. They identify the Republican Party, not without some reason, with businessmen playing golf. You join the party in which you feel at home."

Kristol is among the most influential intellectual catalysts in the higher circles of the Counter-Establishment. In 1978, with William Simon, he founded the Institute for Educational Affairs to pour millions into the "war of ideas" with the "adversary culture." His positions as co-editor of *The Public Interest,* professor at New York University, columnist for the *Wall Street Journal,* board member of five corporations, and senior fellow of the American Enterprise Institute merely hint at his activity. "I raise money for conservative think tanks. I am a liaison to some degree between intellectuals and the business community," he claimed modestly.

Conservatives, building the Counter-Establishment, envied the grants and jobs that liberal intellectuals seemed to accrue effortlessly. Who better to learn the methods of advancement from than renegade liberals? Neoconservatives, at the heart of the New York intellectual world, would teach conservatives, at the peripheries, the ancient arts of promotion that could win in the marketplace of ideas. The neoconservative who filled this role best was known to movement adepts as "the Godfather." They avidly sought audiences to supplicate him for sinecures and funds; and he could arrange offers from institutes and foundations that no conservative would refuse. Kristol is this *capo di familia.* "Irving," said supply-sider Jude Wanniski, whose career was boosted by Kristol, "is the invisible hand."

While many use analogies and metaphors of the Mafia and the market to try to describe Kristol's efforts, their precedent, in a much more direct and literal sense, comes from the Old Left, of which he was once a dedicated cadre. With his constant improvisation of front groups, magazines, and conferences, Kristol resembles no figure so much as Willi Munzenberg.

During the 1930s, Munzenberg was the great organizational genius of the German Communist Party, an audacious blend of commissar and entrepreneur, who virtually invented the front group. On any issue he could put together a committee of notables. For any audience he could field a journal. And then there were books and films and cabarets. Kristol has not quite matched Munzenberg's enterprise, but it has not been for lack of trying.

Where other neoconservatives were tentative, anxious about their political assimilation into the right wing, Kristol followed his ideas to their logical conclusion. The rise of ideological politics presented to him an immense opportunity. "American politics has become more ideologized," he said. "There is no question that as politics become more ideological, intellectuals become more significant. That is the reason intellectuals like ideological politics. The ideological energy has left the center and has either gone to the right or to the left. What new young interesting liberal columnist has been produced in the last fifteen years?"

When Norman Podhoretz entered the *Commentary* office in the early 1950s, Kristol, working there as an editor, greeted him. In the 1930s, as a student at CCNY, he had been a Trotskyist. "His party name was Perry or Ferry. I can't really recall," said Irving Howe, who recruited Kristol into the Trotskyist movement. It is something he still regrets, because Kristol learned the fine arts of ideological politics there.

Kristol left the movement, but carried an anti-liberal attitude away with him. In March 1952, he wrote in *Commentary* about the crusade being conducted by Senator Joseph McCarthy: "There is one thing that the American people know about Senator McCarthy; he, like them, is unequivocally anti-Communist. About the spokesmen for American liberalism, they feel they know no such thing."[22] The liberals, he believed, were colored by fellow-traveling, a Stalinist tinge that a Trotskyist could easily detect.

The next year, Kristol left for London, to become co-editor of *Encounter* magazine, a publication of the Congress for Cultural Freedom, intended to counter the "anti-Americanism" of British intellectuals. *Encounter* was viewed by its founders as a symbol of the freedom that intellectuals in the West exercised. But this particular venture in free thought was covertly funded by the CIA. When this fact was revealed in 1966, long after Kristol had left, he insisted that he knew nothing about relations with the agency.

In 1965, Kristol helped found *The Public Interest* as a journal to study public policy using the methods of non-ideological social science. The first issue of the magazine declared that the principal stumbling block in making effective public policy was "a prior commitment to an ideology, whether it be liberal, conservative, or radical. For it is in the nature of ideology to preconceive reality; and it is exactly such preconceptions that are the worst hindrances to knowing-what-one-is-talking-about."[23] It was a basic tenet of many who later became neoconservatives that socialism was exhausted and social problems had become mainly technical and administrative. The end of ideology had arrived.

In the past, intellectuals had propagated ideology; now they would be technocrats of knowledge. They were in fact rising in America, mainly because theoretical thinking as a skill and knowledge as a commodity was becoming central to the economy and the government. The necessity of expertise transformed what was once a narrow intelligentsia into a mass New Class.

Neoconservatives soon found themselves between a rock and a hard place. They asserted that the end of ideology was a social condition, yet they were defending the notion against all sorts of new ideologies. They regarded themselves as the last fortress of the old intelligentsia, defending high culture against the New Class human-wave assault: "beneficiaries of postwar mass higher education, scientists, lawyers, city planners, social workers, educators, criminologists, sociologists, public health doctors, etc.—a substantial number of whom find their careers in the expanding public sector rather than the private," wrote Kristol. "Though they continue to speak the language of 'progressive reform,' " he added, "in actuality they are acting upon a hidden agenda: to propel the nation from that modified version of capitalism we call 'the welfare state' toward an economic system so stringently regulated in detail as to fulfill many of the traditional anticapitalist aspirations of the Left."[24]

To Kristol, the phrase "the New Class" meant not only a new class struggle but a generational one as well. To defeat the New Class, the generation schooled in the sixties would have to be denied. *"The enemy of liberal capitalism today is not so much socialism as nihilism,"* wrote

Kristol.[25] The neoconservatives became so busy contriving an ideology that they forgot about the end of ideology.

The provenance of Kristol's ideology is the work of the philosopher Leo Strauss, whose magnum opus is *Natural Right and History.* In it Strauss argued against what he called the "moderns" in favor of the "ancients." He believed that truth and virtue are prior to history, rather than unfolding through time. By virtue he meant a harmonious balance within society, achieved by a higher morality promoted by the state. Monarchy could be as just as a republic if it promoted virtue, and it could be more just than a republic that produced folly. By virtue he meant a natural law independent of any ephemeral circumstances. The undermining of virtue, according to Strauss, began with that devilish diagnostician Machiavelli, whose realistic depiction of the mechanics of power stripped it of a loftier justification. Machiavelli and his gimlet-eyed successor, Thomas Hobbes, paved the way for liberalism, "that political doctrine which regards as the fundamental fact the rights as distinguished from the duties of man and which identifies the function of the state with the protection or safeguarding of those rights. . . ."[26] Where rights begin, virtue may end.

Following Strauss, Kristol formulated a version of history and economics to bolster his own political position. The goal of society must not be the protection of "entitlements," or rights, but the promotion of virtue. He considered the sixties a decade of rampant individualism, during which "do your own thing" was the prevailing philosophy, and riots were a mode of politics. Kristol set out to place neoconservatism on a firm philosophical foundation so that it might withstand the hurricane of nihilism.

During the 1976 Bicentennial celebration, Kristol delivered a paper at AEI entitled "The American Revolution as a Successful Revolution," in which he attempted its deradicalization. Our revolution, he argued, was not a revolution in the sense that we commonly understand the term, but a "restructuring," an essentially conservative event, an effort to preserve the status quo. We must "ignore" that rabble-rouser Tom Paine, "an English radical who never really understood America."[27] The Founding Fathers, in Kristol's account, were men of dampened enthusiasm, sober to a fault, and the shot heard round the world launched "a reluctant revolution." Their success, he argued, could be proven by the fact that "this was a revolution which, unlike all subsequent revolutions, did not devour its children."[28]

Kristol's bid to sever the American Revolution from the stream of revolutionary history, even world history, makes him a revisionist. By stacking the deck at the beginning, excluding characters who don't fit, like Tom Paine, Kristol offered a one-sided interpretation that failed to explain most of what followed.

"If there's any amnesia in the story of America after the revolution, it is Professor Kristol's omission of the Civil War from the perspective in which he views the American past," wrote the political philosopher Harry V. Jaffa, a Straussian and conservative. "No one aware of that ordeal or who has contemplated the dilemmas from which it has sprung can call American politics unproblematic. If the generation of the Civil War was the offspring of that of the revolution—the grandchildren if not the children—it must be acknowledged that the American Revolution, as much as any, devoured its progeny."[29] In order to give neoconservatism roots, Kristol created an American past in the light of an ideal image he wished for the present. His historical reconstruction was an effort to restore the American spirit, the spirit of virtue, but he tried to do so by denying the fundamental principles that led to the founding itself, especially the *right* of revolution. His version of the revolution, where the Founding Fathers resemble no group so much as the senior fellows of AEI, is a history for the self-satisfied corporate executive who would like to see himself as the heir to Jefferson and Madison.

Kristol's economic revisionism matched his history. In an essay, "Adam Smith and the Spirit of Capitalism," he strained to prove that individualism was not at the core of Smith's universe, which would then enable Kristol to capture him for the neoconservative pantheon, assuming a place alongside the Founding Fathers. To accomplish this feat, Kristol separated lowly "economic man" from the higher "bourgeois man," associating Smith with the latter specimen. Kristol inferred a moral architecture undergirding *The Wealth of Nations* that Smith himself neglected to articulate. And he supplied the reason for Smith's omission by claiming that Smith and the Founding Fathers, too, implicitly assumed a *"coherence* in the private sector achieved through the influence of organized religion, traditional moral values, and the family."[30] The effort to reconcile Smith, who began with the self-interested individual, with Strauss, who began with doctrine preexisting any individual, would stretch any philosophy to the limit, particularly an ideology under construction.

Kristol's revisionism has earned him less fame than his argument that liberal social policies prove a "law of unintended consequences": whatever the intention, an opposite effect is achieved. By this approach, neoconservatives tried to demonstrate the shortcomings of the Great Society. Kristol called himself a believer in a "conservative welfare state," but the hinge on which his analysis turned was not so much conservatism as irony. In this, at least, he remained closer to Trilling than did Podhoretz.

Through *The Public Interest*, Kristol gained a new prominence. In the aftermath of the Kent State massacre and the Cambodian "incursion," Nixon beckoned him to discuss the student rebellion. Kristol pondered, and then declared that the protesters didn't "know what country they're in."[31] His support for Nixon, however, faded quickly. As the Watergate affair unfolded, Kristol tersely responded to all questions about it: "No comment."

In 1972 Kristol's book *On the Democratic Idea in America* drew even more praise and attention. A rising star at the *Wall Street Journal*, Robert Bartley, a devoted reader of *The Public Interest*, wrote a brief profile, and a year later, when Bartley became the *Journal*'s editor, he installed Kristol as a columnist. Bartley's own thinking and the editorials in the *Journal* were informed by Kristol's ideas, which provided a new basis for attacking liberals, environmentalists, and Ralph Nader.

Kristol's influence was adding up. Through assiduously cultivated contacts in foundations and institutes, the press and academia, among corporate and political leaders, he was beginning to define an ascendant conservative faction. Soon he served as the intellectual mentor to the charismatic congressman Jack Kemp, published Jude Wanniski's first article on supply-side economics in *The Public Interest*, and then secured grants for Wanniski to write *The Way the World Works*. Supply-side economics has been perhaps the most consequential project for which Kristol has been "Godfather."

"What if this new conservative political economy doesn't work? To which one can only reply: It had better work," he wrote in the *Journal,* a month after Reagan's election. "It is the last, best hope of democratic capitalism in America, and if it fails—well, then conservatives can concentrate on nostalgic poetry and forget about political economy. Someone else will be in charge of that."[32]

In his attempted unification of the higher and lower realms of politics, it was apparent that Kristol still believed that while philosophers have interpreted the world in various ways, the point is to change it. "We studied radicalism in the 1930s," he said. "It was great training in polemics and sustained political analysis. Being a Trotskyist was highly intellectual. I learned a lot. The neoconservatives are the political intellectuals, and that's what the Trotskyists were. Not the Communists. The Trotskyist movement produced political intellectuals, which is why so many went into sociology and achieved distinction. It was much more rigorous intellectual training than you could get in college. If someone came up with some matter on which you were not well read, my God, you were humiliated. It was jesuitical. The Republican Party, meanwhile, produced antipolitical intellectuals. Those people are not in my tradition."

The neoconservatives are the Trotskyists of Reaganism, and Kristol is a Trotskyist transmuted into a man of the right. He remains a free-floating, intense political intellectual in the vanguard. *"We* had to tell businessmen that they needed us," he said. "They are still not convinced. The cultural differences are so varied and will remain so for a long time. But slowly bridges get built, contacts get made. The neoconservatives, the Republican politicians, and the business community do not make an easy mixture. They don't meld all that well. But at least they mix, whereas they used not to mix at all. Business understands the need for intellectuals much more than trade unionists understand it, but not enough. Basically, it wants intellectuals to go out and justify profits and explain to people why corporations make a lot of money. That's their main interest. It is very hard for business to understand how to think politically. I think business is changing. An academic generation is only four years. A business generation is more like twenty. It takes time to change."

The neoconservatives would do for business what the old immigrant Hollywood producers did for small-town America: idealize and celebrate it. Some of the neoconservatives and Hollywood producers felt culturally marginal in the mainstream. By casting a warm glow around places they believed to be at the center of national life, which they were never part of, they gained a vicarious sense of belonging. These roseate visions betrayed a subtle and inchoate contempt. The pretty small-town images projected by Hollywood were calculated to appeal to the lowest common denominator, what the producers imagined the unwashed masses out there wanted. Similarly, the neoconservatives' defense of business patronized the businessmen, who were thought to be too dull to defend themselves. The neoconservatives also had a vested interest in elevating business to the level of myth, thereby making themselves seemingly indispensable and thus ceasing to be outsiders; without them, the bright picture they painted might fade. Appropriately, Ronald Reagan acted against backdrops created by both the Hollywood producers and the neoconservatives. He took the celebrations of small towns and business at face value and improved upon them.

One of the businessmen Kristol attempted to tutor was Nelson Rockefeller, whose contacts and money Kristol coveted for the neoconservative cause. When Rockefeller retired from public life, after his brief stint as Vice President, and began immersing himself in his art collections, Kristol tried to coax him back into politics. "I told him there was a big role for him," said Kristol. "I had several conversations with him. I spoke to him about supply-side economics before he died. He didn't quite understand it. But he was very interested in us. He liked the neoconservatives. He was saying that the old liberal Republican idea was empty now. His staff was somewhat less receptive; they had less intellectual curiosity than he did. He lacked the staff to keep reminding him of what he learned yesterday. The only intellectual he had ever had was Henry Kissinger. If Rockefeller were alive today there's no question he'd be a neoconservative. He could have gotten interested in the American Enterprise Institute, the Heritage Foundation, publications. He could have done an awful lot with his prestige, his name, his money. Why he retired I don't really know."

Kristol must have been a very good Marxist-Leninist because he persistently engages in sweeping class analysis at the same time he is keenly aware of short-term tactical imperatives. As a vanguard intellectual of the Counter-Establishment, he is constantly offering advice to cadres on how to blunt the political thrust of the "New Class." And he has urged businessmen to learn the limits of "thinking economically" —the shortcomings intrinsic in concentrating only on the maximization of profits—and to learn the long-term benefits of "thinking politically."[33] The tension between these two modes of thought and the kinds of activity they breed is exactly the subject at the heart of Lenin's *What Is to Be Done.* In that book, Lenin described how an exclusive focus on trade-union demands led to what he called an "economist" cast of mind. Larger political considerations, however, brought to the working class from outside by cadres of revolutionists, can catalyze a class consciousness; initially these cadres are overwhelmingly intellectuals, but in time advanced members of the proletariat are won over, are trained as activists, and take over the revolutionary party.

Yet the feelings of alienation among the political intellectuals are never dispelled. "Traditionally," said Kristol, "the Republican Party has been very suspicious of intellectuals. Some people within the Republican Party now do understand the intellectuals. An awful lot still don't. The philistinism still deeply rooted in the business community, if not anti-intellectual, is so utterly non-intellectual. It is very hard to get people who run things in Republican politics to run things in ways other than what they are used to thinking."

Almost immediately after Reagan assumed office, the neoconservatives mounted their first action, fighting the foe in a demonstration of firepower that could only be made by self-consciously superior intellectuals. What they demonstrated most clearly was the new politics of ideology. Kristol was the point man.

In February 1981, the President nominated as Assistant Secretary of State for Human Rights Dr. Ernest Lefever, director of the Ethics and Public Policy Center, a small Counter-Establishment institute funded by the conservative foundations. He envisioned the State Department post as a place from which to exercise what he called "silent diplomacy." "The U.S. government," he declared, "has no responsibility—and certainly no authority—to promote human rights in other sovereign states."[34]

The neoconservatives had a special interest in defending Lefever. Not only was he related to them by virtue of common foundation funding, not only was he a former Humphrey aide, but the issue of human rights was one they felt they owned. After all, they had been in the vanguard attacking Carter's policy. Jeane Kirkpatrick, a neoconservative American Enterprise Institute scholar, had come to Ronald Reagan's attention because of an article she wrote in *Commentary,* entitled "Dictatorship and Double Standards," positing a distinction between authoritarian and totalitarian dictatorships. Kirkpatrick asserted that the power of authoritarian regimes was personal in nature, flowing from the patriarchal figure of the dictator; while he ruled the state, he left the private lives of the people alone. However, the authority of totalitarian regimes was grounded in ideology, and the politicization of all aspects of life was relentless. In the worldwide conflict between the Free World and Communism, the authoritarian regimes tended to be our allies, while Communist nations and revolutionary liberation movements were totalitarian. Under Carter, our human rights policy penalized our friends and rewarded our enemies, according to Kirkpatrick's logic. Lefever was seen by neoconservatives as personifying the Kirkpatrick thesis.

Liberals, however, regarded his position as an abandonment of human rights. Traditional Republicans, too, came to oppose Lefever during his Senate confirmation hearings in late May 1981. They objected when he called his critics "Communist-inspired" and then denied he had made such a charge, even though the senators had clearly heard him.

The emotional rallying point for opposition to Lefever was Jacobo Timerman. The editor of the Argentine newspaper *La Opinion,* Timerman was imprisoned and tortured for two and a half years by the military junta. His jailers, during lengthy torture sessions, accused him of being a kingpin in an international Jewish-Communist conspiracy against Argentina. His searing experiences, recounted in a book, *Prisoner Without a Name, Cell Without a Number,* were published during the Lefever fracas. Timerman credited the saving of his life to the personal intervention of Patricia Derian, Jimmy Carter's Assistant Secretary of State for Human Rights. The neoconservative repudiation of Carter's policy and the nomination of Lefever raised the question of whether people like Timerman would now be left in the jails of regimes that were merely authoritarian. Timerman himself appeared at the Lefever hearings; although he was requested by senators to testify he declined, instead serving as a symbolic witness, an icon of human rights.

On May 29, the *Wall Street Journal* published a column by Irving Kristol entitled "The Timerman Affair," in which he attempted to salvage the Lefever appointment by making Timerman's ideological motive the issue. Then, his shadow leftism coming to the surface, Kristol wrote: "The politics of polarization, in which the left crusades against the right under the banner of 'human rights,' while the threat from the totalitarian left is altogether ignored, appeals to their ideological bias as well as to their self-righteous passions. One might almost say it is their secret agenda."[35]

Kristol's column set off a whirlwind of controversy. But while the neoconservatives succeeded in elevating Timerman from a relatively obscure figure into a man of renown, they failed to rescue Lefever, who was rejected on June 5 by a thirteen-to-four vote of the Senate Foreign Relations Committee. Five hours later he withdrew his name, saving the administration further embarrassment.

The neoconservative argument on Timerman had great positioning logic for a Manhattan literary firefight. Its logic was much less compelling in Washington and almost inexplicable in the rest of the country. The neoconservatives thrive on ideological combat; it's their daily bread. To them, conflict is to be expected and even reveled in. It is how they advance themselves and their ideas. In the Old Left, and among the pluralist Democrats, contentiousness is universal. No one is frowned upon for throwing food and screaming at the dinner table; it's all in the family. When everybody has bad manners, nobody can be singled out. But this was not the ethic prevailing in the Senate, which was dominated by regular Republicans. They do not believe in making bad scenes worse. In Lefever they knew they had a loser. By holding their fire they thought they would call less attention to the problem. The other side would shout for a while but, on another issue, Republicans would eventually even the score. Performing dirty work, even if it must be done, does not merit esteem among Republicans; the work, after all, is dirty. To the neoconservatives, however, making a target of Timerman seemed natural. The issue made Old Left sense; ideological charge demanded ideological countercharge.

The denouement of the Timerman case occurred almost a year after Lefever's nomination had been defeated. On April 2, 1982, UN ambassador and theoretician Jeane Kirkpatrick attended a dinner held in her honor at the Argentine embassy. The Argentines were not sure she would show up, and when she did they were vastly relieved. For while toasts were proposed and the repast consumed, Argentine troops were invading the British-held Falkland Islands. To the Argentines, Kirkpatrick's presence that evening most likely indicated tacit U.S. approval of the Argentine action; at the least, it demonstrated cordial passivity in the face of aggression. The British were outraged by her behavior. If there was a double standard at work here, it worked in favor of the "authoritarian" dictatorship and against democracy.

Kristol, for his part, still had some influence with the administration. He was able, for example, to lobby successfully for the appointment of neoconservative William Bennett as chairman of the National Endowment for the Humanities, knocking out a candidate favored by more traditional conservatives. (In the second term, Bennett became Secretary of Education.)

Like Podhoretz, Kristol continued to write, trying by persuasion to steer the movement. More important, he continued to place comrades in key positions within the Counter-Establishment, a circuitry of influence that blinks like a Christmas tree when he plugs in.

In 1985, he plugged into the Olin Foundation and a $600,000 grant came his way. The money subsidized a magazine, pointedly named *The National Interest,* with Kristol acting as publisher. *The National Interest* recalled *The Public Interest,* the journal devoted to domestic issues. Yet that magazine was founded with an anti-ideological intent, while *The Natinal Interest* was calculated to be a weapon in what Kristol called the "war of ideology."

Kristol's war would be simultaneously waged on several fronts. "The basic conflict of our times—that between the USSR and the

United States—is ideological," he wrote in the premier issue of *The National Interest.* The American ideology, "liberal internationalism," first enunciated by Woodrow Wilson and based on notions of self-determination and international rule of law, is "naive and utopian," tragically inadequate in the world struggle. In its place he proposed a "new conservatism," which is "self-consciously ideological," especially when it comes to the "basic conflict" with the Russians, a conflict "we should aim to win . . . instead of pursuing a defensive policy that sees stalemate as the goal."[36]

At every juncture in their journey the neoconservatives have been propelled by a feeling of disillusionment. This venture was no different. "A neoconservative," Kristol quipped, "is a liberal mugged by reality." Now the neoconservatives believed they had been mugged by Ronald Reagan, whose foreign policy they viewed as a succession of dismaying events. Though the president excoriated the "evil empire," he ended the Polish sanctions, lifted the Russian grain embargo, disastrously withdrew from Lebanon, and did business with Shiite hostage-takers. These episodes, neoconservatives feared, might be a prelude to the greatest betrayal of all—a debilitating arms-control agreement with the Soviets, the moral equivalent of appeasement. So they launched *The National Interest* to help instruct a benighted administration.

Neoconservatism is not likely to have generations. It is less a coherent intellectual expression than a political movement of people joined by shared background. By definition, this experience is exclusive, reserved only for the older set. Yet there is a species of young neoconservatives, which is more a collection of like-minded individuals than a successor generation.

"They may think of themselves automatically as Republicans," said Nathan Glazer. "The younger people may have an easier transition. Some of them have come out of the already strong tradition of conservatism in the colleges and universities, in which case, if they are Republicans, it wouldn't bother them. There is a real generational difference."

"The second-generation neoconservative intellectuals are really conservative intellectuals," said Kristol. "They learned their neoconservatism from many of the neoconservatives. Who else writes the books? The old right did not produce any distinguished social scientists, except economists. Intellectually, the young neoconservatives will be at home within the Republican Party, if the Republican Party lets them."

Who are the young neoconservatives? "Well," said Podhoretz, "there's my son-in-law." For Podhoretz, neoconservatism had become a family-run dry cleaners. There is his wife, Midge Decter, a one-woman lecture series on the evils of women's liberation, nuclear disarmament, and the sixties. ("As far as making the bed is concerned," she once wrote, "I plead guilty to thinking it right and proper a woman should do so.")[37] Her blunt opinions lifted her to the board of the Heritage Foundation and the directorship of the Committee for a Free World, a neoconservative sect funded largely by the Olin Foundation. The committee's newsletter, *Contentions,* is edited by the Podhoretzes' son-in-law Steven Munson, the former public-relations aide to Ambassador Kirkpatrick. And it is characterized by ad hominem attacks on the Podhoretz family's perceived ideological enemies. Then there's Elliott Abrams, who filled the post Lefever failed to achieve and in the second Reagan term became Assistant Secretary of State for Latin American Affairs, where he became the chief promoter of military aid to the Nicaraguan *contras.*

"Norman tends to take positions in an extreme way," said Glazer. "He's a romantic. Neoconservatism's identification with a tough foreign policy is almost entirely Norman and Midge and their in-laws and relatives."

"Norman and Midge are the golden couple now," said Abrams, shortly after the 1980 election. "It's strange."

The shadow leftism of young neoconservatives like Abrams does not have its emotional center in the 1930s. Instead, they are obsessed by the sixties, when, unlike their mentors, they could not withdraw into their own society. They could not escape their peers; but by attaching themselves to the Counter-Establishment they hope to defeat them.

"I'm *sorry,* but John Lennon was not that important a figure in our times," said Abrams a week after Lennon's killing. "I do not believe he created the culture of the sixties. Come on! I've actually formed a political opinion of this. Why is his death getting more attention than Elvis Presley's? Because Lennon is perceived as a left-wing figure politically, anti-establishment, a man of social conscience with concern for the poor. And, therefore, he's being made into a great figure. Too much has been made of his life. It does not deserve a full day's television and radio coverage. I'm *sick* of it."

Elvis's demise, of course, was hardly ignored by the press. Abrams's insistence that it was reveals his political assumptions, a parochialism characteristic of neoconservatives bred in certain insular New York circles and perhaps a resentment against perceived slights.

"My parents were strict," he said. "Everybody went to a movie, and I always had to call home at nine-thirty. I don't think I'm the worse for it. I went to my high school reunion and I saw wreckage. A startling number of talented people—waiters, bookstore clerks. It's awful." Were these the people who didn't have to call home?

When Abrams graduated, he entered Harvard. (He later attended Harvard Law School, and during his second year he rented the top floor of Nathan Glazer's house.) He was on the cusp of his generation, precisely the right age to be fully affected by the fusion of politics and culture in the sixties and to be fully self-conscious about it, neither too old by a few years nor too young. In 1968—before the assassination of Robert Kennedy, before the harrowing Democratic convention, before the fall campaign—young people chose sides against the Johnson administration. Many were attracted to the cool intellectualism of Eugene McCarthy, many were attracted to the heated existentialism of Robert Kennedy, and many disdained and despaired of all hopeful possibilities. Abrams supported Hubert Humphrey. He was, in fact, national chairman of Campus Americans for Democratic Action, founder of the Harvard chapter, and an ex-officio member of the national ADA board. "I quickly discovered that CADA was a paper organization, in which anyone could immediately rise to the top. So I did." After he declared for Humphrey, he attended his first national board meeting in Washington. "I arrived all excited and delighted and happy." As he recalled, the first person to approach him said, "Resign!" He was, he said, "diselected," booted out of office for the Humphrey heresy. "It didn't change my feelings about liberalism," he said. "It changed my feelings about liberals. I thought I was doing the right thing. The ADA liberals were doing something very wrong. I was one of the people to drop away from what we called the New Left. I was at that tender age in the vanguard. No sooner did I enter than I left. There was no sense of past loyalties or friendships gone. I was so new to it."

Yet his experience placed him in opposition to his peers, making him an outsider. "If you are my age, you broke with your generation," he said. "While everyone was up in arms about Vietnam and involved with the youth culture, you didn't share it; you reacted against it. I spent a good portion of my time in college working against SDS. There aren't many of us. We have a feeling of swimming against the tide. You feel isolated, embattled."

"Elliott's still living in the world of the 1960s, where Harvard is about to be destroyed by revolutionaries, who happen to be his fellow students," said one of his friends. "He has a deep and abiding resentment about what went on and he sees it in all sorts of inappropriate contexts. He sees about half the Democratic Party as SDS taking over University Hall. I would describe it as a fixation in the past. But Elliott's no lunatic. It's not a weirdness waiting for an ideology to happen. He just doesn't see how times have changed in any way. Why has he been fixated? I'm not sure. He was not the only person affected this way. It's a political ideology he became part of."

Working for Reagan was something about which Abrams had no ambivalence. "I was especially for Reagan because he was harder line than any of the others," he said. Abandoning the Democratic Party was no hardship. "The conclusion I come to is that the Democratic Party for the foreseeable future is not the right place for neoconservatives. The Republican Party is. Either the Democrats will stay with the big-government/weak-America policy or they will begin to say 'me, too.' There is no reason neoconservative intellectuals should say 'me, too,' rather than being on the frontiers. Neoconservatives will probably, most of them, end up as Republicans. There isn't any reason to stay in the Democratic Party these days."

His longest statement of principle was a contribution to a forum of young neoconservatives published on the eve of the 1980 campaign in *The American Spectator.* He wrote:

Grant that injustice, poverty, disease, and war are in part simply endemic to the human condition, and in fact the result of ignorant or mistaken or evil acts by individuals and a very different result emerges. Where liberals see "problems," neoconservatives see "conditions."[38]

Problems can be solved, but conditions are a result of human nature, even perhaps conditions like human-rights violations.

On the cover of this special issue of *The American Spectator* was a cartoon of his father-in-law, Norman Podhoretz, clutching a saber and leading the charge.

The *Spectator* is perhaps the most important journal of the younger conservative generation, occupying a unique niche within the Counter-Establishment. While the older generation speaks in a self-consciously grave tone, the voice of *The American Spectator* is self-consciously outrageous. Its editor, R. Emmett Tyrrell, claims his prose follows in the tropes of H. L. Mencken. But while Mencken's sarcasm was directed against sacred cows like Calvin Coolidge and the banalities of the "booboisie," Tyrrell worships at the shrine of those who still worship Coolidge. Like many younger conservatives, the figure he tries to emulate is William F. Buckley, Jr., whose early posturing established him as a liberal nemesis. By mimicking the Buckley manner, the youthful set hope to capture a similar fame. Covering the Buckley stations of the cross is now an established ritual: the precious liberal-bashing tract *(God and Man at Yale);* the affected Englishness; the conspicuous use of big words. They offer themselves as originals, one after another, with eyes cocked at the Buckley icon.

Tyrrell is the president of this particular fraternity house. He has produced the obligatory book *(The Liberal Crack-Up,* a postgraduate effort in the tradition of Buckley's *Up from Liberalism),* and he often produces near-perfect absurdities. (On Jimmy Carter: "a scamp mountebank from jerkwater America.") Tyrrell has the rare ability to deal exclusively in invective and derision without achieving satiric effect. His efforts have proven so noteworthy that he was hailed by Jeane Kirkpatrick as "a major neoconservative voice of the new generation." Tyrrell in fact is no neoconservative. He's from Indiana, he's not old enough, he's never been a Democrat (much less a Trotskyist), he's no scholar. He fits too few of the categories to make the cut. Neoconservatism is too exclusive a movement to include him; it is far too exclusive to have a true successor generation. The neoconservatives may breed conservatives, who have never known the joy of disillusionment, but not neoconservatives. Generational experience cannot be replicated.

In late 1978, Tyrrell organized two field trips for young conservatives to meet Richard Nixon, then secluded in a Manhattan apartment. Among those joining the expedition were William Kristol, a political scientist and Irving Kristol's son; Robert Bartley, editor of the *Wall Street Journal;* Leslie Lenkowsky, director of the Smith-Richardson Foundation; and Elliott Abrams. For some, who went out of morbid curiosity, visiting Nixon was like a trip to the wax museum. Others felt differently. "We were impressed with Nixon's intellectual abilities," said one. For them, the encounter banished any remaining misgivings they might have had about their mission; they were emboldened, not chastened, by their meeting with the specter of disgrace.

Among the neoconservatives it had become conventional wisdom that the Watergate affair was a "coup d'etat" overturning Nixon's 1972 landslide victory. Back in 1972, the neoconservatives were in the middle of their journey. They were a faction without a home, and the Counter-Establishment was a home without enough people. It was a match. Now they staffed the think tanks, wrote for the journals, and helped create the new ideas. Thus they prepared the way for Reagan's election, which they viewed as an improvement over Nixon's lost mandate.

CHAPTER SEVEN

A LOST

CONTINENT

During the first week of January 1980, on the eve of the presidential primaries, Ronald Reagan was formally briefed on supply-side economics by the doctrine's major advocates, Jack Kemp, Arthur Laffer, and Jude Wanniski. Though an old guard of conservative economists and political operatives was wary of these upstarts, campaign manager John Sears was eager to explore the notion's political possibilities. It might be just the thing, he reasoned, to attract the middle-class rebels of the still unfolding tax revolt.

A collection of Counter-Establishment brain-trusters, enough to staff a think tank, had assembled in a conference room at the Beverly Wilshire Hotel, to tutor the prize pupil. The supply-siders sat quietly in a corner. "I was really alarmed the first day," said Wanniski. "It was all military and defense. All of these global chessplayers who move missiles around in their minds were tossing ideas back and forth. Every now and then Reagan would interrupt and ask something and make a little joke and seem to say something irrelevant to the discussion as though it were off an index card. He didn't literally have an index card in front of him, but it sounded like it. I was alarmed at how shallow the guy seemed, even though I didn't know what was going on either."

Then it was Wanniski's turn to lecture. "The second day I had to give a presentation on supply-side theory and energy policy, which can get pretty dense in its own way. Again, Reagan was interrupting with his little index-card examples and I said, 'Yeah, that's right. You got it.' I was groping toward a definition of what this was all about, and then Reagan would find something in his past, some little story, some little anecdote, and say, 'Is this what you mean, this thing that happened to me in 1939?' He seemed to put it all on an index card. But I saw within my own area of expertise what he was doing. *Yeah!*"

He viewed Reagan as something of a Jedi master who had plumbed the mysteries of the Force, which is the marketplace. "Reagan does listen and he listens hard. When somebody understands what you're saying, do you know what you feel? Love. That's what love is all about. I feel like a kid about Reagan. I'm delirious."

Wanniski believed that Reagan listened attentively at least partly because of his own economic education. "The most important thing about Ronald Reagan is worth his weight in gold," Wanniski said. "He is the *only* political leader on this entire planet who has a degree in economics from Eureka College before Keynesian economics was taught. He has classical training."

Supply-side economics was a theology spawned almost overnight. It developed its own hierarchy of wizards and divinities, but it wasn't spontaneously generated. A political force—the Counter-Establishment—made possible the economic doctrine. On the surface, the supply-siders were an odd assortment of types, but they shared a common passion for ideology. The dramatis personae included *Wall Street Journal* editorial writer Jude Wanniski; economists Arthur Laffer and Robert Mundell; *Wall Street Journal* editor Robert Bartley; neoconservative intellectual Irving Kristol; Representative Jack Kemp; foundation executive Leslie Lenkowsky; political strategist John Sears; and, of course, Ronald Reagan. Each was essential in bringing the idea to fruition. Supply-side economics was an example of the Counter-Establishment in motion, an intricate meshing of media, money, and ideas. It was also an illustration of how a handful of self-described "wildmen," consumed by monomania, would try to change the course of history.

Supply-side economics was presented as radically innovative but ancient wisdom. It was a revival of the oldest chestnut in classical economics, Say's Law, once the Alpha and Omega, but refuted by John Maynard Keynes. "So far from being new or revolutionary, supply-side economics is frankly reactionary," wrote Irving Kristol. " 'Back to

Adam Smith' can be fairly designated as its motto."[1] Jean-Baptiste Say was a French follower of Smith. His enduring contribution to economics was his law: "Supply creates its own demand."* Until the 1930s, opinion in the economics profession was nearly unanimous about Say's Law. It was believed to be a neat and accurate description of reality. Those who supplied goods and services in the marketplace generated their own demand. Some succeeded and others failed, proving the market's neutral genius. Yet an equilibrium was achieved without outside interference. If the market was unbalanced, it was accidental and would soon right itself. Under Say's Law, there could never be a shortage of purchasing power; full employment was just around the corner and new investment was always coming to the rescue. During the Depression, these truisms were no longer self-evident. It took Keynes to say so. In 1936 his masterpiece, *The General Theory of Employment Interest and Money,* was published. His intention was to demolish the postulates of classical economics. He argued that supply did not create demand; that equilibrium was not achieved at full employment; that savings did not necessarily translate into investment. He advocated government spending to stimulate the demand for goods and thereby spur production. In time, John Kenneth Galbraith wrote, "Say's Law sank without a trace."[3] It was a lost continent of economics.

We were all Keynesians now, said Richard Nixon. The doctrine was laid along the exact lines of a graph. The Phillips Curve, describing the trade-off of unemployment and inflation, became the guide for fine-tuning the economy, which seemed to require no more than sensitive adjustments. But the Phillips Curve could not explain stagflation— simultaneous high unemployment and high inflation—which persisted throughout the 1970s. So Keynesianism was called into question.

In 1972 an international group of economists called the Club of Rome issued a report forecasting "limits to growth." This disturbing idea contradicted traditional American optimism; we would no longer be a people of plenty. Then the economist Lester Thurow of MIT argued that America was becoming a "zero-sum society." "As we head

---

*Say's work was referred to as the "vulgarization of Adam Smith" by Karl Marx in *Capital.* Marx was always merciless about those he thought second-rate.[2]

into the 1980s," he wrote, "it is well to remember that there is really only one important question in political economy. If elected, whose income do you and your party plan to cut in the process of solving the economic problems facing us?"[4] Once again, the dismal science offered dismal visions.

Just as Keynesianism emerged when free-market doctrine seemed incapable of resolving the pressing problems of the Depression, supply-side economics appeared when Keynesianism seemed incapable of resolving those of stagflation. Supply-side economics was a lightning storm in the intellectual atmosphere. It lit up the darkening skies with electrical energy; peals of rolling thunder could be heard. Eureka! It was so old that it seemed incredibly new. Supply-side economics balanced all of the theorems of classical doctrine on the Laffer Curve. It was so reductionist, so simple, so obvious, that it appeared brilliant.

The Laffer Curve was a direct riposte to the Phillips Curve. It intended to describe how cutting taxes would increase incentives to work and therefore increase investment, production, and even government revenues. It was more suggestive than precise, although various econometric models were built around the idea, making several economic consulting firms prosperous and Reagan administration forecasts uncertain.

Supply-side economics provided the theoretical underpinnings for old-fashioned optimism. The doctrine restated the free-market myth with verve and originality. In an era when the "limits to growth" were proclaimed, the gnostic supply-siders made claims to knowing the secret of endless wealth: the magic of the marketplace. And in an era when political solutions to fundamental problems were widely considered nearly impossible because of a "zero-sum" paralysis of interest groups, supply-siders declared that their formula required only a willingness to implement it for the world to be saved. They did not accept the premise that we inhabited a closed system in which all factors were already in play. To them, the most important factor was the invisible hand of the market, which brought unexpected and dramatic changes. When few could see a way out of the impasse, the supply-siders emerged as visionaries with faith, confirmed optimists among dour pessimists. They knew for a *fact* that a return to the first principles of the free market was the path to a dazzling future. Here was no gloom and doom, no Spenglerian maunderings about an inexorable turn to the dark side of history, none of the grim caution of the older conservative economists. Supply-side economics was the high note of the Restoration. The supply-siders, moreover, did not reiterate the free-market myth with the inflection of an Austro-liberal like Frederich von Hayek. Supply-side economics was *echt-*American, a theory for the multitude of go-getters, promising that the cornucopia was bottomless. Supply-siders were enthusiastic but vague in their populism, while grandiloquent in their reference to historical precedents. The doctrine was philosophical lore, at the same time obscure and readily accessible, sweeping and banal, novel and trite. It demanded from its believers half-knowledge; the other half was faith. The doctrine promised hope and opportunity; it discounted sacrifice and complexity; such pessimistic themes were banished.

Because supply-side economics struck so many as something out of the blue, its advocates felt the need to invoke historical authority. Examples from the past demonstrated that the theory was not invented slapdash yesterday morning, but the wisdom of the ages. Perhaps it was even part of Divine Providence's plan. Wanniski explained to Reagan that supply-side economics actually played a role in the birth of Jesus Christ: "Supply-side's birth coincided with the birth of Christ and Christianity. It was Emperor Caesar Augustus who decided to revive the idea of his adoptive father Julius and conduct a tax census of the empire. By identifying the whole of the citizenry, the burden of taxes could be spread, avoiding the necessity of burdening the few with the entire load. Joseph and Mary were en route to his home to be enumerated for this supply-side economic purpose when Jesus was born."[5]

Another great exponent of supply-side economics (after Emperor Caesar Augustus) was the fourteenth-century Arab sociologist-historian Ibn Khaldun, whose little-known writings were cited at a presidential press conference on October 1, 1981. Reagan said:

If you look at our reductions in capital gains tax, if you go back to the 1920s when Mellon was the Secretary of the Treasury under Coolidge and was doing this every time, that kind of a tax cut brings us back, I've told, I think, some of you before, to a principle that goes back, at least I know, as far as the fourteenth century when a Moslem philosopher named Ibn Khaldun said: "In the beginning of the dynasty great tax revenues were gained from small assessments. At the end of the dynasty, small tax revenues were gained from large assessments." And we're trying to get down to the small assessments and great revenues.*

America, of course, was founded on supply-side principles. The theory was not "just another version of late-nineteenth-century robber-baron social Darwinism," wrote James Ring Adams, an editorial writer for the *Wall Street Journal* with fervent supply-side sympathies. "The supply-side approach was in fact so well known to the founders of the United States that it can claim to be the foundation of the American economic tradition. . . . Far from being radical and untried, the basic principles of 'Reaganomics' were common currency at the founding of the United States and through much of its history. Their legacy has been the extraordinary development of a continent."[7]

Just as Alexander Hamilton was conversant in supply-side theory, so was Andrew Mellon, the Pittsburgh millionaire commonly referred to in Coolidge's day as "the greatest Secretary of the Treasury since Hamilton." Mellon, after all, cut taxes.

So did John F. Kennedy, claimed as yet another supply-sider. Arthur Laffer, during the 1980 campaign, in a private report to his clients, entitled "The Reagan-Kennedy Nexus," wrote: "The basis of Ronald Reagan's vision of the future is the restoration of economic incentives from the top to the bottom of American society. To accomplish this he has proposed policies amazingly similar to those of President John F. Kennedy."[8]† Kennedy's tax cut, however, was conceived as a Keynesian measure to spur demand. It may be interpreted as an incomplete policy, since Kennedy never proposed the kind of sweeping program that John Kenneth Galbraith suggested in *The Affluent Society* to

---

*Ibn Khaldun also said: "No intelligent person doubts the existence of sorcery."[6]
†During the 1960 campaign, Reagan wrote a letter to Nixon in which he suggested that Kennedy's program be smeared as "Marxist."

remedy the grievous contrast between private wealth and public squalor. The supply-siders' claim to Kennedy's tax cut may also lead to a designation of them as perverse Keynesians. Whatever the case, their assumptions differ markedly from Kennedy's. Kennedy applied a fiscal measure to compensate for the perceived failure of Say's Law, where the supply-siders apply it to prove Say's Law. One acted on the idea that the classical model was faulty—a "myth"—the other on the idea that it was truth.* Regardless, Kennedy was taken as a supply-side hero, the latest in the line stretching back to Emperor Caesar Augustus. Reagan, in his adherence to the supply-side doctrine, was acting on vast historical experience, at least according to the supply-siders.

The true history of supply-side economics, in fact, can be best traced not to Imperial Rome but to Minersville, Pennsylvania. And the story really begins not with Emperor Caesar Augustus, but with John Rusinskas, a miner, Lithuanian immigrant, and staunch member of the Communist Party.

During the early years of the Depression, the coal industry collapsed. About a third of mine workers earned less than $2.50 a day. Hunger was routine, disease expected, and the death of children by starvation not uncommon—all consequences of a supply-side nightmare. The historian and economist Irving Bernstein, in his definitive book, *The Lean Years: A History of the American Workers 1920–1933,* wrote:

> Capacity vastly exceeded demand; the business units were all small and much too numerous; the horizon of the typical operator was fixed at the line of his own property. The consumers

---

*Walter Heller, chairman of the Council of Economic Advisers under presidents Kennedy and Johnson, writing in 1982, challenged the notion that "Mr. Reagan's tax cut is just a replica of the successful Kennedy-Johnson tax cut in 1964. It's no such thing. Not only is it about half again as large, but it is sharply regressive in contrast with the mildly progressive tax cut in 1964. Even more important, the Kennedy tax cuts were enacted in a setting of virtually no inflation—just over one percent per year —and a budget that moved into surplus just fifteen months after the 1964 tax cut was enacted. The foregoing combination of circumstances enabled the Federal Reserve to accommodate expansion. Monetary and fiscal policy worked hand in hand, rather than clashing head to head."[9]

... mainly steel, railroad, and utility corporations—played one operator against the other in fixing prices. ... To describe the price market as disorderly would be an understatement; it was a classic illustration of cutthroat competition.[10]

Throughout the coalfields, class warfare was not a slogan but a reality. Workers struck in order to have enough to eat; owners resisted to stay in business. Both sides were armed.

The established union, the United Mine Workers of America, was in shambles and in retreat. So desperate workers turned to the Communist-led National Miners Union. In 1931 the NMU led a bitter strike in Harlan, Kentucky—"Bloody Harlan"—which ended in ignominious defeat. Armed thugs were employed by the owners; there were many killings. A song written by the wife of a union organizer involved in "Bloody Harlan" became an anthem:

> Oh workers, can you stand it?
> Oh tell me how you can.
> Will you be a lousy scab
> Or will you be a man?
> Which side are you on?
> Which side are you on?

John Rusinskas was a Communist militant who boarded NMU organizers in his Minersville home. He was on the editorial board of a Lithuanian-language (party) newspaper, regarding himself as a class-conscious proletarian and committed revolutionist, unwavering in his faith. And he was constantly bickering about politics with his son-in-law, Michael Wanniski, who worked as a butcher, carpenter, and chicken farmer to make ends meet. He lived in nearby Pottsville, where the novelist John O'Hara grew up and which was the setting for his stories of an enclosed society sharply gradated by caste and class.

Jude Wanniski was born in Pottsville. As a boy he was a quiet witness to the perpetual debate between his grandfather and father. John, the believer in the one true faith, never ceased in his labors to convert Michael, who never conceded a point. "What I got in all the early years was a discussion of supply-side Marxism," said Jude. "My grandfather always had the Kremlin line. Whatever the line was on anything, he had it. The debates that went on were about my father resisting my grandfather and me listening to both."

In 1938 the entire family left the coalfields and settled in Brooklyn. The debates continued. When Jude graduated from high school his grandfather gave him a precious gift to guide him in the wide world: Marx's *Capital*. Judge attempted to read it from cover to cover, but says he never finished. His early political position was defined more by family dialectics than by Marx. To take one side would mean betrayal of either his father or grandfather; someone would be finally outvoted or outshouted. Since this was not really a contest of competing candidates but an extended family, the stakes were ultimately not political. "I wanted to feel I was splitting the difference between my father and grandfather," said Jude. "So instead of being a Marxist, I'd be a Fabian. When I was twenty years old, I would tell people, 'I'm a Fabian.' " The Fabians were British socialists who were by temperament reformers, not insurrectionists; they believed that public education in proper ideas was the road to power. Jude now diligently read books by such Fabians as Sidney and Beatrice Webb.

After attending Brooklyn College for a year and a half, Wanniski transferred to the University of California at Los Angeles. Every Tuesday night he participated in a discussion group organized by the Young Peoples' Socialist League, the Socialist Party youth group, the closest thing to the Fabians in America. But he didn't fit in. He wanted to argue and shout, just like at home. "I'd irritate the Marxists," he said.

In July 1959, a month after his graduation, drawn by "the idea of adventure" that journalism and the "last frontier" seemed to offer, he moved to Alaska, which had just become the forty-ninth state. He was not escaping from settled society. By getting a job on an Anchorage newspaper he embarked on the first part of his self-conscious quest for fame and influence. The hero he sought to emulate was James Reston, columnist for *The New York Times.* "I'd succeed him," said Wanniski. "His position was so thoughtful, and he was anti–Joe McCarthy." Anchorage was intended to be the beginning of a journey that was supposed to wind up with Wanniski acclaimed as the most respected and admired journalist of his generation. It was a good starting place, bustling but not overwhelming. A bright young man could make a name for himself while learning the rudiments of his craft.

After a couple of years in Alaska, Wanniski got a job with the *Las Vegas Review Journal,* another frontier. He approached journalism in the spirit of his father and grandfather. "They were jacks-of-all-trades," he said. "They were both the same kinds of characters. They believed that if there are a million things to learn about anything, you can learn the first half-million in the first thirty days." So in Las Vegas he got himself assigned to cover each of the major beats for a month: the hotels, the state house, the courthouse. "I wound up seeing that there were few people in Nevada who understood the way the state worked the way I did. I just had an understanding of the Nevada political economy, pieced together like a jigsaw puzzle. I wound up having a massive amount of experience." He was ready to be a columnist, and for five years he wrote a daily column on local politics. The *Review Journal,* which carried James Reston's syndicated column, featured both Wanniski's and Reston's pictures on advertising billboards. "I had become a celebrity," Wanniski said. "I had gotten to be Reston without going to Washington."

In 1964, Democrat Howard Cannon was challenged by Republican Paul Laxalt for a U.S. Senate seat. Wanniski was an innocent bystander hit by a shot. The *Review Journal*'s publisher supported Cannon, and he issued orders that coverage should be "blatantly tilted," according to Wanniski. The editor, Robert Brown, quit on the spot. Wanniski felt he had no choice but to resign, too. It was time, he reflected, to proceed immediately to Washington.

Since his Alaska days, he had been a stringer for the *Wall Street Journal.* When he moved to Nevada, he continued to provide the paper with a stream of stories. In the 1960s, the *Journal*'s parent company, Dow Jones, began publishing a weekly newspaper, *The National Observer.* Now, from Las Vegas, the embattled Wanniski made a telephone call to the *Observer*'s editors. "I got to get out of this place," he said. He was hired instantly. Though he had lost his status as a political columnist—a Reston—he was installed in Washington, the center of the political universe, the object of his ambitions.

In 1966, two years after he arrived at the *Observer,* the paper launched a political column without a columnist. Various staff members tried out for the position. After Wanniski got his chance—he *knew* how to write a column—he was awarded the plum. "I did it the same way I did my column in Las Vegas," he said. "I wound up covering everything, having a general view of the different power lines being crossed." He wrote about Congress, the FBI, the Supreme Court, presidential politics, defense strategy, almost every subject, except one with which he had only a slight acquaintance—economics. It was early 1971, and he felt that he had better learn something about it. The Nixon administration had just issued a projection that the Gross National Product would rise $1.65 trillion that year, a figure considered laughable by most established economists. The source of the number was traced by bloodhound reporters to the Office of Management and Budget, and from there it was traced to the OMB's chief economist. "It came," said Wanniski, "from none other than Arthur B. Laffer."

Arthur B. Laffer studied economics as an undergraduate in the early 1960s at Yale, a bastion of Keynesian teaching. The leading light of the economics department, James Tobin, was serving as a member of President Kennedy's Council of Economic Advisers, and occasionally returned to Yale to lecture. On June 11, 1962, Kennedy himself came to Yale to deliver a forceful defense of Keynesian economics and an even more forceful attack on what he called the "mythology" that "fails to reflect the true realities of contemporary American society." He said:

The stereotypes I have been discussing distract our attention and divide our effort. These stereotypes do our nation a disservice, not just because they are misleading, but because they stand in the way of the solution of hard and complicated facts. It is not new that past debates should obscure present realities. But the damage of such a false dialogue is greater today than ever before simply because today the safety of all the world—the very future of freedom—depends as never before upon the sensible and clear-headed management of the domestic affairs of the United States.[11]

176

Laffer was thrilled by this flashing rhetoric, and Kennedy became his hero. The sensation of the moment stayed with him longer than the message.

Laffer was a poor student, more active in his fraternity and secret society than in his studies. His father, William Laffer, the CEO of the Clevite Corporation, manufacturer of bearings, of Cleveland, Ohio, was sorely disappointed. A year in Germany, studying at the University of Munich, helped straighten Arthur out. In his senior year he performed well and graduated with honors in economics. He received a master's in business administration from Stanford and began working on his doctorate. He considered himself a political liberal. In 1967, he was hired as an economics professor at the University of Chicago by George Shultz, dean of the faculty, who was influential with the economics department where Milton Friedman presided as gray eminence. In 1970, Shultz, who had become director of the OMB, hired his protégé Laffer as his chief economist.

Laffer was a cipher, just another drone in the federal hive, when his economic projection about the GNP became an overnight sensation, one of those significant but quickly forgotten issues that arise weekly in Washington. Laffer—inexperienced, exposed, powerless—was an ideal target for public ridicule. His name, too, lent itself to obvious double entendres. Moreover, as it turned out, he had used only four equations to reach the projected number of $1.65 trillion, whereas most economists achieved their results from painstaking calculations of numerous formulas that were formidable in their complexity. The press portrayed Laffer as an idiot savant. Senator William Proxmire derided "Arthur Laffer and his money machine." Understandably, Laffer was hurt. "I stopped seeing anyone from the press," he said. Then Wanniski called.

"I couldn't figure out what was going on," said Wanniski. "I called and asked if he could explain this to me. I was an economic ignoramus." Laffer agreed, hesitatingly. "Jude promised he wouldn't write about what I said. He just wanted to get to know me." Laffer was dealing with his stressful predicament by gluttonous eating. He was short, but had ballooned to 235 pounds. His physical absurdity contributed to his sensitivity and reclusiveness. "He was Mr. Five-by-Five," said Wanniski. "He was so nervous, eating all the time. We went out to lunch together. He told me how thrilled he was that I wanted to learn. The others just wanted to get headlines. The importance of my meeting with Laffer was that he was willing to spend unlimited time teaching me macroeconomics. One of the keys of my success in Las Vegas was that I went to the superintendent of schools and asked him to teach me how the fiscal system of the state worked. With Laffer, I had the same thing. I knew he was heretical, but I had someone in the middle of all the debates."

But not for long. In 1972, Laffer left the government. "He had become the laughingstock of the profession," said Wanniski. "The faculty at Chicago felt he had brought dishonor." (The GNP in 1971 was $1.32 trillion, not the $1.65 trillion that Laffer projected, making his error enormous.) Laffer landed a job as a consultant to the H. C. Wainwright investment firm. Although he worked in New York, he kept in close touch with his former colleague at Chicago, Robert Mundell, an economist with whom he had great affinity.

Mundell was imperious, audacious, and fearless in challenging the assumptions of the profession's elders. In 1971, during the first oil shock, he began advocating a unique combination of policies. He stood alone, neither Keynesian nor traditionally conservative. These policies were the harbinger of supply-side economics.

In April 1971 he attended a conference of leading international economists and financiers held in Bologna, Italy, under the auspices of the Johns Hopkins Bologna Center, where he first spelled out his position. "The right policy, I think," he declared, "is to split monetary and fiscal policies, using monetary restraint to check inflation, and tax reduction—which would reduce upward wage pressure—to increase employment." Conservatives were aghast at the prospect that this mix might result in enormous deficits, which always worried them. Mundell sloughed off their concern. "I'm frankly not worried about this problem at all," he said. "I think it's a mirage."[12]

Laffer followed Mundell's progress with great diligence. In 1974 the two economists co-chaired a seminar at the American Enterprise Institute on "The Phenomenon of Worldwide Inflation." Once again Mundell urged a simultaneous tight-money policy and a tax cut. He offered a theoretical explanation for his program. "Mundell argued that you can't ignore the 'substitution effects' of inflation," said Laffer. What were these "substitution effects?" Taxes, mainly. High taxes removed incentives for people to work because any gains they made would be taken away by the government. Productivity and investment suffered; inflation was encouraged. Laffer had never before heard the problem stated quite this way. "When you pay people not to work, it does not increase production," he said. "Don't be surprised if people don't increase their work effort. You couldn't find that anywhere in the literature. The fault of economics until the mid-1960s was that no one considered the 'substitution effects' of fiscal policy. I was impressed. I hadn't thought about it. It made sense. It just clicked."

Mundell's logic was classical theory, Say's Law approached anew. It was also an entrepreneurial understanding of human nature: People earn what they deserve; they need obvious incentives to work harder; and hard work lends new respect to the dollar. From this point of view, inflation ultimately became a crisis of character. If the problem was one of human motivation, the answer must be proper incentives. Laffer listened raptly to Mundell's talk about "substitution effects." And Laffer was talking almost every day to Wanniski, who had become his trusted confidant.

By this time Wanniski was writing for the editorial page of the *Wall Street Journal,* which would become the principal publicist for supply-side economics. "In the supply-side debate, our page was the forum," said Robert Bartley, editor of the *Journal.* "These people [supply-siders] had to find each other. And they had to have publicity to get other economists thinking about it. It wouldn't have happened without someone playing the role of broker of ideas."

Although the *Journal* was synonymous with business, it was not widely read until relatively recently. Founded in 1880 by Charles Dow and Henry Jones (the original Dow Jones), the paper had a circulation in 1941 of only 33,000. By 1980 its circulation was over two million, and about half the subscribers held top management jobs. "The commercial success of the *Wall Street Journal* is important," said Bartley.

"We're so large and pervasive that we can't be ignored."

Bartley's success story was critical to the rise of supply-side economics. As director of the paper's editorial page, he as much as anybody was responsible for injecting the doctrine into the national debate.

Robert Bartley grew up in an Iowa family whose Republicanism seemed as natural as the corn harvest. His father was a veterinarian. Robert received his bachelor's degree from Iowa State, where he was editor-in-chief of the *Iowa State Daily*, and got his master's degree in political science from the University of Wisconsin. He started working for the *Journal* as a reporter in Chicago in 1962. "Then I volunteered to write some book reviews for the editorial page," he said. Vermont Royster, the editor, was impressed with the quality of his prose. He asked Bartley, age twenty-five, if he would like to spend a summer writing editorials. "He said writing an editorial is like writing a book review, except you don't have a book," said Bartley. He became Royster's bright young man.

In 1969, Bartley told his mentor that "I'd like to go to Washington for a while and find out what that's about. He didn't like the idea much. But he made the arrangements for me. Immediately after I got there, in December 1970, I got a note from Royster saying he was going to retire. He got ill." Royster's successor was Joseph Evans, who was in his early fifties. Less than a year after assuming his duties, Evans had a heart attack and died. Warren Phillips, Dow Jones's chairman, called Bartley and offered him the editorial page. "When I was appointed," Bartley said, "Phillips laid down some broad guidelines—free enterprise and individual freedom. Those were the basic marching orders."

In the pre-Bartley era, the *Journal*'s editorial page had been a forum of predictable conservative opinion, publishing mostly free-market economists whose views were already well known. Bartley wanted to shake things up. "The time was coming to make conservatism respectable," he said. "I could see hooking up conservative ideas with erudition to capture some of the intellectual appeal traditionally associated with liberalism, which liberalism lost in the 1960s. In the 1960s, a turbulent time, the world was coming apart at the seams. I was gratified to run across Irving Kristol's magazine [*The Public Interest*]. Here were some people talking sense."

Bartley considered himself a neoconservative, although he didn't fit the strict definition of one who had moved from left to right. Rather, he was shifting his points of reference without altering his position. He did not believe that the older conservatives—the Remnant—could command the intellectual authority of the disillusioned liberals. The neoconservatives knew the arts of discourse Bartley wanted to master. "Unquestionably," he said, "Kristol had a big influence on me. It was possible to be intellectual, erudite, and conservative. The demonstration of that was encouraging. You shouldn't underestimate the *National Review* crowd, but they couldn't have done it. They weren't able to generate the same kind of support and acceptance in the intellectual community as the neoconservatives."

The day after Bartley became the *Journal*'s editor, he attempted to hire as an editorial writer a young right-wing aide to Senator Gordon Allott named George Will. "That didn't work," said Bartley. "He didn't want to move to New York City. Then I put the works into motion to hire Wanniski. Here was someone who thought for himself. He was working for Dow Jones already. Jude's big talent has been to find news. That's what editorials are—the ideology finds the news."

Wanniski joined the *Journal* in February 1972. Soon he became one of Richard Nixon's principal defenders among the press corps during Watergate. "We were running a complicated rearguard action," said Bartley. "I thought they'd get Nixon—but let's make them prove it. Jude got out in front." "I felt it was an obligation," said Wanniski. "I love the idea of defending lost causes. Saint Jude is the defender of lost causes, hopeless cases." But his defense of Nixon earned him the enmity of many of the *Journal*'s reporters, who felt that extremism in the defense of Nixon was a vice.

Wanniski was soon moving on to other issues, becoming the main editorial writer on international economics. "I wound up talking to Laffer every day, to get the line," he said. Laffer was trying to expand upon Mundell's insights. And Wanniski was convinced that they had constructed the framework of an original worldview; he was enthralled. "All of a sudden," said Bartley, "Jude is trying to sell me a policy of enormous tax cuts accompanied by tight money. It seemed crazy. I couldn't understand it. It didn't make any sense. He was all steamed up, so I said, 'Write an article.' It was our story, and we ran with it."

Almost every week, beginning in 1972, Wanniski and Bartley had a ritual dinner with Laffer at the Michael Two restaurant in Hanover Square in the Wall Street area, a custom that lasted until 1979. The assorted players of the supply-side drama would occasionally pull chairs up to the table: Robert Mundell (teaching at Columbia), Irving Kristol, and later, George Gilder. Their discussions were distilled into articles that popularized the ideas.

Bartley paid homage to Kristol by making him a member of the *Journal*'s board of contributors, which meant that he wrote a monthly column. Among other perquisites, he received an invitation to the annual *Journal* Christmas party, which was where he first met Wanniski. They shared two interests. "Irving and I would talk about the [old] Brooklyn Dodgers," said Wanniski. "He was a big fan. Also, he loved Las Vegas. He loves to shoot craps. Once a year he sneaks away to Reno or Vegas."

In mid-November 1974, Kristol telephoned Wanniski and invited him to lunch at the Italian Pavilion, "Irving's favorite joint." Kristol, always orchestrating ideological offensives, had a new project in mind. "Irving spend the lunch attacking the press for its economic ignorance. This had to do with the oil crisis. The press was blaming Exxon and Mobil. Everyone was blaming the oil industry, and business circles were alarmed about the press writing all this radical stuff. In the air was a massive takeover of the industry. Irving asked me to write a piece for *The Public Interest* on the economic ignorance of the press corps. Irving argued that we had to call the press to account. I said journalists reflect, they don't create. The problem we have is not the ignorance of journalists; we have the ignorance of economists. Irving said, 'You want to write that instead?' He wanted *something* to cover the problem, and he wanted ten thousand words in six weeks. So I wrote 'The Mundell-Laffer Hypothesis, A New View of the World Economy.' "

In it Wanniski spelled out, for the first time in print, the framework of supply-side economics. The "hypothesis," he claimed, was nothing less than a "Copernican revolution" in thought. He restated Mundell's policies in italics: *"If the world economy has inflation and unemployment at the same time, the proper policy mix is tight money and fiscal ease.* "[13] Wanniski argued that this doctrine rested finally on a free-market view of human nature, and he believed this was the hypothesis's great strength. He wrote:

> It is so uncommon to hear economists analyze the nation's economic problems . . . in terms of what makes people want to work and produce. It is a distinctly different approach from the monetarist who sees everything as depending on the proper amount of money printed by the Federal Reserve, or from the neo-Keynesian who sees everything as depending on demand management by the government. Both of these "macroscopic" theories are inherently managerial in nature. Mundell and Laffer go back to an older style of economic thought in which the incentives and motivations of the individual producer and consumer and merchant are made the keystone of economic policy.[14]

Before Wanniski submitted his manuscript to Kristol, he gave it to Laffer and Mundell to read. "They didn't know the 'hypothesis' existed before," said Wanniski. Even if there was now a "hypothesis," there was still no "Curve." The essence of the Laffer Curve was explained in a dense footnote, but not labeled as such.

The story of the Laffer Curve's origin has an apocryphal quality. The day after the congressional elections of 1974, in which the Republicans were trounced, Wanniski wandered about Washington, attempting to sell the tax-cut idea to Ford administration officials. He wound up in the office of presidential assistant Donald Rumsfeld. Rumsfeld remembered Laffer—"brilliant," he said—and he asked Wanniski to get Laffer together with his top aide, Richard Cheney. They met in December 1974 at the Two Continents restaurant for drinks. Cheney couldn't really comprehend the earthshaking message. So, according to Wanniski, Laffer drew a bell-shaped curve on a cocktail napkin, which explained how cutting taxes would actually increase government revenues because of increased production. "I don't remember explicitly drawing that curve," said Laffer. "But it sounds great." Who knows? Perhaps it was Wanniski who invented the Curve just as he constructed the hypothesis. Certainly he was the chief promoter of both. These two elements were essential for the cause. "The Curve as a pedagogical device was immense," said Wanniski. "It saved us years. You could, in drawing the Curve, persuade someone."

The Curve, however, did not have the power to lend the hypothesis respectability among economists. A case for it would have to be made by someone within the profession who was not an enthusiast. Then the doctrine would have the stamp of official approval; it would not be dismissed as an aberration. In May 1975, Wanniski attended a conference sponsored by the First National Bank of Chicago devoted to "What's Wrong With the World Economy," where Mundell gave his by-now-patented presentation. Wanniski was seated between a banker, Paul Volcker (later to become chairman of the Federal Reserve), and an influential economist, Marina von Whitman. This seating arrangement was, according to Wanniski, "the most important thing" about the conference; for he spoke to von Whitman about the hypothesis. Soon she produced a paper touching on it, published by the Brookings Institution. "These views," she wrote, "pose a direct challenge to the current orthodoxy."[15] But she criticized the new approach for consigning "to irrelevance the problems of economic stabilization with which most policy-makers are primarily concerned. . . ."[16] "That piece gave our ideas credibility. She had sufficient standing to elevate it," said Wanniski.

Still, no political figure of stature had hitched his wagon to the Curve. Wanniski the salesman was relentlessly scouting the market. He would draw the Curve for any politician he could corner, even Senator Walter Mondale. "I wondered if I'd ever find a politician who would take us seriously," he lamented. Then, both Bartley and Kristol told Wanniski that he must meet Jack Kemp, the former professional quarterback turned congressman. "I always imagined Kemp was a 'Vinegar Bend' Mizell type, first and foremost an athlete," said Wanniski. "But Irving and Bartley told me that there's more to Jack Kemp than meets the eye."

Jack Kemp grew up in southern California, where his father and uncle owned a thriving package-delivery service. Kemp attributed the success of his family's enterprise to "diligent effort and a good idea." It was a "story of people, not of systems."[17] He did not go into the family trade. Instead he became a quarterback for the Buffalo Bills. When his football career ended he was a local celebrity without a profession; he decided to capitalize on his fame and enter politics. His previous experience consisted of a summer internship on the staff of Governor Ronald Reagan. In 1970, Kemp was elected to Congress from a Buffalo, New York, district suffering a protracted economic decline.

He was a rather rigid Republican, a new face with old ideas. "I came in as a balance-the-budget, root-canal, austere Republican," he said. "Then I looked around and realized that my career was going to be ended very quickly if I couldn't come up with something more hopeful. There were too many people unemployed; there were too many blacks that didn't have jobs; there were too many young people moving out of the city and out of the state. And I had won by 51 percent."

He began to study the question of capital formation, which led him to the question of taxes, and that led him to the history of President Kennedy's fiscal policies. Kennedy was Kemp's personal hero because, among other reasons, they shared the evocative initials "JFK." "Kennedy," said Kemp, "was the last President to have a vision of the nation that wasn't zero-sum."

Kemp's staff economist, Paul Craig Roberts, joined with conservative economist Norman Ture to craft what they called the Jobs Creation Act. (Both would later become assistant secretaries of the treasury.) It was not a true supply-side measure, but a bill intended to grant corporations tax breaks to stimulate investment.

One day in early 1976, Wanniski was roaming the marble halls of the Longworth House Office Building, gathering material for a story on Representative Wayne Hays, a tyrant of vast pettiness, who was being disgraced for having maintained on his payroll Elizabeth Ray, a glamorous secretary who could not type. Wanniski was to interview the congressman leading the charge against Hay's malfeasance, Robert Baumann (a conservative moralist who later admitted to alcoholism and homosexual tendencies). Wanniski noticed that he was marching right by Jack Kemp's office. He had fifteen minutes to spare, so he walked in and handed his card to the receptionist. "Kemp came dashing out," said Wanniski. He had been closely reading and clipping Wanniski's columns, and he believed that his own Jobs Creation Act was partly inspired by the *Journal*'s new emphasis on tax cuts. "He showed me all my writing," said Wanniski. "And he asked how come it's taken me so long to get there." All too quickly, Wanniski's fifteen minutes passed. Wanniski had to see Baumann, but he canceled the rest of his day's appointments and returned to Kemp's office, where they talked and talked. Kemp brought him home to dinner and kept him talking late into the night. "We talked about the model," said Wanniski. "He took to it like a blotter. I was exhausted and ecstatic. I had finally found an elected representative of the people who was as fanatical as I was. Kemp would grab people by the lapels."

The congressman soon scrapped his Jobs Creation Act and replaced it with one that would mandate a 30-percent, across-the-board personal income tax cut over three years. This measure, co-sponsored by Senator William Roth, became known as the Kemp-Roth Bill, the Laffer Curve in action.

Kemp wasn't ponderous in handling ideas; he didn't fumble. "What people don't appreciate about Kemp is that he's smart," said Bartley. "He has gushes of enthusiasm. That has advantages for a politician, but it obscures that he's smart."

Wanniski and Kemp became fast friends. The journalist offered the politician a way to make a national reputation and secure reelection, while Kemp offered Wanniski a way to move his ideas into politics. "Jude was Kemp's contact" within the small group of supply-siders, according to Laffer. "Jude talked to him every day. Jude lived on Kemp's doorstep."

Kemp's new associates rescued him from anonymity and the New Right. "Irving Kristol had much to do with moderating my conservatism," he said. "And that's why I never fell into the New Right. Irving shaped my consciousness to recognize the necessity of the welfare system, or the safety net. It is absolutely incumbent upon a society to organize itself collectively and share whatever is necessary to make sure that people survive." Instead of yielding to the temptation to build his career on the social issues—abortion, busing, lapsed morality—he devoted himself to the economic issues. "I think, basically, that people vote on a higher plane than just against something. There are many, many wonderful people on the New Right, but unfortunately, in certain instances, it's coming to an element of fear. Fear. Resentment. I would rather have a campaign that is not based on a negative."

Kemp was pure optimism. He insisted that liberal policies, by contrast, were based upon a "zero-sum proposition": "It's 'dog eat dog' in a contracting economy."[18] Against zero-sum liberalism he called for a "rising tide" of prosperity that he promised would "lift all boats," a phrase lifted from John F. Kennedy. The American character, Kemp believed, was enduring. He had seen its wondrous workings, how virtue was manifested in his own family's enterprise. Only big government obstructed the free market from operating as it should, which confounded American values. The new conservative themes came naturally to Kemp. His philosophy also rested upon an interpretation of dreams. In his book *An American Renaissance* (whose title itself expressed the restoration myth), Kemp wrote:

> Opportunity, the chance to make it and to improve your life, that's what the American Dream was and is all about. What poisons that dream is when government stands in the way, throwing up roadblocks that are really unnecessary.[19]

Like Reagan, Kemp was explicit about the conservative ideology. More than any other political figure of the younger generation, Kemp was on his wavelength. Sometimes in large meetings during the early Reagan presidency, those present would suddenly become aware that Reagan and Kemp were conducting what seemed to be a private conversation. Their remarks in the group were directed only to each other; they spoke almost in code. They shared a common spirit of good-natured camaraderie, which contributed to their ideological rapport. Kemp, the former football player, could keep up a constant locker-room chatter, while Reagan (the college football player who felt he had a calling to play George Gipp in the movies) reveled in old stories. If they were not father and son, they were an uncle and his favorite nephew. The older man, however, had arrived at his philosophy through harsh experience: he was once a liberal, but became bitterly disillusioned. Kemp's philosophy was his birthright: among other things, he was a native Californian, not someone remaking himself on a new frontier. His family was Republican and entrepreneurial, not Democratic and working-class. Kemp never switched sides; he underwent no personal crisis in which he saw the world turned upside down. He came to conservatism the easy way. Yet his precarious political position, representing a northeastern congressional district, made him receptive to some new ideas. He had Reagan's certitude, but he was still searching for self-definition. Thus he was open to the neoconservative "Godfather" and the supply-side innovator.

"We were," Wanniski said, "ammunition in search of a weapon." Senator Paul Laxalt, one of Reagan's closest friends, whom Wanniski had known from his Nevada days, told him: "If you have Kemp you have a weapon."

The same year that Kemp was recruited to the cause, the movement received its indelible name. Herbert Stein, a traditional conservative economist and former chairman of Nixon's Council of Economic Advisers, gave a speech mocking those who embraced the deviant new strain of economic thought as "supply-side fiscalists." He meant the label to be uncomplimentary, but Wanniski, always keen for clever rhetoric and publicity, appropriated the derisive term for his own purpose. He dropped "fiscalists" and kept "supply-side," trumpeting the new name in an article in the *Journal*. Stein's mischief, in Wanniski's hands, turned into a favor.

Thus, having framed the hypothesis, popularized the Curve, helped catalyze the transformation of the *Wall Street Journal*'s editorial pages, inducted Kemp into the inner circle, and seized upon a name for the cause, Wanniski looked forward with anticipation to the 1976 presidential election.

In the spring of 1976 he had a three-hour lunch in Washington at Duke Zeibert's (a popular power-lunch restaurant frequented by politicos, lobbyists, and journalists), with John Sears, Reagan's campaign manager. Sears often appears meticulously impassive, although his mind is constantly ticking. He is a consummate strategist, seeking the key to open doors. As a young lawyer he worked in John Mitchell's firm, aiding senior partner Richard Nixon in his 1968 campaign. Sears's political specialty was the Northeast—he was a New Yorker—and he had helped unlock crucial Northeastern delegates at the Republican convention for Nixon. But Nixon's palace guard, H. R. Haldeman and John Ehrlichman, shut Sears out of White House decision-making. Now he was looking to get support in the Northeast for Reagan, whose cowboy image seemed indigenous to a far coast.

Wanniski explained to Sears the idea of "bracket creep"—how inflation pushed people into higher tax brackets without necessarily raising their real incomes. Inflation benefited government, which gained increased revenues and was therefore able to avoid deficits while paying for expensive social programs. "There was no argument that the tax burden was killing the goose that laid the golden egg," said Sears. ("Sears was fascinated," said Wanniski.) But the Reagan campaign did not adopt the notion as a major issue, although Reagan did mention "bracket creep" in a television speech during the North Carolina primary, where he won a surprise victory. Yet Reagan didn't repeat the thought. Instead, he harped on the Panama Canal Treaty, an old favorite.

Before the Republican convention commenced in Kansas City, it seemed apparent to most informed observers that Gerald Ford had clinched the nomination. Then, in a breathtaking move, Reagan announced his choice for the vice-presidency, Senator Richard Schweiker, a "moderate" from Pennsylvania, to forestall the inevitable. The ploy was Sears's attempt to keep the convention open and win votes from Northeastern delegations, where Ford appeared solid.

Wanniski came to Kansas City as a journalist, but he was more participant than observer. Kemp, who was scheduled to give a convention speech, showed a copy to Wanniski. It was turgid and uninspiring, quoting Ludwig von Mises, an Austro-liberal free-marketer, author of numerous recondite volumes and a complete blank to the average Republican delegate. "I told Jack to tear it up," said Wanniski. He took out his portable typewriter and wrote Kemp a new speech about how "it's time to go off defense and go on offense." Touchdown time.

Ford was trying desperately to secure his nomination, Reagan was desperate to stop him, and Wanniski was trying to thrust himself into the thick of the maneuverings. Kemp arrived on the scene uncommitted, an advantageous position since both camps felt compelled to woo him. "I really liked Reagan, but Ford was the incumbent," said Kemp. "I felt strongly the nomination was going to go to him. I thought Ford deserved the nomination." So he stayed above the fray. But Wanniski, on his own initiative, began wheeling and dealing with the Reagan team. He proposed a deal, his version of a Schweicker gambit: if the candidate would endorse supply-side economics, Kemp would publicly throw his support to Reagan and try to persuade northeastern delegates to support him. "I was the intermediary," said Wanniski. "It was a secret. It wasn't the correct thing for a working journalist. But the overriding thing was the problem of the world economy."

Wanniski approached Sears, who was not opposed to the deal but insisted that it first be approved by Martin Anderson, campaign chief of research. "I don't recall the exact quid pro quo," said Sears. "But I do recall that Marty was supposed to pass judgment on what degree we were to commit ourselves to tax cuts." Wanniski claimed that Anderson turned the deal down, but Anderson said flatly, "There was no deal presented to me. Jude may have talked to John Sears during the convention but I don't remember talking to him." Wanniski then beseeched Paul Laxalt and Edwin Meese—to no avail. "Meese gave me a blank stare," said Wanniski. The deal was dead.

Wanniski was certain that Kemp's support would have made Reagan the Republican standard-bearer. "It was my view," he said, "that it [the convention] would have turned around and he would have got the nomination." Kemp offered another opinion. "I knew Jude was talking to Sears," he said. "I was skeptical of Jude's move. He did it on his own. Wanniski couldn't deal me and I couldn't deal the northeastern delegates."

(In 1977, Arthur Laffer met Ronald Reagan at a dinner. Laffer, briefed by Wanniski on his behind-the-scenes politicking, brought up Reagan's purported refusal to support supply-side economics to win Kemp's support. "Gee," said Laffer, "it seems awful funny that you'd do that." "I never did that," Reagan replied. "I supported it!" Laffer was conveying the gist of a story that wasn't quite true, and Reagan earnestly claimed something he had not done. Since there had been no deal to begin with, there was nothing for him to support or reject. Thus, in the early history of supply-side economics, the distinction between fact and fable was already blurred.)

Shortly after the Kansas City convention, Wanniski flew to Atlanta to meet with the entourage of Jimmy Carter, the Democratic nominee. He thought he might as well try to win acceptance of supply-side economics in this camp. He met briefly with Hamilton Jordan, and he spent some time with members of the staff of Stuart Eizenstat, Carter's issues director. "I gave them the whole background on Ford and Reagan," said Wanniski. "I told them I thought Carter was on the right track until he got into the redistribution guise. That's where the Eastern Establishment and the AFL-CIO made peace with him." Just before Wanniski put in his Atlanta appearance, he had written a *Journal* editorial entitled "Jimmy Robin Hood," praising Carter for his critical view of the tax system, but attacking him for his attachment to "the same old liberal tax-the-rich ideas." "The Carter people responded very positively," according to Wanniski. "But Eizenstat wasn't there. Then the problem in the last six weeks of the campaign was that Carter was losing ground. The more his lead dissipated, the more his advisers told him to get the rich. Ford had an equally stupid campaign. It was the old guard versus the old guard."

Wanniski didn't feel defeated, though. "Within hours after Carter's election, we're talking about how to gear up for 1980," he said. "How do we get Jack to run for President? And I decided to write my book."

Wanniski knew exactly what kind of book he would produce—*The General Theory* of its time, demolishing the postulates of Keynesianism and establishing supply-side economics as the ascendant doctrine. But he didn't know how he would find the time or the money to write this seminal work. He couldn't take a leave of absence from his duties at the *Journal* unless he had other means of support. He went to Irving Kristol.

Kristol had recently made the acquaintance of Randolph Richardson, heir to the Vicks VapoRub fortune, whose family charity, the Smith-Richardson Foundation (created in 1935), had given funds in the past to the Boy Scouts. In the 1950s the foundation subsidized some foreign-policy studies, including the work of a then-unknown Harvard professor named Henry Kissinger. In 1973, Richardson gained control of the foundation. A North Carolinian living in Manhattan, he had gotten the idea that the foundation ought to "defend" free-market capitalism. His friendship with Kristol was cemented when the foundation began the defense by picking up the annual debt of Kristol's journal, *The Public Interest.* And when Richardson scouted for a new chief program officer, someone who would dispense the yearly grant budget of about $3 million with maximum effect, Kristol suggested a candidate. On Christmas Day 1975, Leslie Lenkowsky was interviewed by Richardson and offered the job.

Lenkowsky was a graduate student at Harvard during the late 1960s and early 1970s. Professor Daniel Patrick Moynihan was his principal adviser, and he also studied with Nathan Glazer. (Lenkowsky got to know another Harvard graduate student who was Moynihan's live-in babysitter, David Stockman. "He was just like he is now, a zealot with a cold eye," said Lenkowsky.) He studied welfare systems in the United States and Britain under Moynihan's tutelage. In 1975 he was named assistant to Pennsylvania's welfare director, becoming part of a new reform team that was supposed to redesign the entire program. Governor Milton Shapp, who had given the team its mandate, however, was sprinting vainly around the country, running for president. Reform took a back seat to ambition. Thus Lenkowsky came to his job at the Smith-Richardson Foundation as a young neoconservative, trained by neoconservatives, disillusioned by liberal policies and politicians, and recommended by Kristol.

The first major project that crossed Lenkowsky's desk was Jude Wanniski's book. It had been preceded by a letter of recommendation from Kristol in which he described Wanniski as "pregnant." Wanniski's proposal was entitled *The Modern Political Economy.* He wrote:

My first thought months ago was to write a modern translation of Adam Smith's *Wealth of Nations.* But as worthy a project as that may be, I quickly realized that it could only have ephemeral interest, a whimsical curiosity. What I intend instead is a book of such provocation, logic and lucidity that opinion leaders will be provoked to read it and learn in spite of themselves. . . . I want nothing less than to change the world.

Lenkowsky didn't know what to make of this. He was self-conscious about his inexperience as a philanthropoid, and he didn't want to make a terrible mistake with his very first grant. "Here's this wildman," said Lenkowsky. "The general thesis was plausible. The only question was how to do it as a project, get peer reviews that assessed it adequately. What do you say to your trustees? It was a hot potato because it was so wild."

Lenkowsky decided to run the idea by his trustees. (By this time, Wanniski had abandoned the sweeping title and replaced it with an even more sweeping one: *The Way the World Works.* This title was suggested by Wanniski's daughter, who had explained to a neighbor that her father was writing a book "on the way the world works." Lenkowsky presented the project to one North Carolinian trustee, who replied that it reminded him of a local eccentric who used to stand outside a drugstore in Greensboro and explain the way the world works. Was Wanniski just the town crank?

Lenkowsky wanted to fund him, but he couldn't figure out the precise mechanism that would win everyone's assent. He sought the counsel of Hoover Institution scholar Martin Anderson, who Wanniski believed had undermined the "deal" at the Republican convention.* Anderson was paid a consulting fee of one hundred dollars to review the proposal. "I said it was risky to support," said Anderson. "While Jude was a good writer, he had no training in economics. But neither did Adam Smith. I said Jude would benefit from an environment in which he could bounce his ideas off people."

Lenkowsky promptly telephoned William Baroody, Sr., president of the American Enterprise Institute. "How would you like to have a

---

*Anderson was a follower of Ayn Rand, author of *The Fountainhead,* a popular novel extolling unfettered individualism, and *The Virtue of Selfishness,* a tract whose title neatly summarized the Randian view. Anderson belonged to the initial sect of Randians that met at Rand's apartment for instruction and discussion. Another member of this circle was Alan Greenspan, President Ford's chief economist, who would later play a key role in the development of Reagan's policies.

resident journalist program, and we'd fund it?" he asked. "A journalist would spend a year at AEI and produce a book. It's mutually beneficial. The reason I ask is that I've got this project that needs a home." Wanniski, as it turned out, was no stranger to Baroody, whose son, William junior, and Wanniski were "buddies," according to Wanniski; they had lunch once a month during his Washington days. And Kristol, AEI's leading neoconservative, put in a good word for Wanniski, too. "Baroody just wanted to make it happen," said Wanniski.

He promptly went through AEI's formal procedure. He submitted his proposal, which was reviewed by the academic screening committee, chaired by Paul McCracken, former chairman of Nixon's Council of Economic Advisers. Wanniski's personal interview with McCracken and Baroody took place over a breakfast of bacon and eggs at Washington's Madison Hotel. Wanniski made his case, and McCracken told him that although he disagreed with the position he considered it respectable; he was curious to see the evidence that would prove the veracity of the Curve. The request was approved: Wanniski would become AEI's first resident journalist. On January 1, 1977, he was off to spend a year there writing his book.

Lenkowsky, in the meantime, had profited from the experience. "In the process I learned how to run a foundation and that this was a fruitful area to do some funding," he said. He decided to use a substantial portion of his $3-million-a-year budget to promote supply-side economics. Smith-Richardson was responsible for funding what Lenkowsky called the supply-side "trilogy": Wanniski's *The Way the World Works,* George Gilder's *Wealth and Poverty,* and Michael Novak's *The Spirit of Democratic Capitalism.* "Wanniski talks about taxes, Gilder talks about taxes and faith, and Novak talks about faith," said Lenkowsky. He also gave a grant to Harvard professor Martin Feldstein for research into the Social Security system. (Feldstein was later appointed chairman of the Council of Economic Advisers by President Reagan.) James Ring Adams, *Wall Street Journal* editorial writer, was funded to write a supply-side book on state and municipal finances. And specific projects at AEI and the Heritage Foundation received large grants.

To Lenkowsky, supply-side economics was part of a broader ideological strategy. "Supply-side economics is less an economic theory than a philosophy, an ideology," he said. "It's an effort to reorient policy. Foundations are not involved in politics directly. We're in the world of ideas. The kind of infrastructure we create is a network of people who know there is a place to go for funding and contacts. Primarily it's an educational process. That's what the infrastructure is all about. That's where the lasting changes come." But Lenkowsky discovered that it was not easy to find the thinkers he wanted to cultivate. "What I've learned," he said, "is that ideas are always scarcer than money, and talent is always scarcer than ideas. We're a huge talent search."

In 1983, Lenkowsky was appointed deputy director of the U.S. Information Agency, where he intended to wage the "war of ideas" in the international arena. He took office before he was confirmed by the Senate, and according to several high-ranking USIA officials, he maintained a systematic log of liberals to be blacklisted as government-sponsored speakers abroad. Lenkowsky denied the charge. But his testimony at his confirmation hearing before the Senate foreign relations committee was disastrous. "I am prepared to stand by what I meant to say," he said. Several key senators were led to disbelieve Lenkowsky because of his seemingly contradictory testimony.

"They were baiting me," he remarked. "There was no doubt what I was saying." Of the blacklist, he said: "I did not compile a blacklist. It existed two years before I got there." Later he commented, "I did participate in a review process. I had no idea it was a blacklist."

On May 15, 1984, his nomination was rejected. He retreated for a while into the recesses of AEI. Then, in 1985, he was appointed director of the Institute for Educational Affairs, a Counter-Establishment foundation he had helped create a few years earlier.

During Wanniski's sojourn at AEI, he was joined by Kristol. "Irving caused me difficulty," said Wanniski. "He wanted to talk me out of my first few chapters, which were about my political model. But this was pure Wanniski. I took the Mundell-Laffer model and grafted it onto my political model. Irving said it was probably wrong. He said my economic theory was so innovative, so radical, that there was no reason to have it carry the extra burden of the political model. I thought Irving was right." Wanniski was depressed and confused; he felt that his work was being blocked. "Then," he said, "I thought that if my political model was wrong, my economic model was wrong." And since he never believed that his economic model was in error, it followed that his political model must be correct, too. Although Kristol and Wanniski were both attracted to supply-side economics, their political philosophies were sharply divergent. Kristol had a deep suspicion of modern democracy and what he felt to be its excesses. He was a follower of the philosopher Leo Strauss, who urged a retreat to premodern thinkers. Wanniski, on the other hand, had no fear of the masses and no belief that democracy had any dark impulses. He wedded supply-side economics to the populist idea that the people were never wrong. Therefore, let them make the marketplace decisions: tax cuts must be universal, across the board, and not merely for vested interests. Elections, Wanniski wrote, "always turn out right . . . given the choices."[20] He added, "The welfare of a nation state . . . is limited by the capacity of politicians and philosophers to understand the wisdom of people."[21] His was a democratic faith, more consonant with the American tradition than Kristol's. And in his extravagant optimism, Wanniski was at one with Kemp and Reagan.

Wanniski wanted to be the herald of a golden age, not a stern preacher of sacrifice. In *The Way the World Works,* he argued that "empires and golden ages have been built on one end of the Curve; when political leadership fails, it crushes empires and produces the friction of war against the other end of the Curve."[22] All great historical events were laid by Wanniski along the Curve, for it could explain them. He even attributed the fall of Saigon to its tax rate. With the Curve as an instrument of guidance, the Vietnam calamity might have been avoided.

Wanniski's rhapsody on incentives included a funereal motif—the "wedge," or government-created obstacles to production. The "wedge" consisted mainly of taxation, although Wanniski mentioned population in passing. The tax rate was the source of global crises; hence the supreme importance of tax cuts.

The Way the World Works concluded with a discussion of the state of the Republican Party. Wanniski wrote:

> The Republican Party is now in dismal condition. But if there is to be a Pax Americana during the next century, its foundation will rest on a Republican renaissance. The solutions to domestic and global economic problems now require primary commitments to income growth, not redistribution, and the GOP will always win a competition with the Democrats over which is more passionate over growth. The decline and fall of the GOP since 1930 resulted not from its lack of passion, but from its failure to understand the nature of the Laffer Curve.[23]

Yet there was hope on the horizon. Kemp's tax-cutting measure was "adopted formally by the Republican National Committee in New Orleans, Louisiana, on September 30, 1977. This was the necessary first step toward a renaissance of the GOP."[24]

In 1978, tax cuts became a red-hot national issue after a convulsive tax revolt broke out in California. This was no peasant uprising, but an almost spontaneous social movement of the middle class, whose inflated housing prices pushed their property taxes ever higher, until it appeared to many that government was expropriating their homes. Howard Jarvis, a feisty and eccentric seventy-five-year-old director of a landlords' association, emerged as the revolt's leader. From the failure of a previous effort, he had learned many lessons in staging a successful tax revolt. In 1973, former aides to Governor Reagan had put on the ballot a state constitutional amendment known as Proposition 1, which would reduce the size of government. Prop 1 was 5,700 words long and contained so many technicalities that Reagan himself publicly admitted he didn't understand it. So it was defeated. Jarvis framed his Proposition 13, which would require immediate tax cutting in direct language. On June 6, 1978, voters approved it overwhelmingly, 65 to 35 percent.

John Sears, shrewd and calculating, believed that taxes had enormous potential as an issue, but he wasn't certain how far it would carry.

Could Ronald Reagan use it in a presidential campaign? Or was the tax revolt an ephemeral, local event of the sort that California seemed to produce with frequency? "It was interesting to see to what degree voters could be aroused over high taxes," Sears said. Jeffrey Bell's primary campaign in New Jersey against incumbent Senator Clifford Case, a "moderate" Republican, offered a test case. Bell had been a political aide to Reagan, and he had become a fervent supply-sider. (He had sought out Wanniski and brought him to his office. The journalist was astonished. "It was a Wanniski shrine," he said. Bell had assiduously clipped his columns from the *Journal* and decorated the walls with them: supply-side wallpaper. He and Wanniski became close friends.) Although Bell had been one of Reagan's staffers, Reagan declared his neutrality in the New Jersey contest. He had proclaimed early in his political career an "Eleventh Commandment"—"Thou shalt speak no ill of another Republican"—an excellent device for deflecting criticism by others of himself. But he had to adhere to it to make it credible. Sears, however, was quietly advising Bell. He said he did so as a "friend," adding, "Jeffrey was strongly drawing on that [tax] issue." Wanniski observed, "The important thing in Jeff's race was that Sears watched it closely. No one knew that he was advising Jeff. He was impressed with the economic issue." When Bell, who campaigned heavily on supply-side themes, upset Case, it seemed apparent that the doctrine was not a purely theoretical construct; it had practical political uses.

To Sears, supply-side economics was an attractive way of approaching the 1980 campaign. "One thing that was wrong with all sides was that no one had any new handle, aside from the difference of opinion on who should pay the sacrifice," he said. "This was a new idea in terms of handling the nation's economy. It addressed itself to a matter on the minds of the public. It was worth investigating and moving towards."

Wanniski felt increasingly restless. He was finding it harder to maintain the balance between the detachment of the journalist and the commitment of the politico. It was a tension he couldn't maintain for long, and probably didn't want to. "When Jude came back to the paper after writing his book, he really wanted to leave," said Bartley. "I kept trying to persuade him not to. But he kept getting more involved with

Kemp and getting more political. I tried to get Jude to pull back. But then he got involved with Jeff Bell in the New Jersey race." One day Wanniski joined Bell and some of his volunteers passing out leaflets at a commuter train station. Among those handed the literature was Raymond Shaw, president of Dow Jones, who was not delighted to see his editorial writer in a partisan pose. "Jude," Bartley implored Wanniski, "you said you wouldn't do this." The next day he resigned. "The real story," Bartley claimed, "was that he wanted to leave and this was his way of getting my consent." (The *Journal* kept up the drumbeat for supply-side economics. Bartley hired Kemp's staff economist, Paul Craig Roberts, to replace Wanniski on the editorial board.) Wanniski promptly joined Arthur Laffer in an economic consulting business. He also began plotting a presidential campaign for Jack Kemp.

In January 1979, Wanniski convened a meeting of what he called "the Cabal" in a Washington hotel suite at One Washington Circle. (Among those present was supply-side novice David Stockman.) Irving Kristol urged Kemp to run. Wanniski and Bell were enthusiastic for a race, too. Bell argued that the other Republicans were running on "old guard" themes. Kemp would stand out. And Bell claimed that all he needed in the New Hampshire primary to win in a crowded field was 30 percent. "Kemp," according to Wanniski, "was noncommittal, but he sounded positive." Wanniski and Bell appointed themselves cochairmen of an unofficial exploratory committee.

That month they flew to Miami to attend the festivities surrounding the Super Bowl. Jack Kemp, the former gridiron star, annually uses this climactic sporting event to mobilize his national fund-raising base; his biggest contributors congregate in the city where the Super Bowl is being held, and throw him a party that lasts several days. "We came to convince his power base," said Wanniski. In the sportive atmosphere, they lobbied the money-men. "We got general enthusiasm," said Wanniski. "We converted some of the pessimists." On the morning of the big game, Wanniski and Bell left Miami. By late May they were conducting negotiations with pollsters, professional fund-raisers, and media consultants about working on a Kemp-for-President campaign. "Kemp said that if we could sign up these consultants, it's doable," said Wanniski. Kemp, however, insisted that he never encouraged Wanniski's effort. He believed that Wanniski was engaged in "a process of dialectical politics, not presidential politics." He was campaigning for an ideology.

One charter supply-sider who was never on this particular bandwagon was Arthur Laffer. He had become an authentic Southern Californian, living in the Santa Barbara suburbs in a large home with extensive grounds, where his children's exotic pets, including weasels and peacocks, roamed in a peaceable kingdom. The Reagans lived a freeway drive away in Pacific Palisades. Laffer, in fact, had become a junior member of Reagan's "Kitchen Cabinet." Justin Dart, the irascible entrepreneur and Reagan friend, established an especially close relationship with Laffer. Dart even set up the Center for the Study of Private Enterprise at the University of Southern California (where Laffer was a professor), and then had Laffer named director—a capsule Counter-Establishment institution. "Laffer's mentor is Justin Dart," said Wanniski. "He just loves Laffer. Justin has been to Art what Irving has been to me." Laffer mingled socially with Reagan's "Millionaire Backers," and occasionally he had Ronald and Nancy over to his house for dinner. (During one of these evenings, Laffer's daughter, without warning, tossed a squirming weasel into Nancy's lap.) "They're neat people, if you've ever been to a dinner with the Kitchen Cabinet," said Laffer. "I had a lot of 'ins' in that group." His link to Reagan dated as far back as 1966, when he contributed to the governor's first economic report. And when Reagan visited Washington during the early 1970s, Laffer was invited to meet with him. He was always the well-connected Reaganite.

John Sears, whose sensitive antennae picked up signals of the nascent Kemp effort, tried subtly to stymie it. "The conventional wisdom in 1976 was that Ronald Reagan was too far to the right to be nominated," said Bartley. "Between then and 1980 the ideological climate had changed. The fact that conservatism gained intellectual respectability no doubt helped Reagan." But he might be threatened by Kemp, whose candidacy would implicitly underline the age issue—Reagan, if elected, would be the oldest president in history—which was then felt to be significant. Kemp was a young Reagan; he might eclipse the older man with his vigor. In 1978, Sears attempted to persuade Kemp to run for governor of New York. He believed his advice was in the best interests of both Kemp and Reagan. "I felt it might be a good time to try it," said Sears. "I told Kemp I did not feel that as long as Reagan was going to run for President he should do that. My advice was in the cast of what was good for him."

Early in the summer of 1979, Laffer threw a fancy dinner party for the Kitchen Cabinet. The Reagans and the Kemps were also invited. "All through this time period," said Wanniski, "Sears is getting reports and trying to talk Jack out of running. Sears never figured Reagan could be defeated by anybody except Jack Kemp. So Sears arranges that the Reagans have lunch with the Kemps on the day they are supposed to have dinner." The lunch lasted two and a half hours. Kemp asked many questions about Reagan's commitment to supply-side economics. "I was very pleased with where he was," Kemp said.

That evening, at Laffer's, their discussion continued. Laffer recalled, "Kemp said that he was going to run. He and Reagan would get more delegates than Reagan alone. If push came to shove, Kemp would then turn his delegates over to Reagan." Reagan gently asked Kemp to stroll with him down to the guest house in Laffer's garden to speak privately. When they returned, Kemp announced that he would support Reagan. Laffer remembered Kemp as being "very excited and pleased with the outcome of the evening." Kemp, however, recalled the evening as purely "social." He claimed he had already made up his mind to support Reagan.

Back in Washington, Kemp broke the news to Wanniski and Bell. "We go berserk," said Wanniski. "We say Kemp's been outfoxed by Sears. Jack says that Reagan is for 85 percent of the ideas. Why were we against Reagan? I said that now that you've told him you won't run against him, he'll be 75 percent and then 50 percent and then 5 percent." Two weeks later, Reagan told a group of Oklahoma farmers that he favored restricting beef imports, a free-trade heresy. Wanniski pointed out this slippage to Kemp. "Jack got all upset," he said. "Sears was no longer talking to him as much. Jack let it be known that his offer to support Reagan was no longer operative because Reagan's staff made it public. He gave us the green light again. [Kemp denies this.] There were calls from Reagan and calls from Sears. Sears came to Jack's office, where Jack was promised to be made chief campaign spokesman to replace Laxalt. They made a deal. Jack would be a spokesman and supply-side themes would be employed. As soon as Laxalt heard about it, being a spokesman became meaningless." But Kemp's endorsement gave supply-side economics an advocate inside the campaign who was regarded by Reagan's aides as a weighty political figure.

"I didn't trust the Reagan group," said Wanniski. "I thought we'd lose another four years. Then I began to see that things were beginning to come together. I was more in communication with Martin Anderson's policy shop."

Reagan himself was becoming an open supply-sider. Sears insisted that he had to be coaxed. "On the matter of cutting taxes to put more money in the private sector, Reagan had no trouble in the early stages," Sears said. "The notion of how it related to budget deficits took longer. He had preached the Republican religion that deficits are bad. There was a ring of inconsistency." Laffer, however, believed that Reagan was a supply-sider from the start. "There was no conversion that I know of," he said. "Reagan believed those things long before I was born. A fair day's work for a fair day's pay—that's basically supply-side economics. Reagan is really into the issues." Kemp agreed: "He was a supply-sider before it was called supply-side. It's instinctive."

At the January 1980 briefing of the candidate, all of Wanniski's doubts were swept away. "We were absolutely thrilled," he said. "We saw that Reagan vibrated with all our arguments. Reagan not only favored the policies but understood them. For a brief period, we were giddy with joy, thinking we had it all."

The campaign, however, was wracked by internal turmoil. One after another, as in a version of Agatha Christie's *And Then There Were None,* Reagan's closest advisers from California were forced out by Sears. When Sears was about to move against Edwin Meese, Reagan fired him on the day of the New Hampshire primary. The candidate coasted to victory, winning the Republican nomination, employing Sears's strategy without Sears. It relied heavily on supply-side themes, expressed straightforwardly in two television commercials aired in primary after primary.

Announcer: Ronald Reagan believes that when you tax something, you get less of it. We're taxing work, savings, and investment like never before. As a result, we have less work, less savings, and less invested.

Reagan: I didn't always agree with President Kennedy. But when his 30-percent federal tax cut became law, the economy did so well that every group in the country came out ahead. Even the government raised $54 billion in unexpected revenues. If I become President, we're going to try that again.

In short advertisements, unadorned by any image other than Reagan speaking directly into the camera, liberal policies were criticized and the supply-side alternative was proposed and defended as having worked before. These spots, according to Reagan's polls, were crucial in winning voters' support, even as George Bush, a rival for the presidential nomination, was attacking supply-side policies as "voodoo economics."

"There's falling demand for demand-side economics and rising demand for supply-side economics," proclaimed Jack Kemp in the early fall of 1980. "The liberal Democratic left was the thesis. The Republican Party was the antithesis. Now the Democrats are the party of the antithesis. We are the thesis. We're on offense, they're on defense."

Even before Reagan's inauguration, a celebration of supply-side economics began. Capturing the zeitgeist at perfect pitch and at the perfect moment was George Gilder's *Wealth and Poverty,* a panegyric resonating with religious organ notes. The book was a pure Counter-Establishment product, and Gilder had an ideal history to prepare him for the composition of the movement's hymnal. His emergence as a supply-side celebrity was itself evidence of a political shift, the demise of Republicanism and the rise of conservatism.

George Gilder, a Harvard graduate, junior fellow with the Council on Foreign Relations, was one of Nelson Rockefeller's bright young men, serving as a speechwriter. A young leader of the Establishment, Gilder became a leading figure in the Counter-Establishment. By 1980 he wasn't writing speeches anymore for "modern Republicans." At the request of William Casey, Reagan's campaign manager, who would become CIA director, Gilder wrote a draft of Reagan's acceptance speech at the Republican convention.

Gilder's relationship with the Rockefellers was more intimate than that of a campaign operative. When Gilder's father, who had been David Rockefeller's roommate at Harvard, was killed during World War II, David assumed some responsibility in raising George; he became very much a part of the Rockefeller family circle. David tried to imbue in George the virtues of the Protestant ethic, the family heritage. In his conservatism, Gilder would cast these principles as a defense of "Robber Barons" and an assault on the Liberal Establishment.

When Nelson Rockefeller was running for President, an ambition that spanned a full generation, he built around himself a government-in-waiting, staffed by policy intellectuals such as Henry Kissinger, producing plans and projections that would be tested once their patron assumed his rightful place. The cutting edge of Rockefeller's "modern Republicanism" was the Ripon Society, a group of youthful, liberal Republicans who believed the GOP could become a majority party if it gazed at least as much upon the present as the past. George Gilder was a charter member. In 1966 he wrote, with Bruce K. Chapman, a penetrating analysis, *The Party That Lost Its Head,* diagnosing the political and intellectual drift of the GOP in the wake of the Goldwater debacle. What was needed, they asserted, was an "ideology" for the "Progressive Republican." The entrance onto the stage of a certain fresh California face struck them as an absurd distraction. "Reality," they wrote, "is to be shut out altogether as the GOP eschews the problematical and mentally taxing world of politics for the more glamorous, exhilarating, free-floating world of entertainment. This is the home of the pop-politician, ruggedly handsome, blond, alliterative Ronald Reagan—the party's hope to usurp reality with the fading world of the Class-B movie."[25]

Reflecting on the perilous practice of putting one's thoughts into writing and therefore on the record, Gilder said, "It depends on how much pejorative content you wish to put into the words. It's not far from a pop politician to a populist politician. And Reagan certainly was a B-movie star, and he certainly does come from California."

By the fall of 1980, Gilder saw things differently from the way he had in 1966. "I am still a member of the Ripon Society. My role is to move it toward supply-side economics and to obstruct where possible the clutching of various flags of social liberalism. They brought me into politics and I continue to associate with them. But I'm very sympathetic to the New Right because they're tough, and I think the threat of government in America at the moment is very serious. Moderate, compromising political figures don't have any backbone to resist the new absurdities that issue from established powers. Without the New Right, I suspect Reagan would be conducting virtually a liberal Republican campaign. The New Right is the militant edge to the cause."

In 1973, Gilder wrote *Sexual Suicide,* an attack on the burgeoning feminist movement, the premise of which was that "the woman's place *is* in the home, and she does her best when she can get the man there, too."[26] Gilder followed this performance with *Naked Nomads,* in which he warned of the dangers to society of tribes of unmarried men, whose existence was owed partly to the irresponsibility of feminists who refused to do their duty. Then he wrote *Visible Man,* "a nonfiction novel," a study of a nomadic black man and his families in the North and the South. All the families he wrote about, whether abstract or real, seemed to have lost fathers.

From this concern with family life came Gilder's attachment to the New Right, and he soon became a featured speaker on its circuit. "The New Right is no more motivated by resentment than is American liberalism," he said. "It's motivated by very deep feelings about the course of the country. I think the New Right is right that ignorance of family issues has risen and that adoption of all sorts of federal policies betrays the worst contemporary tragedy, which is the destruction of the black families of the inner cities, directly traceable to government programs. The worst experience for the black family since slavery has been the war on poverty. It was a catastrophe because it refused to acknowledge that family structures are essentially based on man the provider and woman the homemaker. Female-headed families are incapable of raising little boys, and they are incapable of escaping poverty under any circumstances. The New Right recognizes that family life is the very foundation of civilized life." Little boys needed strong fathers, and America needed the New Right.

Although Gilder was a prolific writer, his books did not sell well. He lived as a free-lancer on New Grub Street, reveling in the freedom of poverty. It was then that he began writing his paean to wealth. In search of a grant, he presented the first draft of his manuscript to Leslie Lenkowsky, of the Smith-Richardson Foundation. "Have you ever read a Gilder first draft?" asked Lenkowsky. "How could he afford the time to do the second draft? We helped create Gilder's institute. We needed a program director." The institute in question was called the International Center for Economic Policy Studies (later renamed the Manhattan Institute), founded by William Casey. This Wall Street speculator, later to become Reagan's campaign chairman and CIA director, had deep roots in the conservative movement. He had been the lawyer who incorporated the *National Review.* (William Simon was on the board; Anthony G. A. Fisher, chairman of the influential British Counter-Establishment think tank, the Institute for Economic Affairs, was a vice-president; and Alan Walters, Thatcher's monetarist adviser, was on the Academic Advisory Board.) Gilder was promptly appointed program director. "I thought it'd be a good job for George," said Lenkowsky. "Most of his time was devoted to revising his own book." The Smith-Richardson Foundation had funded Wanniski's breakthrough book, and Gilder's book, Lenkowsky reasoned, would further advance the cause. So a Counter-Establishment think tank was created to allow Gilder to make his signal contribution. With the publication of *Wealth and Poverty,* he emerged as a leading supply-side theoretician—a theologian of the movement.

Initially, *Wealth and Poverty* was to be called *The Pursuit of Poverty.* "Then," said Gilder, "I discovered that you couldn't understand poverty without understanding wealth." In his book, he argued that bad ideas perpetuate poverty. "Rather than wealth causing poverty," he wrote, "it is far more true to say that what causes poverty is the widespread belief that wealth does."[27] The source of this belief was the Liberal Establishment, and particularly certain members. The "war against the rich" was "led and inspired by the declining rich, to arouse the currently poor against the insurgently successful business classes."[28] The only member of the "declining rich" he mentioned by name was David's daughter, "young Abby Rockefeller, the most eloquent of radicals in the younger generation of the family."[29] Gilder had turned the family tie into a theory of power. The unproductive heirs of old money control "the media and the foundations, the universities and the government, all the secure but ultimately unenriching havens for those who refuse to enter the real arena of upward mobility."[30] Blacks are held in poverty by "myths of discrimination," and "liberalism, not racism, accounts for the enduring poverty."[31]

Gilder performed several astounding feats in his book, among them flipping Karl Marx on his head, substituting a capitalist theory of value for the Marxist theory of surplus value. In Gilder's version, only capitalists are the creators of wealth. "A successful economy depends on the proliferation of the rich, on creating a large class of risk-taking men who are willing to shun the easy channels of a comfortable life in order to create new enterprise, win huge profits, and invest them again," he wrote.[32] But the true goal of capitalists is not the maximization of profits, which Gilder characterized as an "unexpected return," a means to an end.[33] For him, the "function of the rich" is "fostering opportunities for the classes below them in the continuing drama of the creation of wealth and progress."[34] Wages and salaries, then, are philanthropy, trickled down from above; capitalism as a system rests on noblesse oblige, the grace of the parvenu.

Marx's "emphasis on the means of production shows the fallacy of liberal thinking," said Gilder, who, apparently inspired by Hegelianism, believed that the course of history is the dialectical progress of spirit. "Capital," said Gilder, "doesn't just consist of mechanical contrivances. The metaphysical component is the most crucial. The metaphysical means of production is human creativity in conditions of freedom. It's really as simple as that. Most of the capital of any economy is in people's heads."

In *Wealth and Poverty,* Gilder sought to link entrepreneurial individualism with traditional culture, the former represented by supply-side economics, the latter by the New Right's sexual politics. This was Gilder's reconciliation of family and free-market myths. The New Right, with its "pro-family" social issues, was the patriarchal community; supply-side economics was the entrepreneur's world of perpetual progress. "Faith in man, faith in the future, faith in the rising returns of giving, faith in the mutual benefits of trade, faith in the providence of God are all essential to successful capitalism," wrote Gilder.[35] "Imagination precedes knowledge."[36]

Gilder's best-selling version of conservatism was a history colored by uplifting romance. Yet the original American entrepreneurs, the farmers, were unacknowledged by Gilder. Until the close of the nineteenth century, individual shareholders constituted a majority of the population. Thomas Jefferson's vision of America was of a self-sufficient yeomanry, granted enough land to sustain itself into the far distant future without succumbing to the ills of a manufacturing urban culture marked by antagonisms of extreme wealth and poverty. (It's worth noting that Jefferson, the most cosmopolitan American of his generation, did not see a village until he was fourteen years old.) Jefferson, in fact, once elaborated the case for American exceptionalism to Jean-Baptiste Say, the disciple of Adam Smith, whom the supply-siders claim as the founder of their doctrine. "The differences of circumstance between this and the old countries of Europe furnish differences of fact . . . in questions of political economy, and will consequently produce sometimes a difference of result," wrote Jefferson on February 1, 1804. He noted that the reason he failed to find Say's arguments compelling was that "you wrote for Europe . . . while . . . I think for America."[37]

The promise of the Republican Party, in its beginning, was of unbounded opportunity for a yeomanry facing an expansive slave power that threatened to engulf and close off the West. Victory in the Civil War, the founding of the land-grant colleges, and the passing of the Homestead Act were fulfillments of the promise. The Republicans used as their instrument a vastly enlarged federal state. Another outcome of the Civil War was the rise of a new industrial order, and the yeomanry faced destruction of their way of life. The result was rural populism.

The new industrialists, possessing no spiritual justification and unable to find a rationale in tradition, freely appropriated the individualist rhetoric of republicanism. By individualism, the Robber Barons meant that the fittest survive—Social Darwinism. Individualism became the mythology of the winners, not the common property of citizenship.

According to Gilder, individualism started with "the greatest of capitalists—the founders of the system," who he complained are unfairly called "robber barons." He even chided conservative thinkers for failing to "give capitalism a theology or even assign its results any assurance of justice."[38] He endowed entrepreneurs with moral legitimacy and divine sanction; they are part of a great worthy tradition denigrated by modern cynics.

For Gilder, entrepreneurial activity is sacred, which leaves employees in an awkward, profane realm. Since only capitalists create wealth, only they can administer the sacraments of the marketplace. Workers, however, are accorded the democratic right to aspire to be entrepreneurs. Gilder wrote that all individual advancement was based on "work, family, and faith."[39] Unions do not figure into Gilder's "system."

In his book, Gilder identified cultural authenticity with the New Right and economic authenticity with entrepreneurship. His archetypal hero might well be William Jennings Bryan in his dotage, the premature Moral Majoritarian, peddler of "magic Miami" real estate, upholder of parochial orthodoxies, scourge of evolution. Certainly, Gilder did not have in mind the youthful Bryan, the populist tribune railing against the perfidies of the Robber Barons in the name of an older individualism.

To Gilder, entrepreneurship was an ethical calling, not the war of each against all. *Wealth and Poverty* was a hymn to the altruism of the capitalist instinct, buttressed by idiosyncratic history. Gilder believed that technology in the hands of entrepreneurs would recreate a world of traditional values—individualism *is* community. The free market would teach us (as Nelson Rockefeller used to say) "the brotherhood of man and the fatherhood of God." Gilder's version of history corroborated his faith. And faith permitted him to believe in the compatibility of a traditional order and a capitalism that inexorably overturns established customs. The issue of this union was a faith for our time—Reagan's time.

CHAPTER EIGHT

THE

PROTESTANT

ETHIC

During the year before Reagan's election, George Gilder befriended an obscure, intense, and intellectual congressman from rural Michigan named David Stockman, who had been inducted by Jack Kemp into what Wanniski now called "the Cabal." Stockman was eager to occupy a niche as both politician and ideologue for the movement. Throughout 1980 he labored over a manuscript on supply-side theory, contracted for by Gilder in his role as think-tank program director. Stockman, in turn, had helped Gilder with his work by writing a ten-page single-spaced critique; many of his suggestions were incorporated. When he was appointed director of the Office of Management and Budget, Stockman launched a publicity campaign for *Wealth and Poverty,* even contributing puffery to the dust jacket: *"Wealth and Poverty* is promethean in its intellectual power and insight." One of his promotional schemes involved distributing copies of the book during a cabinet meeting in the full glare of the press. Unfortunately, Gilder's publisher couldn't deliver the books in time for the grand media event. Gilder was disappointed, too, that Stockman wouldn't finish his own book. "I tried to build a school of thought that would lead to taking power," said Gilder. "But we took power first, before the school could be built."

Stockman believed that his masterly management of the budget and his intellectual leadership could reconcile the contradictory theories of conservative economics. Monetarism would suppress inflation, supply-side policies would foster expansion, and cutting government spending would lead to a balanced budget. If this program could, in fact, stimulate booming prosperity, conservatives would establish them-selves as the leaders of a governing majority that might last well into the twenty-first century; if the experiment failed, the conservative renaissance might unravel. Much, it appeared, depended upon Stock-man.

In the early 1980s, various elements of the Counter-Establishment battled over whose definition of the Reagan economic program would prevail. Great demands were placed upon Reagan's skills in projecting the ideology and maintaining its coherence in order to maintain public support. And at the height of the greatest economic crisis since the Depression, Stockman's faith itself faltered. In his failure to make the Reagan program work lies the origin of the enormous federal deficit that will shape the economy of the future.

The Stockman story is an essential Counter-Establishment tale, for Stockman has had the complete conservative career. He was educated by neoconservatives, endowed with ideas by supply-siders, and then lifted on the strength of his friends' recommendations to appointive office, where he attempted to implement the ideology.

He was not the usual Republican cabinet appointment, neither a lawyer nor a businessman, but a Counter-Establishment intellectual-politico, a wholly new species. He never lived in a big city, except Washington, and he never held a job in the private sector. Further, he had no intervening experience between graduate school and political life.

At thirty-four years old, he was one of the first of his generation to be invested with national power. He lacked deference for the customary ways, categorically rejecting the old centrism in the belief that tradi-tional conservatism was sterile and traditional liberalism fatuous. About his own ideological position he had absolute certitude.

In his new job he maintained an eighteen-hour workday, propelled by gallons of coffee and endless packs of cigarettes. Stockman was driven by more than ambition; he was driven by an ethic of ambition. In his search for his calling, he has been an exemplar of what Max Weber, in *The Protestant Ethic and the Spirit of Capitalism,* called "worldly asceticism."[1] Stockman disciplined himself as he sought to control events. Few could measure up to his standards of moral stringency. He cast himself between an imperfect world and a perfect goal; the imperfect world would always make the perfect goal appear to be just out of reach. And Stockman would always redouble his efforts.

He came to power by a circuitous route, his career a series of startling transformations—from farmboy to Harvard scholar, from student radical to neoconservative.

David Stockman grew up in St. Joseph, a small town in the southwest corner of Michigan, where his father, Allen, is a fruit farmer. As a teenager, he echoed an inherited conventional wisdom. "I was a country conservative from a Republican family," he said. "I thought Goldwater was the greatest thing since sliced bread."

He followed the expected path of the bright boy with a good high school record. In 1964 he began his studies at the East Lansing campus of Michigan State University, "when the whole process of the unraveling cultural and political consensus was just starting," he said. As the Vietnam War escalated, he lent his name to an ad, paid for by the local chapter of the radical Students for a Democratic Society, that appeared in the student newspaper, declaring his intention "to refuse to fight against the people of Vietnam and refuse to be inducted into the armed forces of the United States."

In 1967, between his junior and senior years, he served as the chief organizer of the Lansing area Vietnam Summer project, which sent volunteers into neighborhoods to urge residents to oppose the war. Stockman's duties included writing antiwar literature, mailing it, organizing antiwar coffee klatches, giving political education sessions at weekly dinners for volunteers, and speaking before various groups such as the Kiwanis. H. Lynn Jondahl, a liberal Democrat who became a Michigan state representative, chose Stockman for the post. Jondahl recalled: "He was strongly committed to it. The financial reward was minimal. One had to have a lot of commitment because we encountered a lot of opposition. He was dependable and aggressive on that issue; he was very articulate and could speak convincingly on the war. Dave felt that the government of Ho Chi Minh was a legitimate government and that the war was a manifestation of an imperialist goal. The National Liberation Front was seen as indigenous and popular. There was a heavy sense of the immorality of the war. Dave became our spokesman.

He was excellent at that because he knew the data."

In East Lansing, Stockman came under the influence of the Reverend Truman Morrison, senior minister of the Edgewood United Church, the first of a series of mentors who would help the young man along his way. Stockman taught Sunday school at the church, and out of church funds he was given a no-interest student loan. "We knew David as a radical," said Morrison. "He had a kind of relationship with SDS. I thought he would go on developing his liberal and radical ideas."

Morrison had taken his divinity degree at the University of Chicago, writing his thesis under the guidance of Reinhold Niebuhr, and Stockman and Morrison had long discussions about Niebuhr's work. Shortly after Stockman's appointment as OMB director, the minister said: "David missed the point on Reinhold Niebuhr, who was a socialist with qualifications and knew better than to be unskeptical about concentrated economic power. Niebuhr wrote: 'Man's capacity for justice makes democracy possible; but man's inclination to injustice makes democracy necessary.' He felt that no matter how immoral we are, we are motivated by more than self-interest. And all allocated power and authority must be checked. I'm very worried, frankly, about what I'm learning about David. He thinks of himself as hard-nosed and tough-minded, but there's something naïve about him. Compassion. That's what I'm looking for from David. I wish David and I had done more theological investigations than we did."

Stockman began to drift rightward as a senior. "I discovered," he said, "that the world wasn't as neatly explained as some pamphleteers at the time believed." (Of course in Lansing he was the leading pamphleteer.) "I became," he said, "more of a skeptical intellectual." Jondahl recalled: "He had strategic qualms, whether we should protest in the streets or go inside organizations." And Morrison said: "I remember having a conversation with David before he left here about C. Wright Mills's *The Power Elite.* He felt it was a simplistic analysis." Despite his purported reservations, Stockman served that year as a member of the steering committee of the Greater Lansing Community Organization, a multi-issue left-wing group that was an outgrowth of the Vietnam Summer project.

Jondahl and Morrison wrote recommendations for him to attend

the Harvard Divinity School, and in the fall of 1968, Stockman en-
rolled, intending to devote himself as a layman to the study of Reinhold
Niebuhr. He was disappointed to discover that "nobody was interested" in Niebuhr, and much of his course work became centered in the
fields of government and politics. Seeking a place to live cheaply—and
perhaps a political home as well—he became a house- and baby-sitter
for the family of Daniel Patrick Moynihan, an early advocate of neoconservatism, who was teaching at Harvard and commuting to Washington, where he was President Nixon's special assistant for domestic
policy. "He was very much part of the family," said Moynihan, whose
household became Stockman's reeducation camp. "I was looking for a
way out of the left," Stockman said, "and here was a respectable,
impressive, thoughtful, alternative, antileft ideology. If your present
ideology is disintegrating, you have to find something to replace it. I
came under the influence of people like Moynihan. I read all of his
books and articles and the memos he brought home. He had a great
influence." One thing Stockman did not acquire from Moynihan, however, was his abiding faith in the Democratic Party. Other noted neoconservatives also influenced Stockman, including two under whom
Stockman studied at Harvard, James Q. Wilson and Nathan Glazer. It
was Glazer who said, "When one is moving in a certain direction, one
finds people to be influenced by." At a time of often difficult relations
between faculty and students, Stockman was exceptional, an eager
protégé.

In 1969, Stockman attended a study group taught by David
Broder, political columnist for the *Washington Post,* then a fellow at
Harvard's Kennedy Institute of Politics. "He was antiwar, as almost
everyone was," said Broder. "But he was listening to Pat [Moynihan]
and had second thoughts about his liberal position. He identified himself as a Republican."

Among the guest speakers at Broder's seminar was John B. Anderson, a Republican representative who was at the time little known
outside his Illinois district. Broder recalled: "He wrote me later that he
had a staff job on the House Republican Conference (of which Anderson was chairman) and said that he'd be interested in my students. I

mentioned Stockman." Moynihan also recommended him. And so Stockman left Harvard without completing his divinity degree, in order to take on a new calling and a new mentor.

Although Anderson had a formal position of power, he was not particularly influential in party affairs. He was a traditional Midwestern conservative, from a background much like Stockman's, but he was slowly drifting away from orthodoxy. "When I worked for Anderson my job was to keep him a Republican," said Stockman. "I began to focus on all the Republican issues he felt comfortable espousing—fiscal policy, revenue sharing, deregulation. Those were heretical ideas then. Since he was out on the fringe of the party on social issues, there was a great danger he'd be knocked out of his caucus chairmanship unless he could constantly remind the Republicans by initiatives, speeches, and floor activity that at heart he was a Republican. That was my role."

"I don't share Dave's view of the past, although Dave did very good work for Anderson," said Bob Walker, a Washington-based political consultant who was chief domestic policy adviser for the Anderson-for-President campaign, and who had earlier been Anderson's legislative assistant and had worked intimately with Stockman. "If you look back at Dave's views then, he was mainly a Keynesian. The memos he wrote for Anderson were Keynesian in their assessments. I don't think Anderson ever envisioned Dave's role as keeping him fiscally conservative. Dave was soul-searching in the area of economics. He's self-taught. He was picking up bits and pieces and trying to blend them into a new version."

Stockman was cool, calm, and dry. "For him, nothing exists but work," said Walker. "He was not the type of person to whom you would say, 'Hey, let's have a beer.' To Dave, life is work. He's a very ambitious person. That consumes his work as well. I don't feel hostile to him, but I don't feel friendly to him."

Anderson himself refused all along to comment on Stockman, a telling silence implying perhaps a feeling of betrayal. The two men had been close—Anderson, for example, gave jobs to two of Stockman's brothers. The relationship was irreparably damaged, according to those close to Anderson, by Stockman's realistic impersonation of him during

Reagan's preparation for the Anderson-Reagan debate—a role that enabled Stockman to make his first personal impression on the President-to-be.

Not long after beginning his service with Anderson, Stockman began studying his home district with an eye to running for Congress. And he was beginning to find his way toward an economic vision to match his neoconservative revelation.

Stockman was introduced to supply-side economics by Jack Kemp, a different kind of mentor—more an equal than an elder, a political older brother, a football player who could tutor a Harvard graduate student. "He got supply-side economics from Jack. There's no question of who the teacher was," said Irving Kristol. "Dave spent a lot of time in our home," said Kemp, who introduced him to Arthur Laffer and Jude Wanniski, Laffer's Boswell. "I discussed with him the whole intellectual underpinnings of supply-side economics."

Stockman came to believe that an unrestrained market operates as a self-balancing order, its own best guardian. Supply-side economics was a contemporary recasting of the original liberal doctrine expressed by Adam Smith, who wrote in *The Theory of Moral Sentiments:* "Every man is by nature first and principally recommended to his own care."[2] Thus, Stockman's new conservatism was ancient liberalism. "We are trying to move ahead by restating the classical principles of incentives and markets," said Kemp. "The ultimate *liberal* institution is capitalism." Stockman, too, came to believe that private gain is public benefit and that the successful self-seeker becomes the public benefactor. The addition of all individual acquisitiveness computes to the social good; wealth is its own justification.

This once revolutionary doctrine, used by political thinkers to overturn medieval institutions and ecclesiastical philosophy, was to Stockman a weapon against a new "feudal" system. "Government is a new feudalism," he said. It was artificial, the market natural; government was not a response to market failures, but the cause. Stockman's protestantism was against the established church of latter-day liberals.

His first major public statement was an article entitled "The Social Pork Barrel," published in Kristol's *Public Interest* in 1975. In it he described how the federal budget was used by politicians and bureaucrats to create self-perpetuating constituencies, a destructive process abetted by liberals and conservatives alike. Stockman vehemently protested: "The aims of social policy have been subordinated to the exigencies of the new fiscal politics, and what may have been the bright promise of the Great Society has been transformed into a flabby hodgepodge, funded without policy constituency or rigor, that increasingly looks like a great social pork barrel. . . . Conservative duplicity and liberal ideology both contribute to the dynamics and durability of the social pork barrel."[3]

Stockman elaborated his notions further in a torrent of articles; some of these were lengthy monographs, and others were barbed op-ed pieces for the *Washington Post*. Perhaps the most comprehensive revelation of his logic was an unpublished, untitled, forty-one-page critique of *Politics and Markets* (a book published in 1977), in which Yale political scientist Charles E. Lindblom disputed the tenets of classical liberalism. Lindblom wrote that "the major specific institutional barrier to fuller democracy may . . . be the autonomy of the private corporation. . . . The large private corporation fits oddly into democratic theory and vision. Indeed, it does not fit."[4] And if the corporation did not fit, how valid was the hallowed doctrine of free markets?

Stockman responded with a fierce attack. Every one of Stockman's challenges to Lindblom's axioms was a declaration of his own assumptions. Stockman contended that there was not "anything even closely resembling Lindblom's nebulous 'business elite.' "[5] There just wasn't a "business class possessing mega-influence." It was "impossible to conclude that business has a superior position of influence of power." Rather, what Lindblom defined as the "business elite" was just another one of many "special interest constituencies." These "special interests," according to Stockman, encompassed virtually every group that placed demands on the federal government: "social workers, educators, research scientists, nutritionists, homebuilders, environmentalists, etc." The "nutritionists" and the "elite Fortune 500 executives" were equivalent "special interests." Stockman could thus conclude that "the business interest turns out to be indistinguishable from the cacophony of claimants seeking advantage."

"Special interests" was a phrase lifted from the lexicon of the early

Progressives. To Stockman, the "special interests" all seek the same thing: "an array of special indulgences by government." This word—"indulgences"—defined in this way, was original with Stockman; no other contemporary conservative used it. It marked him as a protestant militant. If his paper on Lindblom had been called "Disputation on the Power and Efficacy of Indulgences," after Martin Luther, it would have been appropriate. In the Middle Ages, indulgences were sold by the Catholic Church to mitigate punishment for sin. To the protestants of the Reformation, indulgences were a sign of the Church's profound moral corruption. To Stockman, "indulgences" were programs awarded "special interests" by government: *Government is a new feudalism.* Max Weber, in *The Protestant Ethic and the Spirit of Capitalism,* wrote that "the practical use made of certain institutions of the Church, above all of indulgences inevitably counteracted the tendencies toward systematic worldly asceticism. For that reason it was not felt at the time of the Reformation to be merely an unessential abuse, but one of the most fundamental evils of the Church."[6]

Even "government investment in public goods," Stockman wrote, "are really special interest subsidies." He believed his notion was a historical truism, and he offered a citation from history to prove his economics—the Erie Canal. This "indulgence," he insisted, was worse than worthless, because "there were thriving business enterprises in both eastern and western New York State long before the Erie Canal was built." This was, he claimed, an early example of private initiative overwhelmed by the demonic state. A voyage down the canal, however, is not a route to the supply side.

The Erie Canal was a government enterprise underwritten by the public credit of New York State. This opportunity fell to New York partly by default, for financiers in Boston and Philadelphia maintained exclusive practices, limiting participation in key investments to a favored clientele; they lacked the imagination and initiative of politicians such as De Witt Clinton. The state helped pay for the unprecedented venture by an increase in taxation, an increase that resulted in vast enterprise and prosperity. Among the unforeseen consequences of the canal was the establishment of Wall Street as a financial center to rival and eventually supplant Boston and Philadelphia. The government-

guaranteed credit for the canal unleashed a torrent of individual investors, and investment houses and banks sprang up to catch the flood.
Anticipation of the canal made New York the financial capital, and its
completion turned the city into a commercial capital. By breaching the
Appalachian chain, farmers in the Northwest states such as Michigan
had a ready market for their produce. By means of the government-
sponsored "internal improvement," demand and supply were joined.
Growth extended well beyond the actual end of the canal, far into the
West, accelerating the development of what would become the great
cities of the interior. The canal more than paid for itself in tolls. But
its significance lay beyond just commerce. The canals and waterways,
and later railroads, that moved relentlessly from east to west helped
weld together the Union that would quell the Confederacy. Finally,
without the Erie Canal there would have been no metropolis called
Buffalo, no Buffalo Bills for Jack Kemp to quarterback, no congressional district to represent, and no one to introduce David Stockman,
son of Michigan fruit farmers, whose markets were first opened up by
the canal, to the supply side. Stockman's astringency demanded a
purification not only of the present but of the past.[7]

Government, he argued, must always, in all cases, be the dead hand
that stills the invisible hand, black magic against the magic of the
marketplace. "Most current government economic promotion activities," Stockman wrote, "are not only absolutely unessential to induce
business performance, but actually undermine profit opportunities in
the aggregate, to say nothing of the general economic welfare of the
nation." By taxation and regulation, government supplants the market.
For example, Stockman attributed high black teenage unemployment
to "the minimum wage," part of the conventional wisdom of the right,
a Friedmanism. What's more, "indulgences" by government "override
the outcomes of the marketplace . . . introducing inefficiencies, arbitrary wealth transfers and resource misallocations." The result is a
strong state, not free individuals—the fabled "road to serfdom," redis-
covered.

Stockman was not surprised by the existence of monopolies, because this transgression of the free-market ideal was due to the "indulgences" of government. "Monopolies are only created by government,"

he claimed. "The marketplace always defeats monopoly unless the monopoly is sanctioned by government." He defined politicians, bureaucrats, and planners as the monopolists. Planners constitute a self-aggrandizing priesthood—a New Class—whose very existence is predicated on foiling the market. And so they appear in a devilish guise, driving a Faustian bargain. Stockman wrote that "the planner's logic must inevitably lead to a dubious bargain: exchange of the benign uncertainty of the market for the ominous uncertainty of a world in which the wealth-creating process has been foolishly shackled."

The major premise of Stockman's critique of Lindblom was that classical liberalism was both an accurate description of reality and a goal: the market always, eternally, exists as a natural system and could be restored by a conservative politics. Only the state and its planners caused scarcities. Abolish regulation and abundance would result.

What followed from Stockman's analysis was a theory of rights in which "indulgences" were a form of illegitimate "entitlements." In 1981 he announced: "I don't think people are entitled to any services. I don't believe that there is any entitlement, any basic rights to legal services or any other kinds of services. The idea that's been established over the last ten years that almost every service that someone might need in life ought to be provided, financed by the government as a matter of basic right, is wrong."

Stockman posed liberty against equality, defining equality as injustice because it could only be attained by the unfair advantage of state power. Modern liberalism, he believed, impinged upon liberty, and more restrictions were implicit in the idea of "limits to growth." Yet he argued that limits on equality were now necessary for growth. "I don't accept that equality is a moral principle," he said. "That's the overlay, the idea around the welfare state. A safety net is different— it's the minimum to which you'll allow anyone to fall. To go beyond that and seek to level incomes is morally wrong and practically destructive."

It was here, Stockman believed, that the strands of conservatism converged. "The thing that marries supply-siders of the more recent vintage, classical free-market-oriented people, and neoconservatives is that they are all suspicious of state power. The classical free-marketers, because they know the state always screws up the market; the supply-siders, because they know the state uses the tax system to discourage production; and the neoconservatives, because they see the state as the instrument to achieve equal outcomes."

Stockman's virtues were readily apparent to the supply-side leaders. "Some people were intimidated by the vast knowledge he had," said Kemp. "He's a threat to ignorance." Stockman was only one of four people Wanniski trusted to read *The Way the World Works* while it was still in manuscript. In 1976, Laffer and Wanniski rented two adjoining suites in a Washington hotel, where they cooked hot dogs, drank iced beer, watched televised football games with Kemp, and debated the manuscript with the few local true believers. "We were plotting and scheming how to take over economic policy," said Wanniski. Even as Stockman and the others plotted, he was taking what would be a major step in that direction—closing in on his dream of having a congressional career of his own.

When Stockman looked around for help with his own congressional ambitions, he decided to approach Chester J. Byrns, a Michigan Circuit Court judge and Republican, who had made an unsuccessful run for Congress in 1962. "I developed contacts and I knew where the power-houses were," Byrns said. After meeting with Stockman, he was favorably impressed and willing to help. "He knows how to respond to an older person," Byrns said. "He knows how to ask them for advice. He went out of his way to get to know me. I could see how he and Reagan could come together."

In 1975, a year before the primary, Stockman assembled the first modern campaign apparatus ever to operate in the solidly Republican district. He set up campaign committees to which he appointed hundreds of influential citizens, who suddenly had a stake in his effort. He also won new stature that same year with the publication of his article on "The Social Pork Barrel." There were not many subscribers to *The Public Interest* in Stockman's Michigan district, but when Irving Kristol, co-editor of the magazine, wrote a column in the *Wall Street Journal* promoting Stockman's contribution, he became something of a celebrity to local businessmen. "That's like getting into the Bible around here," said Byrns. The Counter-Establishment connection,

Stockman demonstrated, could reach far into provincial politics.

Representative Edward Hutchinson, an old-fashioned Republican, was the incumbent. "Hutchinson was a cipher," said Byrns. "But nobody recognized what a nonentity he was until the Watergate investigation. He was the senior Republican on the House Judiciary Committee. He didn't know what to do. This came as a dreadful shock to people around here. The ice and hard ground cracked under Ed." Hutchinson pulled out of the contest before primary day. There were no obstacles in Stockman's way, except his past. "It didn't come out until late in the campaign about his antiwar activity," said Byrns. "If it had come out earlier . . ." But by then Stockman's election was assured. Said Byrns, "Dave could have been congressman forever." (Stockman would later tell a top OMB aide who had been an SDS member that he didn't fully trust peers who hadn't been radicals in the 1960s. "It was an intellectual test to him," said the aide.)

As a new House member, Stockman's ascribed status was that of a back-bencher, but he quickly won a reputation as an aggressive gadfly, pouring out a torrent of bills and research papers. "He would get into some project, do exhaustive research, and come up with a thoroughly buttressed argument, which he would defend very inflexibly," said former Republican Representative Barber Conable, from New York. "He didn't have a wide influence, but he gained respect for his intellectual abilities. He's not a tremendously outgoing person. In a convivial place like Congress, thoroughgoing individual hard work is a surprising attribute."

As the jockeying began for the 1980 presidential campaign, Stockman broke ranks with his fellow supply-siders and supported John B. Connally. "Dave told me that Reagan wasn't going to be firm enough with the special interests and Congress," said Wanniski. "He felt Connally would be strong." Connally did not pledge to resurrect the classical free market. He did not speak about a community that could start the world over again. He did not appeal to metaphysics, but to megabucks. He was the candidate of "indulgences" for the big money. But Republican primary voters were repelled by this coarse vision. Reagan's supporters, especially, believed that Connally represented the purest degeneration of the New Deal—the ex-Democrat turned Republican in the unvarnished quest for power, substituting one set of interest groups for another. Stockman, however, was attracted by Connally's will to power, his greed for office. Connally was not ascetic, but he was certainly worldly. In this case, Stockman apparently did not distinguish between the unfettered dominion of the dollar and the unfettered dominion of the market.

When Connally's bid failed, Stockman promptly transferred his allegiance to George Bush, the Establishment candidate running on his lengthy resumé and empty slogans. Only after Bush was beaten in the New Hampshire primary did Stockman decide to support Reagan, who was by then the clear front-runner. Stockman was late in his plunge into the Reagan market, and he had to make up for time lost on bad investments. He had not even met the candidate. Soon Stockman issued a ringing personal declaration of support for Reagan and the Republican platform in the form of an article in *Commonsense, A Republican Journal of Thought and Opinion,* published by the Republican National Committee. He hailed the candidate's unification of communal and free-market themes: "The Republican platform combines the moral traditionalism of the earlier Reaganite constituency with the bold policy departures of the new Reagan idea—supply-side economics. Both are a response to the excesses of the American superstate."[8]

In short order, Stockman became convinced that the directorship of the OMB was potentially the most significant economic post. At the Republican Convention, he began talking to friends about getting a supply-sider into the job. "Stockman had the idea the OMB director would be almost a deputy president," said Wanniski. "But he didn't have himself in mind." Stockman's choice was William M. Agee, the chairman of the Michigan-based Bendix Corporation; its political action committee had supported Stockman financially in the 1978 congressional campaign. "I had a party at my house for Jack Kemp during the convention," said Agee. "Just as Dave was about ready to leave, he said, 'If the governor is elected, there's an appointment for you,' referring to the OMB. I said, 'No, I'm a private enterprise man. But that's the job for you.'"

Quickly and unexpectedly Stockman gained Reagan's undivided attention. As preparation for the debate with Anderson, Reagan decided to engage in a mock encounter. He needed a sparring partner, someone who could offer a reasonable facsimile of Anderson's style and position. By mimicking the mannerisms of his old mentor in an effort to destroy him, Stockman found the main chance. The exercise took place in the old garage on the Wexford, Virginia, estate Reagan had rented, a place that had once been John F. Kennedy's home. The audience consisted of advisers, and for realistic effect, the debaters stood on a stage, in the glare of spotlights. Reagan, in a red turtleneck sweater, was casual; Stockman, in a dark suit, was not. He so impressed Reagan, the veteran actor, with his bravura performance that he was cast for a later mock debate as Jimmy Carter. Stockman prepared by studying a pilfered Carter campaign blueprint, with George Will, the conservative columnist, serving as his coach.

In this debate, Stockman read old quotations of Reagan's and demanded to know if he still held such outrageous opinions. "That's the most ridiculous thing I ever heard," he replied to the candidate's answers. He pointed an accusing finger at Reagan at one point and said, "This just demonstrates his shallowness." Stockman's performance eerily foreshadowed the charges he made in his disillusioned memoir about a shallow president.

"If I had an Academy Award to give, I would have offered it," said economic consultant and campaign adviser Alan Greenspan. "Not only was Stockman exceptionally close to Carter's position—he took the position in a sophisticated way—but he tried to capture the Carter style. Had Carter played Carter as well as Stockman did, he might still be president. Reagan was very impressed. I remember a dinner party during the transition. Stockman and I were standing together. Reagan came up and said to him, 'You sure beat me in that debate.' " From one trouper to another, it was the ultimate compliment.

In September 1980, Stockman asked Kemp to help him draw up a memo about the President-elect's economic program that would be ready for presentation the day after the election—a first strike. During the campaign a fierce argument had raged between the supply-siders and the traditionalists, who were mostly former Nixon and Ford era officials. In the view of the supply-siders, the traditionalists focused their attention on consumer demand, not on supply, and didn't really accept the supply-side model, even though they had begun to "package their ideas with supply-side words," according to Wanniski. "The risk is that even with an electoral mandate to change the direction of economic policy in the U.S., politicians may inadvertently initiate seemingly different policies when, in fact, they are simply extending those very policies that have sapped much of the vitality from the U.S. economy."[9]

Wanniski called his faction the "populists" in the debate and the other faction the "elitists." At the end of March 1980, he gave an interview to the *Village Voice*, elaborating his version of the titanic struggle for Reagan's mind going on within the campaign. "We are the wild men," he said about the supply-siders.[10] The *Washington Post* and several other newspapers reprinted the *Voice* piece. The immediate result was Wanniski's loss of access to the campaign's inner sanctum, and the supply-siders were momentarily put on the defensive. Even Arthur Laffer claimed to be "offended beyond belief" by Wanniski's indiscretion. "It almost got me knocked out," said Laffer. But Wanniski kept up his own campaign from the outside, while Kemp carried the ball on the inside. Now, during the transition, a period that set the mold for what would follow, Stockman positioned himself as the movement's point man.

Reagan summoned his issue task forces to Rancho del Cielo to outline an agenda for the coming New Beginning. A memo was drawn up by the traditionalist, George Shultz, urging the traditional approach, not the radical tax cuts. The moment, however, was seized by Stockman, who unveiled a dramatic twenty-three-page statement written in portentous Churchillian rhetoric, "Avoiding a GOP Economic Dunkirk." (His co-authors were Kemp and Lewis Lehrman, drugstore mogul and Counter-Establishment funder and leader.) "The momentum of short-run economic, financial and budget forces," they wrote, "is creating the conditions for an economic Dunkirk during the first twenty-four months of the Reagan administration. . . . In order to dominate, shape and control the Washington agenda, President Reagan should declare a national economic emergency soon after the inauguration. He should tell the Congress and the nation that the economic, financial, budget, energy, and regulatory conditions he inherited are far worse than anyone had imagined." The particular genius of the "Dunkirk" memo was not its economic prescription, but its political aptness. It offered the new conservative President a method to galvanize the country behind his leadership, holding out the promise of a lasting political realignment. The traditionalists promised merely more Republicanism. Stockman and friends suggested a great leap forward.

Reagan's political operation was also calculating the uses of policy. Pollster Richard Wirthlin was named director of planning during the transition, and David Gergen, the managing editor of *Public Opinion* magazine (published by AEI) and former Bush aide, was put in charge of what became known as "The First Ninety Days Project." They reported to Reagan that the character of his administration would be set decisively in his first hundred days in office. To apply policy for maximum political effect, Gergen advised, "Keep a simple focus and go strong on the economy."[11]

In December, without consulting anyone, the irrepressible Wanniski leaked the "Dunkirk" memo to *The New York Times.* For the first time, the public became aware of the new influence wielded by the supply-siders. They also became aware of David Stockman. "It elevated Stockman into a pivotal force," said Wanniski. "He was the guy with the framework."

Meanwhile, Stockman had begun actively seeking his own appointment as OMB director, while making it clear that he would not accept the job of Secretary of Energy, which was headed his way. Inside the Reagan camp, Kemp, of course, pushed for him for the OMB, but there were others as well. Richard Whalen, the former Nixon speechwriter, who had years earlier lamented the absence of a conservative policy-making elite, physically escorted Stockman to an audience with Senator Paul Laxalt, Reagan's "First Friend." Whalen and Stockman handed Laxalt a copy of the "Dunkirk" manifesto. "I'm for you," Laxalt said. "And you've got support elsewhere." Although Laxalt hadn't met Stockman, he was familiar with his views. "He was the only Michigan congressman," said Laxalt, "who stood up on the Chrysler bailout [voting against federal loan guarantees for the ailing automaker]. I took an article he wrote on the Chrysler issue for the *Washington Post* and mailed it to Reagan. This was our kind of guy. Reagan didn't need any selling on Stockman. Dave was solidly there. The only one ahead of him was Cap Weinberger." Then Weinberger was named Secretary of Defense. So Stockman had the job.

Among Stockman's friends, only George Will advised him against taking the post. "I had anxieties," Will said, "about who would come to his defense when the shelling got heavy. People don't like prodigies."

The supply-siders saw Stockman as their broker of legitimacy within the administration; through him, their ideas would cease to be abstractions. Wanniski said, "He is the most important supply-sider we have in the administration, with the exception of Ronald Reagan." Kemp said, "Reagan is the Oldest and Wisest, and Dave is the Youngest and the Wisest." And Gilder said, "He carries the hopes of the supply-siders. He is surrounded by old businessmen. The question is, what happens to a young idealistic intellectual as he assumes vast power?"

One of the first items on Stockman's agenda was a whirlwind tour of Wall Street investment houses, arranged by Whalen. Stockman was accompanied by Kemp. The public circulation of the "Dunkirk" memo, followed swiftly by Stockman's appointment, did not sit well with many financial experts, who looked askance at the supply-side theory and dismissed talk of an "emergency." So Stockman marched in and out of investment houses, assuring the money managers that he meant to save the system.

That evening, a dinner in his honor was held at Manhattan's Century Club. In attendance were leading Counter-Establishmentarians: Lehrman, Whalen, Kemp, Kristol, Wanniski, Bartley, and Jeffrey Bell. In days past, the talk had been theoretical; now one of their own, a Counter-Establishment intellectual, had suddenly been invested with tremendous power. "We want to change the world," said Kemp. "We talked about what we could do as a next step to advance the cause." Stockman's power was now at the center of that cause.

His power flowed from the special nature of the OMB itself, and from the special function of the budget in defining the workings of the American government. All federal agencies must filter their requests for funds through the agency. These requests are studied by a professional field staff of more than three hundred examiners, who forward their recommendations to the OMB director. This constant flow of information about the bureaucracy gives the OMB ways to exercise control over the agencies. The OMB also offers the President a means of dealing with Congress: legislators have many pet projects, such as home-district military bases and water projects, which the OMB can fund or cut. Without an effective OMB, a president cannot govern well. The director burns the midnight oil for the President. When Jimmy Carter lost Bert Lance as OMB director, too often he burned it for himself. Stockman burned it for Reagan.

To Stockman, the budget was not a telephone book, a blur of unrelated names and numbers, but a tragic saga of recent American history. He knew all the corruptions, all the "indulgences," all the sinners. The budget was the way the "superstate" regulated production, undercutting the pursuit of wealth. Stockman believed the budget rendered the entrepreneur an involuntary steward of the superstate, denying him the liberty of the market. The budget erected false gods, sanctified by the secular words of the New Deal about comforting the afflicted; but these words justified morally corrupt material relationships. To a theologian, this would be a confusion of realms.

In January, after his first major meeting on the budget with Reagan, Stockman gave his troops the order of battle. Examiners began producing dozens of large black loose-leaf notebooks, listing programs to be slashed. The notebooks were passed on to senior aides, who were faced with the task of making virtually instantaneous recommendations about the future of incredibly complex programs. "There's no way to make it objective," a top OMB aide said of the process.

Even as the budget review process was proceeding, a group of economists was gathering two or three times a week to develop a picture of how the entire package would affect the economy. Discussion revolved around an economic model produced by the Claremont Economic Institute. OMB chief economist Lawrence Kudlow happened to be a director of CEI.* And at Stockman's behest, Kudlow brought in

---

*At OMB, Kudlow and Stockman became fast friends. They shared a similar political background. Kudlow had been a leader of the left-wing Students for a Democratic Society chapter at the University of Rochester, where he led an occupation of college buildings. In his off-hours, classmates recall, he drove a Porsche around campus. He later moved to New York City and attempted to enter political life through the

his associate at CEI, John Rutledge, to run computer simulations of the economy. The goal: to project the future behavior of investors under the Reagan scenario. The computer model made assumptions that reflected a free-market view—that the removal of government from the marketplace would cause a spurt in economic growth, and that the marketplace, when liberated from government intervention, would naturally enter into a state of equilibrium. When the Reagan policies were programmed into the computer, investors behaved enthusiastically, with very positive results for the economy.

"To some extent it's a theology, a model of the world," said a senior OMB aide who participated in the forecasting. This aide regarded himself as a student of von Hayek, the author of *The Road to Serfdom* and fountainhead of contemporary conservatism. Stockman read deeply in von Hayek, according to the OMB aide, and they often had long discussions about the Austrian's ideas. But these talks weren't simply philosophical ruminations. "Just plug the numbers into von Hayek, and it works," said the aide. "It works!"

Sides formed around the model. Supply-siders, led by Norman Ture, a Treasury under secretary, and Paul Craig Roberts, Kemp's former aide, now a Treasury assistant secretary, argued that the model proved that the Reagan program would produce widespread prosperity and lower inflation. Ture snapped his fingers to emphasize the speed with which the change would take place.

Monetarists were led by a Treasury under secretary, Beryl Sprinkel,

---

1976 senatorial campaign of Daniel Patrick Moynihan. Within the campaign there were two principal camps, the neoconservatives and the political professionals. Kudlow aligned himself with the pros, who he believed would have the inside track. They did not. And the neoconservatives, according to one of them, considered Kudlow a blatant opportunist, so they shut him out of the inner circle. Kudlow then went into business, becoming chief economist at the Bear Stearns investment house. Through his Wall Street position he discovered the supply-siders, in particular Jack Kemp. He also became a confidant of William Simon's, whose speech before the 1980 Republican convention he helped to write. After Reagan's election, Kemp sent his resumé to Stockman. Kudlow and Stockman immediately hit it off, and Kudlow became the OMB's chief economist. Eventually he left the supply-side faith and became a bitter opponent of his former comrades within the administration. Whenever his name was mentioned among them, there were dark mutterings. In 1983, Kudlow quit government to set up a lucrative practice as a consultant, another Washington success story.

who accepted the validity of the computer model's free-market assumptions. The monetarists, however, were more anxious about the inflationary consequences of the plan than were the supply-siders; they advocated, according to formula, slow growth in the money supply, which would mean a lower rate of growth in the Gross National Product.

In the middle were Alan Greenspan, the only outsider, and Murray Weidenbaum, who, as CEA chairman, was responsible for defending the official economic assumptions of the plan and the reliability of the figures on which it was based. Weidenbaum had become a leading critic of government regulation. He had headed a Counter-Establishment think tank, the Center for the Study of American Business, located at Washington University in St. Louis; he also edited a journal, *Regulation,* under the auspices of the American Enterprise Institute. He put a price tag on federal rules, asserting that in 1978 they totaled $100 billion, a sum he did not revise after a Library of Congress study described his data as being of "doubtful validity," replete with "double accounting and errors of addition."[12] Weidenbaum's credo for the administration: "Don't just stand there, undo something!" He was not a member of any particular conservative camp but an avuncular advocate of all.

Greenspan and Weidenbaum believed that the monetarist and supply-side positions were compatible. But they disputed the CEI model's projections, which they claimed were far too optimistic. "I'm Peter Pan," Weidenbaum told the forecasters. "I want to believe. But you have to convince me, and you haven't done that."

On February 7, Stockman and Weidenbaum made a command decision about what the future would hold under the Reagan economic plan. By 1986, they agreed, inflation would drop to 4.9 percent, unemployment to 5.6 percent, the rate of growth of the GNP would almost quadruple, and the federal budget would show a *surplus* of $30 billion.

On the morning of February 18, the day the President would announce his economic program to a joint session of Congress, Stockman breakfasted with fifteen reporters at eight o'clock, briefed the cabinet and the congressional leaders, held a full-dress press conference, and then spoke to the House Republican Conference. Shortly before nine o'clock that night, he marched into the Capitol, where he had been a back-bencher a few months before. Now, first among equals within the cabinet, he sat up front and listened to President Reagan present "A Program for Economic Recovery."

The speech proposed a 30 percent across-the-board income-tax cut, to be applied over three years—the supply-side remedy that Reagan had pledged to try during the campaign. To inhibit inflation, he called upon the Federal Reserve to maintain a stable money supply. Critics charged that the loose fiscal and tight money policies were analogous to stepping on the accelerator and the brake at the same time. Supply-siders and monetarists, too, believed that their nostrums were at odds. In fact Reagan's program was nothing less than the programmatic version of the original Mundell-Laffer Hypothesis, which exactly prescribed this combustible mix. Stockman would make the policy fit reality by wielding a deft meat cleaver. To begin with, he calculated, eighty-three major budget cuts would be necessary to bring the economy and the government in line with an ideal form. He would make the world perfect by the exercise of sheer individual will.

Some of Stockman's cuts were aimed directly at programs such as the Legal Services and Environmental Protection agencies, which he believed were used by the New Class to pursue its nefarious goal of equality. Stockman declared that "the need to curtail the influences of the New Class assault on American institutions" was among his personal "causes." "They're stashed all over the government," he said about the New Class. "We'll find out where they are and throw them out. The environmentalists, the solar power freaks, the Naderites— whatever their particular cause, they're hostile to the status quo, the social order. I'm not hostile to it. I think it's pretty good."

Immediately after the President's speech, Stockman began selling the program with the intensity he had brought to bear in framing it. His sales efforts, however, were hindered by a recurring arithmetic problem. His estimates of the budget had been off the mark by $3 to $6 billion. On February 25, Stockman had lunch in the cabinet room at the White House with the President, Weidenbaum, and Treasury Secretary Donald Regan to discuss the miscalculation. The President told Stockman, "You just have to cut more." Stockman tried to deal with the strangely expanding deficit by cutting more and even proposing a two-cent tax on gasoline, a supply-side heresy that Treasury under secretary Ture called "a boo-boo." Reagan quickly dismissed the idea. None of this seemed very consequential at the time, perhaps not even to Stockman, but it was his first realization that the program wasn't working just according to plan.

But that was not the President's worry. Above all, as Reagan said in a March 2 speech, he was concerned about "parochialism." And, in fact, more than 150 groups, ranging from labor unions to feminist and religious organizations, formed coalitions to lobby Congress against the budget cuts. In Congress itself, the administration faced Tip O'Neill, the man who said, "All politics is local." In Stockman's world, O'Neill represented the "special interests."

The House Democratic leadership had no strategy, but just haphazard tactics, in its attempt to block Stockman. In any case, Stockman had a spy in the enemy camp in the person of Representative Phil Gramm, a friend with whom he had rehearsed budget-cutting in the past. Gramm soon emerged as a Democrat eager to cosponsor the Reagan budget proposal.

O'Neill, after some fruitless maneuvering, tried to stop Stockman through an arcane gambit—a budget reconciliation bill. If passed, this measure would require congressional committees to meet the administration's budget targets, but the Speaker believed that with a Democratic majority he could defeat it. Then the proposed cuts would have to come before Congress as separate items. Legislators would not want to alienate pressure groups that could influence an election, and so Stockman's initiatives would not succeed. Interest-group politics would prevail.

The key swing group in Congress were the conservative Southern Democrats, called the "boll weevils." To achieve his triumph over the "special interests," Stockman bargained with this particular "special interest." For example, he negotiated the dropping of White House opposition to new sugar price supports, a move that secured votes from the Louisiana and Florida delegations. On June 25, the budget reconciliation measure passed the House. Stockman immediately proclaimed that there were no "deals made," but only "adjustments and considerations."

In the meantime, Weidenbaum, who had to defend in public the rosy scenarios the administration was projecting, was growing uneasy because he believed the scenarios were false. He commissioned aides to devise a new forecast. At a meeting of White House senior advisers on June 5, 1981, their numbers were presented, far more pessimistic than those the administration was offering to Congress and the public. "You mean," said James Baker, "it really is voodoo economics after all?" A vote was taken. Should the new forecast, based on the less optimistic figures, be released? Weidenbaum voted in favor. The other senior aides voted against. "It was a political call," said a participant in the meeting. "The whole focus was on getting the tax bill passed. It would be the wrong signal to send to Congress. Anything that would interfere was disloyal." Thus, solely on the basis of political expedience, the White House staff pushed forward an economic program that most of them no longer believed in. Time and again these aides would try to get Reagan to change the course, but he would resist them because he remained a true believer.

By now the administration was lobbying hard for its supply-side tax-cut bill. And in the effort to win its passage, Stockman was participating in the granting of what he used to call "indulgences." The Democrats, too, contested for business support by offering the lure of assorted "indulgences." Dan Rostenkowski, House Ways and Means Committee chairman, proposed a tax bill, based on supply-side premises, that would have given more to small business than did Reagan's bill. This was an attempt to split the business coalition. "We had to appeal to their patriotism on that one," said a presidential aide about the small-business constituency. But it was big business that shaped the tax bill.

Shortly before Reagan introduced his economic program in February, Stockman invited representatives from the Business Roundtable over to his office for a meeting. "We hope you'll express disagreement," he said, "because that would be helpful in selling the package. Otherwise, people would be concerned this program was only for business."

The Roundtable representatives regarded this statement as cynical and foolish. "We didn't make much of a reply," said one. "It was a fallacious argument."

The business coalition had been crucial in the budget reconciliation fight. In the battle for the tax cut it would again demonstrate its prowess. And in this matter the tax lobby, led by Charls Walker's American Council on Capital Formation, had its own agenda. "The tax bill was a compromise between the supply-side and the business tax lobby," explained a presidential aide. "By buying into that group we bought into ideological help and political inroads on the Hill. By tapping into all that we had a ready-made structure. We had to graft their stuff onto our own program. It was easy to grab what was in place. They brought all of their baggage with them, but that was fine. Politically, this was the only way to go. Otherwise, the other guys control the debate and derail the President's plan. Your choice is winning or losing. That's not a choice."

The business tax lobby is a small circle of friends possessing the "mega-influence" Stockman once disputed. This "special interest" is not like other "special interests." It is, in fact, more powerful than, say, the nutritionists. "It's interlocking directorates," said a presidential aide. "There are a few players and they each wear six hats. Look at what Charlie Walker's got." Indeed, he is influential: Richard Rahn, his former chief economist on the Capital Formation Council, is chief economist for the Chamber of Commerce; Jack Albertine, a Council board member, heads the American Business Council, one of the biggest corporate lobbying groups in Washington; and Walker himself has the Roundtable and many of its corporate members as clients. He lives for tax bills.

On July 29 the House and Senate approved a three-year, 25 percent tax-cut bill—a victory claimed by the administration, the supply-siders, and the Capital Formation Council. Out at the Rancho del Cielo, where the President basked in euphoria, his senior advisers gathered. At last his program was in place. He expected the boom soon to begin; he felt that he was presiding at the beginning of a new age. In this buoyant mood, the President listened as Murray Weidenbaum explained to him that a recession was about to begin, that it would create large federal deficits, and that the budget would not be balanced. Reagan was "stunned," according to an administration official. He flatly refused to believe his chief economist and he refused to speak to him.

On July 30, the President met with Weidenbaum, Stockman, and Secretary of Defense Weinberger. Stockman and Weidenbaum were disquieted by the prospect of potentially enormous deficits. Stockman gave the President a memo calling for cuts in military spending as a way for dealing with the problem. Reagan always responded to demands for such cuts by saying that he would never choose between national security and economic factors—as Commander-in-Chief he must never compromise national security. In his memo, Stockman had called the national security argument "Pentagon blue smoke." Weidenbaum openly challenged the feasibility of the vast military buildup. But Weinberger answered: "I don't have to demonstrate it is feasible. You have to demonstrate it is not feasible." Reagan decided in favor of Weinberger. "What is national security? It is whatever Cap Weinberger says it is," said a despairing administration official who had been present at the meeting. Huge deficits now were inevitable.

Stockman's budget balancing became an overwhelming obsession. He seemed to be returning to the faith of his Republican fathers, the neolithic economics of gloom which the supply-siders intended to eradicate with their blinding optimism. The theory of "rational expectations" he had banked his hopes on was working perversely. In 1981 it was rational for money managers to be pessimistic, and they failed to invest as expected. Stockman conjured up recurring nightmares of "Dunkirk."

But was he really a victim of a theory gone wrong, or was he a perpetrator of the crime he professed to be solving? The game he played had several elements, all of which were self-serving. To carefully cultivated reporters he acted as a background source, leaking them inside stories about his fearless attempt to control the deficit by overriding the crazy ideologues and detached President. Then the press would trumpet his claims, which he would show to his White House colleagues as evidence of a public clamor in support of his position.

Another element involved speeches in which he portrayed himself as an austere thinker standing alone against the forces of mindless extravagance. In these dramatic recitations, the federal deficit was declared to exist because he was not heeded. Greed (everyone else) was triumphing over principle (Stockman). On June 5, 1985, for example, Stockman told the board of the New York Stock Exchange: "The basic fact is that we are violating badly, even wantonly, the cardinal rule of sound public finance: Governments must extract from the people in taxes what they dispense in benefits, services and protections. . . . Indeed, if the [Securities and Exchange Commission] had jurisdiction over the executive and legislative branches, many of us would be in jail." Those who break "the cardinal rule" must be committing a cardinal sin. A harsh penalty—jail—would be justice.

But to what degree did Stockman share in the guilt he was liberally apportioning to others? According to Daniel Patrick Moynihan, Stockman told him in 1981 that "the plan was to have a strategic deficit that would give you an argument for cutting back the programs that weren't desired. It got out of hand."[13] Thus the deficit was deliberately created as the instrument of conservative policy.

An eerily appropriate witness to this strategy materialized—Friedrich von Hayek, the Remnant philosopher. "I really believe Reagan is fundamentally a decent and honest man," he told a Viennese magazine in 1985. "His politics? When the government of the United States borrows a large part of the savings of the world, the consequence is that capital must become scarce and expensive in the whole world. That's a problem. You see, one of Reagan's advisers told me why the President has permitted that to happen, which makes the matter partly excusable: Reagan thinks it is impossible to persuade Congress that expenditures must be reduced unless one creates deficits so large that absolutely everyone becomes convinced that no more money can be spent. . . . [Reagan] hopes to persuade Congress of the necessity of spending reductions by means of an immense deficit. Unfortunately, he has not succeeded!"[14]

Von Hayek's account squared with Moynihan's. They appeared to substantiate Stockman's actual role. But what did the President know and when did he know it?

All along, Stockman was Reagan's puritan. Through him, the leisure-class President proved his sincere belief in the work ethic. While

Reagan relaxed, Stockman worked. He was delegated the cultivation of facts, a division of labor that allowed Reagan to devote himself to generalities.

On September 2, 1981, Stockman attended a political fund-raiser for a congressional candidate in Gladstone, New Jersey, where he answered questions from the Republicans assembled for the occasion. He was a big draw. Among those in the crowd was the prophet outcast, Jude Wanniski, who felt that Stockman was "betraying the supply-side movement." The two men had not talked since March because Stockman, angry at Wanniski's criticism, wouldn't return his telephone calls. Wanniski followed Stockman outside the hall. "You might as well be Jimmy Carter's budget director," Wanniski shouted. Stockman "looked at me like he wanted to hit me with a baseball bat," he recalled. Then, according to Wanniski, Stockman icily replied, "Why should I believe you instead of the Wall Street bond traders?" And he stalked away.

"I don't feel vulnerable," Stockman said, chain-smoking cigarettes, in the heady days of his power in early 1981. "I'm used to being attacked." He gestured toward his dozens of black notebooks scattered around the room. "That's what all those books are, people losing their benefits from government. That's a lot of enemies in those pages. No, it doesn't bother me. Most of them have unjust claims. You've got to choose your enemies, I guess."

In December the *Atlantic* featured an article by William Greider entitled "The Education of David Stockman," in which the OMB director offered unusually candid opinions on the administration's budget projections ("none of us really knows what's going on with all these numbers"), business allies ("the hogs were really feeding"), and the supply-side tax cut ("a Trojan horse to bring down the top rate"). Stockman's odyssey appeared as a classic in the annals of disillusionment. "The whole thing," he said, "is premised on faith." But faith was something the former divinity school student lacked.[15]

Stockman keenly experienced the collision of the world of dreams and the world of consequences. To try to realize a dream risks it. The threat to Reagan's dream was a threat to his presidency because he had equated the two; he had argued, after all, that dreams do come true. But Stockman had to deal with Reagan's dream in minute detail, eighteen hours a day. And when the numbers did not add up, he began to lose faith. Could a program based on faith be destroyed by apostasy? Stockman, however, was not so much a casualty of reality as of dreams.

Max Weber, in *The Protestant Ethic and the Spirit of Capitalism,* wrote:

> Since asceticism undertook to remodel the world and to work out its ideals in the world, material goods have gained an increasing and finally an inexorable power over the lives of men as at no previous period in history. Today the spirit of religious asceticism—whether finally, who knows?—has escaped from the cage. But victorious capitalism, since it rests on mechanical foundations, needs its support no longer. . . . No one knows who will live in this cage in the future, or whether at the end of this tremendous development entirely new prophets will arise, or there will be a great rebirth of old ideas and ideals, or, if neither, mechanized petrification, embellished with a sort of convulsive self-importance. For of the last stage of this cultural development, it might well be truly said: "Specialists without spirit, sensualists without heart; this nullity imagines that it has attained a level of civilization never before achieved."[16]

At the beginning of Reagan's second term, Stockman landed a $2 million contract to write a book, entitled *The Triumph of Politics.* According to the Stockman jeremiad, his warnings of hellfire had been ignored by unrepentant Democrats and Republicans alike. And so America went down a rat hole. When Stockman's book was published, he began a lucrative job with Salomon Brothers investment banking house. It was his first job outside the federal government.

Stockman believed that only his prescriptions made sense, that only his statistics were valid, that only his vision could save the country. He played a game of winners and losers, and his self-importance was an implicit denigration of Reagan. With his new millions, Stockman attained the state of grace the Reagan program presumed to seek for everyone. Yet there were obvious limits to Stockman's powers of political redemption. If the conservative movement had rested its hopes on him, they would have been dashed almost as soon as he assumed office; talk of realignment would have instantly ceased, too. Stockman's politics were all blood, sweat, and tears—Dunkirk again, not "morning again in America."

CHAPTER NINE

THE MYTHOLOGY

OF REAGANISM

In 1960 William F. Buckley, Jr., was a featured speaker at a Nixon-for-President rally held in a Beverly Hills school auditorium. The man who was to introduce Buckley to the throng was the California chairman of Democrats for Nixon and a subscriber to the *National Review*—Ronald Reagan. The microphone, however, was dead and there was no one in sight to turn it on. The only route to the locked control room was a foot-wide ledge running outside the building, two stories above the ground. Buckley recalled: "Hollywoodwise, [Reagan] climbed out on the ledge and sidestepped carefully, arms stretched out to help him balance, until he had gone the long way to the window, which he broke open with his elbow, lifting it open from the inside and jumping into the darkness. In a moment the lights were on, the amplifying knobs turned up, the speaker introduced."[1] Here, at last, was the natural. Reagan was even his own stuntman.

In 1966, Buckley attended a debate between Ronald Reagan, just elected governor of California, and Senator Robert Kennedy on the Vietnam War. In private, Kennedy was going through a profound crisis over the issue, which would eventually lead him to challenge for the presidency. He was filled with doubts. Reagan, on the other hand, had no ambiguities; he was for the war. Almost all observers at the debate agreed that he was the victor. Among those who happened to be in the audience was Richard Nixon, then a Wall Street lawyer, already planning the miraculous resurrection that would result in his election to the presidency. He was impressed with Reagan's performance. "Suppose he makes a very good record as governor of California?" Nixon told Buckley. Reagan must then be considered presidential timber. Buckley scoffed at the suggestion, refusing to believe Americans would ever accept a former actor in the Oval Office. Reagan was just too "implausible" to imagine as President.[2]

Buckley did not recognize that Reagan would make the key breakthrough for the movement, performing political tasks that no other conservative could manage. Conservatives had repeatedly attempted to fuse the various doctrinal creeds of the movement into a single force. But precisely because the movement was based in ideology it was rent apart; inconsistent logic could not be reconciled as consistent politics. What Reaganism represented was the effort to unify in politics the disparate strands of conservatism. He animated the intellectuals' theories with a resonant symbolism—images of idyllic small-town life, enterprising entrepreneurs whose success derived from moral character, and failure induced only by federal bureaucrats. By translating a complex ideology into a soothing vernacular he made it accessible to Americans yearning for reassurance of their own special grace. Reagan's popular rendition of conservatism was in one sense a simplification, but in another sense an improvement. For he turned the movement outward by transforming a sectarian interpretation of the world into a political mythology, a civil religion. The point, he demonstrated, was to get people to participate in the myth-making.

In the days of the Remnant, conservatism had been dismissed by almost all political analysts as an eccentric movement whose origins could be traced to deeply rooted pathologies. The ideology, it was believed, could never withstand exposure to empirical examination. But Reagan's ability to present conservatism as a mythological system insulated it from much criticism. With him, facts don't determine the case; they don't make his beliefs true. Rather, his beliefs give life to the facts, which are tailored to have a moral. Reagan doesn't use stories the way experts use statistics. They seek mathematical certainty, whereas he has moral certainty. He asks listeners to trust the tale, not necessarily the detail. If the facts belie his premises, then the facts are at fault, and he can shift ground without making any fundamental change in his beliefs. His policies might be contradictory and counterproductive, but his mythology remains appealing. Throughout his presidency, Reagan has maintained support by persuading many Americans to value the mythology even above their own economic interests. He stages a superb theatrical production, but it's no act. Greed is not enough to explain this kind of presidency; an analysis that patronizes Reagan simply as a front man for special interests, a man who became president because he was the available pretty face, is too narrow. His life experience vindicates his nostalgic approach to the future; he feels what he says, and that gives it authenticity and force.

No previous conservative leader had been capable of his astonishing feats. Barry Goldwater was able to mobilize true believers but could not persuade others. His statements were those of a sectarian prophet, reflecting a minority claiming to speak for the majority. Goldwater projected a militant ideology, often as arid as the Arizona desert from which he came. He was born a Westerner, whereas Reagan had gone West as a young man. The difference is crucial. Reagan knew from his own life that there could be a new beginning; he knew the frontier was open to all. His vision had far horizons and his tone was always optimistic. He didn't appeal to resentments, but to the American dream he had had the good fortune to live. Unlike Goldwater, he had originally been a liberal Democrat, but had converted—another new beginning. And unlike Goldwater, Reagan projects the message outward, drawing people in. Goldwater's slogan was: "In your heart you know he's right." Reagan's tack is different: In his heart he knows you're right. And he wants to give you the opportunity to prove it in the free market. His ideological politics wasn't constricting, but attracted support beyond the usual Republican constituencies.

Conservatism, as Reagan practices it, is partly a consequence of the old California Progressivism, which was an anti-party movement led by people for whom ideas were paramount. In 1910, Californian political parties, which had been pawns of the Southern Pacific Railroad, suffered de facto abolition when the Progressives won control of the state government. All state jobs became civil service appointments, rendering machine politics impossible. The Progressives also made it legal for politicians to cross-file as both Democratic and Republican candidates, undermining the meaning of partisanship. (California representative

Richard Nixon ran in his second campaign for Congress with both parties' designation.) Since then, movements rather than parties have dominated politics in the Golden State. It is hardly surprising that the first political consulting firm, Whitaker and Baxter, emerged in California. Politicians and special interests, lacking the party vehicle to sustain ambitions, required image-making machinery to mobilize public opinion.

Reagan himself has not depended on the party to promote his career, as have regular Republicans like Gerald Ford. Reagan, moreover, does not believe in the party as such. He has always been much more the movement figure than the stodgy partisan; he believes he represents values beyond party. During the long wilderness years after Goldwater's defeat, Reagan's career was sustained by the movement, just as he sustained it. And because of his indispensability he has been able to use the movement without becoming shackled to any of its factions. His unique position has confounded many political observers, who attempt to pigeonhole him as a "pragmatist" or an "ideologue" without reference to his relationship with the conservative movement.

Reagan's purpose has never been the resurrection of the traditional Republican Party. His mission is Reaganism. His ideology naturally comes to him, partly because he has crafted a mythology from his own life, which he believes exemplifies the themes of Reaganism.

Time and again, he has used an autobiographical vignette to clinch a political point. For him, Reaganism begins at home, a deduction from the Ronald Reagan story, which illustrates broad forces at work in American society. He presents himself as the self-made man. He tells us that he's just like us and that through the free market we can succeed as he did. For decades he has been surrounded by image-makers in Hollywood and in politics. But ultimately he has been his own myth-maker: the self-made man invents himself.*

. . .

*Like all major political figures, Reagan has speechwriters. But his White House aides insist that his speeches are really his own. He almost always rewrites them. In any case, he often doesn't pay any attention to his staff. What makes Reaganism genuine as a social creed is not that Reagan writes much of his own material, but that many Americans could write it instinctively. He expresses widely shared feelings and beliefs.

Jack Reagan was an alcoholic traveling salesman who never succeeded. He was a staunch Democrat in the Republican heartland, a nonpracticing Catholic among devout Protestants and an outspoken opponent of the ascendant Ku Klux Klan. His wife, Nelle, an active member of the local Christian Church, a Protestant sect, was always performing good deeds, regularly inviting just-released convicts to board in her home.

Ronald Reagan remembers his early childhood as "one of those rare Huck Finn–Tom Sawyer idylls." When he was nine, his family moved from Tampico, Illinois, to the larger Dixon, population 10,000. "All of us have to have a place to get back to; Dixon is that place for me," he wrote in his autobiography, *Where's the Rest of Me?*[3] His memories are of a golden age whose tempo was measured by the seasons, not by the clock. Small-town life was the natural world.

Growing up, Reagan says he was "an inveterate reader."[4] A book that "made a lasting impression on me at about the age of eleven or twelve, mainly because of the goodness of the principal character" was entitled *That Printer of Udell's,* a Horatio Alger–style success story, written by a popular turn-of-the-century author, Harold Bell Wright.

The hero of the novel is a young Midwesterner named Dick Falkner, earnest and poor. His benevolent mother dies and his father is a drunk. He must leave town to find work. He moves to Boyd City, where he becomes a printer by day and a student at the night school. There he solves a murder and rescues a beautiful, wealthy young lady in distress. Dick and the other young members of the Jerusalem Church seek "to apply Christ's teachings in our town." They aim for "civic Christianity" and "municipal virtue"; social welfare, they believe, is a matter of individual initiative. So they set up their own charitable agency—the Institution for Helping the Unemployed—which makes sure that only the truly needy are aided. Traditional values are good business, and Boyd City becomes a paradise.

In place of the saloons that once lined the east side of Broadway and the principal street leading to it, there were substantial buildings and respectable business firms. The gambling dens and brothels had been forced to close their doors, and their occupants driven to seek other fields for their degrading profession. Cheap variety and vulgar burlesque troups had the city listed as "no good," and passed it by, while the best of musicians and lecturers were always sure of crowded houses. The churches, of all denominations, had been forced to increase their seating capacity; and the attendance at high school and business college had enlarged four-fold; the city streets and public buildings, the lawns and fences even, by their clean and well-kept appearance, showed an honest pride, and a purpose above mere existence. But a stranger would notice, first of all, the absence of loafers on the street corners, and the bright, interested expressions and manners of the young men whom he chanced to meet.[5]

A traveling salesman, passing through Boyd City, remarks upon viewing this incredible transformation: "I'm sure of one thing, they were struck by good, common-sense business Christianity." In the end, Dick Falkner marries the girl he saved, is elected to Congress, and leaves home to carry his message to Washington.

Reagan was encouraged at home to emulate heroes like Dick Falkner. Jack Reagan taught his son: "All men are created equal and man's own ambition determines what happens to him the rest of his life." By taking this maxim to heart, Ronald may have had ambivalent feelings about his father, whose alcoholism Nelle explained as a "sickness . . . beyond his control," a character flaw that undermined ambition.[6]

Jack's dreams never came true. He never owned his own home; the one he rented had a leaky roof. He never earned more than fifty-five dollars a week, and he was able to afford a new car only once. Ronald had to wear his older brother's clothes until he at last outgrew him. One Christmas Eve, Jack received a dismissal notice in an envelope in which he expected a bonus (a story his son told countless times on the campaign trail). Then, Jack's dream of owning his own store was shattered by the Depression. Fortunately, big government saved him. His campaign activity on behalf of the Democratic Party landed him a patronage job as Dixon's top bureaucrat with the Work Projects Administration during the early days of the New Deal. The local relief agency, however, wouldn't allow all of its charges to work for Jack's WPA. His life, according to his son's later interpretation, "became one of almost permanent anger and frustration. However, his rage was directed only at his local tormentors. Being a loyal Democrat, he never criticized the administration or the government."[7] But did Jack's "rage" begin with the New Deal? He was, after all, a dyed-in-the-wool lifelong liberal Democrat who was rescued from ruin by his party's program. Was there no connection between his economic failure, his alcoholism, and his "rage"? His son prefers an explanation that suits his political views.

Reagan's family's humble state fits a classic motif of success fairy tales. Jack's alcoholism, the leaky roof, the do-good but ineffective mother, the layoffs, the bankrupt business, the hand-me-down clothes —these are Ronald Reagan's log cabin. The most successful people are those who have risen the furthest; the humbler the father, the nobler the son.

After Reagan graduated from Eureka College, he worked as a radio announcer at WOC (World of Chiropractic) in Davenport, Iowa. He went on to broadcast Chicago Cubs games, and when he followed the baseball club to California for spring training he took a screen test at Warner Brothers. He left town before his test was reviewed. Reagan believed that returning home helped him get his Hollywood contract. He didn't sacrifice his authenticity to "go Hollywood," he needed only luck. "Actually I had done, through ignorance, the smartest thing it was possible to do."[8]

Reagan's dream as a young man was to become a leading man in what he later called the "house of illusion"—in Hollywood. Eventually this dream of stardom matured into a political vision that would be officially embraced by the Republican Party. The importance of Hollywood to Reaganism does not lie mainly in Reagan's ability to peer professionally into a camera lens. He gives a sense of being at home with himself not because he's an actor, but because he knows his place in the cosmos. Hollywood has at least as much to do with Reagan's substance as his technique.

When Reagan signed his first contract with Warner Brothers, the movie colony was a dream to millions of young people aspiring to become silver-screen legends. During the Depression, Hollywood helped sustain the hope that anything was still possible in America, the opportunity society. Leo C. Rosten, in his classic 1941 study, *Hollywood*, wrote:

> Our culture is saturated with the dynamic attributes of what Max Weber called "the Protestant ethic": Work hard, be virtuous, and you will succeed. But our world, particularly in an era of crisis, does not fulfill these promises, and to the degree that our economy fails to reward those who try hard and train themselves and shun evil, the role of luck becomes increasingly important, and the individual becomes increasingly aware that luck is a crucial part of success. The very fact that opportunities have shrunk, that millions are caught in depressions as in an iron trap, that neither ability, intelligence, nor training seems to guarantee success any more—these make the role of luck more desperately cherished, more desperately invoked in fantasy or prayer. There is an unconscious point to the dream of Hollywood which millions keep alive in their minds.[9]

The star system was the basis of Hollywood box-office success. An actor became a charismatic celebrity because people could see in him their private dreams. A star was an archetype: There was only one Clark Gable, but producers searched for a "Gable type." New contract players at the studios may have thought that they were hired because of their own radiant qualities, but more often than not, they were on the payroll because they reminded producers of someone else. Reagan learned "some time" after his film debut that "I was in Hollywood and at Warner Brothers because of a similarity in voice to that of a promising young actor, Ross Alexander, who—on the verge of stardom at Warner Brothers—was a tragic suicide."[10] Ross Alexander's lingering image made Reagan's film career possible. As an actor he never achieved the status of an archetype, a failure that liberated him for another kind of stardom.

Reagan's most affecting role was in *Knute Rockne,* playing George Gipp, a young football player for Notre Dame, whose death was used by coach Rockne to inspire the team to victory: "Win one for the Gipper." Reagan's silliest role was in *Bedtime for Bonzo,* in which he was upstaged by a chimpanzee. And his best role was in *Kings Row,* which is particularly interesting because it can be interpreted as a dream picture about the New Deal. (When the film was made, in 1941, Reagan was an ardent liberal who idolized Franklin D. Roosevelt and regarded the Republican Party as "the party of big business.")

Kings Row is set in a midwestern small town. Reagan is Drake McHugh, a carefree young man who lives off a trust fund (symbolically: the Roaring Twenties). He courts the town physician's daughter, but his bid for love and respectability is rejected because he is too carefree. The wealthy doctor, played by Charles Coburn, is a sadistic surgeon (the "economic royalist"). When Drake's trust fund is embezzled by the local banker, he is without work or cash (the Crash). He must move to the wrong side of the tracks to live with his new girlfriend, Randy Monaghan, played by Ann Sheridan. Her father, a railroad foreman, gets Drake a job. But one night Drake is hit by a train, and the cruel doctor is summoned. Drake's legs are amputated. "Where's the rest of me?" he cries upon awakening. He's crushed (the Depression). But his best friend, Parris Mitchell, played by Robert Cummings, who has been studying psychoanalysis in Vienna, is informed about the accident by Randy. Parris writes a letter, describing the accident as a "ghastly tragedy," especially because Drake "lived by his freedom and independence." Above all, care must be taken to "avoid the helpless invalid complex." Drake must *"make a new beginning."* Soon Parris arrives on the scene. He tells Drake that he has nothing to fear but fear itself. He lends Drake money to get him on his feet again. Parris is a doctor who fixes bodies and souls (Dr. New Deal). By the time Parris tells Drake that losing his legs was unnecessary, Drake has regained his old confidence. "Let's give a party. I feel swell," he says in the last line of the movie. (Happy days are here again!)

Reagan's movie career, poised to take off after the success of *Kings Row,* was grounded by World War II. He served in Hollywood, making films for the army. Although he didn't leave California and never heard enemy fire, he contends that his wartime experience jolted him.* He wrote:

> The story of my disillusionment with big government is linked fundamentally with the ideals that suddenly sprouted and put forth in the war years. Like most of the soldiers who came back, I expected a world suddenly reformed. I hoped and believed that the blood and death and confusion of World War II would result in a regeneration of mankind. . . . I was wrong. I discovered that the world was almost the same and perhaps a little worse. . . . [This] crystallized a determination in my mind. I would work with the tools I had: my thoughts, my speaking abilities, my reputation as an actor. I would try to bring about the regeneration of the world I believed should have automatically appeared. This introduced me to the world of reality as opposed to make-believe.[11]

Shortly after the war, Reagan became president of the Screen Actors Guild. All political groups jockeyed for power inside the Guild, including the Communists. In the beginning of Reagan's involvement in Hollywood politics, he characterized himself as having the "uncomfortable consciousness of being unusually naïve."[12] He regarded himself as a "near-hopeless hemophilic liberal."[13] Within a couple of years he became such a realist that, when he felt his life threatened, he packed a .32-caliber Smith and Wesson revolver on a shoulder strap. He discovered that instead of harmony, shared values and trust in the liberal community, there was conflict, faction, and deceit. He came to believe that if Communists like those he encountered in Hollywood won, the world would fall apart.

Reagan was a premature neoconservative. Like the neoconservatives, he first became personally disillusioned with the left and then

---

*In 1983, Reagan told the Israeli leader Yitzhak Shamir that at the end of the war he personally helped liberate the Nazi death camps as an army photographer and, deeply moved, made a filmic record. By this method, the preserved memory would presumably prevent historical distortions.

attributed the world's fall to the left's activities and programs. He believed that his mission was to restore the rightful order of things.

His conversion from left-winger to right-winger wasn't the result of a single epiphany, but the outcome of a series of upheavals, including his tangle with the Communists in Hollywood, his encounter with the stiff British tax system, his bitter divorce from Jane Wyman, and his marriage to Nancy Davis, whose wealthy stepfather was a staunch conservative. Reagan continued moving rightward when his movie career stalled. In 1954 he became a traveling salesman for General Electric and the virtues of free enterprise. He also became a star in the new medium of television, hosting *GE Theater* and *Death Valley Days.* His standard GE speech, about "encroaching government control," was a litany of engaging anecdotes and facts culled from magazines like *Reader's Digest.* He was continually clipping pertinent articles and underlining brief stories to enliven and update "the speech."

One day, in 1959, he added a paragraph to "the speech" in which he attacked the Tennessee Valley Authority. This alarmed GE's executives because the company did $50 million worth of government business. Reagan was pressured to drop the offending remarks. In 1962, when GE officials demanded that he drop the ideological pitch from "the speech," he refused. Twenty-four hours later, the corporation canceled *GE Theater.* In analyzing what happened in this confrontation of conservative principle and corporate interest, Reagan turned to the writing of another former left-winger, Whittaker Chambers. In a passage cited by Reagan in his memoirs, Chambers wrote: "When I took up my little sling and aimed at Communism, I also hit at something else. What I hit was the force of that great Socialist revolution which in the name of *liberalism,* spasmodically, incompletely, somewhat formlessly, but always in the same direction, has been inching its icecap over the nation for two decades. I had no adequate idea of its extent, the depth of its penetration, or the fierce vindictiveness of its revolutionary temper." Reagan decided that the "attempted hatchet job" on his speech reflected the "vindictiveness of the liberal temper."[14]

Reagan's autobiography stops just as his political career began. The book's final paragraph conveys optimism and restlessness. "The days stretch ahead with promise. The city closes in on the ranch—we prowl the countryside scouting a new location." Had he concluded here, the story that began as a "Huck Finn–Tom Sawyer idyll" might have recalled the last lines of *Huckleberry Finn,* where Huck's impulse is to escape the civilizing clutches of Aunt Polly and "light out for the territory ahead of the rest." But Reagan did not stop here. He was not attempting any symmetry with Mark Twain. Instead, he mustered an appeal to the Zeus of Hollywood. "I should turn to the sages for some profound utterance to close out these words. Still, it is more fitting that a remark by The King of actors, Clark Gable, sticks in my mind. Clark said, 'The most important thing a man can know is that, as he approaches his own door, someone on the other side is listening for the sound of his footsteps.' I have found the rest of me."[15] You can go home again—it's the happy ending that also sets the stage for another new beginning.

In Hollywood, Reagan never made the transition from person to persona. He was a second-rank actor, a player in other people's dreams. He was known as the "Errol Flynn of the B's"—there was no "Reagan type." When Jack Warner was asked what he thought of Reagan for governor, he is reputed to have answered, "Jimmy Stewart for governor, Ronald Reagan for best friend." Stewart, after all, was a superstar, an archetype. (Moreover, he had been a U.S. senator in two movies— *Mr. Smith Goes to Washington* and *The Man Who Shot Liberty Valence.*) Warner understood Reagan only in the context of moviemaking, where a "best friend" couldn't be a brilliant leading man. A "best friend" in politics was altogether another matter. Reagan's inability to rise high in the Hollywood firmament was critical to his political stardom. If he had been a superstar, his celebrity would have been blinding; we wouldn't have been able to see his ideology. Reagan, however, was ordinary enough to make his message sound trustworthy. He failed to become a Hollywood archetype, but cast an ideology into a mythology. He achieved his real stardom by bringing Reaganism to us, by asking us to go back with him to where dreams began.

Reaganism was the star vehicle Reagan had been waiting for all his life, the ultimate treatment of conservatism. Reaganism integrated his dreams and deeds, his inner and outer selves. But he had to live his life before he could master the mythology. Great acting that electrifies audiences is born of conviction. And while Reagan exalted the individual, he stood at the head of a mass movement.

The scene: The 1980 Republican Party Convention in Detroit. The issue: passage of the party platform. The vote: unanimously in favor. The platform's preamble closed with these ringing words: "By reversing our economic decline, by reversing our international decline, we can and will resurrect our dreams." Thus, economic and foreign policies were acclaimed as means to a larger goal—making dreams come true —or, more precisely, bringing dreams back from the dead.

Dreams are the raw material of myth. They are condensed, fragmented, symbolic, super-real; they have a vividness and intensity beyond waking reality. They are an inverted world of wish-fulfillment. They present the answers but not the questions, and so they can seem at once enigmatic and crystal-clear. They're a lot like movies. The substance of Hollywood, of course, is the production of dream pictures. The movies are dreams of what never happened, but what should or could have happened. Movies can create nostalgia and even homesickness for places that are only dreams, like Andy Hardy's small town or John Ford's and John Wayne's Old West. (Movies are fictions, not lies.) Reagan has the special ability to evoke these images and sentiments in politics. He can make us feel nostalgic for the America that never was. He can make us feel that everything will turn out all right. Reaganism is a structure for understanding dreams so that we can make them come true for ourselves and for America.

The first myth of Reaganism—a community myth about an earlier, preindustrial America—honors the traditional world for which Russell Kirk longed. Like many community myths, this one is about a paradise on earth, a land of infinite plenty, open to all, where dreams come true and true merit is rewarded. Those who cleared the land brought order out of chaos. The land gave ungrudgingly, nurturing a special people, a community of faith. "The success story of America," Reagan said on April 24, 1982, "is neighbor helping neighbor." One big happy family lived here. For those who had fled a corrupt Old World, it was a new beginning.

There was a divine hand in this creation. "Call it mysticism if you will," said Reagan in his July 4, 1968, message. "I have always believed there was some divine plan that placed this nation between the oceans to be sought out and found by those with a special kind of courage and an overabundant love of freedom." This is a God of plenty, of "overabundance," who has more than enough for His chosen people.

In the "divine plan" America exists as a New World, or not at all. And the chosen people have the gift to draw upon the primal power of creation itself. "There are no words to express the extraordinary strength and character of this breed of people we call Americans," Reagan said in his 1980 nomination acceptance speech. "Everywhere we have met thousands of Democrats, Independents, and Republicans from all economic conditions and walks of life bound together in that community of shared values of family, work, neighborhood, peace, and freedom. . . . They are the kind of men and women Tom Paine had in mind when he wrote—during the darkest days of the American Revolution—'We have it in our power to begin the world over again.' "*

The second myth that contributes to the grand mythology is the way of Von Hayek. It explains the way the mundane world works, where there's no image of paradise. Outside the gates of Eden, the way of the world is hard work; and progress is the survival of the fittest. (It was Reagan, after all, who as host of *GE Theater* intoned: "Progress is our most important product.") This world is dynamic, and the more risks that are taken, the more luck and fortune result. The free-market myth equates competition with liberty and economic planning with tyranny, individualism with prosperity and government with stagnation.

The third and perhaps most potent myth is about the demonic power of big government, a myth explaining why the world is in such

---

*Paine indeed argued for making the world over again. He regarded the reign of the past over the present as despotism. And he devoted himself to this subject at length in *The Rights of Man,* a reply to Edmund Burke's *Reflections on the Revolution in France.* Burke argued that posterity was bound to honor the laws established by a wise antiquity. Paine countered that "every age and generation must be free to act for itself, *in all cases,* as the ages and generation which preceded it. The vanity and presumption of governing beyond the grave, is the most ridiculous and insolent of all tyrannies. Man has no property in man; neither has any generation any property in the generations which are to follow."[16]

pathetic shape and why the first two myths have been confounded. Through the demonic power of the state about which Whittaker Chambers warned, progress has been limited, competition restrained, the moral fiber of the people weakened, and true merit gone unrewarded. The "compact" of community has been violated and the free market displaced. "For too long now, we've removed from our people the decisions on how to dispose of what they created," Reagan said in 1981. "We have strayed from first principles. We must alter our course." Only a special evil could lead Americans away from their "first principles." There can be no accommodation with this evil.

Of course the biggest big government is Communism, and the New Deal is logically construed as an opening wedge for the greatest evil. "For some decades now," Reagan wrote, "the liberal movement has worked to centralize government authority in Washington and to increase government's power. . . . We find the ultimate in government planning in the Soviet Union."[17] Liberals, by leading in the establishment of the welfare state, deprive us of our liberty. They have made a treacherous bargain. Some liberals, Reagan learned in Hollywood, were in league with those who would destroy us. And he became an FBI informer in order to thwart them. "We are faced with the most evil enemy mankind has known in his long climb from the swamp to the stars," he wrote. "There can be no security anywhere in the free world if there is not fiscal and economic stability in the United States. Those who ask us to trade our freedom for the soup kitchen of the welfare state are architects of a policy of accommodation."[18] The devil gains power by the trick of appealing to our good instincts. "It is in the area of social welfare that government has found its most fertile growing bed," Reagan wrote. "So many of us accept our responsibility for those less fortunate. We are susceptible to humanitarian appeals."[19]

From the perspective of Reaganism one can see just how demonic big government is. It makes you want what doesn't really belong to you. Entitlements, such as welfare or Social Security, aren't seen by recipients as charity or rewards, but as rights. Reagan said, on January 14, 1982, "Did we forget that the function of government is not to confer happiness on us, but to give us the opportunity to work out happiness for ourselves?"

Big government establishes a system that tries to satisfy infinite desires. These desires, by the recipients of entitlements, fuel the expansion of government. "Because no government ever voluntarily reduces itself in size, government programs once launched never go out of existence," Reagan wrote.[20]

Big government turns wants into needs. And if one's desires can never be sated, more is demanded no matter what the ruinous consequences. This makes growth necessary but seemingly impossible because the gluttonous always feel empty. All standards of measurement are lost. Reagan wrote: "Government tends to grow, government programs take on weight and momentum as public servants say, always with the best of intentions, 'What greater service we could render if only we had a little money and a little more power.' But the truth is that outside of its legitimate function, government does nothing as well or as economically as the private sector of the economy."[21] And since government feeds off the deadly sin of gluttony, how can anyone know then who is "truly needy?"

Through taxation, big government takes from those who have made money and gives it to those who haven't, contradicting the lesson of hard work the market should be teaching. "Have we the courage and the will to face up to the immorality and discrimination of the progressive surtax and demand a return to traditional proportionate taxation?" Reagan asked in his memoir.[22]

Because big government promises to solve all of our problems for us without demanding individual initiative in return, it creates rising expectations that can't be met. Riots of the frustrated and envious, gluttonous looting, disrespect for authority, and excessive litigation follow. The demonic power of big government fosters a world of chaos.

This threat to order is manifested politically in interest-group liberalism, which makes people think of themselves first as members of an interest group, not as Americans. Through this system of profane interests, government expands, entitlements increase, and politicians stay in office: tax, spend, elect is the liberal formula. The American identity is shattered, the community violated. "We hear much of special interest groups," said Reagan in his 1981 Inaugural. "Well, our concern must be for a special interest group that has been too long neglected. . . . They are . . . 'We the people.' This breed called Americans."

When big government supplants the free market as a new kind of impersonal force, it reduces the elements of risk and incentive that have made the American character. Our spiritual condition is at stake. "I would like to have a crusade today, and I would like to lead that crusade with your help," said Reagan during his October 28, 1980, debate with Jimmy Carter. "And it would be one to take government off the backs of the great people of this country, and turn you loose again to do those things that I know you can do so well, because you did them and made this country great."

Reagan's "crusade" is a mythic battle for a Restoration. He does not hold Americans responsible for the existence of the national government: I'm OK, you're OK. The devil is an external enemy, whose origin is some mysterious netherworld of history. But the devil's mischief is evident in the disorder of the interest groups and the rigid tyranny of government planners. There is no original-sin motif in his mythology. We can therefore go back in time to the creation, where we will recover our "first principles" and our power. When the Restoration occurs, the dream of a Conservative Opportunity Society will come true. The vivid rhetoric about an ideal community and an ideal free market will be reality.

The Restoration appears like Disneyland, the "Magic Kingdom," an amalgam of various theme parks whose coherence comes from the dreamy sensation they arouse. (Appropriately, Reagan was the television broadcaster at the 1955 opening of Disneyland.) In the world of community, everyone has come home to stay. And everyone shares the same faith, even when it's different; this is the vague "Judeo-Christian tradition," which is timeless. The highest form of knowledge is common sense, and luckily everyone has it. But loss of faith inevitably leads to expulsion from the community.

Then one can enter the world of the free market, where everyone succeeds by striking out on his own. Here time is money, and common sense is no substitute for inside information. One can fall from grace by filing for a Chapter 11 bankruptcy, which, if handled properly by accountants and lawyers, might be a condition for future success. Faith that supply creates its own demand is helpful, but creating demand to meet supply can lead to a higher state than faith: market confidence.

Reagan's economic program is the Restoration in action. Cutting the budget severs the chains shackling citizens to government; the regimen of budget-cutting makes the citizen active in the market again; deregulation slashes bureaucratic authority. It becomes clear that government isn't as important as we had thought and is really a meddler. The supply-side tax cut, rather than encouraging gluttony by giving us more money to spend, provides rewards and incentives so that we can make our own way in the free market. Cutting taxes also starves government, forcing it to reduce its size. "I believe it is clear," Reagan said in his 1980 acceptance speech, "our federal government is overgrown and overweight. Indeed, it is time for our government to go on a diet."

Policies ought to be the gauge of a President's program. But Reagan himself stresses that public actions derive from psychic sources. He wants more than the enactment of laws; he wants a New Beginning. "We have every right to dream heroic dreams," he said in his 1980 Inaugural. We must "resurrect" our dreams, according to the Republican Party platform. "America's future is in your dreams. Make them come true," Reagan said on January 14, 1982. ("If you can dream it, you can do it," said Walt Disney.)

To make the dreams of Reaganism come true, Reagan invokes magic—"the magic of the marketplace," a phrase he uses repeatedly. Here is the underlying principle of the mythological method. "When I spoke about a New Beginning," the President said on January 14, 1982, "I was talking about much more than budget cuts and incentives for savings and investment. I was talking about a fundamental change in the relationship between citizen and government, a change that honors the legacy of the Founding Fathers. . . ." By making one myth—the free-market myth—come true, another myth—the community myth—will come true, too. And then the spell of demonic power will be broken. This is a special kind of magic, early defined by Sir James George Frazer in *The Golden Bough* as "contagious magic." "The logical basis of Contagious Magic," he wrote, ". . . is a mistaken association of ideas;

its physical basis, if we may speak of such a thing . . . is a material medium of some sort which, like the ether of modern physics, is assumed to unite distant objects and to convey impressions from one to the other."[23]

To Reagan, the "magic of the marketplace" restores prosperity and thus community. The magic reconciles economic selfishness and community obligation. The dilemma of private versus public interests is neatly resolved, and the sum of all individuals becomes a nation. No matter that the central values of the community and free-market myths are absolutely contradictory: when government relocates to smaller quarters, neighborly volunteers will assume the running of social services and the rich will be generous, the poor grateful, the hard-working eventually successful.

Reagan has thought about and refined these themes for decades. He expresses them in every important public statement he makes as president. His most stirring and memorable speeches are the most clearly mythological. In his acceptance speech at the 1980 Republican convention, for example, he spoke of a land placed here by "Divine Providence." The chosen community of Americans cherished values that "transcend persons and parties." These values created "a previously undreamed of prosperity." But big government is "eroding our national will and purpose." We must experience a "rebirth," make a "new beginning."

On March 8, 1983, the President spoke to the National Association of Evangelicals, telling them that "modern-day secularism" is "discarding the tried and time-tested values upon which our very civilization is based." American history is the "story of hopes fulfilled and dreams made into reality." Against us stands the Soviet Union, "an evil empire." Reagan quoted Whittaker Chambers, who "wrote that the crisis of the Western world exists to the degree in which the West is indifferent to God."

Reagan's mythology is a variant of what the sociologist Robert N. Bellah has called "the civil religion."[24] (Bellah's intellectual construction has been taken up with a vengeance by the neoconservative Secretary of Education William Bennett, who presents "the civil religion" as some sort of timeless catechism.) Reagan talks about returning to "first principles," as though they were valid for all times. Yet "the civil religion" has not been static, handed down from generation to generation like a meticulously preserved museum piece. It is almost infinitely pliable and has meant different things in different periods. Reagan's version is not a perfect restatement of the original "civil religion." Rather, his account is a major revision, a departure from that expressed by the Puritans, the Founding Fathers, and Abraham Lincoln.

Reaganism is compatible with the traditional "civil religion" in two key respects: Reagan believes that we can start the world over again, with America as the model; and he believes that we need only look at our relationship with America to know where we stand with God. After this, Reagan is a radical revisionist.

In his conception of the chosen people and their obligations, he proposes a direct reversal of both the Puritans' and Lincoln's ideas. For Reagan, it isn't self-denial and sacrifice that make one part of the chosen people, one of the elect. His presidential campaigns, in fact, have been built on derision of sacrifice. In 1980, he sneered at Jimmy Carter for suggesting that the "moral equivalent of war" might be needed to meet "limits to growth." And in 1984, he dismissed Walter Mondale's calls to face the federal deficit as "gloom and doom." The issue in both cases, according to Reagan, was optimism versus pessimism.

But what happens when the Restoration arrives, when it's "morning again in America," as his 1984 television ads proclaimed? In Reagan's "civil religion," election is manifested by conspicuous consumption. What God wants for us is a good description of what Reagan, the self-made man, and his millionaire friends have accumulated. This God takes most pleasure in those who are most pleased. Our enjoyment of the bounty is a sign of piety. The dissatisfied exhibit envy, the sign of failure. And the reason they are malcontents is that big government pretended it could make them happy. Since it's really satanic, those who place their faith in it will always be disappointed. But once they are shaken from their false faith, their chronic agitation will cease. Then, when everyone believes, dreams will be resurrected, the free market will be reopened, like the old frontier, and we will again travel to glory.

Reagan's "civil religion" is soothing. He makes use of the symbols of the past, but requests nothing more than credence. He claims that his "civil religion," his mythology, is eternal. But, above all, it lacks a sense of history. Reaganism is about a time that is out of time, memory without history.

A month after the attempt on his life, on May 17, 1981, Reagan spoke at a packed Notre Dame football stadium, the site of one of his cinematic triumphs, the alma mater of George Gipp. Now Pat O'Brien, the actor who had played Knute Rockne in the movie, was on the stage with him. The film, the President told the crowd, wasn't just about a football team. It was an archetypal story about another "little band of men we call the Founding Fathers," who "gave us more than a nation." It was up to us to restore their dream. "We forgot to challenge the notion that the state is the principal vehicle of social change; forgot that millions of social interactions among free individuals and institutions can do more to foster economic and social progress than all the careful schemes of government planners. Well, at last we are remembering."

Reagan's mythology tells us not only what to remember, but what we can conveniently and without guilt forget. In the course of the battle against demonic government, we must forget, among other things, that the dramatic expansion of the federal government began in the Civil War, under the aegis of Abraham Lincoln, illuminating the American national idea and stoking the fires of economic growth. Reagan wants to take us backward, but the nineteenth century (and the eighteenth century even more) violates all of his precepts and assumptions.

Reaganism, however, cannot be disproved by history or events. To believers, the flaws are in the world, not in the doctrine. Reaganism can always explain the cosmos. Reagan is a radical reactionary because his image of the past is so ahistorical that to return there would indeed be a radical change. Thus, Reaganism can never reach a culmination; the Restoration can never take place. Reagan's dream of the past is beyond our reach. Yet it's indestructible because the path to it is always open in our imaginations.

Followers of Reaganism believe Reagan expresses certain quintessential American ideals, which are summarized by the word "conservatism." But Reaganism is hardly classical conservatism, justifying the status quo as a moral order that must not be tampered with. Reaganism is the popular expression of a sectarian worldview, that of a rising policy- and opinion-making elite—the Counter-Establishment.

Traditional conservatives cherish continuity above all, want to preserve existing institutions and customs, and fulminate against radical innovation. The great English conservative Edmund Burke warned of "metaphysical" politicians who attempt to govern by abstractions. He viewed the state as a father whose failings could not be cured by the voodoo of the son. He urged prudence, caution and patience. And he counseled against new beginnings when he wrote:

> To avoid therefore the evils of inconstancy and versatility, ten thousand times worse than those of obstinacy and the blindest prejudice, we have consecrated the state, that no man should approach to look into its defects or corruptions but with due caution; that he should never dream of beginning its reformation by its subversion; that he should approach to the faults of the state as to the wounds of a father, with pious awe, and trembling solicitude. By this wise prejudice we are taught to look with horrour on those children of their country, who are prompt rashly to hack that aged parent in pieces, and put him into the kettle of magicians, in hopes that by their poisonous weeds, and wild incantations, they may regenerate the paternal constitution, and renovate their father's life.[25]

It is hard to imagine a better summary of the mythological system of Reaganism.

CHAPTER TEN

THE WILL

TO BELIEVE

In February 1982, weary of all the wrangling over his proposed 1983 budget, Ronald Reagan took a vacation in Barbados. He had been invited there by his old friend, the actress Claudette Colbert, who maintained a home on the island. Among the guests at the presidential retreat was William F. Buckley, Jr. The conservative writer was carrying a private message from Richard Nixon: Reagan needed "a nutcutter, someone who can do what Agnew did for Nixon, what Nixon did for Eisenhower. Someone to handle Tip O'Neill." Nixon viewed life, especially public life, as harsh and hostile, where criticism was inescapable and humiliation always possible. A president's role was difficult: he must maintain the dignity of his high office, yet he must also mete out punishment to his opponents. He must therefore have a henchman whose dark impulses are unrestrained by ruffles and flourishes. "Nancy was more interested in this than Reagan was," said Buckley. "But you can never measure the impact of a story. It can lodge itself into his memory and come out someday."

Reagan never acted on Nixon's advice. When one believes in the magic of the marketplace, a "nutcutter" isn't needed. Where Nixon felt the need for vengeance, Reagan counted on optimism and faith. Conservatism, after he became president, was organized around a prediction of spectacular prosperity, the greatest boom of all time, that would come true because we believed it would. "All we need to have is faith, and that dream will come true," Reagan said in a speech on April 28, 1981. He assumed an alchemical process in which individual faith would be turned into market confidence. If the voters believed in his program, Congress would enact it and investors would instantly feel both secure and venturesome. The bull market and capital spending that would follow would be a triumph of positive thinking. His program, however, did not initially catalyze this chain reaction.

Upon the President's return from Barbados, the recession deepened. The winter image of Reagan splashing in the tropical surf had not enhanced his popularity. His program's fairness was becoming a public issue. Already its partiality to wealth and the wealthy had been symbolized by the First Lady's purchase of expensive new china, her extravagant new White House hairdressing salon, and her lavish designer gowns. Reagan and his senior advisers began a public-relations effort to counter the unfortunate political effects of the recession. For example, promptly after his vacation, when the *Washington Post* ran a front-page story about a black family in Virginia on whose lawn a Ku Klux Klan cross had been burned five years previously, the President descended on the scene in a helicopter to comfort them. On the advice of political strategists, the Reagans' Rodeo Drive style of living was altered. No more black-tie dinners. No more riding breeches. A heartfelt expression of sympathy for the unemployed became a regular feature of the standard speech.

To the degree that Reagan's promise of prosperity was unfulfilled the actual conditions of his youth were re-created—the 1920s, a time of yawning inequalities of wealth, and the 1930s, a time of vast unemployment. George Stigler, the University of Chicago economist, a colleague of Milton Friedman, put the matter frankly. He was invited to the White House to be congratulated by the President for winning the 1982 Nobel Prize in economics. Afterward, he appeared at a press conference, a media event at which, shrewd presidential aides assumed, the distinguished free-market economist would praise the free-market President. Instead, Stigler called supply-side economics a "slogan" and observed that the nation was in the throes of a "depression," a forbidden word conjuring unpleasant images of Herbert Hoover and breadlines. For using such illicit language Stigler was promptly hustled out of the press room.

The *Wall Street Journal,* the standard-bearer of supply-side economics, in the meantime expressed great admiration for the President's refusal to resort to Keynesian remedies, even as unemployment lines lengthened. "The economic downturn set postwar records in unemployment and hit some states like a depression, but it is also bound to produce benefits," editorialized the *Journal.* "As the 'Austrian school' of economics teaches, recessions play an important role in economic growth. They weed out inefficient, outmoded enterprises and free resources for new ones. The Reagan administration is the first in memory to adopt this school of thought and to deal with a slump by doing nothing."[1]

Reagan's initial success carried within it the seeds of discord. The ideas the Counter-Establishment had manufactured had helped bring its candidate to the presidency, but because ideology was central to conservative politics doctrinal differences led to intense factional conflict. What had helped elevate conservatism to power now placed its future in doubt.

The corporate managers' early enthusiasm for Reaganomics was transformed into an incessant demand for "mid-course corrections." They lined up with the traditional Republicans, who had never been comfortable with the supply-side solution, which offended their deeply ingrained belief in an economy based on self-denial and self-restraint. They had a habitual fear of deficits, the mechanism by which liberals supported a host of social programs. This point of view had its bastion in the GOP Senate leadership caucus, where Robert Dole spoke for tradition: "People who advocate only cutting taxes live in a dream world. We Republicans have been around awhile. We don't have to march in lockstep with the supply-siders." The CEOs found the Republicans more congenial than the conservatives. And the president's senior staff, generally, shared this perspective. Among them, Stockman carried the day. By the time of the publication of the *Atlantic* article documenting his disillusionment he had already convinced his colleagues; they were chagrined at his indiscretion but protected him from dismissal. They spent much of their time calculating how to get Reagan to accept tax increases to stanch the deficit, even coining euphemisms for his benefit: "revenue enhancers" was a favorite. Leaders of the Business

Roundtable were shepherded into the Oval Office, where Reagan was urged to be "statesmanlike."

The free-market ideologues fell to fighting among themselves. According to the original theory, the Mundell-Laffer Hypothesis, a loose fiscal policy and a tight money policy were yin and yang. Now the supply-siders declared war on the monetarists, whose ranks they believed the traitor Stockman had joined. So long as the recession dragged on, the supply-siders claimed that their theory wasn't being tested. "It has *not* been tried under Reagan," insisted George Gilder. They wanted deeper tax cuts and a restoration of the gold standard, monetarism by other means. The monetarists, for their part, wanted more harassment of Fed chairman Paul Volcker, a kind of Pavlovian punishment drill to make him obey Milton Friedman's money supply targets. "The data," asserted Beryl Sprinkel, the monetarist Under Secretary of the Treasury, "is clear at least as far back as Adam Smith."

On August 19, 1982, the Congress passed a $98.9 million tax increase, molded and maneuvered by Dole. The measure was opposed only by conservatives, rallied by Jack Kemp, who denounced it as a "dramatic U-turn." The Democratic ranks held steady for the Republican bill, and Reagan hailed its passage as critical to his "crusade." Thus a year after he signed the largest tax cut in history, he signed the largest tax increase. This time there was no fanfare when he affixed his signature to the bill, no desk on the front lawn of Rancho del Cielo, no twenty-four pens, no reporters. Conservatives were aghast. "The collapse of Reaganomics," wrote Buckley, "is testimony to a failure of nerve and understanding."[2] By early 1983, the press was heralding the zeroing out of the conservative presidency. "The stench of failure hangs over Ronald Reagan's White House," editorialized *The New York Times.* "Mr. Reagan's loss of authority only halfway through his term should alarm all Americans."[3]

Reagan, however, still possessed the authority of ideology. He believed in the happy ending, not in econometric forecasts. Even in signing the tax increase he did not believe that any fundamental revision was taking place; this was simply a tactical adjustment. Policy was not the alpha and omega. The appearance of a recession rather than a boom proved to him the tenacious power of the nefarious forces he was fighting. His beliefs never varied. "I'm the supply-side mole in the White House," he told his friends. Without his implacable faith that all would work out well, the conservative project might have shattered on the rocks. No matter how his policy changed, his message was constant. By maintaining control of the ideological wheel he was able to steer public opinion when the recovery finally materialized. His control of the interpretation of events was of greater political significance than the events themselves.

In the midst of the crisis of doubt, in 1982, Richard Wirthlin, the President's pollster, polled for "patience." He discovered that a majority of voters believed they ought to be patient, that Reagan's programs would work in a year, that Reagan himself was likeable. Polling for "patience" was not the same thing as polling for popularity, or even for what survey researchers call "favorability." The data collected by Wirthlin was regarded by the White House as a statistical indicator of faith.

Throughout 1982, major administration figures proclaimed almost weekly that the economic recovery was beginning. Their pious projections were wrong. The Democrats, emboldened by the demonstrable failure of the predictions, escalated their attacks. By fall the Democratic National Committee produced cutting television advertisements that concluded: "It's not fair. It's Republican." The Republican National Committee countered with television spots and a slogan of its own: "Stay the course." The catchphrase referred less to specific policies than to mythology. The persistence of the recession, the growing intensity of the opposition, and the nature of Reaganism led the President and his loyalists in late 1982 to defend his program on the grounds of faith.

Reagan's faith was of the kind that the philosopher William James described in his essay *The Will to Believe.* Faith was not belief in something we knew to be untrue, "some patent superstition." James pointed to cases "where a fact cannot come at all unless a preliminary faith exists in its coming . . . *where faith in a fact can help create the fact*" (emphasis in original text).[4] The more we invested our faith in Reagan, the closer we would come to realizing his goals. If we did not falter, faith could bring on the Restoration. Conversely, disbelief was more than mere opposition—it made the program fail.

The New Beginning was by no means a certainty; predestination was not a tenet of Reaganism. Big government, a demonic power "coming through the windows, underneath the door and down the chimney," according to Reagan, speaking on October 28, 1982, might win. To the extent that we doubted our power to accomplish the ends of Reaganism, these ends would be unfinished. Faith was therefore crucial. On October 21, the President claimed that the "voices of fear and doom" among the Democrats threatened recovery. "There is a psychological element to a recession," he said. "You have to ask those critics in an election year: Do they really want a recovery? Or would they be smiling broadly if things were getting worse simply because it might seem politically advantageous to them?" If we wavered, Reagan and Reaganism were jeopardized. But with faith, they could be fulfilled: "faith in a fact can help create the fact." Faith would reconcile two irreconcilable myths of Reaganism—the free-market myth of a wide-open world of enterprising individuals and the community myth of a close, happy family. For the faithful, the recession and its attendant miseries were no judgment. Rather, economic hardships indicated the epic quality of the struggle, the tenaciousness of the enemy.

On May 25, 1982, Reagan solemnly charged that Tip O'Neill wanted to "cancel the election of 1980." The President said, "We are engaged in an epic conflict. . . . We will never shelve the mandate of 1980 and return to politics as usual." He asked to be judged on the purity of his opponents. If they did not believe in conservatism, his program's shortcomings must be attributed to them. Reagan's insistence that when his program was incomplete it was not his own was compelling evidence of its mythological nature, for myths depend upon a seamless web for their power. Reaganism imperfect could never really be Reaganism. To alter the plan was to compromise it fatally. Yet it could never be enacted whole because in a democracy there is always opposition: "politics as usual." Thus there would always be a convenient explanation for failure.

The President appeared to believe that liberalism was prefabricated when in fact it was improvisatory. In general, the mimetic conservative reaction—"shadow liberalism"—was founded on this misconception. Reagan himself never appreciated that Tip O'Neill always sought specific and limited objectives. The Speaker was not one to engage in any "epic conflict." It wasn't his style. He respected procedure and precedent. He understood that all members of Congress considered their views legitimate, and to the extent that they kept getting reelected, they *were* legitimate. Interests also were legitimate to O'Neill. Conflicting claims had to be weighed, sometimes one against the other. Yet in the end there must be an accommodation. The process must go on.

Reagan, for his part, ascribed coherent intent to O'Neill and the Democrats. He believed that if we had faith in conservatism we would not practice "politics as usual." His own special brand of politics was dependent on media appearances and media events. "Our economic program will work because Americans want it to work," he said. To turn spirit into matter required faith—and publicity. So public opinion had to be constantly rallied by Reagan. The style of his leadership was devoted to the substance of his myths.

Many people saw Reagan's charm as part of his program. They conflated his personality with his public program, which accounted for much of the enduring patience detected by pollster Wirthlin. This popular blurring of image and policy was central to Reagan's position within the mythology. On the one hand, Reagan had risen from humble origins to become a movie star, a millionaire, the President—the free-market myth. On the other, he was just like the next-door neighbor, plainspoken, humorous, commonsensical, authentic—the community myth. Reagan showed that the myths that were theoretically at odds could work well together. Why couldn't they work for society? The mythology could be extended from the body of Reagan to the body politic.

There was something unique yet commonplace about Reagan, who had good fortune and was still without pretension. His extraordinary qualities were ordinary traits magnified. The charismatic individual dreams the dream for the nation. His life is our dream. We don't recognize that we've helped give his persona its power. We are sure he's done it himself. We don't understand that charisma comes ultimately from the crowd. But this is not a one-way transaction. In return for making him our leader, Reagan told us that the hand of Providence was on everyone, not just on him. He offered the possibility of stardom to us all. "We are not trying to help the rich," he said on May 14, 1982. "We're trying to preserve one of the few systems left on earth where people at the bottom of the ladder can still look forward to getting rich." At a $1,000-a-plate Republican fund-raiser in the Washington Hilton on May 5, he had explained, "We're the party that wants to see an America in which people can still get rich." He sprinkled stardust over everyone, what Max Weber called the "charismatic distribution of grace."[5]

When he was in Hollywood, Reagan was never the superstar, the "King," like Clark Gable, whom he quoted reverently in the final sentences of his memoir, *Where's the Rest of Me?* Reagan's incomplete success as a movie star was a precondition to his attraction as a political star. Many movie stars live out fantasies we may want to see projected but don't necessarily want to enter ourselves. A film star whose personal life is out of control may still be an attraction, and his unconventional escapades may be why we pay to see him perform. But he cannot offer us security. A political star, on the other hand, must be in control of himself and the state. He must be able to command dreams so that he can bring them within our reach. And he must, in some way, embody the dreams himself.

Even the aristocratic Franklin D. Roosevelt was accessible to the common man. Young Reagan's hero worship proved the point. FDR had polio, and part of his appeal was his own vulnerability. If he could master his crippled limbs, he could master a crippled nation. He understood common suffering because he had experienced it himself; his own life was an exemplar of willpower. He was thoroughly convincing when he asked us to believe in ourselves: "We have nothing to fear but fear itself." He told us we were all good, that we were not personally responsible for our fall in the Depression, that hope was realism.

How could the ex-Hollywood star Ronald Reagan be the fearless FDR, the President he cited most often? How could Reagan foster a political realignment on the order of the New Deal? From the beginning, he attempted to recreate a sense of crisis equivalent to that which had prevailed in 1932. This was a conscious strategy, articulated by

David Stockman in his memo, "Avoiding a GOP Economic Dunkirk," written during the transition period for the President-elect. By his own account, Reagan's program was designed to deal with a crisis just like that faced by FDR. "When this administration took office," he said on September 28, 1982, "we found America in the worst economic mess since the days of Franklin Roosevelt. . . . Together we've pulled America back from the brink of disaster." FDR, however, had no need to manufacture an image of apocalypse—an "epic conflict." It was manifest.

On January 20, 1983, the White House released a report, "The Reagan Presidency," prepared by Reagan's staff, that summarized his first two years in office. The report stated: "Acting forcefully and fairly, President Reagan had averted the calamity-in-the-making which greeted him when he took office."[6] Was the "calamity-in-the-making" not really here but incipient, a "calamity" that required special vision to see?

The Reagan administration's creation of a sense of crisis was like moviemaking. The ideologue's policies and the pollster's research provided a kind of "script." The special effects of the presidency—dramatic television appearances and a "national economic emergency"—were used to convince us that a crisis was really occurring. Once the camera was rolling, the situation assumed a logic and momentum of its own, and only the original "script" provided a benchmark to the players.

Reagan's image of crisis unfolded as a vivid picture of demonic power. "Runaway government threatens our economic survival, our most cherished institutions, and the very preservation of freedom itself," he said on July 19, 1982. Two months later he spoke of "government careening out of control, pushing us toward economic collapse, and quite probably, the end of our way of life." He insisted that the crisis existed exactly as he pictured it and that it was of a magnitude for which only conservatism was the appropriate response. If the crisis was inevitable, so was Reagan. His vision of the "end of our way of life" was confirmed, not denied, by rapid economic decline. "The poverty and unemployment of today is an outgrowth of the policies and problems of the late 1960s and the 1970s," he said on September 15, 1982.

When circumstances became dire, he called on us for faith; he could work wonders with us behind him.

But questions arose: Was this a crisis Reagan foresaw or manufactured? Can a nice guy do bad things? Why, if we had such a nice guy as President, did the nation suffer? Jimmy Carter, too, was widely perceived to be a good fellow. Eventually, though, most voters came to see him as weak, incompetent, and impenetrable; nice guys finish last. Reagan, by contrast, was perceived as not only nice but strong and familiar. He made us feel comfortable even as he persuaded us the world was on the edge of catastrophe. He was not a distant star; our faith in him therefore could have an effect, for even though he was a star we could help him. If we didn't help him by believing and urging him on, we betrayed ourselves; his program to make us all stars would fail. Carter, who campaigned in 1976 on the slogan that we needed a government as good as the people, by 1979 was testing his own faith and doubting ours. (It was not insignificant that his memoir was entitled *Keeping Faith.*) Reagan said we were all good and asked for our help. With that call he linked the community to the paramount individual. He needed the community's faith to make individualism come true.

The effects of Reaganism, however squalid, need not lead to disillusionment. For those with definite convictions and firm commitments, the unequivocal refutation of belief is insufficient to provoke apostasy. The sociologists Leon Festinger, Henry W. Riecken, and Stanley Schachter concluded in their landmark study, *When Prophecy Fails,* that "when people are committed to a belief or a course of action, clear disconfirming evidence may simply result in deepened conviction and increased proselytizing."[7] For a political cause or a religion or a messianic cult, each new "disconfirmation" raises the stakes. Some drop out, but those who remain believe ever more strongly. And the stronger the belief, the stronger the reaction to "disconfirmation." If a prediction around which the cause has been formed has not been borne out, it cannot easily be acknowledged as false and the elaborate preparations as vain. There is more at issue than just being wrong; the legitimacy of the effort itself is involved. The more one perceives that the world is falling apart, the more likely one is to discount a failed prediction of a redemption. It's not the timing of redemption so much as the promise of it that sustains the believer. The extent of the difficulty proves the desirability of the goal.

When Reagan was confronted with "disconfirmation," he flatly denied its existence. On September 22, 1982, the Harvard economist Martin Feldstein, appointed by the President to head his Council of Economic Advisers, testified at his confirmation hearings: "Extremists among both the supply-siders and monetarists who predicted that inflation would be reduced without raising unemployment have been decisively proven wrong." Three days later, in a national radio address, Reagan contradicted his own expert, charging that it was "the most cynical form of demagoguery" to suggest that the falling inflation rate had any relationship to rising unemployment. Reagan would not permit himself to be confused by contrary data.

Some information, though, was incontrovertible. Reagan knew in advance that on October 8, 1982, the Commerce Department would release an unemployment figure of 10.1 percent, a symbolic double digit, the highest rate since the Depression. This number would give aid and comfort to the Democrats and cloud the electoral prospects of the Republicans. True to the Festinger theory that awkward contradictions provoke missionary activity, the President toured the country, visiting states that were overwhelmingly well disposed to him, to declare that he anticipated and deplored such a sorry statistic. He extended his sympathy to the victims, blamed big government, and asked for "confidence." He needed to take the political sting out of the number. Senior White House aides decided that the President must take to the airwaves. The weapon of the "Great Communicator" must be deployed.

The significance of Reagan's speeches can usually be gauged by the completeness with which he reiterates the mythology of Reaganism. Some speeches are prosaic, containing just a parable or two to illustrate the myths. But when Reagan feels the need to elicit a tremendous public response, he recites it all. On October 13, 1982, he delivered an exceptional speech. It was not a simple campaign speech whose message was tailored just to the situation. It was pure Reaganism, beginning with a testimonial of faith from a citizen and ending with a plea for faith from the President. He asked us to remember that he was trying to make dreams come true. He traced all of our economic problems back to the demonic power of big government. We must reject "the quick fix," which created "trendlines to disaster." And he proclaimed the twin utopian goals of ending "politics as usual" and conquering the business cycle. Prosperity would be permanent, "built to last." No more zigs and zags on the chart, just a rising straight line into the future. Reagan read at length a letter from "a wife and mother named Judith, who lives in Selma, Alabama," which concluded: "We believe. We must—it's all we have." "Well," said the President, "Judith, I hear you . . . and you deserve to know what we're doing in these difficult times to bring your dream—the American dream—back to life again after so many years of mistakes and neglect." In this speech, the "dream" had already died. Heroic measures, a Lazarus-effect, were needed to bring it "back to life." But "all we have" to resurrect the dead is our faith.

Reagan disdained the "quick fix" on principle. He practiced a form of political homeopathy in which the patient is brought to and through the crisis in order to cure him. The crisis was the index to the cure. An unfulfilled prediction, Festinger notes, is often taken by believers to mean that the true crisis point has not yet been reached. Escalating the crisis—refusing the "quick fix"—would heal permanently and completely. All the poisons must come out, none must be suppressed; otherwise, the poisons will return more virulently than ever. If we lack faith, we will never know the extent of the poisons in the system.

Campaigning for the Republican ticket in North Carolina on October 26, 1982, Reagan forecast "a new season of hope." He charged that his opponents—creators of an economic "monster"—were "playing with people's fears, trying to scare them into believing that things will get worse so their own political fortunes will get better." Their criticism prevented the healing climax of the crisis they had produced. "The picture of fear and despair that they paint on the network evening blues is a picture of where America was, not where she's going. . . . It's time others stopped trying to scare people and subvert recovery." Indeed, we had nothing to fear but fear itself.

Reagan spoke as though he were not the incumbent President but the perpetual challenger. All errors had been made in the past by bumbling or fiendish predecessors. These mistakes were still playing themselves out. When asked at a September 28, 1982, press conference, "Does any of the blame [for the recession] belong to you?" he replied, "Yes, because for many years I was a Democrat." During the last week of October, on the eve of the midterm election, he made the most arresting claim of the campaign, accusing "big spenders" for the ban on school prayer. In fact, the Supreme Court had ruled twenty years previously that school prayer was unconstitutional. Reagan's charge was inexplicable outside the framework of his mythology. He attributed everything bad that was happening to an evil power, an external cause. With others always bearing the blame, his image as a nice guy was sustained. This was much of the secret of his so-called Teflon presidency. In some dreams begin irresponsibilities.

But the dreams Reagan had of the future were not prophetic, for the future appeared to him only in the guise of the past. What he recollected was not really history, but fable. His wisdom was not illuminated by a precise memory or erudition, but by archetypal stories in which he always placed himself. He asked us to place ourselves in the stories with him. When our imaginations transported us there, his dreams would come true.

Before he had entered the White House, Reagan dreamed of the best of all possible worlds: Inflation would disappear through monetarist manipulation of the money supply and growth would be stimulated by supply-side tax cuts. This dream incorporated others' dreams. And in Milton Friedman's reverie, recovery must be won by pain.

In October 1979, the Fed had begun the monetarist experiment, but it discovered that its efforts to fine-tune the money supply were notably unsuccessful; it fluctuated wildly. The more volatility, the less credibility the monetary strategy possessed.

Throughout 1981, Beryl Sprinkel, Under Secretary of the Treasury for Monetary Affairs, visited the Federal Reserve every Wednesday for lunch. The board members had initially expected pleasantries and were startled when their guest came to hector them for being insufficiently militant monetarists. Within the Treasury Department, Sprinkel set up a group of orthodox believers called the Office of Domestic Monetary Policy to monitor every Fed lapse.

As the recession deepened, the anxiety within the White House grew. When would the recovery begin? When would interest rates come down? At a February 1982 press conference, the President expressed "confidence" and "support" for the Fed and its money supply targets. In the meantime, Murray Weidenbaum, James Baker and Edwin Meese all made unpublicized visits to Volcker, asking him to ease up.

The economic portents were grim. International Harvester, a major corporation, appeared on the verge of bankruptcy. The Penn Square Bank of Oklahoma City, which had gambled and lost in oil and gas ventures, collapsed, taking with it millions from the Chase Manhattan Bank and Continental Illinois Bank, among others. Then Drysdale Securities, a four-month-old trading firm, folded, defaulting on more than $117 million on loans from Chase Manhattan. And then Mexico, with $80 billion in debts, almost went into default. Mexico's crisis was an alarm that the international economy was on the precipice. Over the past decade, leading commercial banks had made more than $845 billion in loans to debtor nations, with the expectation that the money would be repaid in currency cheapened by continuing inflation. By stemming inflation through monetarism, the Fed had put the Third World countries—and the banks—in peril. Within the Fed, analysts began experimenting with computer-based scenarios. Their projections suggested that a crash of the world banking system was a real possibility. Soon the CIA was engaged in similar scenario-making, coming to the same conclusions.[8]

The Fed blinked. At the July deliberations of the Federal Open Market Committee, the small closed group that sets the Fed's policies, a decision was made to let the money supply grow at the highest targeted rate. A month later, Volcker went public, testifying to Congress that the board might permit money growth to exceed the Fed's previous limits. Finally, on October 9, Volcker told a Business Council meeting that for "technical reasons" the Fed would no longer calculate the movements of Ml. Interest rates fell, the stock market boomed, and the monetarists were bitterly disappointed.

"The experiment has been abandoned," mourned Friedman. Once again, he believed, the monetarist solution wasn't given a fair chance. "It was terrible it wasn't carried out. One step forward and two steps back. You cannot get large bureaucratic agencies to move—period. Inflation has been broken. The question is, will it stay broken? Now they're engaging in a monetary explosion. In both the British and American cases you set out on the correct course of reducing the monetary growth rate. But in both cases you did it in such an erratic and inefficient way that you did not get the assistance of any confidence that you were really doing it. Therefore, you went through a much more severe recession than was necessary and desirable. The best image I can give you for both the Fed and the Bank of England is that they have been trying to drive a car down the center of a road with a defective steering apparatus; they keep in the center of the road because there are two big walls on each side. First, they hit one wall and then they hit the next, and back and forth. They have kept down that road but with these gyrations, with the result that the car is not in very good shape. People don't have confidence that they're not going to break through one of these walls one of these times. Right now the Fed is threatening to break through the wall on one side."

"What is striking," wrote the supply-sider Jack Kemp, "is his conviction that in *every* country which has tried to follow his advice, the monetary authorities have used monetarist rhetoric while pursuing a non-monetarist policy."9

With the attempted countermanding of supply-side economics by tax increases, Stockman's failure to stop the federal deficit by spending cuts, and the scuttling of monetarism by the Fed, the New Beginning, at least as an economic program, seemed to be finished. But these were only facts, and facts do not speak for themselves.

On Election Day 1982, there were a few more facts: twenty-six Republican representatives and seven governors were defeated. It was not an overwhelming repudiation of the President and the GOP, but it was not a vote of confidence. More important, the vote did not realize the grand prediction of a political realignment. After the 1980 election, they argued that a new conservative epoch had dawned, just as FDR's election in 1932 signified the coming to power of a Democratic era. The 1982 contest would ratify the New Beginning, in much the same way that the 1934 midterm election ratified the New Deal. Reagan's eco-

nomic policies were to be the instrument of this realignment, the fruition of decades of conservative efforts. But the policies had unintended
consequences.

And then came the recovery. By consistently adhering to the policy
he had initially laid out—tight money, tax cuts, and an attempt at a
balanced budget—Reagan had helped foster the worst recession since
the Depression. But the more inconsistent he was, the more he departed
from his original plan, the more the economy recovered. By early 1983,
stock market prices were soaring.

Very little that Reagan promised worked as advertised. Monetarism
resembled chemotherapy without any prospect of a cure. True, inflation had dramatically dropped, but so had vital signs of economic
health. When the Fed announced it would cease targeting the money
supply, the bull market thunderously appeared.

The supply side, as it turned out, was the demand side in drag.
Reagan's recovery had its source in the reversal of his policies and
intentions. When money was put directly into the hands of consumers
through the tax cut, an utterly conventional if regressive Keynesian
stimulus, demand increased. The astronomical boost in military spending also had a simple Keynesian benefit, for it was public-sector money
that translated ultimately into consumer demand—big government in
action.

The deficit was the price Reagan paid for the recovery. He covered his debt by paying lip service to a balanced budget amendment
to the Constitution, an ideological promissory note. Reagan was then
freed to campaign for support for his incoherent program by offering
a coherent worldview. His unyielding rhetoric reaped great rewards.
By projecting an unchanging ideology throughout the economic crisis,
he had been able to convince voters that his policies had not under-
gone any substantial revision and were actually the cause of the recovery. A majority of the voters gave him credit for the upturn.
Between January and May 1983, he gained eleven points in the
ABC–*Washington Post* poll. His interpretation of the recent past was
prevailing—a triumph of ideology.

According to Reagan, the economic crisis we had passed through only proved the persistence of our sinister adversary. The Restoration was coming soon after all. Americans, he constantly reminded us, have the power to begin the world over again. And on this point what American, except an authentic conservative, would dispute him? Thus there would always be the promise of a New Beginning. His policies may have been in tatters, but his mythology was intact. Reagan and the conservatives were fortified for 1984.

MORNING

AGAIN

The sun rose, the flag was raised, and everyone went to work. "It's morning again in America." A young couple is getting married. A family is moving into a new home with a white picket fence. "Just about everyone in town is thinking the same thing—now that our country is turning around, why would we ever turn back?"

The images in this Reagan campaign commercial were so familiar that their artful arrangement required only the merest suggestion of a narration, a suggestion in the form of a question, to supply their meaning. But what "town" had we landed in? It was nowhere and everywhere, and the people were nobody and everybody. The place was home and they were us. Here, in Our Town, the Restoration was an accomplished fact.

The mythic tone of Reagan's campaign was not something his handlers happened to stumble upon. "Paint Reagan as the personification of all that is right with, or heroized by, America," wrote the senior presidential assistant Richard Darman in a memo. "Leave Mondale in a position where an attack on Reagan is tantamount to an attack on America's idealized image of itself—where a vote against Reagan is, in some subliminal sense, a vote against a mythic 'AMERICA'."[1]

Reagan didn't campaign on a platform of issues. He ran on a worldview, one so stratospheric that issues disappeared from sight. The big blue marble could be seen whole, but the distinguishing features were nebulous patches of color. The myths Reagan employed required no discussion of policies to be understood. Contrary to the conventional wisdom, the imagist does not always substitute style for substance; if he is good at what he does, he condenses ideas into their essences, using a poetic shorthand that moves our emotions before our reasoning. The apparent absence of content in Reagan's ads confounded the literal-minded. To them, candidates campaign on the issues, not on the mythology. Reagan, however, was hiding nothing and explaining a great deal. His campaign was entirely comprehensible in terms of conservative ideology and history, and its through-the-looking-glass relationship with liberalism. The free market and traditional values, spirited away and gagged by the Liberal Establishment, were being brought back to life; the movement had passed through the crisis of the early 1980s and, almost miraculously, was standing in the sunshine. America, at least for a season, a long Indian summer, became a small town where the ideology assumed human shape. (The Soviet Union, in one of his campaign ads, assumed the shape of a bear—"if there is a bear," said the narrator.)

Reagan was able to campaign on his ideology because of his apparent economic success. But he was awarded credit for the recovery only because of his adroit and stubborn use of ideology during the recession. Once the boom appeared, Reagan never had to descend to the material world; that was already paid for by the deficit. In the past, when Democratic presidents had presided over a growing economy, stimulated by government spending, they were quick to claim credit. Reagan, however, never openly assumed responsibility for the economic gain of his spendthrift military Keynesianism; yet he received plaudits from the voters anyway. He preferred to take credit for that which he wasn't responsible for. Because he asserted that he was liberating the market, he could share the private success of those seemingly untouched by federal largesse. Thus, for what government did (pump up the economy by means of the deficit) and for what it didn't do (the market), Reagan was the political beneficiary.

Among the political advantages of the recovery was that it allowed Reagan to unify his elites behind him. Throughout the early years of his presidency, a disintegration of his support threatened to turn his base into rubble and plaster dust. The supply-siders hated the monetarists; the monetarists hated the Fed; the neoconservatives hated the

State Department; the Senate Republicans, abetted by the corporate managers, hated the supply-siders; and nobody trusted David Stockman. Yet once prosperity returned, all calls for "mid-course corrections" were temporarily abandoned. The doctrinal schisms within the Counter-Establishment remained as sharp as ever, but they receded in prominence. Conflict was submerged in a mood elevated by cash and patriotism.

Walter Mondale had expected the coming struggle to be a classic match-up of interest groups against interest groups. Because the interest groups that made up the Democratic Party were more numerous than those of the Republican Party, he foresaw victory. He dickered publicly with every conceivable factional and constituency group leader, establishing early on the gathering of such endorsements as the chief qualification for the nomination; those who failed to acquire the full roster were not, he charged, "real Democrats." He neglected, however, to justify the necessary mechanics of coalition-building by reference to a larger design. Jesse Jackson's campaign added to the problem by highlighting the impression that the Democrats were breaking down into their raw coalitional elements. Then Jackson's jabber about "Hymietown" and his alliance with Black Muslim leader Louis Farrakhan, who called Judaism a "gutter religion," triggered a rupture between blacks and Jews, the two most stalwart Democratic constituencies.

To discipline this coalition and to convince the general public that it was not simply a grab-bag of "special interests," a leader must advance a strong vision of the national idea. Mondale, however, had made the test of leadership the ability to court the factions. He insistently reduced all political matters to the currencies of race, religion, gender, and region. This was how the Democratic Farmer-Labor Party in Minnesota had operated, how Hubert Humphrey had operated, and how Mondale expected all "real Democrats" to operate.

Reagan's interest groups, however, couldn't be seen beneath the high tide of good feelings, which the Summer Olympics in Los Angeles elevated to euphoric heights. The President did not go out of his way to make public appearances with trade-association lobbyists. Instead, there he was with the Olympic medal winners, with Michael Jackson, and at the Grand Ole Opry with Roy Acuff, and *(quack)* talking with the man who was the voice of Donald Duck. Reagan was never lowered to Mondale's level, and Mondale was incapable of rising to Reagan's. The President's interest groups were real enough, but only Mondale's could be spotted with the eye. Mondale's metabolism, it seemed, was regulated by others; he appeared to be a creation of his coalition, not an autonomous figure. His quality of leadership became invisible.

Reagan had argued that he was returning the country to its original principles; now, in the campaign, he insisted that he would return politics to its original basis. Only then would the rightful order of things be restored. But in Reagan's cosmos there was no reference to Republicans; the political Restoration did not include them. Conservatism only made sense by analogy to liberalism. And what made Reagan so elusive a target in 1984 for the Democrats was his shadow liberalism.

At the Republican Convention the true keynote address was delivered by the neoconservative Jeane Kirkpatrick, then still a registered Democrat. Her speech was a screed against the "San Francisco Democrats," pretenders to the mantle of the true Democracy. She contrasted their false congregation to the assemblage before her, loyal to the principles she always espoused. Was this really the convention of the Dallas Democrats?

Throughout the campaign, Reagan never once mentioned the name of a Republican President. Instead, he gloried in playing the roles of Democratic heroes—John F. Kennedy, Harry Truman, and—his hero of heroes—Franklin D. Roosevelt. On September 19 he traveled to Waterbury, Connecticut, a historic Democratic bastion, where every man, woman, and child had turned out to cheer Kennedy in 1960. "Even though it was the fall it seemed like springtime, those days," Reagan recalled to the crowd. "I see our country today and I think it is springtime for America once again." The age of Reagan is the restoration of the age of Kennedy. Then: "You know, I was a Democrat once. . . . The only abandoning I see is the Democratic leadership abandoning the good and decent Democrats of the JFK, and FDR, and Harry Truman tradition." According to his reasoning, the Democratic leaders were on some demented detour. The Democrats, however, were still the normal majority party. Reagan didn't abandon anything; *he* was the "real Democrat." Vote for Reagan and remain what you were.

Shortly after his turn as Kennedy, Reagan boarded the very train Harry Truman used to conduct his whistle-stop campaign against the real Republicans. The '84 campaign was the '48 campaign upside down. This time the honest Democrat was the Republican and the honest Republican, stumping on the quintessential GOP issue of the deficit, was the Democrat.

For Reagan, the figure who meant the most was Roosevelt. He incorporated into his own identity more than FDR's confidence, more than his style. He operated according to a construct that could be understood only in the terms of New Deal liberalism: Jimmy Carter became Herbert Hoover; the late 1970s became the early 1930s; Grenada served the function of D-Day, which happened to be the centerpiece of his campaign film shown at the convention; and Mondale became the stand-in for Carter, the stand-in for Hoover. The circle was complete with the appearance of Roosevelt/Reagan. Mondale was the incumbent of the bad times, "gloom and doom." Reagan was the challenger, the restorer of happy days. Appropriately, the New Deal theme song, "Happy Days Are Here Again," was played at the Dallas gathering, but not at the San Francisco affair.

The formal Democrat, Mondale, claimed linear title to the New Deal. He believed that the endorsement of all the establishment Democrats and the constituency groups constituted FDR's inheritance. He also had the notion that policy is created in Washington laboratories of experts; perforce, he embodied the fundamental fallacy in the thinking of the policy elite that compresses everything into discrete, rational categories. Stationed in long-standing bureaucracies like the Brookings Institution, these experts believe that discussion of particular issues is the highest stage of politics; in all other cases, politics is the enemy of policy. Their aim is a neutral "center," managed by the indispensable technocrats, no matter which party holds electoral sway. The only thing missing in this conception is contemporary political reality. By combining their particularized approach to issues with a particularized approach to interest groups, Mondale perfected a disintegrative politics. He attempted to paint Reagan as out of touch because he did not know the details of policies. But Mondale was culturally out of touch, even with the New Deal culture, which Reagan reserved for himself.

Reagan's campaign was perhaps the last recapitulation of the popular liberal esthetic of the Depression and war years: *The people, yes.* He still inhabited the mood of Frank Capra's populist movies, Archibald MacLeish's poetic tributes to the brotherhood of the common people, the uplifting social realism of WPA post-office murals. Reagan echoed the spirit of "Ballad for Americans," the Popular Front pseudo–folk song about "nobody who was anybody" and "anybody who was everybody"—"You know who I am: the people!" His mass cultural style of democratic schwarmerei, like that of the old liberal left he once ardently championed, was pitched for ideological advantage. *Let America Be America Again.* Conservatism is twentieth-century Americanism.

The only universality Mondale possessed was his lack of a distinct persona, which gave him the look of the generic Democrat. Having been the Vice President in a discredited administration was perhaps his most uniquely defining characteristic. Within his own party he collected quid pro quos, not devoted followers; he gave little offense because he gave little pleasure. Among the conservatives he struck a far more responsive chord; he was a necessity they could not have manufactured on their own. The conservatives had built the Counter-Establishment as an elaboration of their shadow liberalism. Their rationale might have been shaken if the Democrats had not nominated a candidate who neatly fit their preconceived notions. At this critical juncture, the Democrats seized upon an almost model figure to validate conservative ideology. Mondale's arrival was the confirmation of a complete belief system, like the appearance before the Aztecs of Cortez, who was taken to be the great god Quetzalcoatl. His presence so awed them that their ancient civilization was overthrown by his meager force. In Mondale's case, the fate was reversed; this god returned so that he might be interred, not worshipped. Mondale was still an imperfect substitute for Ted Kennedy, the ideal human sacrifice, but he would do. His humiliating defeat was seen by conservatives as a historical success.

The campaign was mystifying to the Democrats because nothing they did had the expected result. Almost every attempt to save Mondale's candidacy further illustrated the conservative ideology and made the Democrats' situation more desperate. Unwittingly the Mondale team worked as a complement to the conservative effort—so effectively, in fact, that Reagan campaign consultants never bothered to air the harshly negative ads they had produced. The Democrats were acting a role in a story that escaped them; yet they performed perfectly.

The day after the election, Mondale held a press conference to explain Reagan's success. "Modern politics today requires a mastery of television. I've never really warmed up to television and, in fairness to television, it's never warmed up to me. By instinct and tradition I don't like these things," he said, grabbing the microphones in front of him as though he were strangling them. "I like to look someone in the eye." He added: "American politics is losing its substance." To be sure, Mondale was a bad television candidate, that is, a bad candidate, because television is mostly where the campaign occurs. But he would have been a bad radio candidate too, quite unlike that great radio personality FDR. Significantly, the first mass medium Reagan mastered was the radio. If a candidate can't act or sound like a president, he can't *be* the president.

In his ads, Mondale was either abrasive or soporific. His appeals to indignation tried to arouse an enthusiasm about his candidacy that didn't naturally exist. Looking into his dull eyes, one could detect only deep fatigue: Walter Mondale eyes. As a "talking head," he had the vitality of a man talking in his sleep, and his obvious discomfort revealed painful self-consciousness. He treated time before the camera like time under the dentist's drill. In the heat of the campaign, when new ads were in short supply, his media producers were summoned to film him. His poor delivery ruined take after take, according to one of the consultants. Finally the camera broke down, as though it had decided to go on strike. Tense and awkward in the face of the lens, Mondale now recovered his natural bounce. Without ever filming the ads, he exited in a mood of relief to address a nearby rally. He believed that at the live event he could "look someone in the eye."

Mondale did not believe he was looking anyone in the eye when he was on television. Yet the effective use of television requires eye contact, something that Reagan knows well. This skill requires a conscious understanding of the medium, a sensation that one is actually gazing into someone's eyes, a level of abstraction that Mondale didn't have.

Mondale's sorry television performance wasn't just a theatrical failing, but a profound conceptual failing; his technical incompetence was rooted in his notion of politics. He had a narrow view of it as being circumscribed by traditional parties and issues, professional politicians and experts. He constructed his campaign in the same way he put together a deficit-reduction package, like a legislative bill. Like Reagan, he assumed that a normal Democratic majority was still in force; but he assumed too much. For unlike Reagan he believed in the old party system and partisan categories. He also assumed that the voters agreed with him that Reagan was a nonsensical accident of history because he didn't fit the known pigeonholes. In Mondale's restoration, the Reagan mistake would be blotted out; then all would be set right again. He believed that he was in a contest only with some sort of marginal Republican. Conservative ideology and the Counter-Establishment were phantoms to him. He never really grasped whose defeat his victory might signify; consequently, he never understood the magnitude of his undertaking.

By attributing his loss to television, the master of the Democratic establishment in effect confessed that he did not understand the political system. Inescapably, television is the main forum for rhetoric and oratory, classical aspects of politics originally analyzed by Aristotle. When the failure of method is offered to explain the outcome of a presidential election, one must wonder about the logic underlying it. Mondale's hostility to modern technique rested on a dualism in his thinking. In his denunciation of television, he separated substance from the dominant mode of political oratory. He believed that the true product of governing was policy. But he had lost the sense that the consent of the governed must continually be won by more than the endorsement of factional leaders; he forgot that persuasion is the first condition of policy-making. There is no legitimacy without consent, and no consent without communication. Mondale proposed to speak for the public good, but conceded that he could not shape the public spirit. Thus he split society from the state. His failure to communicate was partly a function of his outlook; his bafflement was another measure of his misjudgment.

The Democrats, in chaotic retreat, glanced hastily over their shoulders and saw Reagan looming as a gigantic Sun King. The party's factions scrambled to reposition themselves. In their televised response to the President's 1985 State of the Union address, the Democrats expressed abject self-contempt and promised that the party would undergo a personality change. They were coroners performing autopsies on themselves. Their politics were determined mainly by the fear and trembling induced by the Mondale debacle, not by any critique of Reagan or conservatism.

The Democrats' disarray, however, didn't provoke the conservatives to revise their shadow liberalism, which was fixed. They still had a picture in their minds of the Liberal Establishment, well-coordinated and in control. In the wake of the election, Joseph Sobran, a senior editor of *The National Review,* wrote:

> The left controls the media, the judiciary, the universities that count; it can magnify its own signals and muffle the right's. It has even succeeded in making its own vocabulary the rhetoric of public discourse. . . . How is the right, as a system of communication, supposed to coalesce? Its lines of communication are in disrepair, under constant threat of sabotage. . . . Imagine a society divided into two classes of people, one of which had telephones while the other didn't. Ask yourself which class would rule. Then you will begin to get the picture: Conservatives lack telephones in today's culture.[2]

Within the federal government, however, telephones weren't always needed: conservatives could meet in the White House mess. The cadres of the Counter-Establishment were burrowing into every agency and department, in the West Wing of the White House and the Old Executive Office Building. They comprised an informal but tightly knit network.

But difficulties remained. First, there was a sheer scarcity of qualified right-wing jobholders. Many potential appointees simply refused to consider a sojourn in the capital, so ideologically hostile were they to the idea of the federal government. Most of those willing to leave sinecures at the major factories of ideology—the Hoover Institution, the American Enterprise Institute, and the Heritage Foundation—were already ensconced in office. And by the advent of the second term, many were already out, returned to the think-tank havens, a kind of ideological Taiwan; or else they were seeking their fortunes in the private sector they had extolled.

The Heritage Foundation, for its part, underwent the ideological equivalent of reindustrialization in the effort to produce more cadres. Its recruitment of likely candidates for government slots intensified; its methods of inserting them in place became more efficient. Virtually the entire leadership at Heritage was deeply involved in the job hunt as a matter of routine. Consequently, its influence in Washington continued to rise, surpassing that of the more distant Hoover Institution and the more academic-minded AEI, the latter of which began to suffer a financial shortfall. The cost of respectability was the loss of militance and funds.

Some prominent right-wingers joined the administration for the second term. Hard-edged Patrick Buchanan, the columnist and former speechwriter for Richard Nixon and Spiro Agnew, headed up the communications office. But he soon fell into the disfavor of chief of staff Donald Regan and lost his window with a view. On his birthday in 1985, Buchanan's staff presented him with a framed picture of a window.

Another noteworthy conservative appointment was Linda Chavez, who was placed in charge of the Office of Public Liaison. A neoconservative, she had won the trust of the conservatives as director of the U.S. Civil Rights Commission, striking down the "liberal" agenda. When her name was raised by senior White House officials for the Public Liaison post, the conservative network went into action. But the lobbying from the conservative elite on her behalf was so relentless and so irritating to Regan that her elevation was in jeopardy. Only when she requested a private interview did she win the job. (She left in 1986 to run for the U.S. Senate seat in Maryland.)

Chavez's mentor was William Bennett, a neoconservative himself, the former head of the National Endowment for the Humanities, who became Secretary of Education in the second term. He filled his department to the brim with right-wingers. Among them was a young Harvard professor, William Kristol, son of Irving Kristol, named Bennett's special assistant. The elder Kristol's lobbying had been crucial in Bennett's appointment at NEH. Now Bennett was using his power of appointment to facilitate the generational transition. Young Kristol received a patrimony of disillusioned leftism and abhorrence of liberalism without ever having to pass through the experiences that had led to these attitudes. Like father, like son: William had the character of a right-wing Trotskyist, a vanguard ideologue.

One of the Counter-Establishment groups with which William Kristol affiliated was the Federalist Society, an organization of law students who bring the passion of ideology to the discipline of the law. Many of these young cadres were brought to Washington and given jobs. The Department of Justice particularly favored them. Though their ideological inclinations were entirely predictable, they were something new to the Counter-Establishment. They possessed more than avid belief; they also possessed a strict professionalism and credentials beyond the Counter-Establishment, making them especially valuable properties.

Despite the conservatives' drive to power, everything did not work out as planned. Often, it seemed to them, nothing worked. In the early months of the second term, appointment after appointment fell afoul. Eileen Gardner, a Heritage Foundation researcher named a special assistant to Bennett, was exposed as having written that the physically handicapped had "summoned" their condition from God. She was promptly defenestrated.

Particularly painful for conservatives was the ordeal of William Bradford Reynolds. As assistant attorney general he had overseen the assault on civil rights while presenting himself as the true guardian of civil rights. His appointment as associate attorney general was naturally opposed by civil rights groups. His confirmation hearings before the Senate Judiciary Committee was a theater of self-destruction. When Reynolds concluded his performance, enough senators felt that he had misled them that they struck down his nomination. President Reagan called this exercise in "advise and consent" an "ideological assault." Among the Counter-Establishment minions, it was greeted as a clarifying lesson confirming their ideology, in particular their view of the Liberal Establishment, which, stretching from the media into the Senate, had once again triumphed. So Reynolds's fate was no mere disappointment; it was an incitement.

Reagan's second landslide did nothing to temper the conservatives' impulse to render their politics a shadow liberalism. Their self-consciousness as outsiders was not abated but intensified. They had traveled so far and yet still thought of themselves as a persecuted minority, almost overwhelmed by the Liberal Establishment; they were still insecure, not quite sure of their legitimacy. The liberals were the oppressors, the conservatives the oppressed; they could not reach out and touch anyone because the liberals had cut their lines. If Reagan's second coming did not transform America into the promised land, then the designs of a devilish enemy could explain the confoundment. To the degree that the ideal world did not come to pass, conservatives credited the Liberal Establishment with insidious powers. The Counter-Establishment, it followed, would have to be bigger than ever. So much remained to be done.

Yet Reagan's last campaign conveyed the feeling that American history was nearing its completion. He was the return of the Democratic gods in another guise, the fulfillment of the cycle. His program and our belief were bringing about the Restoration. Thematically, Reagan's claims of success placed conservatism close to the end of days. But if the millennium was almost here, what more really could be done?

CHAPTER TWELVE

THE

SECOND

COMING

Then, as if on cue, new characters marched onto the stage. New proposals, already rehearsed within the Counter-Establishment, were dramatically unveiled. Some notions, introduced without pomp and circumstance during the first term, were now reintroduced as new ideas with loud trumpeting. The Counter-Establishment was in endless production. By constantly adding scenes to the script, the conservatives tried to keep the plot moving. The new tableaux, however vivid, were not spontaneous surprises; they appeared only because a construction crew had assembled and set them before us.

At the start of Reagan's second term, the conservatives waged both conventional and guerrilla warfare against the Democrats. The mighty office of the presidency served as heavy artillery ("Make my day," Reagan fired), while the Counter-Establishment cadres staged black-pajama raids, constantly throwing the enemy off balance.

In Washington the conservatives set up a Potemkin Village almost every month, moving the same bands of ideologues from hotel ballroom to hotel ballroom. A favorite subject was the "Reagan Doctrine," a rationale for supporting Third World insurgencies against Soviet-backed regimes. By the logic of the "Reagan Doctrine," as developed by different advocates, the Communists were either very strong or very weak. Whatever the case, those congressmen and senators who failed to vote for military aid to the Nicaraguan contras and other designated "freedom fighters" were charged with lacking the manhood to defend the West.

Speaking of Communism, in May 1985, at the Madison Hotel, conservatives conducted a conference to dispute the pernicious notion that there was some "moral equivalence" between America and Russia —an idea they claimed liberals backed. Yet "moral equivalence" was a formula contrived by Jeane Kirkpatrick. No liberals stepped forward to defend "moral equivalence." No matter. "Moral equivalence" kept them on the ideological defensive.

The conservatives' tactical mobility, however, was not unlimited. If they were not halted by the catatonic Democrats, they were contained by their own ideology. Their inventiveness stopped at the far edge of their shadow liberalism. Conservatives almost invariably felt uncomfortable in the role of a responsible governing establishment. Because their self-definition was dependent upon their adversarial stance, they always thought of themselves as the opposition. It was always easier for them to define what they were against than what they were for. Even when they came up with a prescriptive program its ultimate intent was almost invariably to counter the foe—regular Republicans, liberals, Communists.

Three distinct horizons appeared in the future the Counter-Establishment was making. First there was the immediate future, a jumble of deficits and budgets. To explain it to us, the Counter-Establishment rolled out a new conservative scholar—Charles Murray, with his critique of the welfare state. Then there was the future that would be judged by a new conservative judiciary who would issue their decisions, precedent by precedent, incrementally changing the law itself, reversing the interpretation that has prevailed for most of the twentieth century. And then there would be the future perfect, which was also the past perfect, a category that "transcends time," as Reagan noted in his second inaugural address. To attain this state of grace we must ascend to the heavens to install a "Star Wars" mechanism, dispel the doomsday anxiety, and usher in universal peace—the final Restoration.

Almost as soon as the election was over, the radiant campaign commercials were packed away and a bleak David Stockman, long under wraps, pulled up a chair in front of the cameras. Unless draconian cuts in the budget were made, the deficit would never be controlled and the economy would be choked: Dunkirk again.

The deficit was now the chief instrument of conservative social policy, just as it had once been for the liberals. In the past, a deficit was defended as essential to economic growth and the provision for social programs. Reagan, too, reaped the rewards of his deficit, which fueled the recovery and his reelection; yet he decried it with the ritualism of the sinner who hates his sin but gets too much enjoyment from it to give it up. By clinging to the atavistic assumption that a deficit was an absolute evil, conservatives could collect its benefits while using it to slash others'.

Stockman took on this Calvinist task with grim enthusiasm. The pain principle, for the moment, was asserted over the pleasure principle. Payment was overdue: liquidate farmers, liquidate students, liquidate small business. "I don't see why we have any responsibility to step in," Stockman said.

On virtually every other desk at the OMB rested the latest conservative best-seller, Charles Murray's *Losing Ground,* the crucial text of the period, serving the same function of justification as George Gilder's *Wealth and Poverty* did in the first term. Gilder, for his part, waved incense over the second term with *The Spirit of Enterprise,* a paean to the successful in the spirit of Horatio Alger. Murray lacked Gilder's rhapsodic prose style, but he more than compensated with at least a hundred pages of dense data. The complex array of statistics was decoded by his astonishingly simple thesis—poverty programs cause poverty. By demonstrating that the number of poor had not decreased since the establishment of the War on Poverty, he seemed to provide more evidence for the neoconservatives' favorite law—the law of unintended consequences. According to Murray, the War on Poverty was imposed from above by a liberal "elite," acting without the approval of the "blue-collar and white-collar electorate."[1] Lyndon Johnson's 1964 landslide was not, then, a mandate for the Great Society. Murray's solution was the dissolution of the welfare state, which he claimed had become a Rube Goldberg contraption preventing the poor from finding their fortunes in the free market. Conservatives believed that Reagan's 1984 landslide was a mandate to undo the Great Society.

They hailed Murray's argument, and overnight he was cited everywhere as one of the foremost experts in the field.

Only two years before Murray's book and Murray himself became celebrated, he was toiling in Iowa as an obscure policy wonk. He had been chief scientist at the American Institutes for Research, a private think tank, but his principal claim to fame was a pamphlet authored for the Heritage Foundation, "Safety Nets and the Truly Needy," which argued that welfare fostered poverty. By now, Murray had befriended Michael Horowitz, the general counsel at the Office of Management and Budget, a neoconservative talent scout. On the strength of his Heritage tract and Horowitz's recommendation, he was invited to a luncheon at the Manhattan Institute, the Counter-Establishment think tank that had helped incubate Gilder. William Hammett, the institute's president, appraised Murray as "a nobody" who could be somebody. After some reflection he decided to take "a flier" on Murray. In short order, $125,000 was raised to support him while he turned his idea into a book.[2] Irving Kristol's connection with the Olin Foundation accounted for $25,000.

Superficially, Murray's argument seemed to be a straightforward demonstration of Kristol's treasured maxim, the law of unintended consequences. Yet Kristol and all other neoconservatives claimed to be critics of the welfare state in the name of its reform. Their attachment to it was a legacy of their left-wing backgrounds, which distinguished them from plain conservatives. Murray, however, advocated the abolition of the welfare state. In their willingness to secure material backing for him, the neoconservatives' commitment to the political needs of the Counter-Establishment took precedence over their expressed belief.

Once Murray completed his manuscript, the Manhattan Institute's responsibility did not end. A big chunk of the money was earmarked for promotion. Conservatives, after all, do not blindly invest their hopes in the marketplace of ideas; they prefer marketing to natural selection.

"Events of the past six months demonstrate that the Manhattan Institute has indeed become a noticeable force in American political ideas and we offer the following summary for our supporters' evaluation," Hammett wrote in a private memorandum on December 26, 1984. In it he described *"THE MAKING OF A CLASSIC":*

Every generation produces a handful of books whose impact is lasting; books that change basic assumptions about the way the world works (or ought to work). . . . Charles Murray's *Losing Ground* could become such a book. And if it does it will alter the terms of debate over what is perhaps the most compelling political issue of our time: the modern welfare state.

Hammett toted up a list of dozens of magazines and newspapers that had excerpted, analyzed, or reviewed the book. The groundwork for the favorable reception of *Losing Ground,* he noted, was laid during the "first three months following publication," which "were largely devoted to making Murray and his book better known to the intellectual and journalistic community." A "key element in that effort fell into place" when the institute secured $10,000 to "gather twenty of the nation's leading scholars from both the conservative and liberal camps, along with some of the best writers on the subject, for a two-day discussion." Then the institute sent Murray into the wider world, for "personal appearances, combined with television and radio interviews." All cash on hand would be spent on his victory tour. "Any discretionary funds at our disposal for the next few months will go toward financing Murray's outreach activities." In just months, Murray was transformed from "a nobody" into an intellectual star.

But almost the instant after he was boosted into the firmament, his luster was dimmed. According to a growing number of critics, *Losing Ground* was beset with errors and omissions. Murray's calculation that the poverty rate had not dropped between 1968 and 1980 failed to factor in the business cycle and unemployment rates. His assertion that the Aid for Dependent Children program was the main source of illegitimacy among black teenagers neglected to consider or even to cite any of the extensive scholarship uniformly showing no such cause and effect. And much of his case rested on the example of an imaginary welfare couple, "Harold and Phyllis," who lived in Pennsylvania, where, critics pointed out, the high level of benefits was atypical. Murray, moreover, figured food stamps into their welfare income, a disincentive to work, then wrongly assumed that they would be denied food stamps if they did find jobs. Also, his statistics never passed 1970, after which welfare benefits in Pennsylvania significantly dropped. *Losing Ground,* charged the critics, built a general premise on a faulty case study. "He has not proven anything," said Senator Daniel Patrick Moynihan.[3]

Murray answered the attacks by reiterating his faith in his own statistics. But he suddenly veered away from his conclusion, asserting that his book never proposed "to scrap the whole system," or to "suggest a threshold or bound to a society's responsibilities to the poor," or to "prescribe a particular size of safety net," or to "grade the performance of the Great Society."[4] Why, then, in *Losing Ground* did he propose "scrapping the entire federal welfare and income-support structure for working-aged persons?"[5] Was the use of the book as a rationale to slash social programs an unintended consequence?

Among conservatives, Murray's book was still accepted as gospel. The criticism was dismissed as a predictable response of the Liberal Establishment—"some of the most intellectually debilitated of Americans . . . mental incompetents . . . limp-minded and lame-prosed critics," according to Gilder.[6] Curiously, the conservatives did not notice that Murray's argument directly contradicted the last major conservative statement against the welfare state, previously accepted as gospel. "The war on poverty that began in 1964 has been won," wrote Martin Anderson in *Welfare,* published in 1978.[7] Anderson, a Hoover Institution scholar who became Reagan's first chief of domestic policy, argued that because poverty had been eliminated, the programs that had worked so well were no longer needed and therefore the welfare state could be safely dismantled. Murray's thesis began from a diametrically opposite point: "We tried to provide more for the poor and produced more poor instead."[8] Who was right? One thing was certain: they could not both be right. Conservatives did not debate this question. Instead they rushed to defend Murray as a movement intellectual. Once saluted by the conservatives as an example of their rigorous intellectual standards, Anderson's book was silently remaindered on a back shelf.

The commotion about Murray subsided almost as rapidly as it began. Yet the Counter-Establishment was still churning its gears, moving simultaneously on numerous fronts. Perhaps the greatest political opportunity for the conservatives appeared in the realm of jurisprudence.

Conservatism is a defense of tradition. Yet Attorney General Edwin Meese III defended tradition by attacking at least sixty years of Supreme Court precedent. His version of conservatism, elaborated in a July 1985 speech to the American Bar Association, was so unprecedented, such a radical departure from settled law, that he provoked two Supreme Court justices, John Paul Stevens and William Brennan, to descend from the bench and upbraid him for his extreme misreading of American history and law.

This extraordinary spectacle was neither politics nor law as usual. It was not the latest Washington sporting event. It was not about who's up, down, in, or out. It was not a contest between personalities or even institutions. Rather, this was a conflict over bedrock philosophy, the meaning of the American past as it applies to current law.

Although the legal back and forth may sound abstract, it was as politically immediate as the conservative movement's ideological agenda, imposed by a newly enthroned federal judiciary, more than half of which will be selected by President Reagan and Meese. On a whole host of issues—affirmative action, abortion, and school prayer, among others—the conservatives sought to rescind the standing law. But they wanted far more than alterations in mere policy; they wanted a fundamental transformation of the philosophy underlying these policies so that such reforms would be impossible in the future. Thus the movement conservatives acted to discredit established canons of judicial interpretation.

Meese may be an unlikely philosopher, but his statement was no spontaneous prank. The concepts he espoused, including the notion that the Bill of Rights should be not applied to the states, have a lineage that runs deep in conservative movement history, particularly the post-1945 writings that have shaped the "Reagan revolution." These ideas, moreover, were aggressively promoted by the foundations and think tanks of the Washington conservative establishment especially devoted to law.

Throughout 1985, in various interviews, Meese suggested that his view of the law is undergirded by philosophical principle, that it was more than an ideological instinct. We must, he said, go "back to basic principles." The Supreme Court ruling legalizing abortion, *Roe* v. *Wade,* is not really "an abortion case." It is, he declared about "the more fundamental principle that's involved there . . . the separation of powers." The court's ruling, he added, is "an arrogation of power away from the states." Then he labeled the Miranda decision, requiring that criminal suspects be informed of their rights, "infamous." "You don't have many criminal suspects who are innocent of a crime," he declared.

In his ABA speech, Meese attempted to explain his various complaints as deductions from a coherent doctrine. At each step of his logic he journeyed farther into the past. First, he assailed the extension of the guarantees in the Bill of Rights to the states, a process that began with a Supreme Court ruling on the First Amendment in 1925. "Nothing," he said, "can be done to shore up the intellectually shaky foundation upon which the doctrine rests." It was, Meese claimed, "politically violent and constitutionally suspect."

In place of decades of court precedent supposedly warping federalism and criminal law, Meese offered something he called a "Jurisprudence of Original Intention"—a jurisprudence based on a correct reading of the Founding Fathers' collective mind—the legal corollary to the Restoration myth.

"We will," he said, "endeavor to resurrect the original meaning of constitutional provisions and statutes as the only reliable guide for judgment." As an example, he noted that "neutrality between religion and irreligion would have struck the founding generation as bizarre."

With "original intention" enshrined as the reigning philosophy, vast areas of the law would have to be rewritten. Yet as Meese and the movement conservatives see it, the courts are already thoroughly politicized. To them, the pre-Reagan federal judges act as a priesthood of "judicial activists," who by attempting to reconcile precedent with changing reality are promulgating a liberal ideology. In their effort to return to "original intention" the conservatives are attempting to cleanse the legal system of the liberal tincture. This places them, they believe, in the position of defending tradition against the liberal cadre dressed in black robes.

Meese provoked a thunderous response. Justice Brennan issued his judgment that the doctrine of "original intention" is "arrogance cloaked as humility." Moreover, it is a cry "from persons who have no familiarity with the historical record." He dismissed "this facile historicism," which seeks to justify itself as "a depoliticization of the judiciary." To Brennan, the hypocritical "political underpinnings of such a choice should not escape notice."

Having dispatched "original intention," Brennan proceeded to train his sights on Meese's Bill of Rights heresy. More than sixty years of law is at stake, he observed. The preemption of states rights by the Bill of Rights, a 1925 ruling, was made possible by the Civil War amendments to the constitution. "It was in particular," he said, "the Fourteenth Amendment's guarantee that no person be deprived of life, liberty, or property without process of law that led us to apply many of the specific guarantees of the Bill of Rights to the states."

On this point stand many of the great decisions of the modern court, from *Gideon* v. *Wainwright,* guaranteeing counsel to all poor defendants, to *New York Times* v. *Sullivan,* which held that libel suits are subject to the First Amendment.

Justice Stevens pursued these questions even more directly than Brennan. He cited Meese by name and then dealt with his propositions about the Bill of Rights and "original intention" as one. To accept the Meese position, he pointed out, "overlooks the profound importance of the Civil War and the postwar amendments on the structure of our government." Almost as an aside, Stevens derided Meese's implicit view that the "founding generation" thought as a monolith.

Why, suddenly, this heated debate about the "founding generation" and the Civil War? What does "original intention" have to do with Meese's intention?

The roots of the controversy spread into the past, an obscure but real past unremarked upon by Meese, but the source of most of his ideas. The thread of this heritage runs from the Founding Fathers to Jefferson Davis and the Confederacy, from the nostalgic twentieth-century Southern Agrarians such as Richard Weaver to the early movement intellectuals like Willmoore Kendall, and at last to the ideological bastions of contemporary Washington.

"Original intention" as a constitutional strategy can in fact be traced to the late eighteenth century. But as the legal scholar W. Jefferson Powell detailed in the *Harvard Law Review,* "original intent" back then did not refer to the Founding Fathers at all, as Meese has insisted. Instead, "intention" referred to "the parties to the constitutional compact—the states as political entities." Meese's idea that "intention" meant the framers is, according to Powell, "historically mistaken."[9]

As the Civil War drew near, the states rights advocates who had spoken of "original intent" began to lace their rhetoric with references to the framers. This view was most succinctly expressed by Jefferson Davis in his Inaugural Address as president of the Confederacy. The Confederacy's constitution, he asserted, is "the Constitution formed by our fathers," differing only "insofar as it is explanatory of their well-known intent."[10]

The banner of the South's lost cause was hoisted in the twentieth century by the Southern Agrarians, who, while not rationalizing slavery, cast a romantic haze over antebellum society. One of them, Richard Weaver, an English professor at the University of Chicago, argued that the South had not really been defeated, but had remained a land of superior values against the liberal modernity of the North. In 1948, his book *Ideas Have Consequences* was published, an outcry against "modern barbarity." The book is widely considered by conservatives to be one of the starting points of their movement, and its title has become a conservative cliché. Weaver's thought did not touch on the legal realm, but he strongly influenced another intellectual founder of movement conservatism—Willmoore Kendall, the Yale political scientist who influenced, among other students, William F. Buckley, Jr.

Kendall taught that modern liberals were the "legitimate offspring" of Lincoln, where the problem really started. This "strong" president injected a "cancer" into the American system that threatened its "very survival." And this "cancer" was the clauses of the Fourteenth Amendment guaranteeing the right of "due process" and "equal protection" under the law. Kendall, however, was not an "original intention" advocate. Instead, he urged conservatives to "get busy and amend the Fourteenth Amendment," from which flowed many of the innovations of the Warren Court.[11]

The law that was made after the North won the Civil War reflected a new political alignment. The attempt now to undo this law reflects a renewed opposition to the metropolitan values of the North as promoted by the federal government.

Movement conservatism is built upon the ruins of Lincoln Republicanism. Inside the GOP, at the height of the civil rights controversy, the conservatives gained control of the 1964 convention by relying on a broad southern strategy encompassing the Sunbelt. This has since become the base of their general election strategy. But after the passage of the civil rights crisis, the proximate cause of the electoral shift in the South, the conservatives have seized upon other divisive social issues in the effort to effect a more sweeping and lasting realignment.

The condition of the conservative ascendancy is the fall of the Republicanism whose philosophical identity has been premised on the Civil War amendments the Republican founders sponsored. The ultimate expression of this stream of thought was the law laid down by Chief Justice Earl Warren, whom the conservatives consider the fount of much evil.

To remove the most stubborn impediment to the conservatives' political ambitions, they challenged the constitutional legitimacy of modern jurisprudence. This was more than intra-party factional warfare. In order to achieve their aims, the conservatives must overthrow more than a partisan position. They must overthrow the larger legacy of Lincoln, a legacy which has long been part of the country's bone and fiber.

Reagan, unlike Meese, had succeeded in cloaking conservatism with his geniality. And yet even he occasionally slipped. In his first Inaugural, he said: "The states created the federal government," an idea that can be traced to John C. Calhoun, a flat contradiction of Lincoln, who said: "The Union is older than any of the states and, in fact, it created them as states." In the movement conservatives' siege of the judicial citadel, Meese unfurled an unadorned ideology, exposing it to an examination from which Reagan mostly protected it.

The Attorney General's enterprise was made possible by a recently emerged conservative legal establishment located around Washington. *Benchmark* magazine, for instance, which deals with legal issues, is published by the Center for Judicial Studies, a think tank directed by James McClellan, a former aide to New Right Senator Jesse Helms of North Carolina. The *Benchmark* book review editor is Gary McDowell, a Justice Department public affairs aide who has castigated the Supreme Court for making the states adhere to the constitutional stipulations on religion, speech, and other rights. Senior editor Grover Rees oversaw judicial selection at the Justice Department, and was then appointed a federal judge. Another senior editor, William Kristol, denouncer of the "judicial activists," is the special assistant to Secretary of Education William Bennett. And contributor Daniel Popeo is the head of the Washington Legal Foundation, which files briefs for New Right causes.

Benchmark's Supreme Court editor, Bruce Fein, the former general counsel to the Federal Communications Commission, is associated with a host of conservative think tanks including the American Enterprise Institute and the Heritage Foundation. He has been perhaps the most direct influence on Meese's formulations. Fein's speech on last year's Supreme Court term, delivered at AEI, was well attended by note-taking Justice Department aides. Unsurprisingly, Meese's ABA speech followed Fein's speech concept by concept, often phrase by phrase.

While these theorists seek to deny the "judicial activists" interpretative latitude, their own legal doctrine also depends on an interpretation of American history. The concept of "original intention," however, implies there are eternal precepts immune to any modernization. For some inexplicable reason, the Constitution of 1787 stands outside history, but the Civil War amendments do not, a selective reverence for the past.

Apparently, what is older is better. In their analysis, the conservatives portray the founding fathers as superhuman seers, the only ones permitted to shape the present. But since the founders are not here, the conservatives must act as their proxies. It seems that the founders' ability to peer into the future is matched by the conservatives' ability to read the minds of men long dead.

But the conservatives' pretension is most threatened by their own ideology, which is on a collision course with itself. In Meese's effort to clarify his July ABA address, he delivered a speech in November 1985 in which he attacked jurists who "have 'grounded' their rulings in appeals to social theories." This "activist jurisprudence," he said, is "a chameleon jurisprudence, changing color and form in each era."

Meese believed that he was setting out the terms for undermining the liberal activists. Yet the "original intention" and "judicial restraint" schools of thought are in direct conflict with the other major conservative school of legal thinking, the law and economics activists whose provenance is the University of Chicago Law School.

The law and economics doctrine is less law than economics. Its founder was Aaron Director, Milton Friedman's brother-in-law, a University of Chicago economist on the law school faculty who shares Friedman's ideological predilection for unrestrained markets. To Director, the law is merely another way of demonstrating the compelling logic of his economics. "A lot of us who took his antitrust course or the economics course underwent what can only be called a religious conversion. It changed our view of the entire world," said Robert Bork, a Director disciple who was appointed by Reagan to the U.S. Court of Appeals.[12]

After founding this school of thought, Director recruited Ronald Coase to the University of Chicago as an economist. Coase argued that legal rules should take account of social costs, which could be minimized by reliance on the market. What became known as the Coase Theorem gave law and economics its rationale. "I hate 'justice.' The word is meaningless," elaborated Richard Posner, a University of Chicago law professor appointed by Reagan to the federal appeals court, who pushed the Coase Theorem into the center of legal debate.[13]

Legal thinkers like Posner reduce the law not merely to economics but to a particular economic doctrine, which is presented as universal truth. The market, in their reasoning, has the correct answer for any legal problem; we need only to discern the intent of the invisible hand.

This Social Darwinist brand of jurisprudence is partly an act of restoration, an attempt to bring back a previously discredited notion. Oliver Wendell Holmes, long ago, assailed those who interpreted the Constitution in the light of "Mr. Herbert Spencer's Social Statics." And Supreme Court Justice Benjamin Cardozo chided those who appealed to liberty as "the masquerade of privilege or inequality seeking to entrench itself behind the catchword of a principle."[14]

Obviously, the law and economics school imports nonjuridical thinking into the law. It is constantly creating new categories by applying its doctrine to changing reality. In the past, other disciplines like sociology and psychiatry were brought into the law to help resolve specific problems such as segregation and insanity. By contrast, the law and economics school has consciously grafted its ideas onto jurisprudence, ideologically motivated by a desire to transform the law into a servant of the free market. The judges who follow this line of reasoning are the supreme "judicial activists."

Yet within the Counter-Establishment, these activists and the condemners of activism easily cohabit. One branch denies it is political at all; the other is fiercely political. One argues the ahistorical fiction that its judgments are rooted in a reading of an enduring "original intention"; the other militantly reads law according to a constantly spinning economic calculus.

What this ideology lacks in intellectual coherence it compensates for with political coherence provided by the conservative movement, which half camouflages the desire for judicial power with strafing of the judiciary. The conservatives attack what they wish to control. In the end, the intention is to entrench conservatism in the courts, insulated even from the electoral tides.

This has happened before, of course. When the Federalist Party, the party of commercial interests and big government, was defeated in the popular arena, its partisans sought to perpetuate their ideology by occupying the courts, the most aristocratic branch of government. Unlike the contemporary conservatives, the Federalists made no pretense of "populism."

More important, the foremost Federalist jurist, Chief Justice John Marshall, who laid down the fundamental tenets of the Supreme Court, addressed himself to the issues underlying the current debate in the 1819 case on congressional power, *McCullough* v. *Maryland.* The movement conservatives who want to invest themselves with the authority of the past will find cold comfort in this founder's words, which ring with contemporary relevance: "We must never forget that it is a

Constitution we are expounding. . . . This provision is made in a Constitution intended to endure for ages to come, and, consequently, to be adapted to the various crises of human affairs. To have prescribed the means by which government should, in all future times, execute its powers, would have been to change, entirely, the character of the instrument, and give it the properties of a legal code. It would have been an unwise attempt to provide, by immutable rules, for exigencies which, if foreseen at all, must have been seen dimly, and which can be best provided for as they occur."[15]

Thus Meese's "jurisprudence of original intention" was refuted at the origin, making his premise disappear.

Unsurprisingly, Meese, in his November speech, argued that "to use *McCulloch,* as some have tried, as support for the idea that the Constitution is a protean, changeable thing is to stand history on its head."

Once again, Meese's confused self-defense provided the occasion for another clash with history. For Chief Justice Charles Evans Hughes, in 1934, directly spoke to Meese's claim: "If by the statement that what the Constitution meant at the time of its adoption it means today, it is intended to say that the great clauses of the Constitution must be confined to the interpretation which the framers, with the conditions and outlook of their time, would have placed upon them, the statement carries its own refutation."[16]

Reagan had already led us through the dark night to the dawn: morning again. But the first term had not completed the cycle. There must be a second coming. Reagan had such remarkable powers of vision that he could explain every step we took as progress on the path to the Restoration. Yet even if we cut the welfare budget, built the MX missile, funded the Nicaraguan *contras,* and turned America into one big Enterprise Zone, from sea to shining sea, we would still not have entered the sacred time. Since the "focus of evil in the modern world" does not come from within us, but from the outside, we must shield ourselves from all penetration by demonic power. We are called to commit a heavenly act. But no death is required for the resurrection; the American spirit becomes immortal when the threat of extinction is removed. Thus we must restore the world to where it was before the

Soviets had nuclear weapons, when we were Fortress America. We must circle the planet with lasers and particle-beam weapons—the Star Wars defense.

The idea of Star Wars did not drop from the sky. It was a product of the hothouse debates among the small circle of nuclear theologians. Appropriately, the father of Star Wars was Edward Teller, father of the hydrogen bomb, an abrasive opponent of liberal policies since his falling-out with J. Robert Oppenheimer at Los Alamos. Another influential proponent of Star Wars was retired Lieutenant General Daniel O. Graham, previously director of the Defense Intelligence Agency and a member of the B-Team, set up at the instigation of conservatives as the CIA shadow to produce an analysis that asserted a rising Soviet threat. Teller and Graham's work was subsidized by a rump group of Reagan's Kitchen Cabinet—Joseph Coors, Justin Dart, Karl Bendetsen (CEO of Champion Industries)—benefactors whose interest was so great that they personally participated in the planning of the study. The Heritage Foundation served as a home, where anonymous policy analysts were attached to the effort.

In the meantime, Gregory Fossedal, a *Wall Street Journal* editorial writer, served as the writer for Graham, and promoted the notion in *Journal* editorials and articles appearing elsewhere. For private guidance the young Fossedal, in his twenties, turned to Jude Wanniski, who had used the *Journal*'s columns to launch supply-side economics, the great precedent. Then Fossedal's wife, Lisa, was placed in charge of a new Counter-Establishment group, the Marshall Foundation (funded by the Olin Foundation), which disbursed grants to Star Wars proponents who produced studies in its favor. Idea, money, think tank, media —the Star Wars project began as an ideally formed Counter-Establishment molecule.

In 1982, the group at Heritage issued a full-color glossy report entitled *High Frontier.* Its authors argued that Soviet power was so great that it "can no longer be counterbalanced." We are "undefended," except that we can destroy our enemy and they can destroy us. This condition—Mutual Assured Destruction—is an "immoral and militarily bankrupt doctrine" that must be replaced by "a strategy of

Assured Survival." (The word *mutual* does not fit into this doctrine.) Space would serve the function once performed by the Atlantic and Pacific oceans as natural barriers to foreign attack. Star Wars is more than a defensive system; it is our manifest destiny: "We Americans have always been successful on the frontiers; we will be successful on the new High Frontier of space."[17]

Star Wars was conceived as a defense that would resist any offense, impregnable forever. Using high technology we could make the great leap forward, but once our defense was perfected, technological change would cease. According to the logic of the Star Wars designers, what could be done for defense could not be done for offense. This was an assumption that defied the entire history of warfare, from the age of the bronze helmet to that of the bomb shelter. Above all, Star Wars demanded a leap of faith—the faith that human ingenuity could devise superior technique to reach the lost horizon.

Before the *High Frontier* book was published, Teller and Graham disagreed over the imminent practicality of the Star Wars device. Teller believed that the system needed new technology, not yet invented, to become a reality. Graham, however, contended that the system could be constructed immediately; and so he spun off, incorporating High Frontier as a separate group.

The idea then began a journey through the official bureaucracy. The Department of Defense commissioned a study that concluded that the notion wasn't feasible. And the Congressional Office of Technology Assessment conducted research, then reported that Star Wars was "a defensive system of extremely limited capability."[18] By now, April 1983, President Reagan had been visited by Teller, Graham, and other advocates, and he had become a fervent convert. All skepticism within the administration and the movement became suspect, support for the idea an acid test of loyalty. The White House even attempted to suppress the congressional study.

On March 23, 1983, Reagan presented Star Wars as nothing less than "our ultimate goal." By doing something totally new, "rendering these nuclear weapons impotent and obsolete," we would "restore our military strength." With this stroke we could create "a truly lasting stability," the final nuclear freeze. During the 1984 campaign, Star Wars was the only specific issue that Reagan offered, his new idea, the completion of the Restoration.

After the election, the Star Wars idea was defended by a host of well-intentioned administration spokesmen as the latest wrinkle in deterrence, the very doctrine of Mutual Assured Destruction it was supposed to replace. Defense Secretary Caspar Weinberger, who had initially opposed the notion, was now among its most avid promoters. He blurted: "If we can get a system which is effective and which we know can render their weapons impotent, we could be back in a situation we were in, for example, when we were the only nation with a nuclear weapon."[19] In other words, Star Wars was not about deterrence; it was a method of restoration.

The conservative intellectuals rallied round the flag. For the neoconservatives, the advocacy of Star Wars was a way to compensate for their overreaching during the campaign. In 1984 they had acted as though they could broker the Jewish vote for Reagan. Publications like *Commentary* were filled with articles attempting to excite Jewish fear of black anti-Semitism within the Democratic Party and allay fear of the evangelical right. Despite their best efforts, the neoconservatives could not shepherd the flock; overwhelmingly, Jewish voters cast ballots for Mondale. Now Star Wars offered a fresh opportunity for them to rehabilitate their standing within the movement by demonstrating their famous skills as publicists and debaters. They marked out a position to Reagan's right, more Catholic than the Pope, supportive of Star Wars but critical of any arms-control negotiations. "We find," wrote Norman Podhoretz, "no rational justification for the faith in arms control." Star Wars, however, "really does hold out the rational hope of an eventual escape from the threat of nuclear war."[20] As the neoconservatives saw it, the issue pitted reason against faith. To be against Star Wars was to be irrational.

The neoconservatives begged the question: What was the underlying reasoning of those who fostered the Star Wars idea? Was this a notion prompted solely by an austere rationality—for example, mathematical calculations of the size of the Soviet arsenal? Or was there tangled somewhere in the logic perhaps a domestic ideological root?

In 1984 the founders, funders, and promoters of Star Wars gathered at a forum sponsored by Citizens for America, a conservative movement group. Karl Bendetsen, a financial backer of High Frontier, explained that Mutual Assured Destruction, or deterrence, had been foisted on the country by liberals, "the same crowd that initiated the disarmament of the United States in 1960 under the first Kennedy administration . . . and the scientists who joined them then and are still on their side."

The concept of "their side" was further elaborated by Daniel Graham, who identified it as the "Liberal Establishment." The conservative movement, he urged, must "get at some of the elites . . . get at the political establishment." The balance of nuclear terror, he continued, was the most insidious and cunning aspect of liberal ideology. "These people really benefit by having the threat of enormous destruction, of catastrophic destruction, of apocalyptic destruction hanging over the heads of Americans. And they don't want us out from under that threat. And the reason they don't want us out from under that threat is because that terrible threat allows them to get Americans to do things they would not otherwise do." According to his logic, Mutual Assured Destruction is the ultimate weapon in the liberal arsenal, deployed to enforce domestic political control. Because of the threat the liberals wield, they are able to manipulate us to support their agenda. Once Star Wars is in place, however, the liberals will lose their shield. Then the window of vulnerability for conservatives—and America—will be closed.

How dangerous are these liberals? Robert Jastrow, a scientist who has become a leading spokesman in favor of Star Wars, noted that liberal scientists who fail to accept Reagan's "wisdom" are in league with "journalist fellow travelers." Their views, moreover, are "accepted unquestioningly by *The New York Times* and by sincere Congressmen and their staffers on the Hill. This group," he warned, "is putting an enormous amount of energy into an effort that can only be described as being in the interests of the Soviet Union. . . ."[21]

Star Wars, according to these conservatives, will accomplish a Promethean feat greater than the ultimate defense of America from Soviet missiles. It will steal the fire of the Liberal Establishment. And by conquering one idea (Mutual Assured Destruction) with another

(Assured Survival) the conservatives will rise and the liberals will fall. Star Wars is shadow liberalism in orbit.

"There is," said Dwight Eisenhower, "a recurring temptation to feel that some spectacular and costly action could become the miraculous solution to all current difficulties," an action like "a huge increase in the new elements of our defense" or "a dramatic expansion in basic and applied research." Yet "in holding scientific research and discovery in respect, as we should, we must also be alert to the equal and opposite danger that public policy could itself become the captive of a scientific-technological elite."[22]

According to almost unanimous scientific opinion, Star Wars would not work as advertised—a perfectly sealed defense mechanism. But the intrinsic merit of the idea matters less than its existence, which heralds a momentous political event—the fusion of "a scientific-technological elite" with a political elite, a Counter-Establishment technocracy.

In the end, the conservative networks that produce the various ideas are almost as important as the ideas themselves. Once in place, the Counter-Establishment can constantly churn out agendas: process determines policy. New doctrines arrive because the Counter-Establishment remains.

CHAPTER THIRTEEN

THE BEGINNING

OF IDEOLOGY

L ong ago, the "end of ideology" seemed so obvious as to be a cliché. It was thought to be less an immediate condition of the postwar era than a reflection of the American character itself. Neither socialism nor continental conservatism had made successful transatlantic voyages. What was called "socialism," even after the fall of the Communist Party USA, was mostly a memory of a distorted image of a foreign model. And what passed as conservatism was eccentric and irrational, and left no trace. Because America lacked a feudal background and a fixed class system, virtually all social scientists and historians agreed that an ideological politics here was, quite simply, impossible. The historian Daniel Boorstin celebrated this as "the genius of American politics."[1]

But even those who offered penetrating insights into American exceptionalism were still bound by an intellectual Eurocentrism. They could not conceive of a native brand of ideological politics because they defined it exclusively in foreign terms. The historians of the "consensus" school were captives of the comparative mentality, unable to disenthrall themselves from Europe, which remained the final authority. They argued convincingly about the uniqueness of America, but then short-circuited their own notion. To them, an ideological politics, a politics motivated by a comprehensive system of beliefs, was unimaginable; a mythological politics, a politics advanced by turning those beliefs into a story beyond history, was considered even more ludicrous. Thus, because they did not fit the proper European slots, the conservative movement and the Reagan presidency could not be explained by the logic of the "consensus" school. "People who talk about an 'end of ideology' are never ready for the next war of ideology," said Edwin Feulner, the Heritage Foundation president. If the "consensus" historians had been correct, there would have been no Counter-Establishment and Reagan would never have been president.

The new ideological politics constantly eludes those using traditional frames of analysis. Because it doesn't appear in the guise of the old Eurostyle, it can be declared not to exist; or because it sometimes inhabits the shell of the traditional parties, it can be pronounced simply the latest mutation of partisan politics. Conservatives are equated with Republicans, and their rise is seen as a shift in the party system. Since some of Reagan's political strategists are seeking what they call a "realignment," an interpretation organized around the concept of conventional partisanship appears on the surface to make sense. Yet after two Reagan victories, most commentators continue to wonder when the predicted realignment will occur. The failure of events to cooperate with the abstract model highlights, more than anything else, the inadequacy of the model itself.

We are not in fact experiencing a realignment of the traditional party system or a realignment of the electorate or a realignment of beliefs. Although some voters have become more reliably Republican and others more reliably Democratic, more voters are more volatile than ever. In any case, the evaporation of party loyalties makes a realignment in the old sense a shallow idea, for the prevailing system is the permanent campaign system.

Despite the conservative dominance over the policy agenda, public opinion on many specific issues is liberal. Much of Reagan's personal popularity as president can be attributed to his studied refusal to challenge these beliefs and enact an unpopular agenda. These factors—the public's operational progressivism and the old party system's decay—contradict the conventional notions of realignment. How then can the relative effectiveness of the Counter-Establishment be explained? Another conclusion must be advanced: We are experiencing a realignment of elites.

Throughout his presidency, Reagan has married the ideas of the

Counter-Establishment to the techniques of the permanent campaign. Star Wars is a demonstration shot, its trajectory illuminating the workings of the actual political system. After the Counter-Establishment does the treatment of the idea, Reagan makes the public presentation on television. Then the "free media" campaign comes into play, with the network news shows broadcasting cartoon versions of the plan. Pow! Zap! We're saved! See, the Star Wars weapons have knocked the Soviet missiles out of the sky. Then, there's the paid media campaign, mounted by the right-wing High Frontier group. On the screen, in the fall of 1985, appeared a child's drawing of a happy scene—Mommy, Daddy, child, and pet. A shield, in fact a line drawn by a crayon, arcs across the sky. Enemy missiles cannot penetrate. The sun smiles.

In the past, a policy became concrete only after it was enacted. But electronic fantasies like Star Wars have changed that. Now the simulation becomes a reality. We know Star Wars can work because we have seen it operational on television. In order not to build the unreal, the earthbound opponents of Star Wars must dismantle a real image already rooted in our minds. To vote against it is to vote against a defense we have seen working. We have bought the project mentally long before the bill comes due, just like supply-side economics. "The Force is with us," said Reagan. All that's required for these ideas to work is our faith in them. This is civics, Reagan-style. What do political parties have to do with it? The Force is something else.

The conservatives are replacing the old party politics with an ideological politics in which the ideas order up the images. In their view, a party is useful only when it serves the ends of ideology. The transformation of the Republican National Committee into a technocratic wonder, combining the functions of a financial clearinghouse and an advertising firm, serves their interest well. By rendering the RNC a robotic factory without a program, the manufacture of the policy agenda is left outside the party. It is an independent enterprise assumed by the Counter-Establishment. These two modes of politics don't conflict, but mesh.

Reagan's pitched battles with such party stalwarts as Gerald Ford and Walter Mondale were more than neat symmetry. These foils embodied the obsolescent party politics in a double sense; neither man was acculturated to the permanent campaign, and neither fully grasped the paramount role of ideas. Unlike most politicians without a traditional party to fall back on, Reagan was not an isolated individual who had to construct an organization around himself from scratch. He was always the favorite son of the conservative movement; his victory was the victory of an ideological elite.

The rise of an ideological politics does not mean that a majority of the voters agree with conservatism, or even that many express themselves in its special language. It does mean that an elite devoted to this brand of politics is flourishing. Its cadres hold some key positions of power under Reagan; they are planning for the long run after Reagan; and they are constantly creating well-funded organizations to wage the endless "war of ideas." Conservatives are not dependent upon the strength of their reasoning alone to ensure future success; the Counter-Establishment is the institutional force that carries the logic. Polls of the general public intended to demonstrate agreement or disagreement with conservative positions don't get at this central point. Only a thin slice of political life can ever be revealed by the statistical matrix of conventional social science. And the polls prove nothing about the nature of the Counter-Establishment.

Reagan's triumph in 1984 was hailed by many commentators as the reemergence of the "emerging Republican majority." They cited the sudden increase of self-identified Republicans as proof. Yet Reagan did not campaign as a Republican and forwarded no positive reason why anyone should become one. He identified himself most often as a "former Democrat." If the word *Republican* has any meaning, it has not been provided by Reagan. This is hardly a mere semantic issue. The crucible of Reagan's politics is not the party, but the conservative movement; and at the head of the movement is the Counter-Establishment. The use of ideology by an elite in an effort to shift policy is not a realignment of the party system. The movement is an extra-partisan force, and when the occasion demands, it is anti-partisan.

Grounded outside the Republican Party, the movement is posed against the GOP traditionalists whose bastion is the Senate caucus and whose leader is Robert Dole. These Republicans still frequently find a natural sympathy in all the old familiar places—the great law and accounting firms; the investment banking houses; the corner offices of corporate executives who still pride themselves on their "responsibility." They may be an Establishment, but they are not what is commonly called liberal. They may even call themselves "conservative," but they are not what the movement conservatives mean by it. If Republicanism is to become strong again, it will have to do so at the expense of the movement conservatives. Conversely, the continuing influence of the conservatives must mean the continuing demise of Republicanism, the ideological end of the historical party. To maintain their preeminence, the conservatives must attempt to render the Republican Party their shadow.

The conflict between the conservatives and the Republicans is not something that occurs at the unconscious level. Conservatives, at least, are acutely aware of what is happening. "Conservatism is emphatically *not* the old Republicanism," explained Feulner. "It's a case of trend lines. Conservatives are in an up trend. Republicans are in a down trend. There's always going to be a rearguard action, but the Republicans are quietly becoming not the dominant element. There will be fewer of the old politicians and more and more of the people who have been through the new kinds of activities. Not only do you have conservative cadres coming into entry-level jobs, but once out of office they will serve as consultants. Come ten years from now, you'll have them ready to go, two or three notches higher, even at the cabinet level. Our infrastructure was never built up in the Nixon administration. By and large Reagan relied on the Establishment to staff his administration. Our bright young people hadn't had the on-the-job training to be really credible. Ten years from now it will be very different. Next time around, there might be fifty percent conservatives—an order of magnitude larger. You won't be counting the Jim Watts one at a time."

Conservatives invariably assert that their ideology is nothing less than the sum total of eternal American verities, the one true faith. But the movement whose origin can be traced to the 1940s is not the same thing as the party whose origin was in the 1850s. When the Counter-Establishment was in its infancy, the Remnant despairingly wailed its helplessness at an alien America. "Stop!" wrote young Buckley in the first issue of the *National Review*—the best short description of the conservative attitude of the time. Conservatism was not the vital center; it was the irrelevant fringe. "We're riding the crest of a process that began when liberalism was in ascendance," said Feulner. "All you have is the logic of your arguments. If you're part of the Establishment everyone grants your premises."

The first principle of conservative first principles is the primacy of its ideology. In the beginning, the movement had little else. But its ideas arrived from different angles, and when they intersected, what was produced wasn't picture-perfect. The cultural conservative's golden past was not the free-marketer's mechanized economy, which was not the ex-Communist's national security state, required to exorcise the nightmarish Communist-liberal Hades. Conservatives have splashed clashing colors on the political canvas at different moments to achieve different effects. But the limited elements of ideology they have worked with have led to some novel distortions. To the extent that conservatism is really not liberalism, it has drawn from sources outside the American political tradition. This has given conservatives a platform to stand on; but even after two Reagan landslides, their ideology has encapsulated them. Most important, it has prevented them from being able to claim the Republican heritage.

"You might be interested to know that the Scriptures are on our side on this," said Reagan on February 4, 1985, arguing against cuts in the Pentagon budget. No previous president has ever presumed in a matter of appropriations to declare that God is on his side. Are Democrats all heathens? Is Congress godless? Just as religious references in feudal Europe signaled a political linkage of church and state, Reagan's scriptural citation is a sign of his alliance with the fundamentalist right, a political force seeking the practical dissolution of church-state separation, the end of a fundamental American idea. How conservatives cope with this crisis they have built into their politics will reveal the degree to which they actually reject liberalism.

The evangelical right has its own peculiar version of shadow liberalism. The Liberal Establishment, they insist, has systematically and consciously made true religion illegal (i.e., the Supreme Court rulings on abortion and school prayer). In its place liberals have substituted a false religion, "secular humanism," whose high priests are trained at the

Columbia University Teachers College and whose temples are the public schools.[2] To combat the Liberal Establishment, the fundamentalist right has constructed a counterculture of television networks and schools, think tanks and political action committees. Their theology does not turn on small ideas like tax simplification, but on big ideas like Armageddon. In conservative ideology, the evangelical right represents "traditional values." But this fulfillment of the ideology is not all milk and honey. The conservative movement can be many movements because its cadres can shift the debate nimbly from issue to issue. The truly religious, however, have limited flexibility because their positions are absolute; their uncompromising theology threatens to restrict the movement's expansion. Yet the movement's failure to accommodate the fundamentalists' unyielding demands may lead to a more intractable situation if the religious rightists decide to take independent action to keep the movement pure. A presidential candidacy from the fundamentalist wing, perhaps that of the Reverend Pat Robertson, the mellifluous television host and multimillionaire owner of the Christian Broadcasting Network, would be an attempt to capture the movement in the way that the movement has attempted to capture the Republican Party.

But if the movement and the fundamentalist right are indistinguishable, then Jews and Catholics almost certainly would refuse to be baptized in that church: so much for realignment. The early warning signs were already present in the overwhelming Jewish vote in 1984 against Reagan and the Catholic bishops' statements on nuclear war and the economy.

The bishops' letters were not aberrant heresies, but derived directly from the Pope's own positions. On the eve of the release of the bishops' economic message, a Counter-Establishment group of lay Catholics, mustered by William Simon and supply-side theologian Michael Novak, issued a counter-manifesto that praised individualism and the free market. The Counter-Establishment effort to displace the traditional teaching of the Catholic Church with the Protestant ethic cannot expect instant success. Those engaged in this project must have great faith that the Counter-Establishment will be around for a long time. In their attempt to transform Catholicism by the customary methods of the conservative movement, they have taken a schismatic leap far beyond shadow liberalism. Will the Counter-Establishment fund a counter-papacy in Orange County?

On point after point, the conservatives have already separated themselves from the secular Republican tradition. Their embrace of the "Christian nation" advocates is merely the gaudiest display of their unorthodox doctrine. The effort by Representative Newt Gingrich, a leader of the movement in the House, to recast the Grand Old Party as the Great Opportunity Party, is the sound of a chain saw severing the ties. Gingrich's exercise is more than sloganeering. Words, after all, do have meaning. And the word most conspicuously dropped in his new formulation is *old*. The cavalier discarding of the Republican past shows what little consequence these conservatives attach to tradition.

To the movement's theorists, the party is less than "grand." "The parties have not declined enough in my opinion," said Irving Kristol. "To the degree that there are strong party organizations, they tend to suppress ideas. Well, that hasn't been true for the Democrats. It is true for the Republican Party. The majority of party leadership in Congress is controlled by the traditional Republican Party, who are linked very much to the CEOs, who believe in managing things." Kristol, of course, is a neoconservative, and the neoconservatives are as anti-Republican now as they were in their incarnation as leftists; they are dedicated to dissolving traditional political bonds even as they exalt an abstract traditionalism. Although Kristol is instinctively sectarian, he also speaks for conservatives on the question of partisanship. "The conservatives and the neoconservatives have come together in the birth of a new ideology," said Feulner. They do not view the GOP, like the traditionalists, as an institution encrusted with a glorious past whose preservation lends society ballast in turbulent seas. The conservatives are ideologues before they are partisans. And their ideology has led them to jettison most of the first principles of the historical Republican Party.

The conservative ascendancy within the GOP has been marked by a curious reversal of positions. On civil, equal, and states rights the conservatives have imported into the party notions that were held dear only by the kind of Democrats who have disappeared from the Democracy. Just a generation ago, the GOP was still a competitor for the black vote—in 1960, Richard Nixon won 32 percent. By 1964 the regular Republicans were still unassailable within the GOP congressional caucus, but the conservatives managed to capture the convention and nominate Barry Goldwater. The split was manifested over the landmark 1964 Civil Rights Act, which the congressional Republicans helped pass and the convention denounced. In 1984, Reagan became only the second Republican candidate for president, following Goldwater, to fail to make a direct appeal to black voters.

The conservative opposition to the Equal Rights Amendment is another dramatic repudiation of the traditional position. It was Republicans, after all, who were responsible for the passage of the women's suffrage amendment. And it was Republicans who first supported an equal rights amendment. From 1944 until 1980, every Republican convention platform contained a statement in favor of equal rights for women. (The first Democratic convention to adopt an ERA plank was in 1972—an act that contributed to the outrage of organized labor, party bosses, and neoconservatives.) At the convention that nominated Reagan, the platform denounced the ERA as a transgression of traditional values. The derision of equal rights as a squalid idea fostered by special interests and motivated by envy is not, however, an attitude consistent with the Republican past.

Instead of upholding the banner of equal rights, the conservatives uphold that of states rights. The two positions are not disconnected, for when the 1980 convention took its stand against the ERA, it justified its break with history in the foreign tongue of states rights. The matter, read the platform, is "now in the hands of state legislatures." States rights, banished at long last as divisive and discreditable from the Democracy, was picked up by the conservatives as a "bloody shirt," a banner in the war against big government. It was a strange garment in which to dress the Republican Party. Yet Reagan presented it as a revival of original principles. In his first inaugural address, he declared that "the states created the federal government," substituting Calhounism for Republicanism.

Perhaps the most radical conservative departure from the Republican legacy is the movement's unremitting hostility toward the national government. Republicans might have sought to modify certain aspects of federal rule, but never attacked the idea of the government itself. The Republican Party as a governing party rested on the marriage of the national idea with the central government. Republicans were not ashamed of a federal giveaway program called the Homestead Act, or the government enterprise that made possible the transcontinental railroad, or an industrial policy of tariffs. They made the world work, and that's why their politics worked. Even when they were conservative, they were conserving yesterday's liberalism. They were a party of governing, the Democrats a party of protest.

Now, however, conservatives resist any responsibility for the federal government; they are most comfortable in the pose of outsiders. Even when in office, they continue to wage war against what they must manage. Conservatives placed in charge of official bureaucracies often act like soldiers in a free-fire zone; their efforts at reform take on the air of search-and-destroy missions. Their complaint against the size of government is surpassed by their complaint against its autonomy, which they view as a usurpation of the market. And since private gain must be public good, according to their doctrine, they must be serving the national interest.

Some conservatives make little distinction between the market and public service, and so they apply the rules of success to governing. Politics, to them, is often seen as just another market to exploit. Since they are already winners in business, the same precepts of positive thinking should apply to politics. Michael Deaver, who was the presidential aide closest to the Reagans, offers a particularly striking case. As the chief public relations choreographer in the White House, he dramatized the mythology of Reaganism in which the greatest evil is a big government dominated by "special interests." Then Deaver left the White House and cashed in, becoming a lobbyist with extraordinary access—a "special interest" in his own right. When the Reaganites encounter problems, precisely because of their inappropriate behavior, they cast around for culprits. Accordingly, when a conservative such as Edwin Meese is caught taking large loans from people who have been given lucrative jobs, he feels no guilt. Instead, this sort of conservative feels bewildered and angry at his accusers. Once again the conservatives believe they are being unfairly set upon by the Liberal Establishment.

The insiders' status holds both fascination and repulsion for the conservatives. This is one of the many arresting affinities between them and nineteenth-century Populism—a tradition conservatives aver they are emulating and Republicans have always opposed. According to both the conservatives and the Populists, we had a golden age, a lost Eden, a time that can be retrieved. When the power of an intrusive monopoly is defeated, those days can be restored. In this battle there are two sides. The forces of goodness reside in the countryside; the cities are cesspools of crime and corruption. The Populists equated the agrarian West with the values of democracy and posed them against the settled East. This sectional conflict was a shadow war between individuals and big institutions. We were two nations: "the people," and the millionaires. In the conservative version, big business completely recedes from view and big government looms large. Their rhetoric, however, captures some of the earlier tone. "The people" are still fighting "the special interests." Once again the frontier, the Sunbelt, is equated with liberty and serves as a geographical metaphor for the battle of individuals against organizations.

The chief organizing issue for the Populist was money; they argued that the gold standard, the "cross of gold," could be lifted by the unlimited coinage of silver, which would redistribute opportunity. In the conservative account, the Laffer Curve's tax cuts replace free silver as the economic medium of growth. Taxes have been seized from the producers and given to a parasitical monopoly. When taxes are cut, our worth will be determined by the fortune we find. Ironically, the supply-siders, who label themselves the "populists" in their war against the "elitist" demand-siders, call for a return to the gold standard. (The tag they pin on themselves doesn't always apply: George Gilder, for example, argues against "elitists"; yet he pays tribute to the heroic Robber Barons in *Wealth and Poverty*.)

Like many of the ancient Populists, many conservatives reflexively see an unhappy series of events as some sort of conspiracy against them. "Indeed, what makes conspiracy theories so widely acceptable is that they usually contain a germ of truth," wrote Richard Hofstadter. "But there is a great difference between locating conspiracy *in* history and saying that history *is,* in effect, a conspiracy."[3] The Populists of course faced formidable enemies. But some Populists were not content to deal only with their real enemies. They conjured up lurid conspiracies of goldbugs, English diplomats, and Jewish bankers; the octopus and the spider were favored images. For those conservatives who have inherited the belief that there must be some evil, centralized mechanism making the world work according to its selfish design, the enemy is always the scheming Liberal Establishment, its tentacles slithering around the hidden levers of influence—the Trilateral Commission and CBS, the Council on Foreign Relations and Planned Parenthood. This mode of thinking is sufficiently pervasive among conservatives that Reagan himself campaigned in 1980 against the spider's web spun by the Trilateral Commission.

Reagan also cast himself as a "populist" in his second-term campaign on behalf of tax reform. He evoked a symbol he called "Washington," which he insisted was "un-American." It was time, he declared, for a "second American Revolution." Yet this "populism" was hardly progressive, a point Reagan himself observed. At the start of his tax reform effort, in 1985, he denounced the tax system for being too "progressive." His "populism" amounted to an attempt to rid the tax code of its older populist features.

Traditional Republicans, who compose their fair share of the groups excoriated by conservatives, do not think as populists. They believe in institutions, including big ones, which they often run. They have faith in established procedures, disdain plebiscites, and are suspicious of passionate social movements. They do not believe that the market can or should be populated only by Adam Smith's pin factories. They see modern corporations as part of a world of large institutions protected by laws. In short, these Republicans are not populists.

Conservatives who claim the title to the Populist tradition pay an odd homage by using the Populist rhetoric against most of the original Populist goals. While the Populists wanted government to regulate the marketplace in the name of opportunity, the conservatives demand its exit. Conservative antielitism, moreover, is in the ultimate service of a political elite—the Counter-Establishment. If conservatism is Populism, then it is Populism turned on its head and rattled. One thing it is not is Republicanism.

The story of Republicanism in the contemporary age is a story of decline, hastened by the conservatives. During the Eisenhower years, a pudding without a theme was whipped up and packaged as "Modern Republicanism." Nelson Rockefeller and his innumerable panels of brain-trusters served it deluxe. Although the principal ingredient in "Modern Republicanism" was air, it did contain a dollop of old-fashioned Progressive protein. Meanwhile, the Taftite Republicans lumbered to the elephants' graveyard. The new guard of ideological conservatives, whose resources consisted of little more than the word, went virtually unmentioned. By the mid-1980s, however, the institutional force and momentum was on their side. "Modern Republicanism" was as much a relic as the Taftite orthodoxy. The sudden appearance of a messiah like Rockefeller or Willkie was as remote as the possibility that George Bush would criticize the conservatives. Even a political career like that of the twice-nominated Thomas Dewey, Taft's nemesis, was now implausible. Only a few congressmen and outriders traveling under the banner of "Republican Mainstream" attempted to do combat with the movement. Although echoes of the traditional "Mainstream" could be heard in the Senate chamber, it was easily muffled at the 1984 convention.

The Great Opportunity Party is less a house divided against itself than a house that tilts. Conservatives will never be satisfied until they have thoroughly purged it of Republicans. The emblems of their intent were hardly hidden. Conservatives rejoiced when many Lincoln Republicans, led by John Anderson, left the party in 1980. And they celebrated when the New England Brahmins were waylaid. In 1984, Elliot Richardson, the former everything, lost a Republican primary for the U.S. Senate nomination against a former John Birch Society member rehabilitated as a mere conservative. The days of Henry Cabot Lodge were long gone. In New York, the Conservatives conducted a lengthy campaign against the heirs of Dewey. Inspired by William F. Buckley, Jr., they organized a Conservative Party in direct emulation of the Liberal Party—a striking case of literal shadow liberalism. In 1970 they elected one of their own to the Senate, James Buckley, Bill's brother, by displacing the Republican. They demonized Nelson Rockefeller for decades, eventually succeeding in tarnishing him so that Gerald Ford would not run in 1976 with his own Vice President. In 1980 a conservative discovery named Alfonse D'Amato defeated incumbent Republican Senator Jacob Javits, a reprise of the 1970 experience. And two years later, drugstore mogul Lewis Lehrman, a major Counter-Establishment figure, captured the nomination for governor.

By the mid-1980s, Reagan's economic policies, which undermined American exports, threatened ruin for yeoman Republicanism, embodied by the midwestern farmers, the base of the Senate leadership. When a relief bill was passed, Reagan vetoed it. Once again he demonstrated his stand against big government. In doing so, he shut off relief for the family farmers, the traditional economic individualists. Since the reality of a mixed economy could never be acknowledged and accepted in conservative ideology, the stark dogmas of "big government" and "individualism" must prevail. Thus government was passive and individualism suffered.

Reagan's policies undermined more than the GOP's classical farm base. His actions, which inflated the value of the dollar in international markets, also injured the traditional manufacturing upon which the Dewey-Rockefeller wing had rested. A sudden conversion of many Senate Republicans to protectionism resulted. Not even the unexpected fall in the price of oil in 1986, pulling down the dollar, halted the protectionist trend Reagan's policies had set in motion.

Some conservatives privately and happily anticipated the loss of the Senate in 1986; they reasoned that the defeat of the regular Republicans might give them greater freedom at the convention. In New England and the mid-Atlantic and Midwestern states, the old Republican heartland, they were driving traditionalists out of office and, they hoped, out of the GOP. The conservative devotion to the party, of course, was contingent on their ideological control.

Conservatives had already shattered the hegemony of the Republican national elite. Perhaps its last hurrah was the Law of the Sea Treaty, negotiated in good faith by Elliot Richardson and dismissed out of hand by the Reagan administration. Whatever vacuum was created by the Republican demise was promptly filled by the onrushing Counter-Establishment. Though its cadres failed to gain control of all the offices they sought, their debates had become the debates of the executive branch. With their broad supremacy over the Republicans, the conservatives had accomplished at least a momentary realignment of elites.

The Democrats considered none of this in their agonized reconsiderations of what had gone wrong. They had a Ptolemaic view of the universe, in which everything revolved around them. The 1984 primaries, conducted without Republican counterparts, undoubtedly contributed to their narcissism. They accepted their recent setbacks as proof that they were lost in space; yet they had little sense of the next galaxy. During all the post-election self-recriminations, not a single Democratic leader attempted to explain who the conservatives were, how they worked, or what they had wrought. Many Democrats confused their confusion with a realignment of the electorate.

If those who forget the past are condemned to repeat it, then most Democratic leaders are fated to travel in an unending circle. They attributed the 1984 defeat to their own failure to occupy the "center," which they were convinced they had forfeited. Mondale, they believed, was among the chief culprits for this fatal drift. Yet throughout his campaign, Mondale had obsessively tried to station himself in the "center." At the Democratic Convention, in his acceptance speech, he spelled out the character of his "centrism" in great detail, even giving it a name—the "New Realism." "Look at our platform," he said. "There are no defense cuts that weaken our security; no business taxes that weaken our economy; no laundry lists that raid our Treasury." Having succinctly stated the dilemma, he then locked himself inside it:

> I want to say something to those of you across the country who voted for Ronald Reagan. . . . I heard you. And our party heard you. After we lost, we didn't tell the American people that they were wrong. Instead, we began asking you what our mistakes had been.

Thus Mondale acknowledged the circumstances that made his politics seemingly unworkable; he rejected his old views while still clinging fast to them. Here was a man practicing the eulogy for his own funeral, an oration delivered virtually word for word by many Democrats after his campaign expired.

As self-described "pragmatists," they continued their quest for the "center," just as Mondale had before his defeat. After two thrashings they regarded Reagan as a right-winger who, through occult powers, had spirited away this "center." Could it be won back by an even more intense "pragmatism"?

In the conventional wisdom, pragmatism is the rightful opponent of ideology. To be pragmatic is to be moderate, realistic, and sensible. Moderation, of course, may refer to an implicit belief in due process and a measured approach to citizenship. But the "moderation" of the self-conscious "centrist" is less a matter of principle than of positioning asserted as principle.

According to common political usage, pragmatism has no philosophical content, except the absence of such content, which is why there is often a bias in its favor; it means tactical adjustment within the current arrangements. Pragmatism is the politics of status quo maintenance, and it is ultimately inflexible because it rules out challenge to established power. Its absolute relativism, moreover, renders it derivative. The pragmatist never initiates, but constantly seeks middle ground. He lives by the spirit of the yardstick, always calibrating some elusive center determined by the distance between others' points. His program is a series of disconnected policies. The self-styled pragmatist rejects Mondale's image yet embraces Mondale's premise. Against that contradiction, the conservative defends his program as thoroughly consistent. But the ideologue's advantage is less his program than his purpose. Proposals divorced from larger principles are mechanical and cold, and however smoothly diagrammed are politically lifeless. The pragmatic concern is not ends but means, which results in the substitution of technique for goals. This inner void of the centrists is a great incentive to the ideologues. And the centrists may even relish the stimulation of extremes because it is the context in which they can position themselves as moderate. Their stance, however, can be defined

by the ideologues because their positioning is a product of outer-direc-
tion. Rather than offering general ideas, the pragmatists assume that
isolated facts by themselves make a convincing case. They have no
story to tell, except that their facts are not the story of nasty extremes.
But power must seek purpose, or wither. The pragmatism of the centrists is a constant rationale, not a purpose itself; it is a true conservatism and a false pragmatism. It has little in common with the spirit of
the philosophy that originated with Charles Peirce, or any philosophy.[4]

Most of the centrists ritually denounced the Mondale campaign
and then typically recapitulated the fiscal gloom and intellectual ex-
haustion of the New Realism. The conditions that Reagan's program
had fostered were implicitly accepted as an impenetrable reality. To the
extent that Democrats gave credence to the conservative dogma about
the absolute evil of all deficits, they had to bear the burden of conservative social policy. But what about the special character of Reagan's
deficit? Extravagant military spending combined with a regressive tax
cut created the debt. Real interest rates were kept at an unprecedented
high level by the Fed, still enthralled by a banker's version of monetarist theology. Consequently, payments for interest on the debt exceeded
payments for social programs for the first time since the New Deal. The
program as a whole operated as a huge mechanism of income distribution. Those who lost were average taxpayers; those who gained most
were holders of bonds and Treasury notes. Demands from conservatives
to cut the tax burden and social programs increased; the taxpayers,
seeking immediate relief, were encouraged in their rage.

In 1985, the Counter-Establishment once again filled the intellectual vacuum. Martin Anderson, the Hoover Institution scholar who had
been the White House domestic policy chief during the first term,
contrived a balanced budget bill in which Congress gave up its constitutionally mandated authority in exchange for certain immutable budget
targets. Anderson's idea was introduced by Senator Phil Gramm of
Texas, a renegade Democrat turned conservative Republican who had
been David Stockman's spy within the House Democratic caucus. Most
Senate Democrats voted for what became known as the Gramm-Rudman-Hollings balanced budget bill, though many of them privately
believed it was crackpot economics. They subjected the future to the

strictures of a Counter-Establishment nostrum while abdicating their own heritage. This was the practical meaning of their pragmatism.

The Democratic bankruptcy was only one of the factors making the conservatives appear larger than life. In fact they were in a fragile political situation—despite the ready access to large sums of cash and foundation grants, the disarray of the once omnipotent Liberal Establishment, and the weakening of the traditional Republicans.

By defining themselves as a movement rather than as a party, they established restrictions on membership: one must believe in order to belong. The movement depends on ideological loyalty above professionalism to bind people together. (Professionalism is often regarded as self-conscious liberalism. When journalists respond to conservative attacks on the press by citing their professionalism, the conservatives usually consider this a hypocritical admission of guilt.)

The reliance on ideology naturally limits the numbers of Counter-Establishment cadres. The Heritage Foundation's *Annual Guide to Public Policy Experts* is a directory listing perhaps a majority of the players in the Counter-Establishment who are not in the administration. The 1985 edition contains slightly more than a thousand names, a substantial increase over the six hundred listed in the 1982 edition. The compactness of the Counter-Establishment engenders a sense of fraternity and morale that is infrequently found in the outside world. Its leaders treasure every one of its people, especially the younger cadres, because they understand that their institutions are still overshadowed. They are no longer a Remnant, but they still are a relatively small band.

Their principal asset is also their principal liability. The belief in ideology has enabled the Counter-Establishment to organize around a set of strong convictions. But because agreement on a fixed ideology animates conservatives, disagreement has enormous disruptive potential. Unlike the constituencies of the New Deal, bound together finally by a common material interest in the role of government, the conservative movement is finally held together by its ideology. But the movement does not escape the Social Darwinism it fosters. At every point of doctrine, there is a sect mobilized around its own internally consistent theoretical system, with the most potentially divisive grouping being the fundamentalist right.

The economic crisis of the early 1980s offered a glimmer of the factionalism that could be ignited within the Counter-Establishment by unanticipated events. Left to the movement's devices, Reagan would have been subjected to endless humiliation at the hands of his ideologues. He was rescued only by a complex deus ex machina: the Republican Senate leadership, the House Democrats, and the Federal Reserve. Without Reagan's talent for explaining the recovery as the logical outcome of faith in conservatism, the movement's fierce factionalism would have lacked a larger rationale. What Reagan actually conserved as president was the conservative movement.

To maintain its momentum, the Counter-Establishment has a constant need to elaborate its ideology; only an incessant agitation keeps the wheels turning. But conservatives can never resolve their own differences by an appeal to party loyalty, which must be secondary. The Hobbesian permutation, where each faction wars against all, always remains a possibility. Reagan's inevitable departure from the stage heightens this chance.

Reagan gave the conservatives legitimacy they had not previously possessed. His reign laid down respectable roots. But his presidency presented a circumstance conservatives had never faced. They had built up a movement and Counter-Establishment in the shadow of their image of the Liberal Establishment. Now conservatives stood in another shadow—Reagan's.

The battle for the succession occurs under his gaze. As the candidates squabble, Reagan remains in the White House. His continuing presence on the scene may have the curious effect of preventing the emergence of another commanding figure. But without one, it may be difficult to sustain the influence the movement has accumulated under Reagan. The next leader, moreover, cannot exactly be Reagan. He must be able to infuse the ideology with a new set of images, vivid for another age. For the first time, the conservatives must cope with a conservative past that is not mythological.

Early on, Reagan defined the ambition of his presidency as nothing less than "starting the world over again," a New Beginning that would bring the country back to the values of the Founding Fathers. These values endure beyond history and do not fluctuate; once we believe, what we build upon them cannot fluctuate either. In the political economy of conservatism, the different spheres—public and private, political and communal—attain harmonious balance. Once we achieve the equilibrium of a Newtonian universe, everything will run like clockwork according to the laws of a benign deity and classical economics. The political realignment and the prosperity that flow from such values must be permanent. Only a lapse of faith could lead to our fall from grace. But what became of Reagan's goals in his own time? Is the legacy as clear-cut as the ideology?

Without the Counter-Establishment thinkers to supply Reagan with notions such as the supply side, his hardened mythology would have lacked the gloss of innovation. He was the interest on their intellectual capital. But without Reagan, conservatism would never have become a mass cultural experience; he gave life to abstractions. Reagan's personality seemed to be the movement and his rhetoric the ideology. Conservatism is contained by his image, which will linger after he leaves.

When the image is focused, an ideological dilemma comes sharply into view. His speeches are laced with references to the puritan virtues of thrift and stoicism. Political self-government is an extension of our personal self-control; the economy is the addition of household economies. Reagan wants us to become a nation of self-made men, to strive and succeed like the self-made president. Our characters will then be measured by the market.

But a curious exchange happens in the ideological marketplace run by Reagan. The self-made man becomes the self-indulgent man; personality defined by appearances replaces character hewn by hard labor; and supply-side rhetoric serves as the boilerplate of the culture of consumption. Nowhere did Reagan make plainer his belief in the consumption ethic than in a speech at St. John's University on March 29, 1985, one of those inimitable performances in which his stark language was so revelatory that few took it at face value. "Perhaps the biggest mistake mankind has made in this century is to think that the big answer is how difficult life is," he said. Negative thinking has led us to the "big thing that will fill the void of the spiritual values . . . the State —that's their idea, the State with a capital *S.* " (Who are *they*? He did not explain.) "Some have said that this is the thing from which all blessings come." But it's a false religion because "our salvation is in ourselves and what we do with our lives and the choices that we make. It is in the things that we choose to worship." What "things" should we "worship"? Reagan was not vague. He told the students that after they graduate, instead of paying a lot of taxes, "a condition of something approaching servitude," they could spend money on "a portable computer, say, or clothing or entertainment. . . ." This was "moral" and, incidentally, a good way of "creating jobs"—a simple demand-side solution. It doesn't matter what "things" we "worship" so long as they can be charged.

One of the disposable commodities we can select in the sprawling mall Reagan describes is a political party. For the conservative activists, the movement, not the party, is the paramount investment good. The party is a fashion label, the wrapping; the contents of the package are designed by ideologues. For the ordinary citizen, whose rejection of the materialism of "the State" comes through the "moral" act of shopping, the party may be an object of self-expression. In the culture of consumption, a realignment may mean temporarily acquiring a party label along with the other "things" that define us; it requires no investment of ourselves.

Reagan's uncanny ability to evoke both the puritan and the pleasure-seeker at the same time is a specialty item. His campaign handlers in 1984 understood that his support rested in great part on this double-edged appeal. But can the package be reproduced? Personality is essential; anyone who strains to fill the image will be disqualified because Reagan never strains. Most important, this is a crisis of ideology. In the absence of a figure who can reconcile opposing worldviews, what happens if the ideological fault lines start cracking open?

Throughout his presidency, Reagan established precedents inconsistent with his stated aims. In the conservative ideology, the market is the frontier, which we can reenter by removing the artificial barriers set in our path by "the State." Yet Reagan increased the powers of "the

State" within the economy. The market for military contractors, where profits are guaranteed, vastly expanded, engulfing key industries such as electronics. While raising the banner of free trade, the Reagan administration in its first term almost doubled the size of the protectionist sector.[5] The supply-siders, for their part, had forecast that "a rising tide lifts all boats." But inequality and poverty heightened; the greatest increase in the ranks of the poor was among the children. According to the new rules laid down by conservative policy, those living on salaries and wages received a shrinking share of national income. Those most rewarded were corporate raiders, merger titans, and speculators, who measured their success by paper profits, not by productive investments.

These conditions fostered a fragmentation of the business community. Industry by industry, the business chieftains desperately sought protection from foreign competition. Interest by interest, the corporate groups moved against Reagan's general effort at tax reform. And the corporate managers, preyed upon by the speculators, wanted some new form of governmental regulation to protect them from the free market gone haywire. Thus the CEOs resisted the Social Darwinism they had helped unleash.

The apotheosis of the corporate culture in the Reagan years was the tenure of Donald Regan as White House chief of staff. The former chief executive officer of Merrill Lynch had been generous in his political donations before Reagan's election, giving to Democrats and Republicans alike. He had even given money to Jimmy Carter. In his early days as Secretary of the Treasury, he was befuddled by the ideological debate. But he was a quick study and soon leveraged influence for his department by presenting himself as an ardent supply-sider. Meanwhile, the contentious supply-siders were quietly purged from Treasury. As chief of staff, he tried to run the White House like a corporation. Politics to him was just another kind of business. He exhibited no strong convictions. Nor did he have a record of long personal devotion to Reagan. In sum, he was a man without a firm attachment to party or person, a man without an idea. He embodied the corporate world's continuing failure to aspire to a larger justification.

These quandaries, however, were ignored or dismissed by the conservative elite. They typically appeared to prefer self-congratulation to self-criticism. So the demand-side recovery was hailed as a supply-side triumph. With every policy defeat, they pointed to the Liberal Establishment as the nemesis. With every policy victory, the conservatives believed we were moving farther from the decadent settlement and closer to the frontier. The Restoration was still within reach.

Reagan's clairvoyance permitted him to see what will happen when the Restoration arrives, when time stands still. "We see and hear again the echoes of our past," he said in his second inaugural address. "So much endures and transcends time." Once we enter this time zone, we live in "golden years." But what is it that "transcends time"? It is a "dream"—a dream, he explained in his acceptance speech at the Dallas convention, "conceived by our Founding Fathers." The political choice we faced in 1984 was between "the dream" and the liberal nightmare that is "ultimately totalitarianism." Winning meant defeating the liberals forever. "If we do our job right," said Reagan, "they won't be able to do it again." Thus the political realignment would be eternal. As he had reminded us before, there would be no more "politics as usual," and prosperity would be "built to last." Thus the recovery would be eternal.

But Reagan did not establish conservatism on a new set of principles that would fundamentally realign our thinking. He could not overcome his own liberal heritage by censuring the most important liberal principle of all—progress. "You ain't seen nothin' yet!" he proclaimed at every campaign stop. This was the progressive interpretation of history as crooned by Al Jolson. And Reagan sang it whenever he also offered the timeless Restoration. In the greatest of vaudeville stunts, we might be agents of history and yet transcend time.

With his incessant glorification of Roosevelt, Reagan did not dispel the ethos behind the New Deal; instead, he attempted to inhabit it. The "former Democrat" had neither the inclination nor the confidence to overthrow his hero. His personal shadow liberalism, rendering him incapable of challenging FDR's accomplishments, defined the limit of a conservative realignment in American philosophy. To truly transcend time, Reagan might have asserted a conservatism rooted in natural law and natural rights, an independent moral order without reference to the oscillations of history. The object in this system would be to align politics with fixed principles, drawn from a fixed human nature.[6] While Reagan occasionally talked about "enduring" values, he preferred a "rendezvous with destiny" and a "springtime of hope." Like the Progressives, he believed that history ebbed and flowed in tides of progress and reaction. There could be new beginnings. Like Jefferson, he accepted the main tendencies of our politics as the aristocratic and the democratic. And he attempted to fit conservatism to this pattern. Government was the monarchy, liberals the royalists, and conservatives the Sons of Liberty. Because he spoke for change, Reagan claimed the authority of history. But by placing conservatism on its merry-go-round, his timeless goals were now subject to its caprice.

The responsibility for sustaining the ideology fell to the Counter-Establishment. Once a motley collection of exiles, ex-Communists, and nostalgists, its organizations were now housed in spacious and elegantly appointed quarters, its journals well subsidized, its cadres' views amplified to the highest reaches of power. But could the Counter-Establishment continue to play the dominant ideological role in politics after what Reagan had done to conservatism? He had created a past that presented problems unimagined by any conservative theorist. Moreover, he proclaimed that his achievement would be permanent. But could a doctrine that failed to account for the present master the future? Could a belief in the automatic operation of the market abolish the business cycle? How thin is this ice?

The Counter-Establishment had not redesigned the doctrines bequeathed it by the Remnant. Instead, its foundations poured increasing sums of money into the manufacture of policies of the moment, the kind of ephemeral intellectual gadgetry perfected by the old Democrats.

But if time does not stand still, can conservatism stand still? Can the Counter-Establishment live comfortably on its accumulated intellectual inheritance? Or can it reconcile a fixed ideology to Reagan's changes? If conservatives cannot accommodate their theories to their own history, will they lose control over the past and thus the future? Or is the conservative ideology inextricably bound up with memories of the 1930s and 1940s, memories that must fade with the generation for whom they are most meaningful?

The test of the ideology's strength will come after Reagan. Revised or not, will it prevent conservatism from fragmenting into a cacophony of sects in the absence of the maximum leader? Will strife in the ranks stimulate the production of ideas, or induce a paralysis? Will movement loyalty, substituting for party loyalty, serve as a basis for a coherent or an incoherent national politics? To what degree is conservative vigor a reflection of the liberals' intellectual weakness? How much longer can that be relied upon? No matter what the results of these questions, the Counter-Establishment will continue to be buoyed by its financial backers. But can transfusions of corporate dollars provide ideological answers? Does money really talk? Does money think?

Reagan had not established a philosophical realignment, so the conservatives were condemned to history: "You ain't seen nothin' yet!" But what if conservatism is not the spirit of reform, like the New Deal, fulfilling the progressive theory Reagan espoused? If American history does run in cycles, is conservatism the spirit of reaction in an age of "normalcy," like the other ages of "normalcy" that passed before?

Will an unaltered conservative ideology be enough to protract endless "golden years?" Perhaps. But nothing would reconfirm the ideology for conservatives more convincingly than defeat. Then they would be swept back to their shadow liberalism. In their Counter-Establishment redoubt, they would return to the opposition, where they began, secure once again in the tenets of their faith. There they could contemplate the next cycle of history and await another chance for Restoration.

NOTES

PREFACE

1. Walter Dean Burnham, professor of political science at MIT, and the leading realignment theorist, has concluded:

"If we view the arena of American electoral politics in historical perspective, we can say that the contemporary status quo extends back to some point in the mid-to-late 1960s. In his recent study, *The Permanent Campaign,* Sidney Blumenthal has advanced the argument that a critical realignment in fact occurred at about the point—1968—where many analysts had been expecting. They were, however, looking for realignment in the wrong place. For crucial to this one, and the 'sixth electoral era' which he argues followed from it, was the exact opposite of all previous events of this type. Instead of being channeled through—and thus revitalizing—the political parties, this realignment involved the conclusive marginal displacement of these parties by the permanent campaign. . . . The older linkages between rulers and ruled become ever hazier, ever more problematic." Walter Dean Burnham, "The 1984 Election and the Future of American Politics," in Ellis Sandoz and C.V. Crabb, Jr., ed., *Election 84: Landslide Without Mandate,* New American Library, 1985, page 206.

INTRODUCTION: SHADOW LIBERALISM

1. Daniel Bell, *The End of Ideology,* Free Press, 1962, page 402.
2. Ibid., page 393.
3. Ibid., page 403.
4. M. Stanton Evans, *The Liberal Establishment,* Devin-Adair, 1965, page 18.
5. Richard Weaver, *Ideas Have Consequences,* University of Chicago Press, 1948.
6. William Simon, *A Time for Action,* Berkley Books, 1980.

NOTES

CHAPTER ONE: THE CONSERVATIVE REMNANT

1. Alfred Jay Nock, "Isaiah's Job," in *Did You Ever See a Dream Walking? American Conservative Thought in the Twentieth Century,* William F. Buckley, Jr., ed., Bobbs-Merrill, 1970.
2. William F. Buckley, Jr., *Rumbles Left and Right,* G. P. Putnam's Sons, 1963, page 30.
3. Frederich von Hayek, *The Road to Serfdom,* University of Chicago Press, 1944, page 70.
4. Carl Schorske, *Fin-de-Siècle Vienna,* Alfred A. Knopf, 1980, page 118.
5. Karl Polanyi, *The Great Transformation,* Columbia University Press, 1949, page 139.
6. Von Hayek, op. cit., page 240.
7. Alistair Cooke, *A Generation on Trial,* Penguin, 1952.
8. Allen Weinstein, *Perjury: The Hiss-Chambers Case,* Alfred A. Knopf, 1978, page 505.
9. Whittaker Chambers, *Witness,* Random House, 1952, page 7.
10. Ibid., page 16.
11. Buckley, *Rumbles,* op. cit., page 189.
12. Chambers, op. cit., page 462.
13. Ibid., page 472.
14. Ibid., page 472.
15. George H. Nash, *The Conservative Intellectual Movement in America,* Basic Books, 1976, page 74.
16. John W. Diggins, *Up from Communism,* Harper & Row, 1975, pages 399–400.
17. Russell Kirk, *The Conservative Mind,* Henry Regnery Company, 1953, page 325.
18. Ibid., pages 7–8.
19. Ibid., page 388.
20. Ibid., pages 396–397.
21. Ibid., page 435.
22. William F. Buckley, Jr., *God and Man at Yale,* Henry Regnery Company, 1951.
23. William F. Buckley, Jr., *Up from Liberalism,* Honor Book, 1965, page 95.
24. Dwight Eisenhower, *Mandate for Change,* Doubleday, 1963 (Volume 1) and 1965 (Volume 2).
25. Josiah Lee Auspitz, "The True Liberal," *The American Spectator,* December 1982, page 20.
26. William F. Buckley, Jr., *The Jeweler's Eye,* Berkley Medallion Books, 1969, page 87.
27. Buckley, *Rumbles,* op. cit., page 194.

28. Diggins, op. cit., pages 343–344.

29. William F. Buckley, Jr., "Publisher's Statement," *National Review*, November 19, 1955.

30. Dwight Macdonald, "Scrambled Eggheads on the Right," *Commentary*, November 19, 1955.

31. Louis Hartz, *The Liberal Tradition in America*, Harvest, 1955, page 5.

32. Ibid., page 57.

33. Clinton Rossiter, *Conservatism in America: The Thankless Persuasion*, Alfred A. Knopf, 1962, page 262.

34. Ibid., page 179.

35. Ibid., page 252.

36. Daniel Bell, "The Dispossessed," in *The Radical Right*, Anchor Doubleday, 1964, page 42.

37. Ibid., page 41.

38. Seymour Martin Lipset, "The Sources of the Radical Right," Ibid., page 369.

39. Buckley, *Up from Liberalism*, op. cit., pages xiii–xiv.

40. Ibid., page 119.

41. Ibid., page 168.

42. Ibid., pages 58–59.

43. Ibid., pages 201–202.

44. Ibid., pages 167–168.

CHAPTER TWO: THE BUSINESS OF INTELLECTUALS

1. Richard Norton Smith, *An Uncommon Man: The Triumph of Herbert Hoover*, Simon and Schuster, 1984, page 419.

2. "Reagan's Think Tank," *Politics Today*, July/August 1979, page 6.

3. Karl Hess, *In a Cause That Will Triumph: The Goldwater Campaign and the Future of Conservatism*, Doubleday, 1967, page 135.

4. Richard Hofstadter, *The Paranoid Style in American Politics*, University of Chicago Press, 1979, page 40.

5. Leonard Silk and Mark Silk, *The American Establishment*, Basic Books, 1980, page 177.

6. *AEI Annual Report, 1980*, page 17.

7. John Kenneth Galbraith, *The New Industrial State*, Houghton Mifflin, 1967, page 71.

CHAPTER THREE: THE BUSINESS OF AMERICA

1. *The Presidential Transcripts*, Staff of the *Washington Post*, Dell, 1974, page 88.

2. Richard Nixon, *RN: The Memoirs of Richard Nixon,* Vol. 2, Warner Books, 1978, page 285.

3. William Safire, *Before the Fall,* Doubleday, 1975, page 550.

4. Ibid., page 551.

5. Ibid., page 691.

6. Richard Whalen, *Catch the Falling Flag,* Houghton Mifflin, 1972, pages 177–179.

7. Ibid., pages 273–274.

8. Kevin P. Phillips, *Post-Conservative America,* Random House, 1982, page 93.

9. William Simon, *A Time for Truth,* Berkley Books, 1979, page 55.

10. Ibid., page 79.

11. Ibid., page 215.

12. Ibid., page 232.

13. Ibid., page 255.

14. William Simon, *A Time for Action,* Berkley Books, 1980, page 56.

15. Ibid., page 131.

16. Ibid., page 76.

CHAPTER FOUR: THE ROMANCE OF THE MARKET

1. Max Weber, "The Social Psychology of the World Religions," in *From Max Weber: Essays in Sociology,* Hans Gerth and C. Wright Mills, eds., Oxford University Press, 1958, page 271.

2. Robert Reich, "Regulation by Confrontation or Negotiation?" *Harvard Business Review,* May–June 1981, page 84.

3. Seymour Martin Lipset and William Schneider, *The Confidence Gap,* Free Press, 1983, page 34.

4. Robert Kuttner, *Revolt of the Haves,* Simon and Schuster, 1980, page 248.

5. *Washington Post Magazine,* November 1, 1981, page 11.

6. Garry Wills, *Nixon Agonistes,* Houghton Mifflin, 1970, page 512.

7. Richard Hofstadter, *The Paranoid Style in American Politics,* University of Chicago Press, 1979, page 110.

8. John Maynard Keynes, *The General Theory of Employment Interest and Money,* Harcourt Brace, 1935, pages 383–384.

CHAPTER FIVE: CAPITALISM AND FRIEDMAN

1. George H. Nash, *The Conservative Intellectual Movement in America,* Basic Books, 1976, pages 287–288.

2. Henry Steele Commager, ed., *Lester Ward and the Welfare State,* Bobbs-Merrill, 1967, page xxx.

3. Eric Goldman, *Rendezvous with Destiny,* Vintage, 1977, page 88.

4. John Maynard Keynes, "The End of Laissez Faire," *Essays in Persuasion,* Harcourt, Brace and Company, 1932, page 312.

5. Leonard Silk, *The Economists,* Basic Books, 1976, page 60.

6. Paul H. Douglas, *In the Fullness of Time,* Harcourt Brace Jovanovich, 1972, pages 127–128.

7. Milton Friedman, "The Methodology of Positive Economics," *Essays in Positive Economics,* University of Chicago Press, 1953, page 4.

8. Ibid., page 6.

9. Ibid., page 15.

10. Ibid., page 14.

11. Ibid., page 15.

12. Ibid., page 38.

13. Ibid., page 41.

14. Silk, op. cit., page 65.

15. Milton Friedman, "The Quantity Theory of Money: A Restatement," *The Optimum Quantity of Money and Other Essays,* Aldine Publishing Company, 1969, page 51.

16. Milton Friedman and Anna Jacobson Schwartz, *A Monetary History of the United States 1867–1960,* Princeton University Press, 1963, page 696.

17. Milton Friedman, *Free to Choose,* Avon, 1981, page 74.

18. For accounts of the 1907 panic, see Frederick Lewis Allen, *The Lords of Creation,* Harper & Brothers, 1935, pages 112–143; Matthew Josephson, *The President Makers,* Harcourt Brace and Company, 1940, pages 246–255; and Henry F. Pringle, *Theodore Roosevelt,* Harcourt Brace Jovanovich, 1956, pages 303–313.

19. Lincoln Steffens, *The Autobiography of Lincoln Steffens,* Harcourt, Brace and Company, 1931, page 507.

20. John Kenneth Galbraith, *Money,* Bantam, 1980, page 150.

21. Allen, op. cit., page 184.

22. Friedman and Schwartz, op. cit., page 159.

23. Silk, op. cit., page 87.

24. Nash, op. cit., page 287.

25. Milton Friedman, *Capitalism and Freedom,* University of Chicago Press, 1982, pages 35–36.

26. See Leonard Silk, *Nixonomics,* Praeger, 1972.

27. Milton Friedman, *There's No Such Thing as a Free Lunch,* Open Court, 1975, page 129.

28. "A Draconian Cure for Chile's Economic Ills?" *Business Week,* January 12, 1976, page 70.

29. Juan de Onis, "Chile's Austerity Curbs Inflation," *The New York Times,* October 30, 1975.

30. Jonathan Kandell, "Chilean Junta Under Fire as Economy Stagnates," *The New York Times,* December 8, 1976.

31. Friedman, *Free to Choose,* op. cit., page 137.

32. Ibid., page xvi.

33. Ibid., page 138.

34. Ibid., page viii.

35. Ibid., page xxi.

36. Ibid., page 287.

37. Anthony Sampson, *The Changing Anatomy of Britain,* Random House, 1982, page 49.

38. See James K. Galbraith, "Short Changed: The Decline and Fall of Monetarism," *Working Papers,* September/October 1982.

39. William F. Buckley, Jr., "Goodbye Milton Friedman," *Washington Star,* August 19, 1971.

40. Friedman, *Free to Choose,* op. cit., page 37.

41. *Newsweek,* October 22, 1979, page 36.

42. Milton Friedman, "Has the Fed Changed Course?" *Newsweek,* October 22, 1979, page 39.

CHAPTER SIX: SHADOW LEFTISM

1. Carl Solberg, *Hubert Humphrey,* Norton, 1984, page 430.

2. Norman Podhoretz, "The Neo-Conservative Anguish Over Reagan's Foreign Policy," *The New York Times Magazine,* May 2, 1982, page 30–31.

3. Norman Podhoretz, "The New American Majority," *Commentary,* January 1981, page 28.

4. Hilton Kramer, "Turning Back the Clock: Art and Politics in 1984," *The New Criterion,* April 1984.

5. Hilton Kramer, "Professor Howe's Prescriptions," *The New Criterion,* April 1984.

6. Diana Trilling, Letter to the Editor, *The New Republic,* December 13, 1983.

7. Norman Podhoretz, "The Neo-Conservative Anguish Over Reagan's Foreign Policy," op. cit., page 29.

8. Lionel Trilling, *The Liberal Imagination,* Doubleday Anchor Books, 1954, page 6.

9. Norman Podhoretz, *Doings and Undoings,* Farrar Straus, 1964, page 111.

10. Norman Podhoretz, *Making It,* Random House, 1967, pages 294–295.

11. Ibid., page 356.

12. Norman Podhoretz, *Breaking Ranks,* Harper & Row, 1979, pages 212–213 and pages 224–228.

13. Ibid., page 265.

14. Ibid., page 306.
15. Ibid., page 216.
16. Ibid., page 298.
17. Norman Podhoretz, *The Present Danger,* Simon and Schuster, 1980, page 12.
18. Norman Podhoretz, "The New American Majority," op. cit., pages 19–28.
19. Norman Podhoretz, *Why We Were in Vietnam,* Simon and Schuster, 1982, page 14.
20. Ibid., page 205.
21. Norman Podhoretz, "The Neo-Conservative Anguish Over Reagan's Foreign Policy," op. cit.
22. Irving Kristol, *Commentary,* March 1952.
23. *The Public Interest,* Fall 1965, page 4.
24. Irving Kristol, *Two Cheers for Capitalism,* Signet Books, 1979, page 14.
25. Ibid., page 61.
26. Leo Strauss, *Natural Right and History,* University of Chicago Press, 1953, pages 181–182.
27. Irving Kristol, *Reflections of a Neoconservative,* Basic Books, 1983, page 87.
28. Ibid., page 83.
29. Harry V. Jaffa, *How to Think About the American Revolution,* Carolina Academic Press, 1978, page 53.
30. Kristol, *Reflections of a Neoconservative,* page 168.
31. Peter Steinfels, *The Neoconservatives,* Simon and Schuster, 1979, page 88.
32. Irving Kristol, "A Guide to Political Economy," *Wall Street Journal,* December 19, 1980, page 24.
33. Kristol, *Two Cheers,* op. cit., pages 69–73.
34. Anthony Lewis, "Advise and Consent," *The New York Times,* May 21, 1981.
35. Irving Kristol, "The Timerman Affair," *Wall Street Journal,* May 29, 1981, page 24.
36. Irving Kristol, "Foreign Policy in an Age of Ideology," *The National Interest,* Fall 1985.
37. Midge Decter, *Commentary,* February 1971, page 35.
38. Elliott Abrams, "Why Are There Neoconservatives?" *The American Spectator,* November 1979, pages 10–11.

CHAPTER SEVEN: A LOST CONTINENT

1. Irving Kristol, "Ideology and Supply-Side Economics," *Commentary,* April 1981, page 50.

2. Karl Marx, *Capital*, Volume 1, International Publishers, 1967, page 522.

3. John Kenneth Galbraith, *Money*, Bantam, 1980, page 268.

4. Lester C. Thurow, *The Zero-Sum Society*, Penguin, 1981, page 214.

5. Jude Wanniski, "There Went Out a Decree from Caesar," *Wall Street Journal*, November 9, 1981, page 29.

6. Bruce Hardcastle, "Reagan's Ibn Khaldun," *The New Republic*, October 28, 1981.

7. James Ring Adams, "Supply-Side Roots of the Founding Fathers," *Wall Street Journal*, November 17, 1981, page 26.

8. Arthur Laffer, "The Reagan-Kennedy Nexus," A. B. Laffer Associates newsletter, August 26, 1980, page 1.

9. Walter Heller, "The Deficit: What Do We Do Now?" *Wall Street Journal*, September 27, 1982, page 22.

10. Irving Bernstein, *The Lean Years: A History of the American Workers 1920–1933*, Penguin, 1966, page 360.

11. John F. Kennedy, *The Burden and the Glory*, Harper & Row, 1964, pages 200–204.

12. John Brooks, "Supply-Side Economics," *The New Yorker*, April 19, 1982, page 134.

13. Jude Wanniski, "The Mundell-Laffer Hypothesis—A New View of the World Economy," *The Public Interest*, Spring 1975, page 49.

14. Ibid., page 51.

15. Marina von Whitman, "Global Monetarism and the Monetary Approach to the Balance of Payments," *Brookings Papers on Economic Activity*, Volume 3, 1975, page 495.

16. Ibid., page 536.

17. Jack Kemp, *An American Renaissance*, Harper & Row, 1979, page 16.

18. Ibid., page 25.

19. Ibid., page 2.

20. Jude Wanniski, *The Way the World Works*, Basic Books, 1978, page 6.

21. Ibid., page 13.

22. Ibid., page xii.

23. Ibid., page 301.

24. Ibid., page 301.

25. George Gilder and Bruce Chapman, *The Party That Lost Its Head*, Alfred A. Knopf, 1966, page 5.

26. George Gilder, *Sexual Suicide*, Quadrangle, 1973, page 248.

27. George Gilder, *Wealth and Poverty*, Basic Books, 1981, page 99.

28. Ibid., page 101.

29. Ibid., page 98.

30. Ibid., page 101.
31. Ibid., pages 128–139.
32. Ibid., page 245.
33. Ibid., pages 21–27.
34. Ibid., page 63.
35. Ibid., page 73.
36. Ibid., page 262.
37. Thomas Jefferson, "To Jean Baptiste Say," February 1, 1804, in *The Portable Thomas Jefferson,* Merrill D. Peterson, ed., Penguin Books, pages 497–499.
38. Gilder, *Wealth and Poverty,* op. cit., page 6.
39. Ibid., page 74.

CHAPTER EIGHT: **THE PROTESTANT ETHIC**

1. Max Weber, *The Protestant Ethic and the Spirit of Capitalism,* Scribner's, 1958.
2. Cited by Harold Laski, *The Rise of Liberalism,* Harper and Brothers, 1936, page 200.
3. David Stockman, "The Social Pork Barrel," *The Public Interest,* Spring 1975, page 13.
4. Charles E. Lindblom, *Politics and Markets,* Basic Books, 1977, page 356.
5. David Stockman, unpublished paper, written while he was a congressman.
6. Weber, op. cit., page 120.
7. Louis M. Hacker, *The Triumph of American Capitalism,* Columbia University Press, 1940, pages 229–230; George Dangerfield, *The Era of Good Feelings,* Harcourt, Brace and Company, 1952, pages 322–323; James MacGregor Burns, *The Vineyard of Liberty,* Alfred A. Knopf, 1982, pages 302–306; *Encyclopaedia Britannica,* Volume 8, 1962, pages 686–687.
8. David Stockman, "Our Grand New Platform," *Commonsense,* Summer 1980, page 1.
9. Jude Wanniski, "An Authentic Guide to Supply-Side Economics," A. B. Laffer Associates newsletter, May 2, 1980.
10. Alexander Cockburn and James Ridgeway, "The World of Appearance," in *The Hidden Election: Politics and Economics in the 1980 Presidential Campaign,* Thomas Ferguson and Joel Rogers, eds., Pantheon, 1981, page 77.
11. Sidney Blumenthal, *The Permanent Campaign,* Touchstone/Simon and Schuster, 1983, page 286.
12. Peter Stone, "I.E.A., Teaching the Right Stuff," *The Nation,* September 19, 1981.

13. Tom Wicker, "A Deliberate Deficit," *The New York Times,* July 19, 1985.

14. Ibid.

15. William Greider, "The Education of David Stockman," *The Atlantic,* December 1981.

16. Weber, op. cit., pages 181–182.

CHAPTER NINE: THE MYTHOLOGY OF REAGANISM

1. William F. Buckley, Jr., *The Jeweler's Eye,* Berkley Medallion Books, 1969, page 84.

2. Ibid., page 87.

3. Ronald Reagan and Richard B. Hubler, *Where's the Rest of Me?* Dell, 1981, pages 18 and 23.

4. Jerry Griswold, "Young Reagan's Reading," *The New York Times Book Review,* August 30, 1981, page 11.

5. Harold Bell Wright, *That Printer of Udell's,* A. L. Burt Company, 1903, page 344.

6. Reagan and Hubler, op. cit., page 12.

7. Ibid., page 65.

8. Ibid., page 87.

9. Leo C. Rosten, *Hollywood,* Harcourt, Brace and Company, 1941, page 16.

10. Reagan and Hubler, op. cit., page 90.

11. Ibid., pages 160–161.

12. Ibid., page 162.

13. Ibid., page 160.

14. Ibid., pages 305–306.

15. Ibid., page 341.

16. Tom Paine, *The Rights of Man,* Dolphin Books, 1961, pages 277–278.

17. Helene von Damm, editor, *Sincerely, Ronald Reagan,* Berkley Books, 1980, page 196.

18. Reagan and Hubler, op. cit., page 356.

19. Ibid., page 347.

20. Ibid., page 351.

21. Ibid., page 344.

22. Ibid., page 355.

23. Sir James George Frazer, *The Golden Bough,* Macmillan, 1951, page 43.

24. See Robert N. Bellah, "Civil Religion in America," *Daedalus,* Winter 1967; and Bellah, *The Broken Covenant,* Seabury Press, 1975.

25. Edmund Burke, "Prejudice, Religion, and the Antagonist World," in *The Portable Conservative Reader,* Russell Kirk, ed., Penguin, 1982, pages 33–34.

CHAPTER TEN: **THE WILL TO BELIEVE**

1. "The Leapfrog Recession," *Wall Street Journal,* July 19, 1982.
2. William F. Buckley, Jr., "On the Right," *National Review,* August 13, 1982, page 16.
3. "The Failing Presidency," *The New York Times,* January 9, 1983, page 22E.
4. William James, *The Will to Believe,* Dover Publications, 1956, page 29.
5. Max Weber, *The Sociology of Religion,* Beacon Press, 1964, page 75.
6. Excerpts of *The Reagan Presidency* appear in *The New York Times,* January 21, 1983, page A15.
7. Leon Festinger, Henry W. Riecken, and Stanley Schachter, *When Prophecy Fails,* Harper Torchbooks, 1956, page 12.
8. John J. Fialka, "World Banking Bust," *Wall Street Journal,* November 10, 1982, page 1.
9. Jack Kemp, "A Student Sallies," *National Review,* July 23, 1982, page 865.

CHAPTER ELEVEN: **MORNING AGAIN**

1. "Avalanche," *Newsweek,* November/December 1984, page 88.
2. Joseph Sobran, "Hollywood: In a Word, Communistic," *The American Spectator,* February 1985.

CHAPTER TWELVE: **THE SECOND COMING**

1. Charles Murray, *Losing Ground: American Social Policy, 1950–1980,* Basic Books, 1984, page 42.
2. Chuck Lane, "The Manhattan Project," *The New Republic,* March 25, 1985.
3. See Jodie T. Allen, "That Charles Murray Book: How Good Is It?" *Washington Post,* September 19, 1984; Robert Kuttner, "Declaring War on the War on Poverty," *Washington Post Book World,* November 25, 1984; Robert Greenstein, "Losing Faith in 'Losing Ground,'" *The New Republic,* March 25, 1985; Daniel Patrick Moynihan, *Family and Nation,* The Godkin Lectures, Harvard University, April 1985.
4. Charles Murray, "The Great Society: An Exchange," *The New Republic,* April 8, 1985.
5. Cited by Robert Greenstein, op. cit.
6. George Gilder, "The Murray Imbroglio," *The American Spectator,* March 1985.
7. Martin Anderson, *Welfare: The Political Economy of Welfare Reform in the United States,* Hoover Institution Press, 1978, page 39.
8. Murray, *Losing Ground,* op. cit., page 9.

9. H. Jefferson Powell, "The Original Understanding of Original Intent," *Harvard Law Review,* March 1985, volume 98, number 5.

10. Ibid., page 947.

11. Cited by George H. Nash, *The Conservative Intellectual Movement in America,* Basic Books, 1976, pages 243–244.

12. Lincoln Caplan, "Supply-Side Judging," *California Lawyer,* May 1985.

13. Lincoln Caplan, "Is the Supreme Court Ready for This Kind of Free-Market Justice?" *Washington Post,* September 30, 1984, page D1.

14. Cited by Harold J. Laski, *The American Democracy,* 1948, page 31.

15. McCullough v. Maryland, 4 Wheaton 316 (819).

16. Home Building and Loan Association v. Blaisdell, 290 U.S. 38 (1934).

17. Daniel O. Graham, *High Frontier: A New National Strategy,* Heritage Foundation, 1982, pages 1–16.

18. Cited by George W. Ball, "The War for Star Wars," *New York Review of Books,* April 11, 1985.

19. Ibid.

20. Norman Podhoretz, *The New York Times,* January 24, 1985, page 25.

21. "A New Shield of the Republic," Citizens for America pamphlet, 1984.

22. Cited by Ball, op. cit.

CHAPTER THIRTEEN: THE BEGINNING OF IDEOLOGY

1. Daniel Boorstin, *The Genius of American Politics,* University of Chicago Press, 1955.

2. Sidney Blumenthal, "The Righteous Empire," *The New Republic,* October 22, 1984.

3. Richard Hofstadter, *The Age of Reform,* Vintage Books, 1955, page 71.

4. On Peirce, see Josiah Lee Auspitz, "The Greatest Living American Philosopher, or the Hero of American Philosophy," privately circulated by the Sabre Foundation. For an abridged version see *Commentary,* December 1983.

5. Robert Lawrence, "Can America Compete?" Brookings Institution monograph, 1984.

6. See Charles R. Kesler, professor at Claremont McKenna College, "The Reagan Revolution and the Legacy of the New Deal: Obstacles to Party Realignment," privately circulated.

INDEX

Abrams, Elliott, 128, 145, 161–64, 165
Abshire, David, 35, 36
Academic Bank, 48–49
Adams, James Ring, 171, 194
Adams, Sherman, 39
"Adam Smith and the Spirit of
    Capitalism" (Kristol), 152–53
Adelman, Kenneth, 145
AFL-CIO, 127, 128, 191
Agee, William M., 223
Agnew, Spiro, 58, 252, 288
Albertine, Jack, 234
Aldrich, Nelson W., 104–5
Allen, Richard V., 33, 34, 35, 46–47,
    141
Allende Gossens, Salvador, 112
Allott, Gordon, 50
Amalgamated Company, 102
America in Vietnam (Lewy), 146
American Bankers Association, 79
American Bar Association (ABA), 297,
    298, 302
American Business Council, 234
American Conservative Union, 34
American Council on Capital Formation,
    80–81, 234
American Economics Association, 90,
    91
American Enterprise Association (AEA),
    32

American Enterprise Institute (AEI),
    4–5, 32–33, 34, 35, 37, 38–45, 88,
    117n, 178–79, 230, 288, 302
  as conservative counterpart to
    Brookings Institution, 38, 41, 42,
    44, 45
  Ford administration and, 41–42, 43
  Friedman and, 108–9
  funding of, 42
  Goldwater campaign and, 39–41, 42,
    108–9
  ideas disseminated by, 43–44
  neoconservatives and, 42–43, 128,
    148, 151, 152, 155, 157
  Nixon administration and, 41
  supply-side economics and, 44
  Wanniski's sojourn at, 193–94, 195
American Institutes for Research, 294
American Renaissance, An (Kemp),
    187
American Revolution, 151–52, 253
Americans for Democratic Action
    (ADA), 162–63
American Spectator, 68, 163–64
Ames, Fisher, 29
Anderson, John B., 214–16, 323
Anderson, Martin, 78, 190, 193, 202,
    224, 296, 327
Anderson, Robert, 79
Annenberg, Walter, 62

INDEX

Annual Guide to Public Policy Experts, 49, 328
anti-Americanism, 143–44, 149
Anti-Ballistic Missile Treaty, 50
anti-Communism, 30, 136
  of neoconservatives, 130–33, 144, 149
aristocracy, 22, 27, 29, 75
arms control, 50, 141, 142, 145, 160, 308
Arms Control and Disarmament Agency, 141, 145
Arnold, Matthew, 12
Assured Survival, 307, 310
A-Team, 140–41
Atlantic, 237, 264
Augustus Caesar, Emperor of Rome, 170
Austro-Hungarian Empire, 16
authoritarianism, totalitarianism vs., 157–58

Baker, George F., 103
Baker, James, 233, 275
Baraona, Pablo, 113
Baroody, William, Jr., 37, 42, 43–44, 52, 84, 194
Baroody, William, Sr., 193–94
  AEI headed by, 38–41, 42–43
  in Goldwater campaign, 39–41, 108–9
Bartley, Robert, 153, 165, 167, 179–82, 186, 198–99, 200, 227
  supply-side economics and, 179, 180, 181–82, 184
Baumann, Robert, 185, 186
Bell, Daniel, 3, 28, 135, 137–38
Bell, Jeffrey, 198, 199, 201, 227
Bellah, Robert N., 258
Belmont, August, 103
Benchmark, 301–2
Bendetsen, Karl, 306, 309
Bennett, William, 38, 159, 258, 288–89, 302

Berkowitz, Herb, 51
Bernstein, Irving, 172–73
big government:
  CEOs' views on, 75–76
  energy crisis and, 64
  Friedman's views on, 92, 115
  in Reagan's mythology, 9, 253–56, 267, 270, 272–73, 320, 324
Bill of Rights, 297, 298, 299
blacks, 123, 205, 207, 219, 263, 281, 308, 319
Bloomingdale, Alfred, 62, 68
Bloomingdale, Betsy, 62
Boggs, Danny J., 34
Bologna conference (1971), 178
Boorstin, Daniel, 311
Bork, Robert, 303
Bozell, L. Brent, 25
Brandeis, Louis D., 18
Breaking Ranks (Podhoretz), 139–40
Brennan, William, 297, 298–99
Broder, David, 214–15
Brookings Institution, 4, 38, 47, 53, 54, 61, 184, 283
  AEI as conservative counterpart to, 38, 41, 42, 44, 45
Brown, Lewis H., 32, 39
Brown, Norman O., 136
Bryan, William Jennings, 62, 105, 209
Bryant, Jane, 62
Brzezinski, Zbigniew, 36, 141
B-Team, 140–41, 306
Buchanan, Patrick, 5–6, 30, 41, 288
Buckley, James, 324
Buckley, William F., Jr., 13, 15, 19, 23–30, 39, 52, 118, 164, 240–41, 262, 265, 300, 315–16, 323
  and attacks on legitimacy of conservatism, 27–29
  celebrity of, 29–30
  in electoral politics, 30, 31
  influences on, 24–25

on Liberal Establishment, 14
National Review published by, 25–28
Buckley, William F., Sr., 24, 25
budget:
cuts in, 231–33, 235, 236, 257, 316
deficits and, 110, 178, 202, 211, 235, 236, 259, 264, 277, 292, 327
review process for, 227–29
Burford, Anne M., 34
Burke, Edmund, 21, 253*n*, 261
Burns, Arthur F., 42, 77, 93, 109, 110, 111
Bush, George, 44, 56, 83, 84, 203, 223, 226, 323
business, 22, 25, 32, 51, 69–86, 217
economic vs. political consciousness in, 156
government regulation of, 37, 72, 74–75, 219, 220, 230, 332
neoconservatives and, 154–56
Reagan's economic program and, 233–34, 332
urban enterprise zones and, 49–50
see also chief executive officers; entrepreneurs
"business coalition," 43, 84–85
Business Roundtable, 52, 55, 56, 68, 69–80, 82, 84, 233–34, 264–65
bipartisanship of, 78
founding of, 77
Knights of Round Table compared to, 72–73
see also chief executive officers
Butler, Stuart, 49, 50
Byrns, Chester J., 221–22

Calhoun, John C., 301
California:
Progressivism in, 242–43
Proposition 13 in, 88, 197–98
Campbell, W. Glenn, 35
Cannon, Howard, 175
Capital (Marx), 174

capital formation, 80–82, 185
capital gains tax, 81
capitalism, 21, 74, 207, 209, 216
Capitalism and Freedom (Friedman), 106–7
Capitol Legal Foundation, 68
Cardozo, Benjamin, 303–4
Carter, Jimmy, 8, 33, 35, 37, 82, 85, 121, 164, 228, 271, 283, 332
economic policy of, 191
foreign policy of, 141–42, 158
neoconservatives and, 128, 129, 141–42, 143–44, 157, 158
re-election campaign of, 120, 134, 224, 256
Case, Clifford, 198
Casey, William, 117, 204, 206
Catch the Falling Flag (Whalen), 60–61
Catholic bishops, encyclicals by, 10, 317–18
Center for Judicial Studies, 35, 302
Center for Strategic and International Studies (CSIS), 35–36, 42, 46
Central Intelligence Agency (CIA), 112, 141, 149, 275, 306
Centre for Policy Studies, 116
centrism, 325–27
Chamber of Commerce, 13, 21, 39, 84, 234
Chambers, Whittaker, 15, 18–20, 21, 23, 30, 122, 134, 139, 254
Buckley influenced by, 24–25
quoted by Reagan, 250, 258
on struggle against Communism, 19–20
Chapman, Bruce K., 204
Chavez, Linda, 288
Cheney, Richard, 183
chief executive officers (CEOs), 27–28, 55–56, 115, 318, 332
AEI and, 42, 44, 52–54, 55
in Business Roundtable, 69–78, 80, 82, 84

chief executive officers (CEOs) (continued)
  conservative intellectuals' alliance
    with, 51–54, 55
  Counter-Establishment's tensions
    with, 85
  entrepreneurs vs., 55, 57, 70, 71–72,
    73, 74
  free-market economics and, 71,
    73–74, 78
  government regulation and, 72, 74–75
  planning by, 72, 74–75
  political clout sought by, 76–78
  public opinion as concern of, 76–77
  Reaganomics and, 56, 264–65, 332
  romantic vision of, 72–74
  sense of power lacked by, 70–71
  supply-side economics and, 44,
    264–65, 281
Chile, monetarist experiment in,
  111–14, 121
Chrysler bailout, 73n, 226
Churchill, Winston, 17–18
Citizens for America, 309
"civil religion," 258–60
civil rights, 126, 289, 301, 318–19
Civil War, 152, 208, 260, 299, 300,
  301, 302
Claremont Economic Institute (CEI),
  228–30
Clearing House, 102
Clifford, Clark, 81
Club of Rome, 168
Coalition for a Democratic Majority
  (CDM), 128, 141, 144
Coase, Ronald, 303
Cohen, Eliot, 135
Cold War, 15, 29, 122, 140
Colson, Charles, 41, 61
Commentary, 128, 149, 308
  foreign policy issues in, 141, 144,
    145, 146, 157
  influence of, 133–34

Podhoretz's direction of, 127,
  133–34, 135, 136, 145
Commerce Department, U.S., 178, 272
Committee for a Free World, 161
Committee on the Present Danger, 128,
  140–42, 144
Committee to Re-elect the President
  (CREEP), 59
Communism, Communists, 14–15, 24,
  29, 134, 154, 249, 250, 254,
  291–92
  authoritarianism-totalitarianism
    distinction and, 157
  capitalism related to, 21
  Chambers's struggle against, 19–20
  see also anti-Communism;
    ex-Communists; Stalinists;
    Trotsykists
Communist Party of Germany, 148
Communist Party USA, 124, 172, 311
Conable, Barber, 222
Confederacy, 299, 300
Confidence Gap, The (Lipset and
  Schneider), 77
Congress, U.S., 8, 71, 77, 79, 80, 81,
  228, 243, 268, 275, 318
  balanced budget bill in, 327–28
  Heritage Foundation and, 47–50
  monetary legislation of, 104–5
  Reaganomics and, 225, 232–33, 234,
    236, 263, 265
  Stockman's term in, 216, 221–22
Congressional Office of Technology
  Assessment, 307
Connally, John B., 56, 77, 78, 79, 82,
  110, 222–23
conservatism, conservatives:
  adversarial stance of, 6
  attacks on legitimacy of, 27–29
  Carter's foreign policy and, 141–42
  Counter-Establishment created by,
    4–5, 9–10, 148

cultural, 15, 20–23
and decline of party system, 312,
    313–15, 318, 331
Democratic bankruptcy and, 286–87,
    325–28
disparaged as fringe element, 3–4
ex-Communists as, 14–15, 18–20, 30
factionalism of, 264, 328–29
federal government disdained by, 287,
    319–21
free-marketeers as, 14, 15–18, 30
fundamentalist right and, 6, 130, 308,
    316–17, 318, 329
historical precedents for, 21–23
history of, 13–31
ideological unity of, 8
infrastructure lacked by, 61
intellectual movement built by, 13
and intellectuals' alliance with
    corporate managers, 51–54, 55
judiciary reforms sought by, 292,
    297–305
Liberal Establishment as depicted by,
    6–7, 14, 287, 289–90, 321, 322,
    333
and mythology of Reaganism,
    241–42, 260
neoconservatives vs., 125, 129, 130,
    134
paranoia ascribed to, 41
Populism and, 321–23
in Reagan administration, 33–34, 35,
    36, 50–51, 287–90
during Reagan's second term,
    291–310
Remnant and, 12–13, 23–30, 38, 181,
    241, 315, 334
Republicans vs., 8–9, 21–22, 314–15,
    316, 318–20, 322–25
and rise of ideological politics, 311,
    329–35
shadow liberalism of, 5–6, 67, 99,
    130, 132, 267–68, 280, 282, 284,
    287, 290, 292, 316, 333
Star Wars and, 292, 305–10
think tanks of, 13, 32–54, 66–68, 85,
    148, 287–88
as twentieth-century Americanism,
    284
welfare system attacked by, 292–96
Conservatism in America (Rossiter),
    27–28
Conservative Mind, The (Kirk), 20–23,
    46
Conservative Party, 30, 323–24
Constitution, U.S., 297, 298, 299, 300,
    302, 303, 305
consumers, 52, 72, 74, 92
consumption ethic, 330–31
Contentions, 161
Cooke, Alistair, 18
Coolidge, Calvin, 32, 164, 170, 171
Coors, Joseph, 45, 47, 66, 72, 306
corporate managers, *see* chief executive
    officers
corporations, 74, 94, 217, 322
Cortelyou, George, 102–3, 105
Cosmos television series, 67
Council of Economic Advisers, 37, 97,
    109, 188, 194, 272
Council on Foreign Relations, 4, 14, 46,
    83, 322
Crane, Philip, 47
Cribb, T. Kenneth, 34

D'Amato, Alfonse, 324
Darman, Richard, 279
Dart, Justin, 59, 62, 64, 68, 200, 306
Dart Industries, 58, 64
Davis, Jefferson, 299, 300
Deaver, Michael, 320
debt crisis, international, 275
Decter, Midge, 10, 145, 161
Defense Department, U.S., 307

democracy, 22, 28, 52, 79, 159, 196, 213, 267
Democratic Party, 8–9, 23, 78–79, 103, 158, 197, 203, 214, 268, 272, 274, 291, 292, 334
  bankruptcy of, 286–87, 325–28
  and conservative ascendancy in GOP, 318–19, 320
  in election of 1984, 281–87, 308, 325–27
  neoconservatives and, 43, 126–29, 130, 142, 144, 163
  Reaganomics and, 265, 266, 267
Depression, Great, 3, 23, 88, 113, 172, 245–46, 247, 269–70, 272, 277, 284
  Friedman's analysis of, 100–101, 106, 115
  Keynesianism and, 168, 169
Derian, Patricia, 158
detente, 131, 140
Dewey, Thomas, 23, 323, 324
"Dictatorship and Double Standards" (Kirkpatrick), 157
Director, Aaron, 303–4
Dole, Elizabeth, 84
Dole, Robert, 264, 265, 314
Douglas, Paul, 93, 95–97

Eastern Establishment, 57, 191
Eastman, Max, 26
econometrics, 97–99
economics, 85–121
  history of, 89–91
  Kristol's revisionism and, 152–53
  laissez faire ideology and, 16–17, 89, 90–91, 93, 97, 100
  law related to, 303–4
  see also free-market economics; Friedman, Milton; monetarism; supply-side economics
Education Department, U.S., 288–89

Eisenhower, Dwight, 29, 48, 59, 79, 262, 310, 323
  conservatism and, 23–24, 26
Eizenstat, Stuart, 191
election of 1952, 25
election of 1960, 61, 240
election of 1964, 31, 39–41, 42, 63, 83, 108–9, 319
election of 1968, 59, 60–61, 109, 126, 162–63
election of 1972, 60, 126–27, 144, 165
election of 1976, 35, 64, 128, 188–91, 200, 271
election of 1980, 44, 50, 58, 61–62, 63, 82–84, 109, 144, 145–46, 165, 252, 259, 276, 322
  CEOs in, 55–56, 78
  debates in, 216, 223–24, 256
  economic issues in, 120–21, 171, 197–203
  Kemp urged to run in, 199–202
  neoconservatives and, 134, 140, 144
  Stockman in, 216, 222–24
election of 1982, 276–77
election of 1984, 279–87, 308, 314, 317, 319, 331, 333
  Democratic heroes glorified by Reagan in, 282–83
  Democrats' response to defeat in, 325–27
  economic issues in, 259, 280–81
  Mondale's blunders in, 142, 281–82, 283–87
  mythic tone of Reagan campaign in 279–80
  populism theme in, 284, 322
Ely, Richard T., 90
Encounter, 149
"End of Laissez Faire, The" (Keynes), 90–91
energy crisis (1970s), 64, 76–77
Enlightenment, 22

entrepreneurs, 51, 69, 228
    CEOs vs., 55, 57, 70, 71–72, 73, 74
    Heritage Foundation and, 45–46
    Reagan supported by, 61–64, 68
    Simon admired by, 64–67
    in Sunbelt, 55, 56–58, 59, 61–62
    traditional culture linked to, 207–9
Epstein, Joseph, 133, 137
equality, 65, 220
Equal Rights Amendment (ERA), 319
Erie Canal, 218–19
evangelical right, 6, 130, 308, 316–17,
    318, 329
Evans, M. Stanton, 4
ex-Communists, 139
    as conservatives and
        neoconservatives, 14–15, 18–20,
        30, 123–24, 144

Fabians, 108, 109, 174
Falkland Islands War, 159
farmers, 208, 324
Farrakhan, Louis, 281
fascism, social, 130–31
Federalist Party, 304
Federalist Society, 289
Federal Reserve, 81, 99, 100–101, 109,
    110, 115, 120, 172n, 183, 231,
    274–76, 277, 280, 327
    creation of, 101–6
Federal Reserve Act (1913), 105
Fein, Bruce, 302
Feldstein, Martin, 194, 272
feminist movement, 161, 205, 318, 319
Festinger, Leon, 271, 272, 273
feudalism, 17, 22, 27, 216
Feulner, Edwin, 36, 45, 46–47, 48, 49,
    50, 145, 312, 315, 316, 318
Finlandization, 142–43
Firing Line, 29
First Amendment, 298, 299
Fisher, Anthony G. A., 117, 206

Fisher, Irving, 100
Ford, Gerald, 36, 64, 66, 79, 84, 85,
    183, 193n, 224, 243, 313–14, 324
    AEI and, 41–42, 43
    conservatives' disdain for, 35
    presidential campaign of, 189–90, 191
Ford Foundation, 4, 5, 61
foreign policy, 82–83, 159–60, 291
    CSIS and, 35–36
    of neoconservatives, 128, 140–47,
        157–59
Fossedal, Gregory, 306
Fossedal, Lisa, 306
Founding Fathers, 22, 259, 260, 298,
    299, 300, 302, 330, 333
    Kristol's account of, 151–53
Fourteenth Amendment, 299, 300
Frazer, Sir James George, 257–58
Freeman, 25, 26
free-market economics, 14, 30, 32, 38,
    53, 110, 192, 201, 209, 217, 229,
    263, 265, 317
    CEOs' views on, 71, 73–74, 78, 85
    Chilean economy and, 114
    decline of, after Keynes, 91
    Friedman's theory of, 87–88, 89,
        91–94, 97–99, 100, 106–8, 114,
        115, 118–19
    Hayek's defense of, 15–18, 170, 253
    law and, 303–4
    in Reagan's mythology, 253, 254,
        256–57, 258, 267, 268
    Reagan's policies inconsistent with,
        331–32
    Sunbelt entrepreneurs' enthusiasm
        for, 56, 57
    supply-side economics and, 169–70,
        183, 216, 220–21
Free to Choose (Friedman), 101–2, 114,
    115–16, 118, 119
Free to Choose television series, 88, 115
Frick, Henry C., 103, 104

INDEX

Friedman, Milton, 84, 86, 87–121, 263, 303
  British economy and, 116–18, 276
  Chilean economy and, 111–14, 121
  econometrics critiqued by, 97–99
  education of, 93–94
  free-market philosophy of, 87–88, 89, 91–94, 97–99, 100, 106–8, 114, 115, 118–19
  in Goldwater's presidential campaign, 39–40, 88, 108–9
  government posts held by, 94–95
  historical analysis by, 100–106, 115
  influence of, 88–89, 91
  Jewish background of, 91–92, 93–94
  monetary theory of, 88–89, 92, 99–106, 109–18, 119, 121, 265, 274
  Nixon and, 109–11, 121
  political economy lacked by, 119–20
  "positive economics" of, 98–99, 105
  as professor at University of Chicago, 97–99, 100, 107, 177
  on Reagan's monetarist experiment, 275–76
fundamentalist right, 6, 130, 308, 316–17, 318, 329

Gable, Clark, 247, 251, 269
Galbraith, John Kenneth, 14, 53, 89, 133, 168, 171
Gardner, Eileen, 289
Garvin, Clifton C., 53, 70–71, 74, 76–77, 78
Gary, Elbert, 104
gasoline shortage (1979), 76–77
Georgetown University, Center for Strategic and International Studies at (CSIS), 35–36, 42, 46
Gergen, David, 226
GE Theater, 250, 253

Gideon v. Wainwright, 299
Gilder, George, 182, 194, 203–9, 265, 293, 294, 296, 321
  Rockefeller family and, 204
  Stockman and, 210, 227
  as theologian of supply-side economics, 206–9
Gingrich, Newt, 318
Glazer, Nathan, 122, 161, 162, 192, 214
God and Man at Yale (Buckley), 23, 25
gold standard, 321
Goldwater, Barry, 83, 204, 212, 242, 243
  as presidential candidate, 31, 39–41, 42, 63, 88, 319
government regulation, 37, 72, 74–75, 219, 220, 230, 332
Graham, Daniel O., 306, 307, 309
Gramm, Phil, 232, 327
Gramm-Rudman-Hollings balanced budget bill, 327–28
Granville, Bonita "Bunny," 62
Gray, Robert Keith, 81
Great Britain, 108, 159
  election of 1945 in, 17–18
  homosexual ethos in, 143
  monetarist experiment in, 116–18, 276
Great Society, 128, 153, 217, 293, 296
Greenspan, Alan, 120, 193n, 224, 230
Greider, William, 237
Gross National Product (GNP), 69, 80, 99, 176, 177–78, 230

Hammett, William, 294–95
Hanna, Mark, 103
Harberger, Arnold, 112
Harper, John, 77
Harriman, Edward, 103
Harris, Ralph, 108, 116
Hartz, Louis, 27, 28

Harvard Business Review, 75
Harvard Crimson, 34
Harvard Law Review, 300
Harvard Salient, 34
Harvard University, 4, 14
Hayek, Friedrich von, 22, 23, 30, 35,
    100, 107, 115, 116, 119, 229, 236
  Austro-Hungarian politics and, 16
  free-market economics and, 15–18,
    170, 253
Hays, Wayne, 185
Heinze, F. Augustus, 102, 104
Heller, Walter, 172*n*
Heritage Features Syndicate, 49
Heritage Foundation, 10, 34, 37–38, 42,
    45–51, 67, 68, 117, 145, 155, 161,
    294, 302, 328
  Academic Bank of, 48–49
  congressional politics and, 47–50
  entrepreneurs' support of, 45–46
  founding of, 47
  funding of, 45, 46
  President's Club of, 51
  Reagan appointees and, 50–51, 288,
    289
  Star Wars promoted by, 306–7
  urban enterprise zones and, 49–50
Hess, Karl, 39, 40
High Frontier, 306–7, 313
Hiss, Alger, 18–19, 122, 134
Hitchens, Christopher, 117
Hobbes, Thomas, 151
Hofstadter, Richard, 41, 321–22
Holmes, Oliver Wendell, 18, 303
homosexuality, 143, 144
Hoover, Herbert, 25–26, 35, 263,
    283
Hoover Institution, 35, 47, 67, 68, 88,
    287, 288, 296
Horowitz, Michael, 294
House Committee on Banking and
    Currency, 105

House Un-American Activities
    Committee, 18
Howe, Irving, 132–33, 149
Hughes, Charles Evans, 305
human rights, 156–58, 164
Humphrey, Hubert, 41, 130, 157,
    281
  neoconservatives and, 126, 127, 128,
    142, 162
Hunt, E. Howard, 41
Hutchinson, Edward, 222

Iacocca, Lee, 73*n*
Ibn Khaldun, 170–71
Ideas Have Consequences (Weaver), 5,
    46, 300
ideological politics:
  American exceptionalism and, 311–12
  Counter-Establishment think tanks
    and, 36–37
  end of, 3, 4, 150–51, 311
  Kristol's role in, 149, 156–50
  Nixon's views on, 60
  party politics and, 312, 313–15,
    318–20, 331
  rise of, 149, 243, 311–35
  Whalen's views on, 61
individualism, 17, 57, 207, 208–9,
    324
  entrepreneurial, traditional culture
    linked to, 207–9
  Smith reconciled with, 152–53
Industrial Revolution, 17
inflation, 230, 272
  monetarism and, 88, 99, 110, 111,
    113, 121, 178, 210, 231, 274, 275,
    276, 277
  Phillips Curve and, 168
  taxes and, 179
Institute for Contemporary Studies, 36
Institute for Economic Affairs, 108,
    116–17, 206

INDEX

Institute for Educational Affairs (IEA),
66–68, 148, 195
Intercollegiate Studies Institute (ISI),
30, 34, 46, 48
International Center for Economic
Policy Studies, 117, 206
investment, 80–82, 185
"Isaiah's Job" (Nock), 12–13

Jackson, Henry, 128, 145
Jackson, Jesse, 281
Jaffa, Harry V., 40, 152
James, William, 266
Jarvis, Howard, 197
Jastrow, Robert, 309
Jefferson, Thomas, 152, 208, 334
Jesus Christ, 170
Jews, 126, 281
    Friedman's background and, 91–92,
    93–94
    as neoconservatives, 123–24
Jobs Creation Act, 185, 186
Johnson, Lyndon, 79, 81, 126, 127,
162, 172n, 293
Johnson, Willa, 48, 49
Jondahl, H. Lynn, 212, 213–14
Jones, Homer, 93
Jorgensen, Earl, 62
Joseph, Sir Keith, 116
judiciary system, 292, 297–305
    law and economics doctrine and,
    303–4
    "original intention" notion and,
    298–305
    Reagan's appointments to, 10
Justice Department, U.S., 289, 302

Kahn, Alfred, 37
Kalmbach, Herbert, 58–59
Kampelman, Max, 126, 142
Kemp, Jack, 49, 50, 153, 184–88, 191,
196, 219, 223, 265, 276
    background of, 184–85

in election of 1976, 189–90
in election of 1980, 199–202
philosophy of, 186–88
Reagan's relationship with, 187–88
Stockman and, 210, 216, 221, 226,
227, 229n
supply-side economics and, 166, 167,
185–86, 188, 189–90, 197, 203
Kemp-Roth Bill, 186
Kendall, Willmoore, 24, 299, 300
Kennedy, John F., 39, 61, 97, 146,
176–77, 224, 309
    assassination of, 109
    economic policy of, 88, 171–72,
    203
    Kemp influenced by, 185, 187
    as Reagan hero, 282–83
Kennedy, Joseph P., 61
Kennedy, Robert, 162, 240
Kennedy, Ted, 284
Kennedy Institute, 61
Keynes, John Maynard, 29, 85–86,
90–91, 167, 168
Keynes, John Neville, 98
Keynesianism, 110, 116, 168, 169,
171–72, 176, 183, 191, 215, 264,
277
    free-market economics opposed in,
    87–88, 97–99
    monetarism and, 99
King's Row, 248
Kirk, Russell, 15, 20–23, 46
Kirkpatrick, Evron, 126, 142
Kirkpatrick, Jeane, 10, 126, 133, 145,
146, 157, 159, 161, 164, 282, 292
Kissinger, Henry, 36, 59, 146, 155, 192,
204
Kitchel, Denison, 39
Kitchen Cabinet, 200, 201, 306
Knickerbocker Trust Company, 102
Knight, Frank, 93, 96–97
Kramer, Hilton, 132–33
Kristol, Irving, 66–67, 68, 135, 137,

147–61, 165, 180, 181, 186, 199, 200, 221, 227, 288–89, 294
as AEI fellow, 42–43
business community and, 154–56
economic revisionism of, 152–53
historical analysis of, 151–52
ideology of, 150–51
as "invisible hand" of conservative organizations, 148–49
journalistic career of, 149–50, 159–60
and law of unintended consequences, 153, 293, 294
Lefever-Timerman affair and, 158
Nixon and, 153
on partisanship issue, 318
Republican Party joined by, 147–48
supply-side economics and, 153–54, 155, 167–68, 182, 183, 184, 191–92, 194, 195–96, 216
Kristol, William, 165, 288–89, 302
Kudlow, Lawrence, 228–29
Kuehnelt-Leddihn, Eric, 46
Ku Klux Klan, 263
Kuttner, Robert, 81

Laffer, Arthur B., 81, 176–79
education of, 176–77
and election of 1980, 171, 201
GNP projections by, 177–78
Reagan's relationship with, 200
supply-side economics and, 166, 167, 171, 179, 181–82, 183, 186, 190–91, 216, 221, 225
Laffer, William, 177
Laffer Curve, 169, 173–74, 183–84, 186, 188, 194, 196, 197, 231
Laird, Melvin, 42, 43, 47
laissez faire, 16–17, 89, 90–91, 93, 97, 100
law and economics doctrine, 303–4
Law of the Sea Treaty, 324
Laxalt, Paul, 175, 188, 190, 202, 226
Lean Years, The (Bernstein), 172–73

Leavis, F. R., 135
Lefever, Ernest, 156–59, 161
Lehman, John F., 46
Lehrman, Lewis, 225, 227, 324
Lenin, V. I., 124, 156
Lenkowsky, Leslie, 165, 167, 192–95, 206
Lennon, John, 126, 138, 161–62
Lewy, Guenter, 146
Liberal Establishment, 4–5, 33, 38, 57, 61, 123, 130, 132, 280, 296, 309, 322, 333
conservatives' depictions of, 6–7, 14, 287, 289–90, 321, 322, 333
conservatives' offensive against, 4–6
entrepreneurs' views on, 46
foreign policy and, 82–83
fundamentalists' views on, 316–17
Gilder's criticisms of, 204, 206–7
Nixon attacked by, 59, 61
Simon's critique of, 65–66, 68
Sunbelt entrepreneurs' views on, 57
liberalism, liberals, 3, 13, 25, 26, 27, 28, 29, 89, 157, 162–63, 180, 187, 205, 207, 267–68, 289, 290, 298, 312, 316
Communism and, 20, 21
conservatives disparaged by, 3–4
defense issue and, 309–10
ex-Communists' views on, 15
foreign policy of, 160
Hiss case and, 18–19
history of, 151
as "natural" in America, 27, 28
neoconservatives' denunciations of, 130–33, 149
Reagan's criticisms of, 250, 254–56
shadow liberalism and, 5–6, 67
Simon's views on, 65–66, 68
Stockman and, 216, 217, 220
in University of Chicago economics department, 95–97
"liberal isolationism," 144

Liberal Party, 323
liberty, 220
Liberty League, 32
"limits to growth," 168–69, 220
Lincoln, Abraham, 259, 260, 300, 301, 323
Lincoln Club, 58
Lindblom, Charles E., 217, 220
Lipset, Seymour Martin, 28, 77, 134
Lodge, Henry Cabot, 323
Losing Ground (Murray), 293–96
Luce, Henry, 25

McCarthy, Eugene, 162
McCarthy, Joseph, 19, 25, 149
McClellan, James, 302
McCracken, Paul, 109, 194
McCullough v. *Maryland,* 304–5
Macdonald, Dwight, 26
McDowell, Gary, 302
McGovern, George, 43, 126, 127, 128, 129, 144
McGovernism, 127, 128
Machiavelli, Niccolò, 61, 151
Macmillan, Harold, 116
Madison, James, 152
Magruder, Jeb, 41
Mailer, Norman, 136, 137, 138
Making It (Podhoretz), 125, 137–38, 139–40
Mandate for Leadership, 38
Manhattan Institute, 34, 67, 117, 206, 294–95
Marcus, Steven, 137
Marshall, John, 304–5
Marshall Foundation, 306
Marx, Karl, 21, 34, 35, 131, 168*n,* 174, 207
Marxism, 7, 123–24, 134
    see also Communism, Communists
Means, Gardiner, 94
Meese, Edwin, III, 34, 36, 48, 51, 82, 190, 202, 275, 297–99, 320

"original intention" notion and, 298–99, 301–5
Mellon, Andrew, 170, 171
Memoirs of a Superfluous Man (Nock), 12
Mencken, H. L., 164
"Methodology of Positive Economics, The" (Friedman), 98–99, 109
Mexico, debt crisis in, 275
Meyer, Frank, 15
military spending, 82–83, 145, 235, 277, 316, 327, 332
Mill, John Stuart, 100
Miller, James E., III, 37
Mills, C. Wright, 213
Mills, Wilbur, 79
Miranda v. *Arizona,* 298
Mitchell, John, 188
Mitchell, Wesley, 93
Mondale, Walter, 6, 184, 259, 279, 281–82, 283–87, 308, 313–14
    centrism of, 325–27
    coalition built by, 281
    as ideal adversary for conservatives, 284
    neoconservatives and, 142
    policy elite and, 283
    television persona of, 285–86
monetarism, 81, 178, 179, 183, 280, 327
    British experiment with, 116–18, 276
    Carter's opposition to, 120–21
    Chilean experiment with, 111–14, 121
    Friedman's historical analysis based on, 100–106, 115
    Friedman's theory of, 88–89, 92, 99–106, 109–18, 119, 121, 265, 274
    history of, 100
    Keynesianism and, 99
    Nixon's experiment with, 109–11, 121

pain associated with, 121, 274
Reagan's experiment with, 210,
   229–30, 231, 265, 272, 274–76,
   277
*Monetary History of the United States
   1867–1960, A* (Friedman and
   Schwartz), 100–106
monopolies, 219–20
Mont Pelerin Society, 107–8, 116
"moral equivalence" notion, 7, 10, 131,
   292
Morgan, J. P., 102–4, 105, 106
Morrison, Truman, 213–14
Moulton, Harold, 38
Moynihan, Daniel Patrick, 145, 147,
   192, 214, 215, 229*n*, 236, 296
Mundell, Robert, 167, 178–79, 181,
   182–83, 184
Munson, Steven, 161
Munzenberg, Willi, 148–49
Murphy, Thomas, 74
Murray, Charles, 292, 293–96
Mutual Assured Destruction, 306–7,
   308, 309–10

Nader, Ralph, 71, 153
Nash, George H., 21, 89, 106
National Endowment for the
   Humanities, 159
National Forest Products Association,
   80
National Interest, 159–60
National Miners Union (NMU), 173
National Observer, 175–76
National Resources Committee, 94–95
National Review, 13, 15, 25–27, 28, 46,
   117, 181, 206, 287, 315–16
   critics of, 26–27
   electoral politics and, 30–31
   founding of, 25–26
National Security Council, 10, 34
"Neo-Conservative Anguish Over

Reagan's Foreign Policy, The"
   (Podhoretz), 147
neoconservatives, 7, 8, 122–65, 181,
   280–81, 293, 294
   AEI and, 42–43
   alienation experiences of, 123–29,
      163
   anti-Communism of, 130–33, 144,
      149
   business community and, 154–56
   conservatives vs., 125, 129, 130, 134
   contentiousness of, 158–59
   definition of, 122–23
   Democratic Party and, 43, 126–29,
      130, 142, 144, 163
   denunciation style of, 131–32
   and election of 1972, 126–27
   and election of 1976, 128
   and end of ideological politics,
      150–51
   foreign policy of, 128, 140–47,
      157–59
   as generalists, 124–25
   Lefever nomination and, 156–59
   liberalism denounced by, 130–33, 149
   Marxist background of, 123–24
   Reagan as, 249–50
   as Reagan appointees, 145
   Reagan supported by, 122, 129, 130
   second-generation, 160–65
   shadow leftism of, 130–39, 161
   sixties radicals and, 125–26, 130,
      138–39, 140, 143, 150–51, 161–62,
      163
   Star Wars and, 142, 145, 308
   Stockman and, 211, 214, 220–21
   see also Kristol, Irving; Podhoretz,
      Norman
New American Majority, 129, 144
New American Right, The, 28
New Class, 6–7, 8, 53, 67, 150–51, 156,
   231
New Criterion, 68, 132, 133

New Deal, 12, 14, 23, 25, 38, 75, 93, 109, 123, 130, 222, 228, 245–46, 254, 269, 276, 283, 327, 328, 333, 335
  Brookings Institution and, 38
  business opposition to, 32
  Chambers's testimony and, 18, 19, 20
  Friedman's work in, 94–95
  King's Row and, 248
New Despotism, 65, 66
New Economic Policy (NEP), 110
New Industrial State, The (Galbraith), 53
New Jersey primary (1978), 198, 199
New Left, 128, 137, 163
New Realism, 325, 327
New Right, 186–87, 205–9
Newsweek, 50, 88, 120
New York, N.Y., default crisis in (1975), 64–65
New York Daily News, 64
New York Times, 4, 5, 21, 31, 106, 113, 226, 265, 309
New York Times Magazine, 147
New York Times v. *Sullivan,* 299
Nicaragua, *contra* war in, 10, 161, 291
Nicaraguan Freedom Fund, 10
Niebuhr, Reinhold, 213, 214
nihilism, 150–51
Nitze, Paul, 140, 141
Nixon, Richard, 36, 43, 48, 58–61, 66, 79, 84, 85, 118, 122, 126, 146, 214, 224, 226, 240–41, 243, 262, 288, 315
  AEI and, 41
  economic policy of, 109–11, 121, 168, 176
  Kristol and, 153
  political realignment attempted by, 59–60
  presidential campaigns of, 127, 129, 144, 171n, 319

  Reagan compared to, 59
  Simon appointment and, 64
  Sunbelt entrepreneurs and, 58–59
  Watergate affair and, 41, 58–59, 61, 66, 144, 153, 165, 181, 222
  young conservatives and, 165
Nobel Prize, 88, 91, 97, 114, 118, 263
Nock, Albert Jay, 12–13, 24, 25
Novak, Michael, 7, 10, 194, 317

Office of Domestic Monetary Policy, 274
Office of Management and Budget (OMB), 37, 176, 177, 210, 223, 226–29, 293
Office of Public Liaison, 43
Old Left, 123, 130, 131, 139, 148, 158
John M. Olin Foundation, 5, 10, 34, 67, 133, 159, 161, 294, 306
  think tanks funded by, 66, 68
Omega Project, 117
O'Neill, Tip, 232, 262, 267, 268
Onis, Juan de, 113
On the Democratic Idea in America (Kristol), 153
"original intention" notion, 298–300, 302, 303, 304, 305
  law and economics doctrine vs., 303–4

Paine, Tom, 151, 152, 253
panic of 1907, 101–6
party system:
  decline of, 11, 43, 45, 76
  ideological politics and, 312, 313–15, 318–20, 331
  realignment of, 8–9
Party That Lost Its Head, The (Gilder and Chapman), 204
Peirce, Charles, 327
Penn Central Railroad, 110
Perle, Richard, 145

Phillips, Kevin P., 58, 59, 61–62
Phillips, Warren, 180
Phillips, William, 137
Phillips Curve, 168, 169
Pines, Burton Yale, 45, 49
Pinochet, Augusto, 111–14, 121
Podhoretz, Norman, 7, 10, 125, 129,
    133–47, 149, 153, 161, 164, 308
  background and education of, 134–35
  as *Commentary* editor, 127, 133–34,
    135, 136, 145
  "culture of appeasement" metaphor
    of, 143–44
  in debate on Vietnam War, 145–47
  "Finlandization" metaphor of,
    142–43
  foreign policy views of, 140–47
  McGovern demonized by, 127
  Reagan administration post sought
    by, 144–45
  on Reagan's 1980 victory, 129
  Trilling's relationship with, 134–36,
    137–38, 139, 140
Poland, Reagan's policy toward, 147,
    160
Polanyi, Karl, 17
political action committees, 69
Political and Social Processes program,
    43
Popeo, Daniel, 302
Populism, 9, 18, 170, 196, 208, 284,
    321–23
Posner, Richard, 303
Post, John, 42, 52–53, 77, 78
poverty, 206–7
Powell, W. Jefferson, 300
pragmatism, 326–27
Pranger, Robert J., 41, 44
Present Danger, The (Podhoretz), 140,
    142–45
Presley, Elvis, 161, 162
Progressives, 3, 4, 242–43, 334

Proposition 13, 88, 197–98
protectionism, 324
Protestant ethic, 204, 211–12, 216,
    218, 236–37, 247, 317
*Protestant Ethic and the Spirit of
    Capitalism, The* (Weber), 211, 218,
    238
Proxmire, William, 177
Public Interest, 8, 128, 148, 149–50,
    153, 159, 180, 182–83, 192,
    216–17, 221
Pujo, Arsene, 105
Pumpkin Paper Irregulars, 122
Puritans, 259

Rahn, Richard, 234
Rand, Ayn, 193n
Ranney, Austin, 43
Rayburn, Sam, 48, 79
Reagan, Jack, 244, 245–46
Reagan, Nancy, 62, 200, 250, 262, 263
Reagan, Nelle, 244, 245
Reagan, Ronald, 11, 13, 14, 31, 37, 44,
    51, 109, 117, 126, 128, 185, 194,
    196, 197, 240–78, 296, 315, 326
  acting career of, 246–49, 250, 251,
    269
  AEI and, 32–33
  ahistorical views of, 260
  "business coalition" and, 43, 84–85
  childhood of, 244–46
  conservatives in administration of,
    33–34, 35, 36, 50–51, 287–90
  conservatives' symbiotic relationship
    with, 36–37
  Democratic heroes of, 282–83
  economic policy of, 56, 70, 85,
    166–67, 169, 170–71, 172, 190–91,
    193n, 198, 201–3, 211, 224–26,
    228–35, 257, 262–78, 280–81, 324,
    327
  entrepreneurs' support for, 61–64, 68

INDEX

Reagan, Ronald (continued)
faith of, 266–67, 271–74
foreign policy of, 142, 147, 160
Friedman and, 87, 88, 89, 118, 119,
    120–21
God's will invoked by, 316
in Goldwater's presidential campaign,
    40, 63
gubernatorial campaigns of, 58, 63
Heritage Foundation and, 50–51
Hoover Institution and, 35
judiciary and, 10, 297, 301, 303
Kemp's relationship with, 187–88
leadership style of, 268–74, 277–78
"magic of marketplace" invoked by,
    257–58
mythology of, 9, 14, 240–61, 267,
    268, 270, 271, 272–73, 278, 320,
    324
neoconservatives and, 122, 124, 129,
    130, 133, 144–45, 147, 155, 156,
    157, 160, 163, 165
Nixon compared to, 59
party realignment and, 8–9
political conversion of, 249–50
political economy of, 119–20
presidential campaigns of, 6, 50, 56,
    58, 61–62, 78, 82–84, 120–21, 142,
    144, 145–46, 165, 189–91, 198,
    200–203, 204, 205, 206, 216,
    222–24, 259, 279–87, 308, 314,
    319, 322, 331, 333
and rise of ideological politics, 243,
    312–14, 329–35
Rockefeller and, 83–84
as running mate for Nixon, 60
sense of crisis created by, 270–71
Star Wars and, 142, 305–6, 307–8,
    313
Stockman's relationship with, 221,
    226–27, 236–39
successor of, 329, 334–35
on Vietnam War, 145–46

Reagan, Ronald, Jr., 62
Reagan Doctrine, 10, 291
Reaganism, 116, 240–61
big government myth in, 9, 253–56,
    267, 270, 272–73, 320, 324
community myth in, 252–53, 254,
    257, 258, 267, 268, 271
free-market myth in, 253, 254,
    256–57, 258, 267, 268
think tanks and, 36–37
recessions, 101
of 1970s, 110
of 1980s, 263–67, 270–78, 280, 329
recovery, economic (1984), 267,
    280–81, 293, 329
Reed, John, 26
Rees, Grover, 302
Regan, Donald, 231, 288, 332
Regulation, 37, 230
Reich, Robert B., 75
Remnant, 38, 181, 241, 315, 334
Buckley's unification of, 23–30
Nock's depiction of, 12–13, 24
Republican National Committee (RNC),
    103, 223, 266, 313
Republican Party (GOP), 18, 23, 28,
    30, 31, 33, 34, 41, 47, 59, 60, 68,
    78, 157, 208, 214–15, 248, 265,
    272, 276, 281, 282, 292, 301
anti-intellectualism of, 156
CEOs and, 264
conservatives vs., 8–9, 21–22,
    314–15, 316, 318–20, 322–25
"Modern Republicanism" and, 323
neoconservatives and, 129, 147–48,
    154, 158–59, 160, 161, 163
Populism vs., 322–23
and rise of ideological politics, 243,
    312, 314–15, 318–20, 322–25
Rockefeller family and, 83
Simon's views on, 65, 66
in Sunbelt, 57–58
Wanniski's critique of, 197

Republican Study Committee, 47
Reston, James, 174, 175
Reynolds, William Bradford, 289–90
Richardson, Elliot, 323, 324
Richardson, Randolph, 191–92
Ripon Society, 204, 205
Road to Serfdom, The (Hayek), 15–18, 107, 229
Robber Barons, 57, 73, 204, 208–9, 321
Roberts, Paul Craig, 185, 199, 229
Robertson, Pat, 317
Robinson, Joan, 99
Rockefeller, Abby, 207
Rockefeller, David, 53, 82, 83–84, 204
Rockefeller, John D., 74
Rockefeller, Nelson, 33, 83, 155, 203, 204, 209, 323, 324
Rockwell, Norman, 9, 10
Roe v. *Wade,* 298
Roosevelt, Franklin D., 9, 12, 23, 40, 90, 95, 276, 285
  Brookings Institution and, 38
  business opposition to, 32
  Reagan's admiration for, 248, 269–70, 282–83, 333
Roosevelt, Theodore, 104
Rossiter, Clinton, 27–28
Rosten, Leo C., 247
Rostenkowski, Dan, 233
Rostow, Eugene, 140, 141
Roth, William, 186
Royster, Vermont, 180
Rumsfeld, Donald, 183
Rusher, William, 31
Rusinskas, John, 172, 173–74
Russian Revolution, 15, 35
Rutledge, John, 229

Safire, William, 60
Sagan, Carl, 67
Salvatori, Henry, 62
savings, 80
Say, Jean-Baptiste, 168, 208

Say's Law, 167–68, 172, 179
Scaife, Richard Mellon, 66
Schachter, Stanley, 271
Schachtman, Max, 127
Schlafly, Phyllis, 83
Schlamm, Willi, 25
Schlesinger, Arthur M., Jr., 14, 133, 146
Schlesinger, James, 36
Schley, Grant B., 103
Schneider, William, 77
Schorske, Carl, 16
Schwartz, Anna, 100
Schweicker, Richard, 189, 190
Screen Actors Guild, 249
Sears, John, 188–89, 190, 197–98, 200–202
Senate, U.S., 157, 158, 195, 324
Senate Judiciary Committee, 289–90
Senate Select Committee on Intelligence Activities, 112
Sexual Suicide (Gilder), 205
shadow leftism, 130–33, 161
shadow liberalism, 5–6, 67, 99, 130, 132, 267–68, 280, 282, 284, 287, 290, 292, 316, 323
Shapiro, Irving, 53
Shaw, Raymond, 199
Sherman, Alfred, 116
Shultz, George, 79, 110, 177, 225
Silk, Leonard, 106
Silone, Ignazio, 19
Simon, William, 6–7, 10, 64–67, 68, 80, 133, 206, 229*n*, 317
sixties:
  hip culture in, 136–39
  Kristol's views on, 151
  radicalism in, neoconservatives and, 125–26, 130, 138–39, 140, 143, 150–51, 153, 161–62, 163
Smith, Adam, 89, 92, 97, 115, 152–53, 168, 192, 208, 216, 265, 322
Adam Smith Institute, 117

INDEX

Smith-Richardson Foundation, 191–95,
206
Sobran, Joseph, 287
social communism, 131
Social Darwinism, 89–90, 171, 208,
303–4, 328, 332
Social Democrats, 128, 130–31
social fascism, 130–31
socialism, 150, 311
"Social Pork Barrel, The" (Stockman),
216–17, 221
Solzhenitsyn, Alexander, 35, 88
Southern Agrarians, 299, 300
Soviet Union, 3, 127, 130, 258, 280,
306, 309
espionage activities of, 18, 19
military superiority ascribed to,
140–41
"moral equivalence" notion and, 7,
10, 131, 292
neoconservatives' views on, 124, 128,
131, 143, 144, 147, 149–50
Spencer, Herbert, 89–90
Spencer, Stuart, 58
Spirit of Enterprise, The (Gilder), 293
Sprinkel, Beryl, 229–30, 265, 274
Stalin, Joseph, 124
Stalinists, 124, 127, 128, 130, 132, 133,
134, 139, 149
Star Wars, 10, 67, 142, 145, 292,
305–10, 313
State Department, U.S., 7, 18, 19,
23–24, 144, 156, 281
states rights, 318, 319
judiciary system and, 297–305
Steffens, Lincoln, 104
Stein, Herbert, 44, 188
Stevens, John Paul, 297, 299
Stigler, George, 263
Stillman, James, 103
Stockman, David, 192, 199, 210–39,
264, 265, 281, 292–93, 327
as antiwar activist, 212–13, 222

background and education of, 212–15
budget-cutting by, 231–33, 235, 236
congressional ambitions of, 216,
221–22
"Dunkirk" memo by, 225–26, 227,
270
and election of 1980, 216, 222–24
faulty budget estimates by, 231–32,
233
government "indulgences" critiqued
by, 217–20
OMB post sought by, 223, 226–27
Protestant ethic and, 211–12, 216,
218, 236–37
Reagan's relationship with, 221,
226–27, 236–39
supply-side economics and, 210, 216,
220–21, 227
Strauss, Leo, 151, 153, 196
Students for a Democratic Society
(SDS), 163, 212, 213, 228n
Sunbelt, 301
Sunbelt entrepreneurs, 55, 56–59
Heritage Foundation and, 45
ideology of, 56–57
Nixon and, 58–59
political clout sought by, 57–58
Reagan and, 61–62
supply-side economics, 8, 44, 72,
166–209, 313, 330, 332, 333
capital formation school vs., 80–81
as Democratic economics, 130
doctrine of, 169–70
first article on, 182–83
free-market economics and, 169–70,
183, 216, 220–21
Gilder as theologian of, 206–9
historical authority invoked in,
170–72, 196
history of, 167–69, 172–84
Kristol's support for, 153–54, 155
Laffer Curve in, 169, 183–84, 186,
188, 194, 196, 197, 231

366

monetarism and, 210, 229–30, 231, 265, 272, 276, 277, 280
naming of, 188
political support sought for, 184–91
Reagan administration's implementation of, 224–26, 229–34, 257, 263–66, 272, 276, 277, 280–81
Reagan briefed on, 166–67, 170, 202
Stockman and, 210, 216, 220–21, 227
Wall Street Journal and, 179, 180, 181–82, 188, 198
Wanniski's book on, 191–97, 206
Supreme Court, U.S., 58, 274, 297, 298, 302, 304–5, 316

Taft, Robert A., 13, 25, 30, 83, 109, 323
tax cuts:
CEOs' dissatisfaction with, 264–65
Kemp's legislation on, 185, 186
under Kennedy, 171–72, 203
under Reagan, 202, 203, 225, 231, 233, 234, 257, 264, 265, 274, 277, 327
in supply-side economics, 169, 170–72, 178, 179, 183, 196, 202, 257, 277
taxes, 185, 219, 221, 255
"bracket creep" and, 189
capital formation and, 80–82
increases in, 265, 276
reform of, 322, 332
revolts against, 197–98
technostructure, 53
television:
Buckley's use of, 29
Mondale's performance on, 285–86
Reagan's campaign commercials on, 202–3, 280
Teller, Edward, 306, 307

Tennessee Coal and Iron Company, 103–4
Tennessee Valley Authority, 250
Thatcher, Margaret, 108, 116–18, 121, 206
That Printer of Udell's (Wright), 244–45
Theory of Moral Sentiments, The (Smith), 216
There's No Such Thing as a Free Lunch (Friedman), 119
think tanks, 13, 32–54, 85
corporate managers and, 42, 44, 52–54, 55
funding of, 66–68, 148
Reagan appointees drawn from, 33–34, 35, 36, 50–51, 287–88
Reaganism made palatable by, 36–37
see also specific think tanks
This World, 67
Thurow, Lester, 168–69
Time, 21
Time for Action, A (Simon), 65–66
Time for Truth, A (Simon), 65
Timerman, Jacobo, 157–59
Tobin, James, 97, 176
totalitarianism, authoritarianism vs., 157–58
Treasury Department, U.S., 79, 274
Trilateral Commission, 82–83, 84, 322
Trilling, Diana, 133
Trilling, Lionel, 134–36, 137–38, 139, 140, 153
Triumph of Politics, The (Stockman), 238
Trotsky, Leon, 26, 124
Trotskyists, 124, 127, 130, 149, 154, 289
Truluck, Philip, 47, 48, 51
Truman, Harry, 95, 282–83
Trust Company of America, 103, 104
Ture, Norman, 185, 229, 232

"Turning Back the Clock" (Kramer), 132
Tuttle, Holmes, 62
Tyrrell, R. Emmett, 164–65

unemployment, 168, 219
    monetarism and, 110, 113, 117, 121
    under Reagan, 230, 263, 264, 270, 272
"unintended consequences," law of, 153, 293, 294
United Copper Company, 102, 103
United Mine Workers of America, 173
Universidad Católica de Chile, 112
University of Chicago, 16, 110
    economics department of, 93, 95–97, 100, 107, 112, 177, 178
University of Chicago Law School, 303
University of Chicago Press, 15
University of Southern California, Center for the Study of Private Enterprise at, 200
Up from Liberalism (Buckley), 23, 28–29, 164
urban enterprise zones, 49–50
U.S. Information Agency (USIA), 63, 144, 145, 195
U.S. Steel, 104

Valis, Wayne, 43, 84–85
Vanderbilt, William, 73
"Vietnam syndrome," 140
Vietnam War, 67, 126, 127, 153, 163, 212–13, 240
    Podhoretz's analysis of, 145–47
Village Voice, 225
Volcker, Paul, 120, 184, 265, 275
Volker Fund, 107

wage and price controls, 110–11
Walker, Bob, 215
Walker, Charls, 78–82, 141, 234

capital formation and, 80–82
    government posts held by, 79
Wallace, Henry, 127
Wall Street Journal, 5, 8, 9, 67, 81, 153, 154, 158, 171, 175, 179–82, 186, 191, 199, 221, 306
    supply-side economics and, 8, 179, 180, 181–82, 188, 198, 263–64
Walters, Alan, 117, 206
Wanniski, Jude, 81, 148, 153, 179, 180, 181–84, 185–86, 202, 210, 216, 227, 306
    background and education of, 173–74
    book written by, 191–97, 206
    and election of 1976, 188–91
    and election of 1980, 199–200, 201, 202
    journalism career begun by, 174–76
    Laffer's relationship with, 177–78
    Reagan briefed by, 166–67, 170
    on Stockman, 221, 222, 223, 226, 237
    supply-side economics first articulated by, 182–84
    Village Voice interview of, 225
    Wall Street Journal quit by, 198–99
Wanniski, Michael, 173–74
Warburg, Paul M., 105
Ward, Lester F., 90
Warner, Jack, 251
Warner Brothers, 246–47
Warnke, Paul, 141
Warren, Earl, 300, 301
Washington, D.C.:
    conservative conference in (1985), 7
    fragmenting, centrifugal forces of, 8
Washington, George, 17
Washington Legal Foundation, 302
Washington Post, 5, 217, 226, 263
Watergate affair, 41, 58–59, 61, 66, 144, 153, 165, 181, 222
Watt, James G., 34, 38, 45
Wattenberg, Ben, 126, 130

Wayne, John, 59
Way the World Works, The (Wanniski), 153, 191–97, 206, 221
wealth, 206–7
Wealth and Poverty (Gilder), 194, 203, 206–9, 210, 293, 321
Wealth of Nations, The (Smith), 152, 192
Weaver, Richard, 46, 299, 300
Weber, Max, 73, 211, 218, 238, 247, 269
Weidenbaum, Murray, 37, 230, 231, 233, 234–35, 275
Weinberger, Caspar, 36, 84, 227, 235, 308
welfare, 127, 153, 186, 192, 220, 254
  Murray's critique of, 292, 293–96
Welfare (Anderson), 296
Westmoreland, William, 68
Weyerhauser Company, 80
Weyrich, Paul, 47
Whalen, Richard, 60–61, 226, 227
What Is to Be Done (Lenin), 156
When Prophecy Fails (Festinger, Riecken, and Schachter), 271
Where's the Rest of Me? (Reagan), 244, 269

Whitman, Marina von, 184
Who's Who, 67
Why We Were in Vietnam (Podhoretz), 146–47
Wick, Charles Z., 62, 63, 68, 144
Will, George F., 30, 50, 181, 224, 227
Williams, Edward Bennett, 81
Willkie, Wendell, 323
Will to Believe, The (James), 266
Wilson, James Q., 214
Wilson, William, 62, 68
Wilson, Woodrow, 18, 105, 160
Wirthlin, Richard, 226, 266
Witness (Chambers), 19–20
Wolfe, Tom, 7
women's movement, 161, 205, 318, 319
Work Projects Administration (WPA), 245–46
World War II, 13, 248–49
Wrather, Jack, 62, 68
Wright, Harold Bell, 244–45
Wriston, Walter, 53–54, 56

Yale University, 23, 176
Young Americans for Freedom, 30

zero-sum proposition, 168–69, 187

WESTMAR COLLEGE LIBRARY

JA 84 .U5 B54 1988
Blumenthal, Sidney, 1948-
The rise of the counter-
  establishment (90-181)

DEMCO